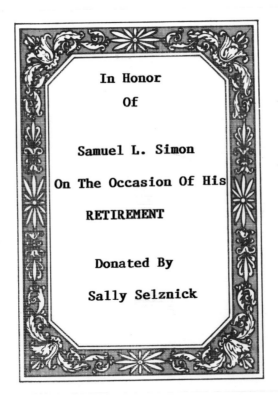

In Honor

Of

Samuel L. Simon

On The Occasion Of His

RETIREMENT

Donated By

Sally Selznick

NO SURPRISES, PLEASE

NO SURPRISES, PLEASE

Movies in the Reagan Decade

• • •

STEVE VINEBERG

SCHIRMER BOOKS
An Imprint of Macmillan Publishing Company
New York

Maxwell Macmillan Canada
Toronto

Maxwell Macmillan International
New York Oxford Singapore Sydney

Copyright © 1993 by Schirmer Books
An Imprint of Macmillan Publishing Company

Schirmer Books
An Imprint of Macmillan Publishing
  Company
866 Third Avenue
New York, NY 10022

Maxwell Macmillan Canada, Inc.
1200 Eglinton Avenue East, Suite 200
Don Mills, Ontario M3C 3N1

Macmillan Publishing Company is part of
the Maxwell Communication Group of
Companies

Library of Congress Catalog Card Number: 92–13847

Printed in the United States of America

printing number
1 2 3 4 5 6 7 8 9 10

Library of Congress Cataloging-in-Publication Data

Vineberg, Steve.
    No surprises, please : movies in the Reagan decade / Steve
Vineberg.
      p. cm.
    ISBN 0-02-872686-3 (alk. paper)
    1. Motion pictures—United States.   2. Motion pictures—United
States—Reviews. I. Title.
PN1993.5.U6V54   1993
791.43′75′097309048—dc20   92–13847
                                   CIP

FOR CHARLEY AND FRANK

• • •

Most of the essays comprising this book appeared in an earlier form in the following publications:

From *The Boston Phoenix:*
"War Is Heaven"; "Les Fleurs de Malle"; "Hallowed Ground"; "Dark Victory"; "Get Out Your Greenbacks"; "Sex Please, We're British"; "The Nuns' Story"; "World of Survival"; "Chet Baker: RIP"; "The Mind's I"; "A Movie Built for Two"; "Little Woman"; "Grief Relief"; "Local Heroine"; "K. C. Superstar"; "The Greek Passion"; "Jarmusch Jumble"; "Tanner of the Times"

From *The Stanford Daily:*
"*Moscow on the Hudson* an Astonishing, Masterful Film"; "Why Good Liberals Go to the Movies—A Defense of *Moscow*"; "*Seeing Red* Lights Up Corners but Raises Few Conflicts"; "*Pixote* Offers No Tender Moment"; "*Personal Best:* The Unembarrassed Camera View"; "*The Godfather* as Comedy of Menace"; "Comedies Show Offbeat Sensibility"; "*The Eyes, the Mouth:* A Drama of Survival"; "*Stop Making Sense* an Ecstatic Film"; "*Lost in America*: Appealing Yuppie Comedy"; "*The Big Chill* Evokes No Warmth"; "*Shoot the Moon:* Domestic Pain in Tears and Blood"; "*Diner:* The Mysterious Power of Pop Culture"

From *The Threepenny Review:*
"DePalma in Vietnam"; "Table Talk" (Spring 1990); "Another Country"; "David Leland's Fictions"; "Upholding the Law of Desire"; "Borrowing Greatness: *Amadeus* on Film"; "Brecht and Freud"; "Coming Up Roses"; "Serving the Text"; "How the Other Half Lives"; "Woman's Legacy"; "Surface and Depth"

From *Boston Review:*
"Thoroughly Maudlin Movies"; "Portraits of the Artist on the Silver Screen"

From *Sight and Sound:*
"*Swing Shift:* A Tale of Hollywood"

From *Cineaste:*
"*The Cotton Club*"

From *Inside Stanford:*
"Movies and the Raised Consciousness"

"A World Apart" Reprinted from *Film Quarterly*, Vol. 42, No. 3, spring, 1989, pp. 38–41, by permission. ©1989 by the Regents of the University of California.

"Thy Kingdom Come, Thy Will Be Done" Reprinted from *Film Quarterly*, Vol. 42, No. 3, Spring, 1989, pp. 31–33, by permission. ©1989 by the Regents of the University of California.

"Drugstore Cowboy" Reprinted from *Film Quarterly*, Vol. 43, No. 3, Spring, 1990, pp. 29–30, by permission. ©1990 by the Regents of the University of California.

"The Fabulous Baker Boys" Reprinted from *Film Quarterly*, Vol. 44, No. 2, Winter, 1990–91, pp. 50–52, by permission. ©1991 by the Regents of the University of California.

Contents

• • •

Illustrations

• • •

Illustrations follow page 146.

Cleavant Derricks and Robin Williams in *Moscow on the Hudson*.
Sebastian Rice-Edwards and Geraldine Muir in *Hope and Glory*.
Jessica Lange and Armin Mueller-Stahl in *Music Box*.
Dylan McDermott and Anthony Barrile in *Hamburger Hill*.
Michael J. Fox and Sean Penn in *Casualties of War*.
Barbara Hershey and Jodhi May in *A World Apart*.
Fernando Ramos da Silva and Marilia Pera in *Pixote*.
Bob Hoskins and Michael Caine in *Mona Lisa*.
Emily Lloyd in *Wish You Were Here*.
Carmen Maura in *Women on the Verge of a Nervous Breakdown*.
Anjelica Huston and Ron Silver in *Enemies, A Love Story*.
Chet Baker in *Let's Get Lost*.
Michelle Pfeiffer and Jeff Bridges in *The Fabulous Baker Boys*.
Lou Castel in *The Eyes, the Mouth*.
Marcelia Cartaxo in *Hour of the Star*.
David Byrne in *Stop Making Sense*.
Mia Farrow, John Wood, Van Johnson, Jeff Daniels, Zoe Caldwell, Milo O'Shea, Edward Herrmann, and Deborah Rush in *The Purple Rose of Cairo*.
Peter and Tatsuya Nakadai in *Ran*.
Donal McCann and Anjelica Huston in *The Dead*.
Daniel Day-Lewis and Juliette Binoche in *The Unbearable Lightness of Being*.
Kyle MacLachlan and Dennis Hopper in *Blue Velvet*.
Jeff Daniels and Melanie Griffith in *Something Wild*.
Judy Davis in *High Tide*.
Goldie Hawn in *Swing Shift*.
Diane Keaton in *Shoot the Moon*.

Acknowledgments

• • •

MUCH of this book first appeared in various publications, in the form of essays and reviews. I would like to acknowledge three original sources that, among them, housed most of these pieces: *The Stanford Daily*, for which I wrote about movies between 1980 and 1985; *The Threepenny Review*, a quarterly that has published my work regularly since 1984; and *The Boston Phoenix*, my primary venue since 1986. Above all I am indebted, for both their editorial finesse and their friendship, to Wendy Lesser at *Threepenny;* to Owen Gleiberman, who hired me at the *Phoenix;* and to Michael Hale—my first, best, and most frequent editor at the *Daily*.

Michael Gorra first suggested that these pieces might make a book. Robert Axelrod, my zealous editor at Schirmer, was the project's first and kindest enthusiast. Charles Taylor, my colleague at the *Phoenix*, came up with a structure and a strategy. He also continues to remind me, through our debates and by his superb example, what it means to be a movie critic.

Dale Bauer, Polly Frost, Pauline Kael, David Long, and Ray Sawhill read sections of the manuscript and gave me many insightful comments as well as unstinting encouragement, for all of which I am most grateful.

I would like to express my gratitude as well to a number of people who have offered me personal and professional support. At Stanford University: Lorne Buchman, William Chace, David McCandless, and Frank Murray. At College of the Holy Cross: Lynn Babcock and Robert Cording. And Jay Carr, Glenda Hobbs, Diane Rafferty, Terrence Rafferty, Lloyd Rose, Howard Shubert, and Michael Sragow. The support of my family—my parents, Sally and Cecil Vineberg, and my brother, David—has been continuous and overwhelming.

Finally, I want to thank my students at Holy Cross, whose fresh responses to movies challenge and deepen my own. In particular, I'd like to pay tribute to a remarkable group in the Film as Narrative course: Sarah Colfer; Jennifer Connorton; Jeanne Marie

Grubert; Beth, Brian, and Mark Gunn; Chip Harper; John Margiotta; Linda Meyer; Jennifer Morello; and Don Whitehead. Not only were they a professor's idea of paradise, but collectively they formed an audience that must be every great filmmaker's dream.

INTRODUCTION. BUCKING
THE ZEITGEIST

• • •

If you wanted to draw up a list of movies made during the 1960s that caught the spirit of their era—*zeitgeist* movies—you might include Truffaut's *Shoot the Piano Player* and *Jules and Jim;* Godard's *Masculine Feminine, La Chinoise,* and *Weekend;* Antonioni's *L'Avventura;* Arthur Penn's *Bonnie and Clyde* and *Alice's Restaurant;* and Peckinpah's *The Wild Bunch,* as well as *Bob and Carol and Ted and Alice, The Manchurian Candidate, Dr. Strangelove, Lawrence of Arabia,* and *A Hard Day's Night.* You'd have to add popular movies that weren't much good but contained elements with a powerful appeal to audiences: *The Graduate, Easy Rider, Doctor Zhivago, Tom Jones, Alfie.* You'd be obliged to throw in *Blow-Up,* 8 ½, and Bergman's trilogy (*Through a Glass Darkly, The Silence* and *Winter Light*), as well as *Butch Cassidy and the Sundance Kid, 2001: A Space Odyssey, West Side Story,* and *The Sound of Music.* An extremely mixed bag, certainly, but on the whole it's no shame to have the spirit of your time and culture represented by the best of Truffaut, Godard, Peckinpah, and Penn.

And here's a suggested list of early 1970s zeitgeist movies: *M*A*S*H*, *McCabe and Mrs. Miller*, and *Nashville*; *The Godfather* (both parts) and *The Conversation*; *Five Easy Pieces* and *Straw Dogs*; *Patton*, *Dirty Harry*, and *The French Connection*; *Last Tango in Paris* and *Women in Love*; *Cries and Whispers* and *Scenes from a Marriage*; *El Topo*, *Love Story*, *Klute*, and *Carnal Knowledge*; *Sunday, Bloody Sunday* and *The Last Picture Show*; *Cabaret*, *Bananas*, and *Play It Again, Sam*; *The Candidate*, *Deliverance*, *Sounder*, and *Superfly*; *American Graffiti* and *The Sting*; *Serpico*, *The Way We Were*, *Chinatown*, and *Shampoo*; *Jaws* and *Carrie*; *One Flew Over the Cuckoo's Nest*, *Rocky*, and *Taxi Driver*. Representing the late years of that decade: *Kramer vs. Kramer*; *Star Wars*, *Close Encounters of the Third Kind*, and *Alien*; *The Warriors*; *Annie Hall*; the 1978 *Invasion of the Body Snatchers*; *Coming Home*, *The Deer Hunter*, and *Apocalypse Now*.

The early seventies were an unparalleled epoch in the history of American sound film, when great filmmakers like Robert Altman, Francis Ford Coppola, and Martin Scorsese found a way to shape their own personal obsessions in movies that caught the national mood: angry, bitter, paranoic (in response to the assassinations, Vietnam, Watergate). These artists may have been natural subversives, but for once the wide, young moviegoing public was, as well (at least in its sympathies), and the demythologizing stance of movies like *The Godfather* and *McCabe and Mrs. Miller* emerged out of a vocabulary these directors shared with their audience. So, even given the quantity of junk loaded in among the gems in the preceding list, the mix reveals an astonishing amount of serious thinking about the culture in the movies we went to see.

At a party in late 1989, some movie friends and I sat around compiling a zeitgeist list for the eighties, and it was a dispiriting experience. There were some marvelous pictures that revealed the mood and obsessions of the decade: *Blow Out* and *Casualties of War*; *Shoot the Moon* and *Diner*; *E.T.* and *Tootsie*; *Something Wild*, *Blue Velvet*, and *My Beautiful Laundrette*; *The Stepfather*, *The Unbearable Lightness of Being*, and *Bull Durham*. But more than half of these flopped at the box office. And in sheer numbers they were overpowered by zeitgeist movies that really were awful.

Not just bad movies but offensive movies, moralistic movies, inept movies; fake movies; movies I didn't want to admit I'd seen (or wanted to forget as quickly as possible), most of which were inexplicably—or all too plausibly—popular. Movies like *Ordinary People; 9 to 5; Chariots of Fire; On Golden Pond; An Officer and a Gentleman; Gandhi; Tender Mercies; Mr. Mom; Risky Business; The Big Chill; Terms of Endearment; Uncommon Valor; Entre Nous; The Natural; Ghostbusters; Places in the Heart; Amadeus; Country; Beverly Hills Cop; The Breakfast Club; Desperately Seeking Susan; Rambo; Cocoon; Out of Africa; The Color Purple; Murphy's Romance; 9 ½ Weeks; Top Gun; River's Edge; Fatal Attraction; Jean de Florette; Wall Street; Good Morning, Vietnam; Cocktail; The Accused; Rain Man; Mississippi Burning; Lean on Me; Field of Dreams; Do the Right Thing; When Harry Met Sally . . . ; Crimes and Misdemeanors; Dead Poets Society; sex, lies, and videotape.*

These were zeitgeist movies of a kind different from *Blow Out* or *Shoot the Moon* or *Casualties of War*; they didn't comment on the culture in any meaningful way—they embodied it. That's not necessarily bad: There was nothing particularly profound about the 1977 *Saturday Night Fever*, but its depiction of a certain contemporary urban lifestyle had the same kind of energy as some of the memorable youth movies from the mid-fifties. But most of the pictures I've listed from the eighties are emotionally tawdry and cautious, morally straitjacketed, rhetorically slick and vacuous. And they're not balanced, as they were in the two previous decades, by movies that dig deeper, that turn up insights into the culture.

I realize how curmudgeonly and unpleasable my list of bad zeitgeist movies makes me seem. But in the eighties it became impossible to maintain *any* kind of standard about what's good and bad at the movies without appearing to come from another planet. At the end of 1985 I sent my Ten Best List to a friend in my hometown (Montreal), and he wrote back that everyone he showed it to assumed it was a gag: Half the films on it had never played there, and most of the others opened and closed with scarcely a murmur. (The list included *The Home and the World*, by the Indian director Satyajit Ray; *The Shooting Party* and *The Return of the Soldier*, by the English director Alan Bridges; Ichikawa's *The Makioka Sisters*; Kurosawa's *Ran*; and *Songwriter, Dreamchild, Heartbreakers*, and

Sweet Dreams. The only movie that sparked any recognition was Woody Allen's *The Purple Rose of Cairo*.)

What happened to movies in the eighties—and has continued into the nineties—was not that good movies no longer got made, though there certainly seemed to be fewer of them. It was that, with shockingly few exceptions, they were ignored, dismissed, buried by a combination of studio publicists who felt they couldn't sell them, critics who didn't understand them or didn't feel secure praising anything that was so clearly falling by the wayside, and audiences that never heard of them (blame the publicists and the critics) or assumed they couldn't be any good if they weren't being hyped and systematically dragged into the national consciousness by massive ad campaigns. When someone I'm introduced to at a party asks me what new movies I've liked and I mention the extraordinary British comedy–fantasy *Truly Madly Deeply*, the response I can expect is a dismissive "Never heard of it" or "Really? Isn't that just a depressing rip-off of *Ghost*?" And I have to try to work out which of the dense overlay of misconceptions is worth addressing—that *Ghost* is a good movie just because it made so much money and got nominated for an Academy Award; that an emotionally wrenching movie is depressing; that when two movies come out on the same subject, the second one released is necessarily a rip-off; or that it might make a difference who *tells* you that a movie is lousy. Usually no one claims these judgments; they're simply in the wind, which isn't the same as "word of mouth," a term that, in the era of the TV critics and gargantuan studio hype that informs you what you're supposed to think of a movie like *Ghost* before you walk in, has stopped meaning anything.

The message that's really being conveyed, all the way down the line from the studios through the media and on through the mass audience, is that you don't want to see a movie that's "weird," i.e., that doesn't conform to current popular taste. You no longer sample a movie on your own; you don't experiment, the way audiences enjoyed doing in the late sixties and early seventies. Americans discovered *Easy Rider* and *M*A*S*H*, but *Thelma and Louise* hurls itself at you. Its debased feminist slogans ("When a woman is crying, she isn't having any fun!" and "I've, like, crossed over. I couldn't go back. I couldn't live") are practically emblazoned across the screen, and its two beautiful women stars are photographed like objects in high-concept TV ads. And *Terminator 2: Judgment Day*, in the tradition of *Total Recall*, is a carefully pre-programmed, inescapable event, like the Fourth of July.

Truthfully, audience response is so preordained these days that I'm not sure it would help the dismal situation if more of the audience for *Ghost* actually took a chance on *Truly Madly Deeply*. Even intelligent, discriminating friends have been suckered in by *Terminator 2*. The $94 million budget (which is the main platform of the hype) seems to have intimidated just about everybody into finding something good to say about this humorless, grindingly monotonous special-effects extravaganza, in which the plot makes absolutely no sense and the trumpeted themes (our inherent destructiveness, the folly of trusting in technology, the importance of releasing the feminine in all of us) have no connection to the action. At $6.50 or $7.00 a ticket, not to mention the cumulative cost of an evening out, it's understandable that moviegoers want some reassurance that they're going to get some value for what they put out. So a false value gets substituted: the comfort of seeing what you'd expected, or what everyone else is seeing, or what you've been told you're supposed to like.

The movies everyone's tuned into these days rarely represent the vision of individuals who are themselves tuned into what's going on in the culture; they're the blockbusters the studios and the loyal press (headed by those eighties creations, the TV critics) have declared are the movies everyone's sure to want to see, like *Ghost*. Thoughtful and provocative, *Nashville* and *Taxi Driver* told us how Americans in the mid-seventies responded to violence and celebrity. *Terminator 2* tells us that as a culture all we care about now are noise, spectacle, slambang cartoon havoc, and conforming to what we think we're meant to cheer for; but it's not a comment on these obsessions—it's just an artifact. In this kind of atmosphere, it's possible for a very smart and very gifted filmmaker like Brian DePalma to make movies like *Blow Out* and *Casualties of War*—two masterpieces bookending the eighties—that penetrate the culture and identify something significant, resonant, disturbing about it, and yet *buck* the zeitgeist, because when audiences ignored these movies or turned against them, they effectively became non-events.

Back in the forties, Robert Warshow pointed out (in his essay "The Gangster as Tragic Hero") the built-in tension between the critical stand of artists and the eternal optimism of our official cul-ture—which is to say not only the movies, the music, the TV (and radio) programs, the painting, the sculpture, and the photographs that receive the sanction and encouragement of our institutions, but also whatever grows up in happy *response to* the standard they set. Because Americans are historically more optimistic and less fond of downbeat (or self-revealing) forms of art than are people of some other nations, the distance between the most exciting work of our filmmakers and the most popular has generally been wide. It just happens that for a brief, incandescent period in the late sixties and early seventies, the whole country was ruled, for once, by the lords of discontent: A lot of glorious movies got made, and audiences re-sponded to them. But in the eighties that distance became greater than ever before—nearly impassable. And as the culture began to go haywire in the Reagan era, moving backwards to a pre–Kennedy conservatism and proclaiming a wholesale embracing of American glory that denied history, not only did our movies grow loonier (*Fa-tal Attraction*, *Field of Dreams*, *Dead Poets Society*), but the dis-senting voices grew dimmer.

I don't mean to suggest that every kind of resistance to the po-litical tide went underground in the eighties. Actually, something even more bizarre occurred: A powerful wave of conservatism turned its opponents into naysayers bound together in consensus just as tightly as were their adversaries. Once Ronald Reagan began his tenure in 1981, most people who felt uncomfortable with him fled to a second camp, just as closed in, just as subject to an imposed vision of the culture and the country and the world: the much-discussed "politically correct" (PC) camp. And if you don't identify with either team—and artists have a way of resisting team poli-tics—then either you're not likely to register at all in the national consciousness, or else you might find youself in the unenviable posi-tion of providing a target for *both* groups. That was Brian DePal-ma's fate with *Casualties of War*.

The Reagan decade was a time when Americans began to re-turn to the homespun values of an earlier time. For a while it seemed like the Eisenhower period was being reconstituted, but we've stretched beyond it, back to the forties—or earlier even, to a *Saturday Evening Post* fantasy of the turn of the century. In 1984 pictures like *Places in the Heart*, *Country*, and *The River*, all set in the heartland, presented us with characters who wore their devotion to family and the land and the community like a blue ribbon identifying them as moral first-prize winners. They wore their obedient Christianity, too: As Pauline Kael observed in her review of *Witness*, the ritual of grace before dinner (familiar from countless M-G-M family movies from the 1930s and '40s) began showing up regularly in several of these movies.

As for acceptable sexual conduct on screen, suddenly Hollywood was caught in what was practically a Hays Code mentality. (The Hays Code, or Production Code, was the Hollywood censorship apparatus that came into full effect in the early thirties and maintained a virtual stranglehold over American moviemaking until the fifties; it disappeared in the sixties.) Our movies don't deny that sex is fun, but do insist that procreation is more important: A movie like the suffocatingly sentimental *Parenthood*, from 1989, is awash in babies. And if a main character has to choose between the sexual impulse and the familial one, well, there *is* no choice. The heroine of the sexy 1985 mystery–comedy *Compromising Positions* (played by Susan Sarandon), fed to the teeth with her boring life as Edward Herrmann's wife, falls for the cop (Raul Julia) working on the case of her murdered dentist. But the movie won't let her have a fling with him; she has to stay true to her insufferable husband, the father of her kids. And Philip Kaufman's magnificent film *The Unbearable Lightness of Being* didn't have a chance at the box office in the eighties: Its hero is a compulsive adulterer. The same can be said for Paul Mazursky's *Enemies, A Love Story*, whose hero is a polygamist.

No one went to see the terrific Patsy Cline bio, *Sweet Dreams*, which makes no bones about the fact that the relationship between Patsy (Jessica Lange) and her husband, Charlie Dick (Ed Harris), is based on sex. Patsy and Charlie have no end of problems as a couple (she throws him out on more than one occasion), yet they're still man and wife when a plane crash hurls her to her death. In this drama for adults the writer, Robert Getchell, and the director, Karel Reisz, remind us that marriages that are shaken up by booze and infidelity and violence and the inequity of finances and careers sometimes stay more-or-less intact when the partners have a great time in bed. *Sweet Dreams* is in the mold of *Shoot the Moon*, perhaps the greatest American movie of the decade (and a box-office bomb), in which a bitterly separating couple (Albert Finney and Diane Keaton), softening toward each other in the emotional turmoil of her father's death, agree to have dinner together, stage a public quarrel, and then, exhilarated and turned on by it all, end up in bed. (The people who made *Shoot the Moon*—Alan Parker, the director, and Bo Goldman, the screenwriter—are no fools; this warm interlude has its unhappy repercussions, too.) In both *Shoot the Moon* and *Sweet Dreams* the filmmakers' refusal to idealize the marital state is an indication of real integrity when that state has once more become a sacred cow in our movies.

Under the tyranny of the Production Code, a woman who had an affair with a married man invariably turned up dead in the final reel; that's the convention Hitchcock plays with in *Psycho*, where Marion Crane (Janet Leigh) is "punished" for adultery and theft by being dispatched while taking a shower—i.e., enjoying her sexuality. (DePalma is even wickeder in *Dressed to Kill*, made twenty years after *Psycho*, when he "punishes" Angie Dickinson for an afternoon assignation by first giving her pickup syphilis and then killing off Dickinson.) The 1987 smash hit *Fatal Attraction* reverts to the kind of moralism Hitchcock was tweaking back in 1960, but takes it much farther. The adulteress (Glenn Close) has snaky locks, and the look she flashes (in her first scene) at a guy who makes an unwelcome pass at her has knives in it. Smoke rises from a subway grating outside her apartment. (It's actually a loft, a setting that smacks of alternative lifestyles.) Her first sex with Michael Douglas takes place against her kitchen sink, initiating a new cliché in American movies: When we're not supposed to approve of two people having sex, it's made to look extremely uncomfortable. (In the nineties, both *Presumed Innocent* and, revealingly, Spike Lee's interracial romance *Jungle Fever* follow suit.)

Alex, Close's character, is a career woman; Douglas's wife (Anne Archer) is a homemaker, and the movie is careful to make her warmer and more feminine than her rival. (In his book *The Gorgon's Gaze*, Paul Coates points out that Alex's name implies that she aspires to male privilege.) Of course it's Archer who has to eliminate the intruder, whose illicit passion for Douglas transforms her into a raging fury. *Fatal Attraction*, which also panders to AIDS hysteria and what was, in 1987, the general tabloid mentality about the disease (be a good monogamous little boy and you won't get it; cheat, and you'll end up with exactly what you deserve—a monster who boils your daughter's pet bunny and goes after your wife with a knife), has become the model for the contemporary sex thriller. The snappy, absorbing novel *Presumed Innocent* turns heavy and solemn in Alan Pakula's 1990 movie version, where the big set-piece is the moralistic confession speech by the murderer, Harrison Ford's wronged wife (the gifted Bonnie Bedelia, transcending her idiotic role). People who read the book marveled at how cleverly it was plotted and how deliciously they'd been taken in; people who watched the movie tended to comment vigorously on the bitch (Greta Scacchi), another career woman, who gets what she deserves for horning in on that marriage. (Bedelia's academic career has been stalled by an unfinished dissertation—which is somehow supposed to be Ford's fault—so her pretty much full-time role is that of wife and mother, and she's very good at it.)

Fatal Attraction ends with a shot of a family photo in the Douglas–Archer home. The filmmakers (Adrian Lyne, the director, and James Dearden, the writer) claimed in interviews that they meant to be ironic, but that's certainly not how audiences took it in 1987, when it was seen as a happy ending. My students, children of the upbeat eighties, want to read even the last moment in *Shoot the Moon* as a happy ending—where Finney, beaten to a pulp by Keaton's lover (Peter Weller), reaches up to her, while she remains detached from him, arms folded on her chest. The jagged, unresolvable domestic realism of *Shoot the Moon* is too close for comfort; it shakes people up. One of my friends insisted it was in bad taste to show this kind of intimate marital battling. My editor at *The Stanford Daily*, where my review of the movie was published in 1982, was so agitated over the film that he followed me out of the newspaper office and across campus, arguing manically, repeating over and over that he couldn't understand how I could possibly have praised it. (Another editor, in the same year, told me he was appalled at my positive review of Robert Towne's *Personal Best*, which he insisted was soft-core porn.)

In the Reagan era every movie, whatever its genre, was supposed to be a feel-good movie, a logical extension of Reagan's invocation to the American people to stand tall and feel great about our country. And this attitude has only intensified in the years since

Bush took over as president. It's practically unpatriotic to recommend a movie that isn't relentlessly upbeat; if you do, you're being "negative." Barry Levinson, who has a reputation for directing serious pictures, pictures of vision and integrity, in fact rarely makes anything *but* feel-good movies: *The Natural*, which alters the downbeat ending of the Bernard Malamud novel it's based on; *Good Morning, Vietnam*, parts of which feel like something made during the Second World War; *Rain Man*, in which the autistic-savant hero (Dustin Hoffman) is a cutie pie who brings out the loving potential in his sleazy brother (Tom Cruise). Even the 1990 *Avalon*, which seems to have been intended as an elegy about the disintegration of a family, has the sappy glow of childhood memories preserved in amber, like *Stand by Me*.

Peter Weir's runaway 1989 hit *Dead Poets Society*, set at a boys' private school in the fifties, is so desperate to send audiences out of the theater feeling good that its ending doesn't make sense. One of the kids (Robert Sean Leonard) offs himself after he's been bullied by an insensitive martinet of a father (Kurtwood Smith, stuck in a role even Olivier couldn't have salvaged), and the cowardly administration shunts the blame onto the talented teacher (Robin Williams) who's been trying to coax the boys' creativity and capacity for risk out of hiding. The headmaster fires him, first intimidating his students into signing a statement against him. Tom Schulman's script is a twenty-four-carat fake; you can't believe in the ways it says Williams has changed his students' lives—and Leonard's character has enough other options that his electing to commit suicide ought to be portrayed as a pathetic failure of imagination, not a romantic, *Young Werther*-like tragedy. However, the movie is at least consistent until, in the final scene, Williams visits his old classroom, now the province of another teacher, to say goodbye to his students, and they pay tribute to him by standing on their desks and dedicating to him the poem he taught them: "O Captain! My Captain!" What are we supposed to make of this flourish of rebellion, *after* the kids have wimped out and signed the headmaster's paper? The movie simply ignores the futility of the gesture. Weir forgets he's shooting a story with an *un*happy ending, and frames this finale as if it were proof of the indomitability of the human spirit.

In the process of finding ways to convert potentially "depressing" material into movies Americans can use to pat ourselves on the back with (reminding ourselves once again of what decent Ordinary People we are), Hollywood invented a new subgenre in the middle of the decade: melodrama without villains. The 1985 *Twice in a Lifetime*, written by Colin Welland and directed by Bud Yorkin, is a case in point. Gene Hackman, leaning on his gift for eliciting audience sympathy, plays a middle-aged steel worker whose affair with a widowed barmaid (Ann-Margret) breaks up his marriage. The filmmakers make sure that the barmaid is sweetly vulnerable to the attacks of her lover's family and friends—she's not in the Glenn Close league—and confirm Hackman's defense that his relationship with his frumpy, unimaginative wife (Ellen Burstyn) went stale long ago. But they also give brownie points to the put-upon wife for emerging from her depression and getting on with her life, and even for displaying indignant anger toward her husband. Jean Renoir believed that everyone has his reasons, but a movie like *Twice in a Lifetime* isn't an exploration of conflicting human motivations. (*Shoot the Moon* is.) It's a smiley face overlaid on a potential real-life situation. *Twice in a Lifetime* treats human interaction as if it were a children's birthday party, where the cake and ice cream have to be doled out with meticulous fairness so no one will feel shortchanged. The evenhanded distribution of points in a movie always ends up turning opposite points of view to mush, just as the noble-minded old codger whom Oscar-nominated James Garner plays so endearingly in Martin Ritt's *Murphy's Romance* (also from 1985) cancels out the very *idea* of political interest when he drives around with an antinuke sticker on his car bumper but identifies with John Wayne.

Twice in a Lifetime and *Murphy's Romance* and Woody Allen's *Hannah and Her Sisters*, which came out the same season, are self-actualization movies. The stories aren't presented as conflicts, but as series of little triumphs—like those athletic obstacle courses you find in some parks that are dotted with challenges of skill and endurance you can meet and reward yourself for before going on to the next one. But since drama is *based on* conflict, movies like these barely crawl forward; the writers have to resort to the most exhausted clichés to lurch the plot from episode to episode. Audiences don't seem to mind; they're happy cheering the characters' breakthroughs. And they really do cheer: Sometimes a moviehouse on a

Friday or Saturday night resembles a pep rally or an AA meeting. (Broadway audiences are just as eager to be revved up, both at terrible plays like Wendy Wasserstein's *The Heidi Chronicles* and Neil Simon's *Lost in Yonkers*, and at such otherwise enjoyable entertainments as the Michael Bennett musical *Dreamgirls*, one of the biggest hits of the decade, where the self-absorption of the characters is glorified in numbers with assertiveness-training titles like "And I Am Telling You I'm Not Going" and "I Am Changing.") Terrence Rafferty, writing in *The New Yorker*, compared the group scenes in Spike Lee's *Jungle Fever* to sessions on confessional TV talk shows (e.g., "Geraldo" and "Sally Jessy Raphael")—all intense, self-absorbed talk and no drama, with spaces built in for audience members to yell their encouragement.

Christopher Lasch called his book about the movement from radicalism to self-help therapy in the seventies *The Culture of Narcissism*, but I doubt that even he could have anticipated a vision of self-actualization quite as cracked as *Cocktail*, a 1988 box-office bonanza. *Cocktail* is like a huge junk sculpture made up of splinters from different American Dream tales and given a late-eighties rock-club paint job. Tom Cruise, who learned the virtues of capitalism as a teen in *Risky Business* (where he operated a whorehouse in his vacationing parents' house and was rewarded for his business acumen with admission to an Ivy League school), achieved hero status as a fighter pilot in an unanticipated tussle with an unspecified enemy in *Top Gun*, and became the first bona fide rock 'n' roll pool hustler in *The Color of Money*, gets out of the military in *Cocktail* and heads for New York to make his fortune. When the men who interview him for Madison Avenue jobs have the nerve to suggest he might want to get a college degree or a little experience under his belt first, he picks up a job tending bar, working under a cynical old hand (Bryan Brown) who passes on everything he knows. Cruise does enroll in business courses, but soon determines that his teachers don't know anything about real life. So he drops out, concentrating on what he now recognizes as his true calling. This movie, which seems to have been written (by Heywood Gould) with a straight face, is all about both a kid who becomes a *star bartender*, and the surface pleasures and deeper perils that accompany that stardom— the gorgeous women, the vertiginous high life, the corrupt values, the cool shirts. Hard-edged Brown, who screws a woman Cruise has been seeing (in order to show him she's worthless), finds himself a rich wife (Kelly Lynch) and opens his own club. Failing to either monopolize her sex life or keep himself solvent, he winds up a suicide. Cruise now has to learn on his own to stop playing gigolo to wealthy older women and return to his true love (Elisabeth Shue). He finally accepts Who He Really Is: a bartender, but *not* a star. At the end he's running his own Irish neighborhood pub, showing off his pregnant wife to the patrons and assuring them the baby's going to be a boy.

It's in the realm of political movies that American filmmaking most fervently embraced the feel-good, walk-tall agenda of the Reagan administration. Political *fantasies*, really: You can't take a movie like *Top Gun* or *Rambo* or the pathetic *Heartbreak Ridge* seriously, except as a cultural artifact. Not only did the political attitudes in our movies begin to change in the eighties—Tom Cruise's dad in *Top Gun*, shot down by enemy planes "over the wrong line on some map," ends up an unsung hero rather than the emblem of American military corruption he would have been painted as a decade earlier—but history itself was being rewritten. In the 1986 TV movie *Resting Place*, supposedly set in 1972, there are no war protesters, no soldiers displeased with their tour in Vietnam, no one at all to challenge the notion that the dead outfit leader whose body is sent home has conferred honor on his town by dying for his country. The blinkered chauvinism of these movies was a kind of crazy reflection of Reagan's creative "interpretations" of world response to American foreign policy.

The subtext of movies like *Top Gun* and the *Missing in Action* pictures—America is a kick-ass military nation that doesn't take defeat lying down—is a message for wartime; the subtext of the heartland pictures—we're at our best when we win through to the basic family and religious values that made our country great—is a message for peacetime. But they aren't as much a contradiction as they seem. During the Second World War, Hollywood split its time between sentimentalizing the war and sentimentalizing the family; the implication was that the second constituted the great American value for which the first was being fought. In actuality, the experience of war, as Hemingway suggested long ago in his story "Soldier's Home," tends to alienate those who have lived through it from both the family and the church. But the movies about Vietnam that caught the popular imagination in the eighties weren't the ones that dealt with the moral complexities of war (like *Casualties of War*) but those that envisioned it as a simplified struggle between the forces of good and evil (*Rambo* and, on a higher level, *Platoon*) and those that emphasized the healing of war wounds (*Born on the Fourth of July*). No wonder we embraced the Gulf War as whole-heartedly as we did, hoisting flags and dotting the landscape with yellow ribbons: As a culture, we'd been behaving for years as if we were *already* at war.

The liberals, meanwhile, were behaving as if they were engaged in an undeclared war of their own. When I wrote about movies for *The Stanford Daily* between 1980 and 1985, the angry letters and phone calls I received were always in response to my reviews of films with political themes and a left-wing slant, such as *El Norte*, *The Ballad of Gregorio Cortez*, and *Atomic Cafe*. Panning pictures like these was invariably seen as a political statement— evidence that I was on the conservative side of the issue. It seemed impossible to persuade these inflamed readers that you can reject a paper-thin, obvious melodrama like *El Norte* just because it's a lousy movie, and keep your own politics out of it. The problem, of course, is that for most moviegoers with strong political convictions (or even generally humanistic leanings), a movie *is* its "message." That's how a genuinely terrible movie like Kevin Costner's *Dances with Wolves*, with its bleeding heart for both native American culture and the environment (two causes virtually no one opposes), became 1990's most beribboned release, the film you pray no one will bring up at a dinner party because you know you'll walk away from the evening with a few more enemies than when you arrived.

The English literary critic I. A. Richards once performed a fascinating experiment with a class of undergraduate men, all freshman English majors. Over the term he gave them a series of unidentified poems to read on sight, and asked them to write a reaction to each. Then he catalogued the results, in *Practical Criticism*. His aim was to get at some of the obstacles that can deter us when we try to analyze poetry. One case that kept recurring was that of students who were drawn to, or repelled by, a poem because of an immediate emotional reaction to something in it—perhaps just a word. Often the student failed to understand what the poem was about because all he could see was that word. Richards's model was a young antiroyalist (this was the twenties) who was appalled by a phrase in a George Meredith poem that hailed the approach of the king; he wasn't able to see far enough past his own politics to understand that the poem was about the coming of spring.

Richards called this reflex "doctrinal adhesion," and it's currently epidemic among the politically correct. Filmmakers are in increasing peril of having their hands tied by members of special-interest groups who don't wish to appear in an unflattering light on screen, or by bands of socially conscious citizens acting on behalf of the hordes they assume will be irreparably damaged by the insensitive, mercenary philistines who make movies. A moviemaker who opposes the current standards for political correctness risks being classed with the brutes. And when empty-headed movies like *Dances with Wolves* draw crowds and Oscars and the general approval of the press, artists who want to do something challenging and complex find either that they can't get their projects off the ground or, if by some miracle they do, that no one will go to see them. (How many *Dances with Wolves* fans have ever rented Irvin Kershner's 1976 *The Return of a Man Called Horse*—a truly great movie about a white man's interaction with native Americans, ignored by almost everybody on its original release?)

People who make movies often *are* insensitive and mercenary and philistine. But the purveyors of *Rambo* and *Top Gun* aren't the only worthy targets of scorn in Hollywood. Ridley Scott, who's been embraced by feminists for making *Thelma and Louise*, is no more highly evolved than his brother, *Top Gun*'s Tony Scott, and makes movies in pretty much the same way. Political correctness sure makes strange bedfellows: The *Thelma and Louise* supporters I've spoken to are always surprised to discover that the film Scott made before *Thelma and Louise* was the stupefyingly racist *Black Rain*, in which the Yankee cop (Michael Douglas) has to school the Japanese cop (Ken Takakura) in aggression, on his own turf. (The only thing that made *Black Rain* amusing to watch was the thought that it must have handed Hollywood's new Japanese executives a huge laugh.)

The main problem, though, isn't that the PC crowd almost invariably lavishes its affection on bad movies like *Gandhi* or *The Accused*; it's that it so often levels its disapproval—which is (as everyone knows) increasingly vociferous and difficult to ignore—on good ones. Most of the few first-rate films of the eighties on political and social topics passed by without attracting the notice of liberal audiences: the Australian picture *The Chant of Jimmie Blacksmith* (made in the late seventies and released in this country in 1980); DePalma's *Blow Out*; the Brazilian *Pixote*; *The Border* (the movie *El Norte* can only dream of being); *Under Fire*; *Utu* from New Zealand; *The Home and the World* from India; *Mrs. Soffel*; *Salvador*; *The Stepfather* (a horror movie that satirizes Reagan-era values); *The Unbearable Lightness of Being*; the documentary *Thy Kingdom Come, Thy Will Be Done*; *A World Apart*; *A Cry in the Dark*; *Music Box*. And filmmakers who are attempting to explore issues rather than reducing them to a slogan or a stand often find they've broken the new PC rules and are being taken to task by culture critics who don't seem to have much understanding—not only of what the directors are trying to do, but even of how movies work.

I remember coming across a humorous example of doctrinal adhesion when I taught high-school English in Montreal in the seventies. Introducing a tenth-grade class to Thomas Hardy's *Tess of the d'Urbervilles*, I found a number of my female students getting angry at the *author* over Tess's treatment; they didn't recognize that their outrage in fact had an ally in Hardy. Of course, they'd made a basic error, assuming that the words or behavior of a character (Angel Clare, in this case) represented the author's attitude, mistaking his tone toward that character's actions. I don't see much difference in the response of those feminists who, in 1980, hung a charge of misogyny on Brian DePalma for making *Dressed to Kill*. (That doesn't include *all* feminists, of course; some are very perceptive about DePalma.) In this ingenious thriller, DePalma deals with women's sexual fantasies, an incendiary topic, and makes a black-comic connection between them and the actions of a homicidal maniac. But the message of the movie *isn't* "All women really desire violent sex and if they are cut up by a sex maniac they get what they deserve." If you thought it *was*, as David Denby argued eloquently in his *New York* column, you were confusing the director's mindset with the killer's.

The link between fantasy and reality in this movie is unconscious. What makes *Dressed to Kill* both funny and frightening is that when the killer strikes, it's *as if he were* tuned into his victims' fantasies—which obviously he couldn't be; their fate is a perverted playing-out of their most sordid private thoughts. What is it that some feminists object to in this movie: the fact that DePalma suggests that women sometimes have kinky fantasies? *Men* do. Is there anyone who really believes that women *don't?* And in what way, exactly, is DePalma's depiction of the heroines in *Dressed to Kill*—Angie Dickinson, the sexually starved wife who picks up a man for an afternoon fling, and Nancy Allen, the spunky prostitute who defends herself against a psychopathic killer—insulting to women? (One of my friends, a DePalma basher from way back, says she'll start taking him seriously when he makes a movie in which he includes a female character who's smarter than the male hero. That strikes me as a very peculiar litmus test for misogyny: Angel Clare is "smarter" than Tess, and so is Alec d'Urberville. As it happens, though, the smartest character in *Dressed to Kill*, aside from the psychopath, is surely Liz, the prostitute.)

I keep hearing that DePalma *enjoys* depicting violence against women. What triggers that notion—the fact that he depicts it at all? In the rape scene in *Casualties of War*, we're told, the camera probes the miserable Vietnamese, Oahn; it participates in her degradation. (Frances FitzGerald, writing in *The Village Voice*, called the movie "sadopornographic.") But what the camera *actually* does in this sequence is remain at a remove from the rape: You can't see Oahn's face, and you barely see her body. Michael J. Fox, as Eriksson, the one soldier who refuses to take part in the gang rape, is in the foreground, on guard duty in the rain, his face turned away. His horror frames what we see—the other men's aggression, and, in the case of the frightened Diaz, who participates because he lacks the courage to oppose the others, a bewildered acquiescence to an act that will, in its way, damage him as much as it damages the nonparticipating Eriksson. DePalma's camera is more than discreet here; it's careful *not* to show us the details of the rape, *not* to catalogue Oahn's reactions. And it wouldn't be justified to say that the victim is simply being blurred into anonymity—that her feelings don't matter—because, when Eriksson confronts her a few hours after the rape, DePalma gives us unforgettable close-ups of Oahn's suffering that couldn't possibly make us feel anything but horror and pity.

Casualties of War isn't the only movie to run into a PC roadblock because it doesn't conform to the expectations—requirements, really—of current modes of thinking. In 1981, the people who made *Fort Apache, the Bronx* (Heywood Gould wrote it, Daniel Petrie directed it) got their wrists slapped because the criminals in the movie were all black or Hispanic; the filmmakers were branded racists. But the movie shows you how the whole neighborhood, which is almost entirely black and Hispanic, is victimized by crime. And the point of the movie is that when white cops are working in a neighborhood like the Bronx, racism inevitably flares up on both sides. The hero, Murphy (Paul Newman, in his greatest performance to date), is a decent cop who sees a colleague (Danny Aiello) throw an innocent Puerto Rican kid off a roof and has to turn his fellow officer in. *Fort Apache* isn't a very good movie in a lot of ways, but it's hardly racist. It's compassionate. And it makes a stab at something deeper: urban tragedy. And in 1984, Paul Mazursky's *Moscow on the Hudson*, about a Russian musician who defects during a New York tour of the circus he plays for, was downgraded by many liberals as chauvinistic, stereotypical, and (most bizarrely) anti-Soviet—adjectives that, juxtaposed in this way, suggest a rabid right-wing fantasy. I was amazed. Could they be talking about the gentle, expansive tragicomedy I'd seen, in which New York is portrayed as a funny, jazzy city where the uprooted representatives of other cultures trade in the currency of American daily life (consumer items, pop, street and business jargon)?

In the first part of *Moscow on the Hudson* we see the hero, Vladimir Ivanoff (Robin Williams), suffering the inconveniences of living in Moscow (the shortage of goods, the crowded apartment buildings, the interminable lines), and the greater indignity of living in a nondemocratic country (the omnipresence of the KGB, the fear of police informers, the constraints on freedom of speech). In the second part, bewitched by his first glimpses of America, he chooses to defect. Were *Moscow*'s critics truly claiming that no such conditions existed in the U.S.S.R., that men and women lived there in perfect freedom and comfort? Mazursky and his co-screenwriter, Leon Capetanos, may have exaggerated (their vision was, after all, a comic one), but nothing I'd read on the subject of Soviet life greatly contradicted what Vladimir endures—and grows to hate. And it would have been the height of political naiveté in 1984 to depict a Moscow in which the citizens move about as freely as they do in America, and where consumers are as spoiled as most of *us* are.

Had Mazursky and Capetanos drawn a collection of Red villains, the way Hollywood did in the bad old Cold War days, there might have been something to grouse about. But even the KGB men in the movie are written in human terms—one is rather stolid and sluggish, the other a sweet, slightly paranoid individual as terrified of the system as any civilian could be. Mazursky deliberately plays *against* type, introducing a sleazy-looking Cuban lawyer who turns out to be both ethical and generous, and a vacuous-seeming Italian salesgirl who, as we get to know her better, displays a complex of ambitions and tensions and emotions. But that wasn't the real sore spot for most critics of *Moscow on the Hudson*. What really rankled some liberals, I think, was that the film is about an immigrant who falls in love with America and, despite a few unfortunate experiences (with muggers and insensitive neighbors), *stays* in love. If Mazursky had chosen to make a modern-day *Candide*, with Vladimir as an innocent abroad who discovers that American life is just as rotten as Soviet life, then presumably the picture would have come in for fewer incredulous sneers; it might have pleased the people who applauded the inarticulate, dead-ended *Silkwood*, or *El Norte*—both romanticized liberal views of suffering. Instead, Mazursky's hero faints in a supermarket when he's confronted with the sheer overwhelming variety of coffee on the shelves, and he hangs American-flag shower curtains in his bathroom (both details derived from true-life incidents). Many people apparently felt this to be a sentimental, dishonest version of immigrant life in America.

Some of the moviegoers I know who called *Moscow on the Hudson* sentimental, manipulative, and moralistic didn't mind being strong-armed by shameless weepers like *Terms of Endearment*, *The Natural*, and *Testament*, all of which came out around the same time. Nothing could be more moralistic than the finish of *Terms of Endearment*, in which the irresponsible little-boy astronaut (Jack Nicholson) finally grows up at his lover's daughter's funeral and begins to take care of her grandchildren. Nothing except, perhaps, the ending of *The Natural*, where the over-the-hill baseball star (Robert Redford) hits a homer for the son he never knew he had, then settles down to teach his boy how to play. It's amazing how broad a sweep this cornball Victorianism encompasses when it intersects with a currently acceptable stance in the culture—in this case, the sensitized father figure forging a bond with his son (or his girl friend's grandchildren). And audiences often don't object to the kind of high-minded manipulation that goes on at something like *Testament*, because they assume that any film dealing with a theme as serious as nuclear war must be worthwhile. I avoided reviewing *Testament* when it came out because I didn't know how to *begin* to explain what's wrong with a nuclear holocaust movie that features a little retarded Japanese boy named Hiroshi.

On the PC side of the spectrum, it's not a matter of how good a movie is, or how legitimate a representation of human experience, but of how trendy the sentiments expressed in it are—pretty much the same criterion you find ruling the conservative camp. The point of view of *Moscow on the Hudson* wasn't fashionable in liberal circles in 1984; the themes put forth in *Terms of Endearment* and *The Natural* were. Writer–director David Leland might have satisfied the art-house audience with his 1987 film *Wish You Were Here* if he hadn't humanized the teenage heroine's middle-aged lover, or if he'd given her an abortion at the end instead of having her return home proudly with her baby in tow. What this kind of rigor reveals, among other things, is the arrogance of people who assume that the *current* standard for political correctness is the *only* applicable one. It's embarrassing to watch that standard applied to older movies, to hear the superior tone with which contemporary "conscious" audiences dismiss movies from an earlier era, put off by outmoded conventions or styles (or, more likely, by the black-and-white photography) and completely insensitive to what may be quite sophisticated and complex examinations of difficult subjects: *The Best Years of Our Lives*, *From Here to Eternity*, *The Men*. Some friends who joined me not long ago in watching *Meet Me in St. Louis*, a 1944 musical set at the turn of the century, said they weren't sure it was the kind of movie they'd want little girls exposed to, because the lives of the two ingenues (Judy Garland and Lucille Bremer) revolve around finding men to marry. (Would they hesitate before handing their daughters Jane Austen?) But then, the knowingness of hip young audiences could be a pain in the ass in the sixties and early seventies, too. Arlene Croce took them on in *The Fred Astaire and Ginger Rogers Book*, published in 1972, in her discussion of the fabulous "Bojangles of Harlem" number in *Swing Time*, a tribute to

Bill "Bojangles" Robinson featuring Astaire in blackface. (The number, of course, is still routinely hissed when it shows up in revival houses.)

These flare-ups at earnest, inoffensive movies like *Fort Apache, the Bronx*, good ones like *Moscow on the Hudson*, and great ones like *Casualties of War* are reminiscent of Richards's antiroyalist student: They expose an unwillingness, or perhaps an inability, to see what's going on underneath the familiar signs. In his marvelous novel *The Ghost Writer*, Philip Roth satirizes a very similar kind of narrow vision. The hero is a talented Jewish writer who bases a story on a skeleton in the family closet that reveals some of his relatives as greedy, materialistic, obsessive, and foolish. He sends it to his parents to read and is amazed to find that they think it's anti-Semitic. They even give it to a notable Jewish judge they know, and—in the book's most painful and hilarious moment—the judge sends the young author a questionnaire designed to probe his motives in writing the story. His climactic question is, "Can you honestly say that there is anything in your short story that would not warm the heart of a Julius Streicher or a Joseph Goebbels?" And how do you begin to argue with someone who thinks the judge's question is a valid one for an artist to consider?

The division of the American audience into the conservative and politically correct camps came at a moment when Hollywood, always both the nuttiest and most terrified of institutions, had begun to spin into hype hyperdrive. It's still spinning. In the early nineties the studios are gambling so much money on blockbusters (like the $94 million heaped on *Terminator 2*) that there's less slack than ever to accommodate filmmakers who want to try something new. At the same time, the invasion of cable and home video have turned a nation of movie lovers into a nation of channel switchers while scrambling the vocabulary and syntax of filmmaking. Wide angle and deep focus are undermined by TV and video pan-and-scanners; structure and progression are devalued by the quick-rush editing of music videos. Suddenly, almost overnight it seems, audiences have forgotten how to "read" movies. To today's young audiences, the allusiveness of a Robert Altman picture may seem insurmountably cryptic; I've stopped teaching *Nashville* to all but my most advanced students, because even very intelligent undergraduates stare at it blankly, waiting for a clue to help them crack the code. The culmination of an elliptical and humanistic and multiperspective approach to moviemaking that rippled through the late sixties and early seventies, a rough cinematic equivalent to the discoveries Virginia Woolf made in literature, *Nashville* now means nothing to them.

In the face of so much opposition to the very nature of artistic endeavor, which is pluralistic and mutable and resistant to the reductiveness of political categorization, it's no wonder that the visionary power of some of our most gifted moviemakers has dimmed, as they've turned to sap or flash or away from the mainstream entirely. With very few exceptions (*Blue Velvet* and *My Beautiful Laundrette* come to mind), the most exciting work from Americans, and from foreign directors sending films over to our art houses, has been condemned or ignored. There's no community around anymore to respond to movies that challenge the accepted doctrine on either form or content. It's exasperating to watch Herbert Ross's *Pennies from Heaven* in a near-empty theater and realize that the moviegoers who applauded the Brechtian musical drama *Cabaret* nine years earlier might have comprehended it, or that audiences who loved Coppola's *The Conversation* in 1974 would certainly have found themselves *simpatico* with *Blow Out* and *Under Fire*. Similarly, college kids who weren't put off by the hipsterism of *M*A*S*H* or the bleaknesss of *Five Easy Pieces* in 1970 or the loose, experimental lyricism (a legacy from the great French and Italian directors) of *Alice's Restaurant* in 1969 would likely have been at home in *The Right Stuff, Shoot the Moon, Personal Best*.

It doesn't take much these days to doom a good movie to an early grave. Was *The Fabulous Baker Boys*, a romantic drama as sexy as it is emotionally engaging, too realistic in its depiction of the seedy piano-bar milieu, or in the relationship between the brothers (played by Jeff and Beau Bridges)? Among the dreary batch of 1990 Christmas movies there was one gem, *The Russia House*, but audiences seemed confused by the dense plot and the point of view, even though the screenwriter, Tom Stoppard, and the director, Fred Schepisi, laid out both with admirable clarity. It seems that almost any film that places even the smallest demand on an audience is crippled before it gets out of the gate. The demand can be emotional (*Shoot the Moon*), political (*Under Fire*), tonal (*Something Wild*), stylistic (*Pennies from Heaven*), or sexual (*The Unbearable Light-*

ness of Being); the results are pretty much the same at the box office. And so filmmakers who do interesting work grow more and more distanced from the spirit of their time, a sad fact reflected as much in an esthetically and emotionally bankrupt art-house winner like *sex, lies, and videotape* as it is in *Fatal Attraction*. Almost anyone who operates like an artist in Hollywood (or abroad, and then tries to get his or her movie seen in this country) is really bucking the zeitgeist. Even an inventive popular entertainer like Steve Martin, who wrote the scripts for *Roxanne* (a movie that made only moderate box-office returns) and the lovely 1991 financial loser *L. A. Story*, can be said to be bucking the zeitgeist.

The great "American Renaissance" movies of the late sixties and early seventies—roughly, the period that began with *Bonnie and Clyde* and ended with *Nashville*—coincided for the most part with my late high school and college years. It formed my own sensibility and understanding of what filmmaking can be and, on the most inspired occasions, is: the efforts of directors and writers and actors to express something new, challenging, even iconoclastic. But this kind of filmmaking is a slap in the face to studio executives who want to grind out carbon copies of the latest moneymakers, to hack manipulators who work at figuring out how many buttons they can push for the widest possible audience, to moralists who aren't comfortable with the probing of certain issues or the burlesquing of others, to cultural conservatives who resist unfamiliar styles, to moviegoers who prefer not to be shaken up, and to film critics who aren't willing to have their expectations upset. For movies, perhaps more than any other art form, are continually smashing expectations. How did Robert Altman pull out of a six-year funk in 1982 to make *Come Back to the 5 & Dime, Jimmy Dean, Jimmy Dean*? Who could have guessed that Great Britain, a country that had turned out fewer than half a dozen interesting moviemakers in as many decades, would suddenly start producing the best pictures in the world in the mid-eighties? After half a century of mostly awful Hollywood adaptations of great texts, how were we suddenly lucky enough to end up with *The Dead* and *The Unbearable Lightness of Being*? Who could have predicted that projects that sounded ideal for certain directors—the Taviani brothers' *Good Morning, Babylon*, Francesco Rosi's *Chronicle of a Death Foretold*—would end up desiccated and dull, while *Choose Me* and *Salvador*, both of which I dragged myself to out of obligation, would be so good? Who could have foreseen a comeback for Martin Scorsese in *New York Stories*, for Costa-Gavras in *Music Box*—or that the spectacularly gifted John Boorman, his movies so cursed by wretched scripts that you had to assume he had no ear for dialogue, would write himself such a sensational screenplay for *Hope and Glory*?

I'd say that the most valuable asset a filmgoer can have is the capacity for being surprised—for applauding a movie that veers from its anticipated route, reveals a side to a character you wouldn't have expected, switches tones to suggest a richer vision of experience, provides an unlooked-for perspective. Or that proves you wrong, as directors, writers, and actors can when they do superlative work long after you've stopped hoping for it: Bruce Beresford in *Driving Miss Daisy*, Paul Schrader in *Patty Hearst*. When the culture is unsympathetic to surprises it grows increasingly suspicious of them, hostile to them, unable to recognize them. That's when a movie that isn't like other movies is put down or ignored, the way *Pennies from Heaven* and *Dreamchild* were; hardly anyone bothers trying to understand what effects that kind of picture might be going for. That is, unless it's given a more uncharitable label (like Frances FitzGerald's supremely ignorant "sadopornographic" for *Casualties of War*). Faced with the strongest resistance to new work of any kind since the Second World War, fighting "I just want to be entertained" on one side and "I really like the message" on the other, no wonder most terrific work gets squashed in the middle. Or, more accurately, floats along on its own peculiar energy, far from the mainstream, far from the zeitgeist.

Most of the original versions of the essays and reviews in this collection were written in the heat of the moment (that is, as the movies arrived), between 1980 and 1989; most appeared the first time around in *The Boston Phoenix*, *The Threepenny Review*, *The Stanford Daily*, or *Film Quarterly*. I've returned to them, pruned them, and in a few cases topped them up with observations I made later when I returned to certain movies in order to teach them in my film courses at College of the Holy Cross. I've tried to gather the pieces together in sections that I trust will help illuminate both the obsessions of the eighties and my own concerns then and now as a movie critic.

GLIMPSES OF HISTORY

• • •

The one constant through all the years is baseball. It's a part
of our past. It reminds us of all that once was good, and
could be good again.
—*Field of Dreams*

Frank Capra stopped making movies in the sixties, so Hollywood
has had to reinvent him. In *Field of Dreams*, adapted from
W. P. Kinsella's novel *Shoeless Joe* and directed by Phil Alden Robinson, an ex-hippie (played by Kevin Costner) plays host to a field
full of ghosts on his Iowa farm, and all his dreams come true. And
not just his, but the big dream of Americans to go back and fix up
all the personal pasts we've thrown away, and relive the collective
heroic past that never existed. The movie, which came out at the
end of the decade, is a piece of insanity—but it transfixes audiences
and causes them to lose their minds. Robinson blends *Lost Horizon*
and *It's a Wonderful Life* with the cant confirming the veracity of
the American Dream we heard all through the 1988 election, and
mixes Reagan-era family values with a back-to-the-land sixties
counterculture wish-fulfillment fantasy. This is the movie *Rambo*

and *Top Gun* prepped us for—the movie that tells us that not only can we pretend the past we don't like never happened, but we can go back and change it to one we like better.

Robinson may be too starry-eyed to be a real shrewdie; he may simply have stumbled onto his big score. But what he's done here is remarkable, in a very creepy way. Other forms of eighties popular entertainment, most notably the TV show "thirtysomething" (one of whose stars, Timothy Busfield, shows up in *Field of Dreams* as a jaded businessman), depicted the members of the sixties generation in a twenty-years-after corporate phase, focusing on the soap opera of their business and family and sex lives rather than on the decay of their counterculture idealism. *Field of Dreams* picked a hero who supposedly has never lost his. The Costner character, Ray Kinsella, and his wife Annie (Amy Madigan) went back to the land and stayed there; he's still a dreamer, she's still a fighter. But, cleaned up and bled of all their antiestablishment cynicism, these hippies have effectively turned into Capra figures. In *Mr. Smith Goes to Washington* and *It's a Wonderful Life* and, looniest of all, *Meet John Doe*, the heroes struggle for goals that are either so generalized or so benign (honesty, decency, the rights of the little guy, politeness) that no one in the audience could possibly get riled up against them. The most pointed battle anyone (Annie) has to fight in *Field of Dreams* is against the tight-assed parents in her community who want to burn books, and that's safe enough, since book burning was still a potent enough image of fascism to repel an eighties audience. Most of the picture is concerned, however, with Ray's dream to build a field for Shoeless Joe Jackson (Ray Liotta) and the other wandering refugees from the exiled Chicago "Black" Sox, and, underneath that, with his longing to forge a link (through baseball) with the now-dead father he could never communicate with while the old man was alive.

What's remarkable about this scenario is that it manages not merely to falsify the past, but to render it completely irrelevant. Shoeless Joe was Ray's father's hero, who the old man believed had been wrongly accused of complicity in the 1919 World Series fix— and the movie accepts his view. It never brings up the relative guilt or innocence of *any* of the ball players who trail Shoeless Joe through the beyond; we're evidently meant to assume that they were all shafted, too—that *no one* who loves our sacred national pastime this much could possibly have conspired to taint it. It's been the unresolved trauma of Ray's life that he never tossed around a baseball with his dad, but Shoeless Joe brings him back, among the ballplaying ghosts, altering the history of the father–son relationship. And Ray, the sixties man, is brought painlessly into the world of the eighties. The ballfield, his young daughter reminds him, will make them lots of money, because everyone will pay to see Shoeless Joe and his buddies play.

Of course, what really happens to Ray—or rather the hippie consciousness he's meant to represent—had already happened during the conception of the movie: It was retooled to bring it in line with the upbeat Reagan–Bush era. And since no one ever suggests that changes have been made, that there's an enormous difference between the Kinsellas and the young people who went to Woodstock and protested the Vietnam War and smoked marijuana, our own quite recent history seems, in *Field of Dreams*, to have been popped down the hole in Orwell's *1984* that swallows up newly defunct perspectives on the past.

The movies I talk about in this section don't cancel out the past; they embrace it, and in doing so preserve the patches of history against which the characters have lived their lives. Rather than simplifying it they celebrate its richness, its contradictions, and the impossibility of gathering it all up into a neat package. Two of these films present the past in an open-ended, humanistic, unexpected, sometimes ironic fashion: Paul Mazursky's *Moscow on the Hudson*, which deals with an era that has only just become history, and *Hope and Glory*, John Boorman's account of a childhood lived among the falling bombs of the London Blitz. One other, the documentary *Seeing Red*, about the American Communist Party, deals with an aspect of U.S. history our movies seldom explore. The three remaining films examine history through the eyes of characters who have been profoundly altered by it—and come of age when they are forced to confront its complexity. *Withnail and I*, by the British writer–director Bruce Robinson, is an idiosyncratic elegy for the sixties; *Au Revoir les Enfants*, by the French director Louis Malle, is set in France during the Occupation; and *Music Box*, written by a Hungarian–American, Joe Eszterhas, and directed by a Greek, Costa-Gavras, focuses on a contemporary American woman who defends her father, a Hungarian immigrant accused of war crimes.

Music Box, neither a commercial success nor a critical favorite, came out in the last weeks of 1989, and addresses, on as profound a level as any other movie released during the entire decade, our relationship to the history we helped to create.

Better Red than Dead

• • •

Seeing Red: Stories of American Communists has such a compelling, underexposed subject—the men and women who belonged to the American Communist Party in the 1930s, '40s, and '50s—and such a vivifying cast of characters that it's an exhilarating experience, even if it isn't a very good documentary. You've never seen such a genial mess of faces. Bill Bailey, seaman and longshoreman, has deep azure eyes and a swollen bottlestopper of a nose; when he recounts the beefs that provoked him into joining the Party he relives all his old battles, sparring with both his voice and his hands. Gentle-eyed, sweet-toned Oscar Hunter describes the action he saw in the Spanish Civil War, burying his emotion in carefully sculpted pauses between phrases. Sylvia Woods, a big, straightforward black woman with indignant fury in her voice, tells how she sent a pair of FBI agents packing, warning them that white men weren't safe walking through her neighborhood after dark. A shrill, head-tossing steel-mill worker, Rose Podmaka, says she got into the Party because they needed someone to take minutes and collect dues; they weren't actually recruiting women at the time. Howard "Stretch" Johnson, a veteran dancer from the Cotton Club days who now teaches college, lets his loose, jovial side leak through his precise, oratorical classroom manner as he talks about the need to relax, even when you're working eighteen hours a day—especially if you believe, as a good Communist does, that life on earth was meant to be lived fully.

You're struck repeatedly by the way passion and articulateness coexist in these people's speech; you can see their training, the years of endless argument and organization, in the shape of their commentary. Dorothy Healey, who joined at the age of fourteen, explains the joys of commitment to an immense cause: "There was absolutely no question in your mind who you were and what you were and why you were. You had that answered." Marge Frantz, a soft-spoken woman of unmistakable intelligence, explains the possibility of dual loyalty: that if you were a true believer, you held up

the shining example of Russia as an inspiration for your own country to follow. Their explanations are spiked with anecdotes—humorous ones like Edna Whitehouse's, about the embarrassment she
felt when she saw her husband getting up to speak in public, potent
ones like writer Carl Hirsch's stories, passed on to his wife in letters
while he was covering a sharecroppers' strike for a Communist paper, of the atrocities committed against the families he had come to
know.

Confronted with so many fascinating camera subjects and so
many resonant issues (why the activities of the Party were kept clandestine; how political and social life intermingled for Party members; how the violent impulses of men and women, whose loyalty
to the organization forbade them to disobey orders and defend
themselves against cops, got translated into military aggression in
the Spanish Civil War; the confusion and bitterness of American
Communists when Khrushchev revealed the horrors of the Stalinist
purges in 1956), the filmmakers—Julia Reichert and James Klein—
are so overwhelmed that they don't do much. They just sit back and
drink it all in. Obviously they're in sympathy with the interviewees—so much so that they've made no apparent effort to challenge
them, by either word or deed. So we meet only those Communists
who stayed in the Party even after the Khrushchev report, or who
remained close to the Socialist ideals of their youth even after leaving the organization. Yet thousands of Americans who had joined
the ranks during the Depression swung dramatically to the right
during the Cold War, and of the *eighty* per cent of the Party mem-
bership who resigned in or shortly after 1956, some of them must
have experienced such disillusionment that they altered their politics significantly. (The radical youth who settles into conservatism
in middle age is the rule, not the exception, in this country: Look
at the activists of the sixties.) But the closest that Reichert and Klein
come to unearthing a dissenter is the segment in which Carl Hirsch
claims he looks back on his days in the Party as just a phase he went
through—and still, when Hirsch reads his letters out loud, he has
to choke back tears.

Reichert, who conducts the interviews, asks no embarrassing
questions; she's a devoted listener, not a journalist. Remarkably few
conflicts are raised, considering the incendiary subject matter.
Marge Frantz and Edna Whitehouse address, peripherally, the con-

tradiction between the querying nature of young people inclined to join a renegade cause, and the rigidity of a centralized, bureaucratic organization that promoted the constant questioning of *other* institutions, but never its own. Yet neither the interviewer nor the interviewees suggest any other reason for uneasiness. Though we're shown samples of grotesque anti-Communist propaganda disseminated by the FBI, no one questions the morality of distributing *Communist* propaganda. And there's an unpersuasive segment in which several of the people we've met, notably Dorothy Healey, insist that the FBI charges of espionage among Party members were not merely erroneous but laughable—and not another word is said on the subject.

Very likely Healey and Bill Bailey and the others in the film never had any connection with spies or spying (what secrets could *they* have offered the Soviets?), but fairly recent political analysts and biographers have tended to give greater credence to the documents implicating other leftists in espionage during the postwar era. In *The Rosenberg Files*, Ronald Radosh and Joyce Milton point out that the ability of American Communists to hold two possibly contradictory loyalties in their heads simultaneously might permit them to share with Soviet agents information that non-Communists would consider the exclusive property of the U.S.—like designs for building the Bomb, which Julius Rosenberg may very well have passed on from his brother-in-law, who worked at Los Alamos. The danger never was that the Soviets might enlist the aid of American Communists to blow up the government, as the popular (FBI-fed) beliefs of the day had it, but that *some* American Communists, who had no reason to support the position of the Truman and Eisenhower administrations in the arms race, might wish to counteract it.

These are errors of omission. There are only two bad errors of *commission* in *Seeing Red*: Reichert and Klein include footage of Richard Nixon in an Army Day parade (any footage of Nixon in a leftist film always brings a cheap laugh), and end an interview with Pete Seeger by pulling the camera back to show him chopping wood outside his snowbound cabin. The filmmakers fall into a fifty-year-old trap here: idealizing and sentimentalizing labor and the laborer. Read Michael Gold, Grace Lumkin, Albert Maltz or other Communist writers of the Depression, or listen to some of the phrases Carl Hirsch used in the letter he reads aloud in this movie, and you understand how the proletarian became the hero of the thirties and how, as Robert Warshow explains in his great essay "The Legacy of the '30s," novels and drama and popular music that embraced this new heroic paradigm came to be accepted as art. (The most ludicrous example of this cultural devaluation is the 1954 film *Salt of the Earth. Because* its heroes are Chicano zinc mine workers striking against their bosses, *because* most of the actors in the picture are real miners, and *because* the filmmakers were all victims of the blacklist, the movie has always had a reputation as a masterpiece, instead of being recognized as the sorry piece of manipulation it is.)

Reichert and Klein don't get into trouble very often in this movie, but they aren't real documentarians, either—or rather, they aren't real directors. In a first-rate nonfiction film the camera has its own point of view, different from that of the people it captures. It may confirm what they're saying or comment ironically on their words, but in any case it ought to show us more than we could see if we did the interviewing ourselves. The camera in *Seeing Red* tells us nothing. So the *dramatis personae*—the Communists themselves—take over, and so does Martha Olson, who supervised the archival research. She's dug up some extraordinary footage, most of which I've never seen anywhere before: Earl Browder, Party General Secretary, addressing a Madison Square Garden meeting in the thirties; John Gates, editor of *The Daily Worker*, tendering his resignation after twenty-seven years of active service in the Party, following the Khrushchev report; Herbert Philbrick, the FBI agent who wrote *I Led Three Lives*, describing Communism as a "lying, dirty, shrewd, godless, murderous, determined international criminal conspiracy." In a newsreel, cops beat up participants in a Communist rally while the mocking voice-over treats the incident as a cartoon. Glimpses of striking tenant farmers camped out beside the state highway to publicize their plight are as heartbreaking as Carl Hirsch's letter implies. In a clip from the House Un-American Activities Committee hearings, author Howard Fast's frustration and indigation when his attempts to defend himself are continually belittled or cut off infect the audience, too: We want to shout the senators down.

Most moving of all are the visual and aural snatches we get of some of the interviewees in their younger days: Dorothy Healey, a pretty, intense, bright-eyed young woman—barely out of her teens, from the looks of it—leading a meeting of striking cotton workers; Bill Bailey answering HUAC senators in the same animated manner we see in today's white-haired retired seaman, full of an unassailable self-confidence. *Seeing Red* fails as a documentary, but it shows us corners of the American sociopolitical map we've never seen before.

February 1984

You Can't Go Home Again
• • •

In Paul Mazursky's magnificent *Moscow on the Hudson*, Vladimir Ivanoff (Robin Williams), a saxophonist with a Moscow circus playing a New York tour, decides at the last moment to defect—in Bloomingdale's, where the Russian performers have been permitted thirty minutes' shopping time. The personnel at Bloomingdale's who assist him in eluding the grasp of the Soviet officials also forge his initial link to America: Lionel Witherspoon (Cleavant Derricks), a black security guard, offers him a temporary home in his family's Harlem apartment, and Lucia (Maria Conchita Alonso), an Italian saleswoman, becomes his lover. The first part of the film, set in Moscow (and performed in Russian, with English subtitles), shows us how the mediocrity of Vladimir's existence and the constant, overarching presence of the KGB instill a spirit of revolt in him without his realizing it's there. So when his best friend, the circus clown Anatoly (Elya Baskin), who has sworn to defect during the tour, finds he lacks the courage to do it, Vladimir realizes he can act in Anatoly's place; the combination of his slowly mounting disgust at Soviet life and his full-hearted response to what he sees in America have already made the decision for him. The second section concerns his adjustment to America and how he copes with the loss of his old life, his old identity.

On one level, *Moscow on the Hudson* deals with the movement from repression to freedom—with what freedom implies and what its constraints and contradictions are. On another level it's a comedy about the seductive appeal of American independence for Russians, like *Ninotchka* was. But there's a lot more to the movie, too. Centrally, Mazursky and his co-writer, Leon Capetanos, are interested in what happens to a man who makes the choice to cut himself off from home and family—from his personal history—forever. The entire story is seen from Vladimir's point of view, so when he waves goodbye to Anatoly outside Bloomingdale's, we see the clown for the last time, too. And we never do learn how Vladimir's family responds to the news of his defection, or if they ever receive the letters he writes them each week.

Mazursky doesn't force us to examine Vladimir's self-imposed rootlessness the way a more conventional filmmaker might; there's no single moment when he suddenly confronts the meaning of what he's done and despairs. Instead, the sadness he must inevitably accept as part of his choice creeps up on us, as it creeps up on him. Like Mazursky's best pictures from the 1970s (*Blume in Love, Harry and Tonto, Next Stop, Greenwich Village*), *Moscow on the Hudson* has a melancholy undertone that takes over the movie—though you couldn't say exactly when. Vladimir's affection for Lionel's acid-tongued grandfather (Tiger Haynes), who reminds him of his own (though he never says so); the unanswered letters to Moscow we hear in voice-overs; his involvement with the Russian immigrant community in New York: All of these elements suggest his attempts to rediscover what he has given up. He tells Lionel, "When I was in Russia, I did not love my life but I loved my misery. Do you know why? Because it was *my* misery. I could hold it. I could caress it."

Mazursky's previous film, *Tempest*, was pretty terrible, but it contained one funny, off-the-cuff scene, where a group of Japanese tourists applauded Jewish musicians in a nightclub in Greece. The TV newswoman who covers Vladimir's defection in *Moscow on the Hudson* is an Asian, Kaity Tong, and everyone he comes in contact with is transplanted from somewhere else—Lucia, his Cuban lawyer Orlando Ramirez (Alejandro Rey), doctors and cab drivers and immigration officers. Even Lionel, who tells the TV cameras, "I'm a refugee from Alabama; I know how the brother feels." Mazursky and Capetanos are fascinated with the problem of assimilation. Lucia, who came over to the U.S. under the sponsorship of an aunt and uncle, has an accent as thick as Vladimir's, but she dreams of a career in sportscasting or newscasting, like Kaity Tong's, and she resists the increasing closeness of her relationship with Vladimir because he doesn't fit into the dream: He's not sufficiently "American." Mazursky is a warm, funny, life-embracing director, but he's also a realist. He respects Lucia's dream, but he knows it isn't likely to come true—and this understanding informs a number of the scenes between her and Vladimir in a touching, painful way. Vladimir and Lucia and all the other immmigrants we meet have hurled themselves into the melting pot, but the glimpses Mazursky offers us of the old Italian mammas dozing on the porch after the celebration of Lucia's newly acquired citizenship remind us that we carry our first homes with us all our lives.

Robin Williams gave a terrific, full-scale comic performance in *The Survivors*, but his only dramatic role previous to *Moscow*, as Garp, didn't stimulate him to do the kind of acting his amazing comedy routines on TV and in clubs indicated he was capable of. Williams's childlike approach to Garp—he looked like a superannuated baby—was rather sweet, and he had some lovely moments (like a scene in which he scrawled a crayon face on his pregnant wife's belly), but he did nothing startling. As Vladimir, he wears a thick black beard that lends him a Russian bear look (stripped to the waist, his chest and arms covered in black hair, he looks even more ursine), and he's buried in his character. This emotionally full, demonstrative Soviet sax player is an ideal part for an actor of Williams's energy and comic imagination—for someone who's bursting at the seams. But you don't catch Robin Williams the stand-up comic peeking through that beard. Vladimir's eyes twinkle like Mork's did, but they're crossed with pain, and when Vladimir speaks English, it's an authentic Russian immigrant's English, not *shtick*. Even Williams's voice sounds different here (especially in the Moscow scenes)—deeper and less fey. This is a brilliant performance, as eloquent in the early, attentive scenes when Vladimir silently registers the indignities he experiences in the Soviet Union as in the New York scenes where, free to express himself, he unleashes his personality. It's one of the wonderful incidental illuminations of this movie that when Vladimir gives vent to his emotions, behaving in an extroverted way he defines as essentially Russian, he does what he was never actually permitted to do in his native land. Mazursky suggests that that's the nature of repression.

The whole cast is marvelous—Cleavant Derricks and hoarse-voiced Maria Conchita Alonso and Tiger Haynes (who doesn't get to do enough), Savely Kramarov as Boris, the circus manager; and especially Elya Baskin, and Alexander Beniaminov as Vladimir's renegade grandfather. Mazursky coaxes hyperbolic performances out of these two, as he has in the past with some of his supporting players, most memorably Shelley Winters as Lenny Baker's over-bearing mother in *Next Stop, Greenwich Village*. Baskin does the first tragic clown number in years that doesn't come across as a platitude, and hawk-eyed Beniaminov, in just a couple of scenes, provides a vivifying portrait of an old man, a one-time comedian, who hasn't permitted age or monotony to dull his perceptions—whose anti-establishment grumbling represents a living, unre-pressed spirit. Vladimir has his grandfather in him, of course. Their scenes together are effervescent and intimate in a way that, signifi-cantly, nothing else in the film is. (This relationship is the most pre-cious thing Vladimir has to discard when he defects to America.) At one point, they spring a vocal improvisation on "Take the 'A' Train," and at another, when Vladimir returns to the apartment late after an evening of lovemaking, laughing with remembered pleasure, the old man throws one arm around his grandson, claps his hand on the young lover's mouth to keep him from waking up the house, and tells him in a conspiratorial whisper, "There are whores in Gorky Park who have carved my name on the trees."

When Mazursky's in high gear, few directors can touch him. At the very end of the Moscow section, Vladimir plays his saxophone in the only place where he can find any privacy—the circus stable, where the camels and zebras watch him in wonder. (Late in the New York section, seeking solace upon hearing that his grandfather is dead, he picks up the sax to play "Take the 'A' Train" in tribute to him, and his upstairs neighbors pound and curse in protest.) The camera tracks way up into the sky and descends again, down the length of a giant billboard depicting Abe Lincoln wearing a pair of earphones, and above him the slogan, "All stereophones are not created equal." This may be the wittiest transition shot in recent American movies (and it's punctuated by the name of the bus company that drives the Soviet visitors around the city: Liberty Lines).

The scene that follows—the Muscovites' first glimpse of decadent America—could hardly be better. Mazursky carries off an amazingly tricky sequence in which Lucia and other immigrants recite the citizenship oath (tricky because it borders on, but never dips into, sentimentality) and comes so close to succeeding with an even riskier scene, in a coffee shop peopled entirely by customers of different ethnic origins, that the attempt takes your breath away. He rarely miscalculates: There's a dispensable bit involving a gay clerk at Bloomingdale's, and Vladimir's encounter with a Texan on his first trip to New York doesn't clinch, but that's about all.

Sometimes Mazursky engages so many emotional tracks at once that you can't analyze exactly which element is having the strongest effect on you. Lionel has a child back in Alabama he's never seen, and at Vladimir's urging he takes a trip home. Vladimir, now working as a chauffeur, drives him to the airport, and Lionel says goodbye to him in Russian and sets off with a fur hat on his head. This beautiful scene made me cry, but I wasn't sure whether I was moved most by the departure of Vladimir's closest friend since Anatoly, or by the way they seemed to swap identities, or by the fact that Lionel was setting off to do what Vladimir never could.

The words "freedom," "home," and "leave" resonate through this movie, and each means easily half a dozen different things. (Freedom, for instance, is what Anatoly is dying for, the word he writes on the window of the Liberty Lines bus with his finger but doesn't have the courage, finally, to grab for himself; it's what Vladimir feels he's deprived of when he gets mugged; it's Independence Day; it's Lucia's right to define her relationship with Vladimir; it's abundance, variety, and a great aphrodisiac. A shower cap looks to Vladimir like a giant condom; Anatoly has a vibrator button for his bed at Howard Johnson's; there's porno on the hotel TV.) I loved *Moscow on the Hudson* in a very special way—the way in which, perhaps, you can love only Paul Mazursky's movies, with their distinctly urban–ethnic comic temperament coupled with a Chekhovian feeling for the small tragedies of human beings. "The saddest

thing in the world is life," Vladimir tells Lionel. It's also the funniest. Mazursky shows you both are true.

April 1984

Confessions of a Misspent Youth
• • •

The icily arrogant Lieutenant Pinson, the unworthy object of Isabelle Adjani's romantic obsession in Truffaut's great 1975 *The
Story of Adèle H.*, was played by a young English actor named
Bruce Robinson. I can't think of another movie I've seen him in,
but his name cropped up on the screenplay for *The Killing Fields*
in 1984, and he's both writer and director of the comedy *Withnail
and I*, which is based on his reminiscences of his days as an unemployed actor in London at the end of the sixties. Robinson has
placed himself in the film in the character of Marwood ("I," who's
never actually called by name), played by Paul McGann, who does
look something like Robinson but has a trembly, small voice and a
permanent expression of psychic dishevelment. A devoted journal
writer whose impressionistic musings form the voice-over narration
of the picture, he shares a flat in Camden Town with another out-
of-work thespian, Withnail (Richard E. Grant).

The movie begins with these two in dire straits: Low on funds
and high on speed (Withnail's been without sleep for sixty hours),
their apartment a shambles (the sink is plugged up with dirty dishes
so long abandoned that they suspect something's growing underneath them), they allow themselves to believe they're becoming
crazy or sick—"drifting into the arena of the unwell," in Marwood's
phrase. Desperate to get out, they persuade Withnail's wealthy Un-

cle Monty (Richard Griffiths) to lend them the key to his country house for a few days' respite.

If you ever hung around with actors, sooner or later you were bound to meet someone like Withnail. He's the actor as aristocrat, a supreme snob who talks to his agent as though to a butler and, though he's never actually *appeared* on the professional stage, still refuses assignments he thinks are beneath him—like merely understudying Constantin in a production of *The Sea Gull*. Withnail's great theatrical triumph is his own ineffable style. In a ragged greatcoat that falls below his knees, and an oversize plaid scarf that coils around his neck, he strides through the London streets (or through the rooms of the flat, at one point in his underwear with soap all over his lanky body like chalk) like an orphan prince, bemoaning his state. Grant plays him as a neurotic version of a Wildean figure, clipped and disdainful. He's a hilarious combination of Oxford indignation and sputtering obscenity—he makes "fucker," his favorite term of invective, sound like he's coughing up phlegm. He's forever grandstanding: In one rural nighttime scene he stands with Marwood on a foggy moor, railing as usual against the cruel, ungrateful world with that wonderful, hollow comic timbre in his voice, his eyes peeled. (They're weirdly light blue, almost transparent, vaguely extraterrestrial.) The wind whips his coat about him; he looks like a possessed scarecrow.

Because Robinson doubled as writer and director, and because the material is so close to him, he's been able to give the characters and their milieu a distinctive flavor. The scraggly, bottoming-out humor of *Withnail and I* is as indigenous as the tone of a comic story by Deborah Eisenberg or Bob Shacochis, and I had a splendid time shut up in it for a couple of hours. Marwood and Withnail's world includes an unbelievably scuzzy pusher named Danny (Ralph Brown), with black hair as thick as a jungle, who wears dark shades inside the house (when he removes them and you see his drug-rimmed eyes, you know why), and whose diction gives new meaning to the word "mealymouthed." In his first scene he's a one-freak vaudeville show, and when, to our delight, he shows up again near the end of the picture with a joint the size of a human bone, he has a pal in tow, a craggy-sub-basso–voiced black dude known as Presuming Ed (Eddie Tayne), whose response to a marijuana buzz is to spin Marwood's globe and recite Hare Krishna verses.

The two aspiring young actors lead a crazy, unstable life, and Withnail, keeping them both drunk much of the time and veering unfailingly toward disarray and danger, makes it even crazier. When they manage to secure the key to Monty's house in the country, they wheel out of London to the strains of Jimi Hendrix's version of the Bob Dylan song "All Along the Watchtower." It's a brilliant choice: The mood of the movie, as well as of this era for self-dramatizing young Englishmen (or, for that matter, Americans) like Withnail and Marwood, can be summed up in the wild, flamboyant guitar riffs and the lyrics, with their luxurious mixture of paranoia and world-weariness: "There must be some way out of here, said the Joker to the Thief/ . . . There are many here among us who feel that life is but a joke. . . ."

The countryside section of the movie (roughly the second half, up until the last twenty minutes or so) contains some good bits involving a chicken and a bull, and a fine drunken row in a tea shop; Paul McGann has his best scene sloshed to the gills, his mouth full of cake. But Robinson's talent isn't really for the Thurberesque travails of a pair of city boys roughing it, and too much time is given over to the attempts of Uncle Monty, who pays them a surprise visit, to get Marwood in bed. Richard Griffiths (he played the accountant, Allardyce, in *A Private Function*), who looks like a British Jiggs, is very funny in his first scene: In his overdecorated art-nouveau London house, he punctuates his dreamy theatrical speeches about Oxford and *Hamlet* with outbursts against the nasty-tempered cat that keeps screeching and leaping around the room. ("It will die!" he cries, wagging his finger like a knife in—more or less—the cat's direction.) He's so porky that when he whispers a line like "As a youth I used to weep in butcher shops," you fall apart. But a little of him goes a long way, and by the time he's chasing Marwood around the sofa, you may find yourself echoing Marwood's sentiments: You really want to get out of the bloody country and back to London.

Withnail keeps getting his friend in trouble, and then when Marwood confronts him he shrugs it off—*noblesse oblige*. You can understand Withnail's appeal, especially to someone like Marwood, who has a strong romantic–masochistic streak in him: The first shot in the film is of Paul McGann, smoking and listening to some lovely, plaintive jazz, and you can see right away that part of him is enjoying the state of crisis he's in. (It's an *experience*.) But no one can live with a Withnail forever. Robinson uses the end of the sixties (which Danny eulogizes) as a metaphor for the end of Marwood's residence in Withnail's world. Marwood gets a role in a play, cuts his hair, and leaves his friend. But not unfondly: The final, touching shot is of Withnail in the rain, swigging red wine and reciting Hamlet's "What a piece of work is man" speech, expostulating once again on the inadequacies of the human race.

July 1987

The Blitz as a Lark
• • •

In *Hope and Glory*, John Boorman's comic reminiscence of a London childhood during the Blitz, the eight-year-old protagonist, Billy Rohan (Sebastian Rice Edwards), first encounters war in the newsreels at the matinees he and his schoolmates attend. A sober voice-over speaks of air raids, but the kids are making too much noise and throwing too many paper airplanes around the theater to hear the dire warnings and the official instructions. This scene (a blackout, really), which opens the movie, sets the irreverent tone for what must be the most joyfully subversive portrait of life during wartime since *M*A*S*H*.

Hope and Glory's wonderfully unclouded child's-eye view of the unanticipated splendors of England under siege puts to rest, once and for all, the solemnity and mawkishness of *Mrs. Miniver* and *In Which We Serve* and the other stiff-upper-lip, catch-in-the-throat movies about this period—the fraudulence, that is, of the way the English have liked to portray themselves (and we have been all too happy to portray them) during their nation's darkest hour.

Hearing Billy's family and neighbors in the first weeks of the war, quipping "A few bombs would wake up this country" and "If they're going to have a war, I wish they'd get it started," or seeing how his teenage sister Dawn (Sammi Davis) continues to search for her misplaced stockings after Chamberlain has made the formal declaration of war via a radio broadcast (she says the war's not her fault—and she still needs her stockings, doesn't she?), you feel like Boorman's knocked the dust out of your brain.

Though the child's perspective links this one to two other great war movies, René Clément's 1952 *Forbidden Games* and the Taviani brothers' 1982 *The Night of the Shooting Stars*, *Hope and Glory* is really a fresh vision. Unlike Clément, Boorman is concerned with the comedy of war, not its tragedy. And where *Shooting Stars* uses the framework of a memory (a bedtime story told by a mother to her little girl) to get at the way myths are created out of experiences too immense to remain as personal recollections, Boorman moves in the opposite direction: He employs the precision and clearheadedness of a child's observations to debunk a sacred national myth.

In this movie, patriotism is synonymous with sentimentality, and it's sheerly the province of grown-ups. Billy's dad, Clive (David Hayman), signs up for the service and then, in the maudlin afterglow of a few drinks, he blubbers to his kids that his besotted companion, an old army buddy he's run into at the recruiting station who won't leave, is "one of the best"; he's so overwhelmed by the emotion of the moment that he fails to notice the poor bugger's got his hand caught in Clive's car door. Billy's headmaster (Gerald James) leads the children in hilariously bloodthirsty prayers for the victory of the British troops. The geography teacher (Barbara Pierson) whacks her pointer at the map at the front of the classroom, yelling at her pupils, "Pink! Pink! Pink! What are all the pink bits?"; the "pink bits," she instructs them, are the British Empire, and the war is being fought to save them for "you ungrateful children." These moments, with their cockeyed music-hall logic, are like extensions of the parlor scene in *Wish You Were Here* where David Leland shows us the banal conversation of adults from the point of view of a little girl who thinks they're ridiculous. But Boorman's tone isn't melancholy, like Leland's; it's loopy and bemused and gleeful—the tone of a gifted schoolboy.

The film is divided into two main sections. In the first, Clive goes off to join the army, leaving his wife, Grace (Sarah Miles), and their three children (Billy also has a kid sister, Sue, played by Geraldine Muir) to fend for themselves as the bombs start falling. (By the time Clive gets out of basic training, he's too old for active service, so he ends up clerking his way through the war. That's another example of how Boorman throws a kick into the old jingoistic sap.) The Blitz changes everything in Billy's life. There's a remarkable scene during the first air raid, when Dawn bursts outside with her brother and dances around the front yard, exclaiming over the dazzling fireworks display. Boorman manages to convey the beauty of those skies as Dawn and Billy see them, the humorous incongruity of their delight, the scary but still distant feeling of the bombs' destruction, and the sad truth in Grace's clichéd response ("Poor old London").

As more and more of the houses Billy knows crumble into rubble under the German attacks, his neighborhood turns into a weird, magical mixture of the familiar and the strange. Boorman, the photographer (Philippe Rousselot), and the production designer (Tony Pratt) derive a wonderful, skewed beauty from the ruined dwellings, the skeletal, twisted staircases, and the scraps of torn curtains waving in the wind. Billy and the gang he joins dig for treasure among the proliferating debris, which also yields his first glimpses of sex—he can hear the groans of couples taking shelter in abandoned buildings. The Blitz is the great adventure of Billy's young life.

When the Rohans lose their own home (ironically, to a banal fire rather than a bomb) and move out to Grace's parents' house in Shepperton-on-the-Thames, the movie enters its second, country-idyll section—which is dominated by Ian Bannen's magnificent performance as Billy's reprobate old Grandfather George. We've already met this character, at a New Year's family party he scandalizes with a drunken toast to all the women he's slept with. In Bannen's hands, a wickedly funny moment acquires, unexpectedly, a touching sloshed grandeur. Clad in proper Edwardian whites, wearing his silvered hair like a crown, Grandfather George, unspeakably irritated that his wife gave birth to a quartet of girls, becomes Billy's ally in the world of women Clive has abandoned him to. The old man teaches him to row and plays riotous, ill-tempered games of cricket with him; his sputtering displays of pique and the mean sexual jokes he cracks at the expense of his daughters' husbands (he thinks they're all fools) act as a tonic against Grace's romanticizing and Dawn's tears when the Canadian soldier she falls for (Jean-Marc Barr) gets stationed elsewhere. Boorman must be the first director who's ever made a virtue out of Sarah Miles's leaky emoting: Grace, whose weakness for soppiness comes to the surface in the vivid days and nights of the war, is the perfect Sarah Miles role. With her thick hair curling wildly over her shoulders, she looks both fatuous and glamorous here.

Hope and Glory contains a superbly understated performance by David Hayman (he was Malcolm McLaren in *Sid and Nancy*), and a marvelously lively one by Sammi Davis (she was May, the young hooker with a craving for ice cream, in *Mona Lisa*). Jitterbugging with her horny Canadian soldier, who treats her to her first sweet taste of sex, or quarreling with her mother, whose repressed romantic visions of true love infuriate her, Dawn whirls across the screen like a comic embodiment of the life force. The way Boorman delineates the differences between this girl and her mother, who married a man she didn't love and has never warmed up to sexually, is one of the movie's incidental pleasures. And the children are sensational: Sesbastian Rice Edwards, with his wide eyes and angelic face, taking everything in with wonder, and round-faced Geraldine Muir, whose pert, miniature matter-of-factness is the film's best running gag. Rice Edwards's finest moment comes during the scene in which the gang leader, Roger (Nicky Taylor), initiates him by forcing him to repeat a swear word. "I only know one," Billy admits, and then, his eyes glistening with the breathless magic of taboo, he intones it. He looks as if he expected a genie to appear— or the sky to come tumbling down.

I watched this movie in a kind of blissful haze; it's bursting with surprises—startling juxtapositions, outrageous throw-away lines, images that are either preposterous (Billy and his classmates reciting the times table with gas masks on their faces) or lyrical (the barrage balloons that draw cheers from the kids) or both (a German parachutist lands gracefully while the neighbors gape and then, with mock-heroic calm, he removes a cigarette from an elegant silver case inside his flak jacket). You begin to feel like Billy Rohan: The movie opens to you like a treasure chest that seems to be constantly expanding. In the most extraordinary scene, the kids learn that one of their friends, Pauline (Sara Langton), has lost her mother during a raid. Boorman supplies so many emotional layers that this sequence is like a classic short story. First there are the other children's responses—a mixture of fascination and incredulousness, embarrassment and sympathy. Then we see the girl's own sense of how the event has set her apart from them and lent her new status: Answering their inquiries, rejecting their invitations to play, receiving their cautious admiration, she seems aloof, proud. Finally, Boorman shows us her confusion and reluctance when a local cop tries to lead her away from the wreckage.

John Boorman has made good movies before (especially *Deliverance* and *Excalibur*), but there have always been obstacles in the writing or absurdities in the conception; he's traditionally been much better at technique and emotion than at thinking things through. *Hope and Glory* is the first of his pictures with the purity and unity to complete the gifts he's brought to his other work. "We define ourselves in the stories we tell and by the stories we remember," he writes in the introduction to the published screenplay. By returning to the endlessly rich scenes of his childhood, Boorman has discovered in himself the spark of a great storyteller.

October 1987

Tough Skin

• • •

When Julien Quentin (Gaspard Manesse), the eleven-year-old protagonist of Louis Malle's semi–autobiographical film *Au Revoir les Enfants* (*Goodbye, Children*), looks out at the world, his eyes narrow and he holds what he sees in an intense, candid focus that makes some of the adults around him uncomfortable, including his well-dressed bourgeois mother (Francine Racette); it puts them on the defensive. Julien isn't easy to warm to. Living at a Catholic boys' school near Fontainebleu in 1944, he's almost encased in his armor of privilege and intellectual superiority, he's often sullen, and his frankness can be piercingly, unkindly challenging—as it is when the confessor tells him "Everyone has evil thoughts," and he snaps back "Even you?" He's the kind of child a teacher admires and wants to shake at the same time; there's a cold brilliance about him. And God knows he's pretentious: He boasts to a classmate, "I'm the only person at this school who ever thinks about death."

But the probing gaze he levels at everyone and everything also betrays a voracious curiosity about the world which is both engaged and frustrated during this final year of the Occupation, the year of his coming of age—the year he befriends Jean Bonnet (Raphaël Fejtö), a Jewish boy the priests are hiding from the Germans, and has all his preconceptions about the way the world works upended. The film lets us get at what's going on inside Julien, and that gaze has to be our point of entry. It's also the movie's emblem, because in *Au Revoir les Enfants* we experience the events of this early spring just as Julien does: as a series of revelations.

You can believe Louis Malle grew out of that unyielding little kid. In his best movies he sets up difficult challenges for his audience, and refuses to renege on them. He's a great humanist. But his films have a moral toughness that's not quite like anything you get from other humanist directors like Renoir, Truffaut, De Sica, Satyajit Ray. At the outset of his mammoth documentary *Phantom India*, he announces that he spent two years in India and didn't understand what he saw, but that nevertheless he's going to show us the things that fascinated him. If you're the type of moviegoer who goes crazy without explanations, this preface is an invitation to walk out, but Malle's point (the same as James Agee's in *Let Us Now Praise Famous Men*, the film's closest literary equivalent) is that it's immoral to pretend you can explain the unexplainable. In *Lacombe, Lucien*, his study of collaboration during the Occupation, Malle places a cipher—a character who lacks the capacity for moral response—at the center of the film, and then asks us to care about the outcome. In his *hommage* to F. Scott Fitzgerald's "Babylon Revisited," *The Fire Within*, his hero is an alcoholic who kills himself because he's tired of waiting for his life to begin. We have to get past our initial impulse to reject this man, whose existence is useless, and accept him, feel compassion for him, on his own terms. Comparatively, what Malle asks of us in his most famous film, *Murmur of the Heart*—to comprehend the incest between a fourteen-year-old boy (a character who represents another side of Julien Quentin) and his mother—is easy, because, unlike the other films I've mentioned, *Murmur* is soft-hued, pliable, charming. Still, the same process is in operation: Malle's gift is always for moving an audience to make concessions they never expected to make. In the case of *Au Revoir les Enfants*, Malle brings us to identify with this brusque, unattractive boy who jabs himself with a compass in the classroom to prove he's insulated from pain, and then lets us feel the other stab wounds that penetrate his protective layer.

Early on in the film, Malle provides a series of allusions to help us locate the realm we're in. An image of the boys strolling through the streets of the village is out of *The 400 Blows*, the roughhousing in the ancient dormitory recalls *Zero for Conduct* (and, more recently, *Get Out Your Handkerchiefs*), and when the boys get up in the morning to perform their ablutions with icy cold water, you may think of *Jane Eyre*. *Au Revoir les Enfants* has a classic coming-of-age movie structure. Julien is both unsettled and intrigued by Jean at first: Jean is the only student in his intellectual league, which makes him both a rival and a potential comrade. Their first conversation is about books—Jean's copy of *Sherlock Holmes* catches Julien's eye; and Julien, playing detective, solves the mystery of this exotic new boy who says he's Protestant but doesn't have a Protestant name (in fact, "Bonnet" is an invention of the priests;

Jean's real name is Kippelstein), and whose story about the where-
abouts of his parents doesn't sound quite right.

What makes these kids friends is the experience of putting
themselves in each other's shoes. In an archetypal rite-of-passage
sequence, the two boys wander far from their classmates during a
treasure hunt and get lost together in the woods. First they encounter a wild boar, then a couple of German soldiers who give them a
lift back to school. By this time Julien has figured out that Jean is
Jewish, and his normal fear of the soldiers becomes nearly unbearable because he takes on Jean's terror as well. It's crucial, for the
movie's purposes, that Malle set up a situation in which Julien is
made to feel for a few minutes what Jean feels all the time. The
twin to this scene occurs at Mass on the next Visitors' Day, when
Jean tries to take communion but the priest, startled by the sight of
this Jewish kid at the altar, refuses him the wafer. These scenes
aren't only about empathy with another human being's circumstances; there's an unmistakable element of schoolboy challenge
here, too, and it's scary—it brings Jean perilously close to exposure.
(A sequence inserted between these two, in which Julien tests Jean
by offering him pâté his mother sent him from home, seems misplaced, since Julien's already learned what he needs to know and
there's no reason for more experimentation.)

If *Au Revoir les Enfants* were just the story of how a sheltered
Catholic bourgeois who's never known a Jew before befriends one
during the war, it wouldn't be much different from dozens of other
movies about Jewish children hidden from the Nazis, except for
Malle's delicacy and the muted elegance of his camera work—and
the superb performances of the two young actors. But what Julien
has to learn in this movie is more than an acceptance of Jews; he
has to learn the great humanist lesson about contradictory behavior
and plurality of motives—that, as Virginia Woolf puts it in *To the
Lighthouse*, nothing is simply one thing. Julien encounters one surprise after another; the moral ground he thinks he's secure on keeps
shifting. The priests he has no use for behave nobly by concealing
Jean (and two other Jews). The German soldiers are kind to the two
boys, wrapping them in blankets as they drive them back to the
dormitory; and one of them, who speaks French fluently, is hurt
when he hears a student alluding to the "Boches"—he believes he's

acted decently, and can't understand the resentment he meets with at the school.

Julien overcomes his class prejudices when he befriends Joseph (François Négret), a scruffy, beef-faced teenager who works in the kitchen and runs a sort of black market, exchanging the boys' treasures for smokes. Obliged to serve well-to-do kids, he's always on the defensive, brawling and whining through his tears, "I'm not your dog!" to those he feels mistreat him. When he's caught for his illicit activities he's summarily dismissed, even though the head priest recognizes that several of the students (including Julien and his older brother) had an equal hand in the system and that therefore Joseph's punishment is really unjust. You can see Julien taking in the iniquity of Joseph's fate and being transformed by it. But when the Gestapo invades the school, unearthing Jean and the other Jews, Joseph turns out to be the informer.

If you've seen *Lacombe, Lucien*, you want to make a connection between Joseph and the hysterical servant at Gestapo headquarters, a lover of Lucien's, who hurls epithets at the young Jewess he becomes interested in: In both cases Malle is drawing a simple equation between the need for avenging private injuries and the convenient outlet of anti-Semitism. But the scene in *Au Revoir les Enfants* doesn't focus on Joseph; Malle concentrates on Julien's amazed silence when he sees his former buddy with the Nazis. What you hear in that silence is a combination of shock, indignation, and hurt. Having so recently learned it's wrong to reject someone because he's poor, now he finds out the poor boy is really a bastard. It's as if the world had turned upside-down—twice—because Jean is identified through a slip of Julien's. And though Malle sees to it that Jean officially lets his friend off the hook, we can't get that slip, which has a strong suggestion of betrayal in it, out of our heads. We know Julien never will, either; that's the legacy of the terrible day when Julien says goodbye to his childhood.

Au Revoir les Enfants received a lot of praise, and an Oscar nomination for Best Foreign Film, but it lost the award to that paean to a complacent bourgeois spirituality, *Babette's Feast*. Some of the praise seemed a bit rote, too, a reflex response to the subject matter and the inevitable sad ending. This movie is much more than a classy tearjerker—it's stunningly complex and unrelenting in the moral demands it places on an audience. The finest sequence is set at a ritzy restaurant where Mme. Quentin takes her sons for lunch on Visitors' Day; Julien invites Jean along. In the middle of the meal an elderly Jewish gentleman who's an habitué of the restaurant is publicly humiliated by an overzealous French collaborationist who demands to see his papers and then orders him to leave the premises. Everyone in the restaurant stands up for the insulted customer— including, finally, an intoxicated German officer at the table next to the Quentins' who castigates the French soldier for his appalling taste, and throws *him* out. Cynically, Julien's brother suggests to their mother that the officer was only trying to impress her (she's the most attractive woman in the room). We don't know if he's right or not—it's possible, but it's also possible that the officer acted humanely out of instinct. Then Julien, responding to Jean's terrified (and fascinated) silence, challenges his mother (who has no idea, of course, about Jean's background), suggesting that *their* family has Jewish blood, that one of their aunts is Jewish. "That's all we need," replies Mme. Quentin, and she assures Julien that the aunt in question is "Alsatian," adding in haste that she has nothing *against* the Jews. This funny, haunting scene is like a seesaw; you're never sure which end is up. Nothing is simply one thing.

March 1988

Knowing and Being

• • •

The director Costa-Gavras and the screenwriter Joe Eszterhas col-laborated on the 1988 political melodrama *Betrayed*, an absurd-ity about a white supremacist (Tom Berenger) who beds down with an undercover Fed—it doesn't seem to bother him that she's Debra Winger, possessor of the most glamorously Semitic looks this side of Amy Irving. When I heard that Eszterhas and Costa-Gavras had decided to follow up *Betrayed* by tackling the subject of Nazi war crimes in *Music Box*, I grimaced. But Eszterhas is the son of Hunga-rian refugees, and perhaps because of his personal connection to the material—a story about a lawyer who defends her Hungarian émi-gré father against the charge of war atrocities—he's gone much far-ther than anyone who's seen the movies made from his previous scripts (they also include *Flashdance* and *Jagged Edge*) could have guessed. In fact, you might wonder as you watch *Music Box* whether he and Costa-Gavras knew when they began the project how profound the implications of the material would turn out to be. I had the feeling they plunged in much deeper than they'd in-tended, and then found the courage and the smarts to shore up the amazing discoveries they'd made. If *Betrayed* reduced a terrifying contemporary subject to a cartoon, *Music Box* takes such a fresh, exploratory approach to a subject we all thought had been worked to death that it ends up moving past it—like *Lacombe, Lucien*—and into the realm where psychology and philosophy meet.

Lacombe, Lucien is the great movie treatise on the banality of evil. *Music Box* takes the opposite tack—it's an illustration of how mysterious evil can be, how unknowable. The story that Ann Talbot (Jessica Lange) has always believed about her father, Mike Laszlo (Armin Mueller-Stahl), is that he was a farmer in Hungary before he came to the States. Here he worked for thirty years in a Chicago steel mill (his son, Karchy, played by Michael Rooker, is still em-ployed there), establishing himself as a respected and valued citizen. Everyone loves Mike: his co-workers, the Hungarian neighbors he meets at community socials, his grandson (Lukas Haas), whom Ann

named for him, even Harry Talbot (Donald Moffat), Ann's first employer and her ex–father-in-law. But then Mike receives a letter
claiming he's "Mishka," a notorious sadist who wore the uniform of
the wartime Arrow Cross—the "special section" of the Hungarian
gendarmes—and threatening to strip him of his American citizenship and repatriate him to Hungary.

As soon as that happens, as soon as Ann takes him into court
to face off with prosecutor Jack Burke (Frederic Forrest), Mike's
long-accepted story begins to fall apart. First he confesses to Ann
that he lied to Immigration about his profession because he needed
to get away from the Communists, and the U.S. had a high quota
for farmers. Actually, he *did* work for the police during the war—
but only as a clerk, he assures her, and he never took part in any of
the dreadful activities everybody heard about, or even witnessed
one. When the Hungarians send a photostat of Mishka's Arrow
Cross ID, with a photo unmistakably of the young Laszlo, Ann argues that it's a forgery and calls a CIA man to the stand who speaks
of a long-practiced ruse on the part of Communist governments to
discredit their enemies in this way. (Mike has been a loud anti-Communist protester, once causing a disruption during a concert by a
visiting Hungarian dance troupe.) But as Burke produces witness
after witness who identifies Mike as the perpetrator of horrible
crimes, crimes Ann can barely listen to the details of, her image of
the faraway monster called Mishka begins to be superimposed on
her image of the loving father called Mike. She can't reconcile
them—and, though she fights her growing understanding of who
Mike Laszlo both was and is, she can no longer separate them,
either.

Eszterhas draws on his skill at building courtroom suspense and
Costa-Gavras rediscovers his editing gifts (his editor here is Joele
Van Effenterre): *Music Box* moves at breakneck speed. It's very exciting—not because you want to find out whether or not Laszlo is
guilty (you accept that he is, long before Ann does), but because
you're breathless to know exactly which piece of evidence will finally break through Ann's resistance. (The title tells you the answer,
but you need to follow Eszterhas's steps to make sense of it.) What
makes the film so remarkable is the way it takes Eszterhas's effective, shallow structure—basically the same one he used in *Jagged
Edge*—and uses it to illuminate three intertwined themes that are

anything *but* shallow: the ultimate unknowability of human beings, the mystery of identity and legacy, and the question of whether you can take a moral stand against your own flesh and blood.

When Ann's team makes a cursory examination of Mike's history, they come up with a long-term love affair Ann knows nothing about; embarrassed, amused, and a little weirded out, she asks him about it. His defense for the secrecy is to remind her that her private life's a mystery to him, too—he has no idea, for example, why she never tried to patch up her marriage. The choice to make Ann's initial discovery of something clandestine in Mike's life a sexual one is very canny, I think. As sophisticated as we may become, many of us never get completely comfortable with the notion that our parents have sexual identities. What better way to bring Ann (who has to operate now as her father's lawyer and not as his daughter) into the cold light of reality about who Mike really is?

In the courtroom scenes, Costa-Gavras keeps shifting perspectives: We see the witnesses from Mike's point of view, or from that of the court artist sketching them; conversely, we see Mike from *their* point of view. Mueller-Stahl, whose steely blue eyes are perfectly reflective, admitting no one, is frighteningly good as Laszlo, and the direction is dazzling—Costa-Gavras may have been influenced by Robert Altman's work with perspective in *Secret Honor* and the TV miniseries *Tanner '88*. Our sense of what and whom we're watching is constantly being scrambled, especially when Costa-Gavras juxtaposes Mike with a blown-up image of Mishka, and the witnesses—superbly played by Sol Frieder, Michael Shillo, Magda Szekely Marburg, and Elzbieta Czyzewska—continue to connect the two and to attribute their horror stories to both. (There's an amazing moment when Shillo's Geza Vamos, who tells the court that no one was permitted to look Mischka in the eye and refuses to glance at his photo, turns his head toward Mike just before leaving the stand and stares him down.) The last story we hear, from a woman Mischka raped (Czyzewska), is the most horrific, and it prompts Mike to leap up, rush toward her, and cry out, "This man didn't do this! It's not me!" And we wonder: Is it possible for a human being to bury his past so thoroughly that he's truly become another person—in effect, to forget he's the man who did these things?

But *Music Box* is more about Ann Talbot than about Mike Laszlo; it's about what it means to *her* that the father she thought she knew was someone else all along. Jessica Lange gives a powerful, unsentimental performance. She puts us directly in touch with Ann's feelings, about herself and her family, and brings us into the way she thinks—her strategies for dealing with the opposition, both in court (where she's brilliantly controlled; she even lets herself appear reticent, allowing the judge to do her arguing for her when he overrules Burke's objections) and outside. Lange isn't afraid to dig into this woman's unattractive side: When Ann invites Burke out for dinner—shrewdly, to a Hungarian restaurant—she tries to get him to back off by waving an unsavory, inconclusive piece of info she's learned about his own past, attempting to force a bogus moral comparison between him and Laszlo. Ann is tough, and when she fights for her father's life (extradition to Communist Hungary would be more or less a death sentence) she's also fighting to preserve the image of Mike Laszlo she's believed in since she was a child. So she has every reason to pull out all the stops.

It wouldn't be exactly accurate to say that *Music Box* is the story of Ann Talbot's moral growth; the movie establishes her as a woman of strong fiber from the beginning (she stopped working for her father-in-law because she quarreled with his ethics), even though, within the framework of her job, she sometimes acts in ways that give us pause. But she does have to face an ugly truth about herself in the course of Mike's trial: that what he has been implicates *her*. It's important that the film send her to Hungary (where another member of Arrow Cross, dying in a hospital, says he can identify Mishka), so she can make that link, see her roots. When she can no longer continue to believe in her father's innocence she confronts him, demanding "How could you do those things? How could you do this to us? To Mikey?" In *Citizen Kane*, when Susan tells Kane she can't live with him anymore, he asks her, "How could you do this to me?" and she replies, bitterly, "Oh, so it's you this is being done to." But when Ann asks the same question, she's comprehending for the first time that her father's war crimes are *her* legacy, and her son's. Lange is fearless in this scene—she uses her whole body to convey how torn Ann is between her old love for this man and her new hatred. (It's the most extraordinary scene she's ever played.) Finally Ann tells her father that she never wants to see him or expose Mikey to him again: "You don't exist," she says.

It's a brave moral stand, maybe the only one that's possible for her if she's going to be able to live with herself. But it's also a kind of self-deception, because if Mike doesn't exist, then Ann isn't the daughter of a monster. The ambivalence of this ending is partly what makes *Music Box* such a sensational movie.

February 1990

FACING VIETNAM

• • •

Although the Vietnamization of America was a subtext of almost every important film put out in this country between *Bonnie and Clyde* and *The Godfather, Part II*, movies didn't deal head on with the war while it was going on. How could they? Hollywood's function during a war (as Paul Fussell makes abundantly clear in his controversial history of World War II, *Wartime*) is to promote patriotism and accelerate the war effort, and there was no question of attempting to present an optimistic portrait of Vietnam when the TV news featured real battles every evening, and every month brought its share of protests. (Hollywood tried once—in *The Green Berets*, in 1968, which offered the official hawk recruiting-poster view of the war—and the result was instant counterculture camp, like Senator Everett Dirksen's singing.) So Vietnam became the great tabled movie subject—until the late seventies, which brought, in a short period of time, *Go Tell the Spartans, Coming Home, The Deer Hunter, Who'll Stop the Rain*, and *Apocalypse Now*.

By now, there have been dozens of treatments of the conflict
or its aftermath. They tend to fall into two categories: movies that
search for a vision of the war, a way of defining it, and movies that
are less interested in examining the wounds than in supplying the
balm, that—overtly or covertly—ally themselves to the great national healing. I'm not just referring to the raft of optimistic pictures
about recovering vets (like, to pick a sample from 1989, *Jacknife*,
Distant Thunder, and the stillborn *In Country*, which had grander
aspirations—a metaphoric portrait of the country's slow return to
spiritual wholeness), but also to the ones that deny history, the wet-
dream, fearless-warrior fantasies about going back to Nam and winning this time (*Uncommon Valor*, *Rambo*, *Missing in Action*). And,
by extension, *Field of Dreams*, whose hero, having come of age during Vietnam, makes a spiritual journey to a mythic America and a
psychic return to a mythic childhood, is the post-Vietnam healing
movie of all time.

Since Vietnam, its brutalities graphically depicted on the television screen, its persistence an international disgrace, and its ending a public humiliation, made Americans feel horrible about themselves, the initial Vietnam movies stressed how different it was from
earlier wars—how bizarre, how exotic, how physically and morally
scrambled. In the Vietnam of Michael Cimino and Francis Ford
Coppola, Yankees bombed islands so their commanders could surf
off them, or were forced to play Russian roulette with their Viet
Cong captors. Coppola was so anxious to create a landscape for
Apocalypse Now resembling nothing our experience with war movies could have prepared us for that he ended up staging a climax
that looked like the last half hour of *King Kong*. And Stanley Kubrick's peculiarly impersonal neoexpressionist style and the ar-
mored, studio look he gave *Full Metal Jacket* produced basically the
same effect: *His* Vietnam War might have taken place on the moon.

Oliver Stone, in *Platoon*, and John Irvin, in *Hamburger Hill*,
were the first directors to place Vietnam on a continuum with other
wars. *Platoon*, with its sentimental, epistolary frame (the protagonist, played by Charlie Sheen, recounts his experiences in letters
home to his grandmother) and its easy identification of good and
evil, was a transplanted World War II picture. The passionate fatalism of *Hamburger Hill*, where the commitment of young soldiers
to taking a hill became an existential act that amounted, in prag-

matic terms, to mass suicide, linked it to such World War I films as *Paths of Glory*. Not too surprisingly, the first was a hit, the second a flop.

Only Brian DePalma managed to produce a film with a truly tragic vision, a vision profound enough to fit the enormity of the Vietnam War. *Casualties of War* came out just months before the end of the decade. But the Vietnam movie that audiences and critics cheered for that year was Oliver Stone's *Born on the Fourth of July*, an astoundingly narcissistic, pseudo-deep movie less concerned with the war than with the self-actualization of its hero, the paraplegic veteran Ron Kovic. *Born on the Fourth of July*, for all its hysteria and the self-professed grittiness of its realism, builds toward an image of personal triumph over adversity that provides an upbeat package to stow away all the strife that preceded it. *Casualties of War*, on the other hand, is an honest view of history, of wartime psychology and morality. A deeply disturbing experience about unresolvable issues, it stays up in your head, each sequence clearly delineated, long after you've seen it. DePalma's film has the effect of obliterating all previous efforts by American moviemakers to put Vietnam on the screen.

Kubrick and Vietnam

• • •

For two decades Stanley Kubrick has put his audience through demonstrations of outsize opaqueness (*2001* and *The Shining*), empty manipulation (*A Clockwork Orange*), and decorator self-indulgence (*Barry Lyndon*). He brings out each new project with such solemnity that a self-important impressiveness has grown up around the very *idea* of a new Kubrick movie. And that's all you get, finally—an idea of a movie. After a few of these experiences I had become conditioned to wanting to throw things at the screen as soon as his name appears. But I didn't feel that way at his Vietnam film, *Full Metal Jacket*; I didn't go numb, the way I generally do in his pictures, even though there are scenes so hermetic that they close out the possibility of an emotional response, and others that so muscle you into a reaction that your natural impulse is to resist. This time I stayed with Kubrick's movie, partly because it contains some terrific sequences and partly because, to be honest, until the very end revealed the director's intentions, I was baffled by it. As it unfolds, *Full Metal Jacket* (the title is Marine jargon for a loaded rifle) appears disparate and contradictory, matching sequences that are explosively funny or authentically harrowing with a style that all but cancels them out—and then, in the second half, scrambling what we've already sat through as if the director were backing up and starting over.

Like David Rabe's *The Basic Training of Pavlo Hummel* (the best of the Vietnam plays) this movie, set among Marines, is divided into two separate but equal sections: basic training, and combat. The basic training scenes at Parris Island (South Carolina) are bald and frontal—Kubrick relies on some of the most assaultive close-ups you've ever sat through—and have the weathered rigidity of ritual. They're dominated by Gunnery Sergeant Hartman (Lee Ermey, a genuine "gunny" and Vietnam vet who's served as military adviser on a handful of movies, including *Apocalypse Now*), responsible for turning a company of recruits into dangerously fit war lovers—for making them (in Marine lingo) "hard" and "salty." Ermey's resilient, leather-skinned physique is a strong camera subject, and his roasted wit sparks this first hour. All of it is at the expense of his troops, most of it is obscene, and much of it is very colorful. (He improvised some of his lines, but a lot of the best ones come straight from the movie's source, former Marine Gustav Hasford's novel *The Short-Timers*.) Hartman is in no way a sympathetic character; he's a brutal son-of-a-bitch who's not above using his fists on his men to drive a point home. He crucifies his most pathetic charge, an overweight half-idiot he nicknames "Private Pyle" (Vincent D'Onofrio), and he rides the rest of them so hard every time Pyle screws up that he ends up rousing them to hatred for the poor sucker. And Hartman's goading has the consequence of turning Pyle into a raging psychotic.

Kubrick's style in these scenes is cold and off-putting. The camera stays on top of the action, the beautiful photography is filtered through steely, smoky blues, and the actors punch even their funniest lines evenly—they're like sardonic robots. But there's a crazy bravado in his aggressiveness, mostly because the writing (by Kubrick, Hasford, and Michael Herr) gets very gutsy in places. Ermey's exchanges with his recruits, which are laced with hetero- and homosexual imagery, really sizzle. He makes them sleep with their weapons, and in one scene he parades them through the barracks in their underwear, one hand on their rifles and the other on their crotches. You have to admit that Kubrick's depiction of the military is farther out than anyone else's (the Marines, after all, are the wild men of the military). It's a hothouse vision, though; he made the whole movie in a London studio. He isn't trying for the kind of authenticity that won Oliver Stone so much praise in *Platoon*—praise, perhaps, that's distorted audiences' view of the movie's real virtues. (The fidelity of *Platoon* to the Vietnam experience, like the heavily publicized reaction of veterans to the movie, is less a dramatic or cinematic issue than a sociological one, and not terribly interesting even on that level.)

Even on its own terms, the first hour of *Full Metal Jacket* is problematic. Kubrick hurls Hartman's vocal and physical insults in our faces, presumably because he wants us to reel as the men do through eight weeks of this kind of treatment. And he makes fat Pyle so exasperating that he begins to wear on *our* nerves, too. If we're supposed to feel dehumanized in some way, implicated when the men tie Pyle up in the darkness and batter him with bars of soap wrapped in towels, then his strategy doesn't work; we just feel alienated. Pyle's metamorphosis doesn't work, either. When D'Onofrio starts muttering to his rifle and grinning dementedly, his eyes shiny and unfocused, as if someone had brained him with a rock, his acting goes familiarly haywire: He seems to be playing a ghoul out of *Friday the 13th* or the George Romero pictures.

You long for a break from the Kubrick approach when, after an hour, there's still no recognizable human interaction between any two characters—that is, a moment that looks spontaneous. The protagonist is a young man named Davis (Matthew Modine), whom Hartman dubs "Private Joker" because of his sly humor, which flirts with insubordination. He's smart and he's very competent, but he has no more warmth than the others, and his collegiate brand of sophistication, his ironic detachment, his more balanced perceptions, rather than deepening the character as they're surely intended to, mostly make you wonder what the hell this guy's doing in the Marines. (He wears a peace button, but "Born to Kill" is scrawled on his helmet; when a higher-up demands an explanation, he mumbles something about the duality of man.)

The film moves to Vietnam after the first hour—a bombed-out, urban Vietnam, with the skeletal remains of colonial mansions eerily bordered by palm trees, a Vietnam that seems thousands of miles away from the jungles of *The Deer Hunter* and *Apocalypse Now* and *Platoon*. There's not much difference at first: Visually, what we see is linked to the Parris Island scenes, and the acting is bombed-out, too. But then Joker, who's been tapped to write for *Stars and Stripes*, manages to get himself hooked up with a battle unit during the Tet Offensive. Its squad leader is his pal from basic training, Cowboy (Arliss Howard), and their reunion cuts through Kubrick's icily deliberate style. The buddies' embrace is the first true human connection we've seen, and it's a breakthrough for the two actors, who can relax and play flesh-and-blood characters for a moment.

A few minutes later, there's a scene in which a TV reporter interviews the men, and Kubrick shifts his actors into a naturalistic mode; the sequence is reminiscent of the documentary episode of the TV show "M*A*S*H" (though it's not as good). And, bizarrely, he *keeps* them there. Is he saying that you can try to turn young men into military robots by slamming the hell out of them in basic training, but the pressures of battle will always melt them down into human beings again? That's certainly not the theme of *The Short-Timers*, which is written with a taut ferocity and unified by its curdled insider's view of Marines on and off the battlefield. I didn't care for the macho corps pride that permeated the novel, but Hasford shows you a side to the war none of the other Vietnam books has, and I couldn't shake it off afterwards. It's a rites-of-manhood novel, with a death's head cackling on the hero's shoulder as he buries his youth. Kubrick uses Hasford's dialogue to juice up his movie, but he ignores the organizing principles of the book because he has something else in mind, something that never comes off. And because it doesn't, *Full Metal Jacket* appears to be two movies—one about the inhumanness of basic training, which culminates in Private Pyle's psychosis, and one about how Private Joker finds himself in a real battle and loses his (military) virginity by making his first kill. Until the very end, finding any link between the two is a game of speculation, like trying to figure out why the actors switch from theater of ritual to the Method two-thirds of the way through.

An interlude involving Cowboy's men and a sassy Vietnamese whore has comic bite—the combat humor feels just right. And the long climactic sequence in which the men try to locate a sniper who's picking them off is tense and upsetting; it's the best work Kubrick's done in more than two decades (since the glory days of *Dr. Strangelove* and *Lolita*). But at the end, when Joker is called upon to kill, the movie shoots back to the robotic style of the Parris Island scenes. This is the moment that's intended to be the picture's crowning glory, where Kubrick finally reveals what he's after: He wants to tell us that when a man does what he's been trained to do—raises his holy rifle and uses it as an instrument of execution—he becomes nothing but a Marine Corps automaton. (Psycho Pyle, who flunks everything else but is so turned on by riflery that he becomes an expert, is evidently located at the outer boundary of Marine mentality.) Matthew Modine, who's a very good actor, does his damnedest to make Joker's moment of truth work, but it has the unmistakable hollow ring of thesis moviemaking. You can't say a movie's a success when it operates on stylistic and tonal shifts that make only theoretical sense until the last five minutes. And though Kubrick wants us to register Joker's action as a rejection of his humanity, we might want to look at it another way: that his victim's suffering just before he fires suggests he's actually behaving in a humane fashion. (Coppola made the same miscalculation when he had Martin Sheen shoot the woman in the boat in *Apocalypse Now* in order to demonstrate his descent into the heart of darkness. The murder came across as more of an act of kindness than Coppola seemed to realize.)

Kubrick's message isn't convincing. There's something precious and even naive about trying to round up this war, of all wars, in a 1960s guerrilla-theater platitude. Far more effective were the messy, contradictory *The Deer Hunter*, and *Platoon*, which, employing a conventional genre approach, ended up exposing the ways in which Vietnam couldn't really be contained *within* the war-movie genre (though, judging from what people said and wrote about the film, I don't think that's the message that made it so popular). In both cases, the directors (Michael Cimino and Oliver Stone, respectively) made more powerful movies than anyone could have guessed from reading the scripts they started out with; there's a flukiness about the success of both projects that has a lot to do with the weirdness of the war and our unresolved feelings about it. In *Full Metal Jacket*, Kubrick starts with material that could have been dynamite on the screen in pretty much its original form—as an authentic first-person account of the Marine experience in Vietnam—and then makes the mistake of second-guessing Hasford, second-guessing the war. What's wrong with the picture is the strong shaping hand of a director who isn't ready yet to throw away his drawing board and make real movies.

July 1987

Feeling the Heat

• • •

John Irvin's movies can be parched and mechanical (*Ghost Story*, *Turtle Diary*), but when he goes to war he really cooks. A one-time documentary and TV director who spent time in Vietnam, he made his theatrical film debut in 1981 with *The Dogs of War*, a lean, acrid thriller about a group of mercenaries who stage a coup against a maniacal dictator in a fictional West African nation. The besieged tension of the first half had some of the outraged authenticity of the early scenes in *Under Fire*, and there was a startling firefight at the end—a model of flamboyantly expressive action direction chiseled into shape by precise, pared-down editing. His Vietnam movie, *Hamburger Hill*, about the horrendous ten-day battle for "Hill 937" (at the base of Dong Ap Bia) in May of 1969 is a taut piece of craftsmanship, and some of the images have a ferocious, visionary beauty. You may think you've seen all the angles on jungle warfare by now, but the mysterious traveling shots that open Irvin's movie, in which the terrain is glimpsed through what seems like miles of chain-link fence, have a stalking, trapped-animal rawness that throws you off guard. And individual shots seem to tremble on the brink of explosion: a sad-eyed girl racing after American soldiers, waving a bottle of Pepsi; a single leaf bubbling with blood; a terrified child crouched beside her mother's corpse, listening to the gunfire (an image that recalls the beginning of *Forbidden Games*). What makes *Hamburger Hill* frustrating is that while Irvin (working in tandem with the photographer, Peter MacDonald, and the editor, Peter Tanner) jerks you into the horror of the battle, the self-righteous script by Jim Carabatsos (*Heartbreak Ridge*, *No Mercy*) too often throws you out again.

The movie is shaped not as a coming-of-age film, like *Platoon* and *Full Metal Jacket*, but as a state-of-siege drama, with the young members of the 101st Airborne, most of them fresh-faced recruits, being picked off as their desperately hurried, on-the-spot military training proves woefully inadequate to the task they've been handed—to take the hill. There's nothing new in the way Carabatsos uses the hill as a symbol of the unattainable war prize that ends up destroying those who fight for it; *Hamburger Hill* recalls the antiwar plays and movies (like *Journey's End*, or the early parts of *Paths of Glory*) that took the trenches of World War I as their setting. What *is* new to this insulated, microcosmic dramatic landscape is Carabatsos's scarred-vet, if-you-weren't-there-you-can't-understand-it attitude. And though it's hard for those of us who *weren't* in Vietnam (Carabatsos, like *Platoon*'s writer–director, Oliver Stone, *was*) to challenge his experience, his tone gives you pause.

For Carabatsos, the tragedy seems to be not so much that the men go through hell, but that back in "the world" no one appreciates them. At first the men receive encouraging, proud letters from their stateside girl friends, but as the war continues, the mail grows infrequent—and one young woman even writes to say that her college pals have persuaded her it's immoral to keep up a correspondence with a soldier. Brittle, roughened Sergeant Worcester (Steven Weber) has a brink-of-tears speech in which he describes the hostility of protesters when he made it home on his last leave. His buddy, grizzled, sleepy-eyed Sergeant Frantz (Dylan McDermott), chews out the press for refusing to "take a stand"—and, as Carabatsos portrays them, the reporters who show up at Dong Ap Bia are as high-handed and obnoxious as the belligerent moron James Caan decked at the garden party in *Gardens of Stone*. By the time the movie's over, you wonder if Carabatsos thinks that all the trouble in Vietnam was caused by the nonsupportive attitude of hippies and journalists.

You can see where Carabatsos is coming from in this movie (as you couldn't in the loathsome, jingoistic *Heartbreak Ridge*): He wants to show us the war from the point of view of the grunts, and their frustration and anger at the unsympathetic response of other Americans to their crippling day-to-day existence in the jungles of Vietnam is certainly part of that point of view. And maybe there's no way to get at those emotions in this setting without going over the edge into self-pity, especially if you're bringing your own experience to bear on the story you're telling. But Carabatsos isn't a good enough writer to beg our indulgence. His dialogue is banal, and he thinks in terms not of scenes that dramatize emotional states but of devices for manipulating an audience. Both Worcester's tirade and the sequence in which one of his men (Tim Quill) plays a tape his girl has sent him are shameless. Ironically, though, the sentimentality doesn't work the way Carabatsos must expect it to, because the sour, resentful subtext of these scenes acts as an automatic distancer.

What Carabatsos's combat experience adds to the movie is an assortment of sharply observed details. None of the other Vietnam movies has shown us field sergeants drilling their troops in the intricacies of dental hygiene or instructing them on how to fill out life insurance forms, and these snippets of army life come across as simultaneously amusing and appalling. *Hamburger Hill* reports on the racial split in the army, too—something we haven't seen before. And though there are natural, cleanly defined performances by Anthony Barrile and Tim Quill, and Dylan McDermott has a few good, seasoned moments, it's the black actors in the cast—Courtney Vance, Michael Patrick Boatman, Don James, and Don Cheadle—who provide most of the heat, especially in their scenes together. (When he flies solo, Vance, as the unit medic, Doc, tends to go over the top. Based on his acting here and on stage with James Earl Jones in *Fences*, I'd say he was a very talented actor who needs to exercise more control on his intensity.) In one scene, Doc's friends employ a ritual chant to cool him out. This moment makes the power and privacy of the bond between soldiers immediately accessible. It parallels the way Irvin's visual command brings the horror of the war freshly to life: We can't look away, we feel part of what's going on before our eyes. When the script doesn't get in the way of that intimacy, *Hamburger Hill* is a very strong experience.

September 1987

Protest Machismo

• • •

Born on the Fourth of July, which spans two decades (from 1956 to 1976), is the story of how a gung-ho patriotic boy, Ron Kovic, wounded in body and spirit in Vietnam, became the most outspoken proponent of Vietnam Veterans Against the War. The director, Oliver Stone, working from a screenplay he and Kovic based on Kovic's autobiography, is out to make the Ultimate Vietnam Movie—the one that will tell the truth at last and locate the American mindset responsible for putting us in those jungles.

Actually, Norman Mailer did all that back in 1967 when he wrote his gonzo parable *Why Are We in Vietnam?*, but Stone isn't Mailer—he doesn't have a subtle bone in his body, and his greatest gift seems to be for rabble-rousing. From the moment the movie begins, he and Kovic rack up points against those who helped instill a sense of aggressive competitiveness in young Ron (Tom Cruise)— his high-school wrestling coach and his hysterical Catholic mother (Caroline Kava), a holy terror who tells him that doing his best at sports is an offering to God and sends him straight to confession when she finds a *Playboy* in his room. There's a Fourth of July parade in which shell-shocked vets are juxtaposed with beaming cheerleaders, and of course the kids in Ron's Long Island neighborhood play nothing but war games.

Stone restages every big set piece you associate with Vietnam movies—the atrocity scene (Kovic's unit blows away a hut full of Vietnamese peasants); the firefights (the first where Kovic, confused and blinded by the sun, kills one of his own men, and later a scene where he receives the wound that turns him into a paraplegic); scenes of homecoming alienation; antiwar demonstrations. Then he adds a few: exposés of conditions at the V.A. hospital, bottom-of-the-bottle confrontations with another wheelchair vet (Willem Dafoe) in Mexico before Ron decides to clean himself up physically, psychologically, and spiritually. And then Stone runs them through that Waring Blender style of his, all jangling zooms and face-the-music close-ups and just-in-case-you-don't-get-it-yet slow-mo. And (as in *Wall Street* and *Talk Radio*) he directs the actors, especially Kava and Dafoe, to give exhaustingly screamy, relentless performances. If you don't come out feeling you've had a great, searing experience, it's not because Stone hasn't used every skill he's got— and his skills are nothing to be sneezed at—to make you believe *Born on the Fourth of July* is an *urgent, important* movie.

But the film is a twenty-four-karat fake. It has its legitimate moments, in the hospital scenes and in one surprising sequence (in the Mexican section) where Kovic, seething with sexual fury, beds a whore who teaches him how to make love to her using the only resource remaining to him, his hands. And it's unusual to find a Vietnam-slaughter episode where *all* the men (who thought the hut they fired on contained only VC) evince horror and remorse over what they've done. But though *Born on the Fourth of July* may possibly have grown out of genuine anger and frustration over the war and over the plight of disabled veterans, it isn't primarily about those subjects and those feelings. It's about Ron Kovic's suffering and Ron Kovic's heroism and Ron Kovic's need to confront who he is and the spiritually bankrupt people and empty ideals that sent him to Vietnam. And, as in the book (which, brief as it is, I couldn't slog through), all the self-pity and self-aggrandizing become mighty sickening, especially considering that they come at the expense of other characters, whose needs are perhaps just as valid as Kovic's and whose motives can be read quite differently from the way Kovic and Stone choose to read them. In the V.A. hospital, a young doctor has to tell Ron that he may lose his leg because the tube pumping fluid out of it—that is, preventing it from getting blocked up and eventually gangrenous—is faulty and the hospital, hurting from government cutbacks, hasn't the money to stock extras. The doctor's not to blame for the situation (he's as trapped by the status quo as his patients are), but by having him repeatedly flub Kovic's name, the filmmakers imply that he couldn't care less.

Visiting his childhood flame, Donna (Kyra Sedgwick), at college, Ron watches her involvement in antiwar demonstrations. But he can't get in to hear the speeches; there's no way for him to manipulate his wheelchair up the stairs into the gym. Sedgwick is lovely in the high-school scenes, but the movie undercuts her performance unfairly here, suggesting that because Donna runs off and leaves Ron outside the gym doors, she (and by extension all protesters who haven't experienced the war at first hand) is nothing but a callow, fatuous hippie.

The worst case of Kovic and Stone's selective reading is the scene where Ron, who's finally made it back from Mexico, travels to rural Georgia to find the family of the boy he killed. Stone portrays them as stereotyped crackers with accents you could cut with a knife. When the father boasts that his family has fought in every war since the one between the states, you can feel your stomach turn: Are Stone and Kovic seriously using the grieving father of an American soldier as a symbol for the corrupt values that brought us into the war? (This moment reminded me of the passage in the documentary *Hearts and Minds*, released in 1975 but containing interviews filmed, of course, much earlier, where another mourning parent says how strongly he supports Nixon. When I saw the movie, the audience laughed at his naiveté: Nixon was a national disgrace in 1975, and even though the man on the screen was only voicing what most voters had felt only three years earlier, the filmmakers saw an easy target in this poor man and couldn't resist leaving the line in.)

Then the parents tell Ron how proud they are of their son's valiant death, which the army has recognized in the form of a medal, and how relieved that he died quickly and without pain. And all the time you sit there, agonized, knowing the truth about the boy's death (which was neither valiant nor painless), and thinking, "He's *not* going to tell them. He *can't* tell them." But he does. And by the way the scene is written, by its placement in the development of Ron's consciousness, we can see we're meant to see his confession not as cruel and selfish, but as a necessary purification. If he doesn't come clean with these people, how can he go on to be the best Ron Kovic he can be?

I can't think of any way an actor could make this scene work, and Tom Cruise isn't even an actor—that is, not if being an actor means connecting with other performers. Cruise is the perfect narcissist; he moves through a scene with an invisible mirror attached to his skull. It's not a vicious narcissism—that is, it's not at the expense of his fellow actors. Paul Newman and Dustin Hoffman have both said they loved working with him, and I don't doubt he's sweet and (personally) accessible. He just doesn't seem to understand how to get beyond himself and onto another actor's wavelength. He re-

ally *tries* to give a performance in *Born on the Fourth of July*; it's
not his usual party-animal *shtick* (which he relied on, pretty much
unaltered, in both *The Color of Money* and *Rain Man*). He's remarkably restrained, really, except for the shouting matches with
Dafoe in Mexico and with his family on Long Island. (He talks so
rapidly in his homecoming scenes—to show us Ron's refusal to consider the moral and political implications of his Vietnam experience—that he sounds weirdly like Martin Scorsese.) But it's a
negligible performance, because it has no real underpinnings and
it's entirely cut off from anyone else's. Tom Berenger shows up in
one scene, early on, as a Marine recruiter with a suggestion of hysteria boiling up under his jingoistic pride, and he makes more of an
impression in three minutes than Cruise does in two and a half
hours.

The idea of casting Cruise as Kovic sounded insane to me when
I heard about it a year ago, but I don't think Stone could have used
a real actor, anyway; he might have gotten in the way. And I suspect that the star of the retro buddy-buddy actioner *Top Gun* was
exactly what Stone and Kovic wanted. The movie is a trip for both
of them—I couldn't dismiss the feeling that Stone was getting off
on Ron's struggles, all that intense hunkering down to the business
of becoming a real man. *Born on the Fourth of July* advertises Kovic's moral evolution, but it doesn't appear that *either* of these men
has evolved very far: This alleged condemnation of the kind of
thinking that sends American men proudly off to war is as thorough
a demonstration of machismo nonsense as I've ever seen.

January 1990

DePalma in Vietnam

• • •

Platoon and *Hamburger Hill* were both strong emotional work-outs and sensational pieces of filmmaking. But when you watch Brian DePalma's *Casualties of War*, which focuses on a single atrocity and uses it to define the way men behave in wartime, your memory barely registers them. You have the sense you've never seen a movie about Vietnam before.

DePalma arrived at this movie through a natural progression; it's just that he was held up, sidetracked, for a few years. Movie-goers who see nothing but a frivolous bent for violence or, worse, a sadistic streak in his extraordinary string of chillers at the end of the seventies—*Carrie* (1976), *The Fury* (1978), and *Dressed to Kill* (1980)—have missed not only his visual wit and daring, his playfulness about delivering what the genre demands, and the dizzying sensuousness of his technique, but the sober issues at the root of the movies. In an article in the Spring 1984 *Sight and Sound*, Terrence Rafferty writes about how DePalma focuses on the experience of adolescence in *Carrie* and *The Fury:* ". . . the feeling that your impulses have gone out of control, that even your own body is alien, even hostile; the powerful sense of isolation, of exclusion from the secrets of the great, organised, social world; the yearning for connection that sometimes takes the form of furtive, inexpressible love, the kind of love that waits and watches, storing images of its object in the mind." The uncompromising nightmare endings of all three of these films confirm the seriousness of what the characters have gone through. At the end of a *Halloween* or a *Nightmare on Elm Street*, we know the monster's not dead, that he'll be back in the next sequel to terrorize us again (just as Frankenstein or the Wolf Man kept coming back in the thirties and forties), but what we know at the end of *Carrie* or *Dressed to Kill*—the far scarier truth that gets sublimated in the unkillable Freddys and Jasons—is that the *horrors* we've gone through will revisit us forever, that they've taken up permanent residence in our heads.

It was the tone and balance that kept these movies in the realm

of entertainment. The desperate story inside *Dressed to Kill*—about
the teenage boy (played by Keith Gordon), a computer whiz, who
tries to use his technological skills to solve his mother's murder and
ends up on the wrong side of a picture window in the rain, impotent
to save a second woman from her psychopathic attacker—was relegated to second place in the narrative. And the boy's failure wasn't
important, because the cops showed up in time. But the following
year, in *Blow Out*, DePalma played out that story, making it clear
how much it meant to him.

    Blow Out is about a Philly sound man named Jack Terry (John
Travolta) who works for a film company that puts out horror
cheapies. One night, while recording sounds in a lakeside park, he
hears and sees a car plunge into the water. Diving in after it, he
manages to save the passenger, Sally (Nancy Allen), but not the
driver, who turns out to be a popular gubernatorial candidate. The
politician's PR man wants to hush up the fact that his married boss
was out with a young woman, but Jack's instinct for the truth keeps
him from playing along. Besides, when he listens to the tape he
inadvertently made of the accident, he discovers it *was* no accident:
He can clearly make out the sound of a tire being shot out before
the car tumbles into the lake. But no one wants to hear Jack's evidence. The cops think he's just a conspiracy nut, and even Sally
isn't bothered by the way the truth about the politician's demise is
systematically being buried along with him—"What difference does
it make?" she keeps asking Terry. (Sally, who doesn't read the news-
papers because she finds them too depressing, dreams of becoming,
appropriately, a Hollywood make-up artist.)

    Jack Terry is a sixties character in eighties America, and he's
as much out of place as Elliott Gould's forties-style Philip Marlowe
in the L. A. of the seventies in Altman's *The Long Goodbye*. Terry
is defeated by a combination of a flaw in his own character—his
too-great trust in technology (like the boy's in *Dressed to Kill*) leads
him to send Sally out on a rendezvous with the politician's assassin
(John Lithgow), linked to Jack by no more than a fragile wire—
and the political climate. It's not a time for truth-telling in America.

    Blow Out was a coruscating indictment of American compla-
cency (and a prescient film about the incipient Reagan era), but
few critics got it. It received generally poor reviews that seemed
premised on the fact that it wasn't as sexy and Hitchcockian as

Dressed to Kill. Despite the red-white-and-blue production design, the parallels to Chappaquiddick, the sly patterning of the John Lithgow character on G. Gordon Liddy, and the setting (Philadelphia on the eve of a mythical patriotic holiday called "Liberty Day"), almost no one who wrote about *Blow Out* understood that it was a political movie. Most hauled out the old complaints about violence and misogyny (though his portrait of Sally, like all the heroines Nancy Allen has played for DePalma, was deeply sympathetic). And audiences, true to DePalma's sad, urgent message, ignored the movie.

After filming Oliver Stone's *Scarface* script, DePalma got some of his anger at what had happened to *Blow Out* onto the screen. (*Scarface* wasn't a true DePalma project, although he managed to bring something restless and queasy to the early scenes, which depicted the Cuba–Miami drug underworld as savagely out of control—a far cry from anything we'd seen from the Mafia in the *Godfather* movies.) The 1984 *Body Double* was DePalma's way of throwing the finger to his detractors, and it was so bitter and furious you could hardly sit through it. For those who had accused him of ripping off Hitchcock, he lifted ideas and images from *Vertigo* and *Rear Window* that (unlike the Hitchcock allusions he built on so ingeniously in *Carrie* and *Dressed to Kill*) went nowhere. For those who said he kept making the same movie over and over, he quoted himself hollowly in just about every sequence. In answer to the steady outcry—call it drone—about violence to women in his movies, he included his most extreme execution yet: death by electric drill. The movie was a joke (it even included a parody of a DePalma trick ending). But it wasn't very funny, and even his most loyal supporters couldn't find much to praise in it besides Melanie Griffith's performance.

Body Double may have done DePalma some good in the end; it exorcised his demons and he went back to work. He tossed off the Mafia comedy *Wise Guys*, with its moronic George Gallo script, and then he assembled a huge popular entertainment, *The Untouchables*. This was a piece of machinery, impersonal and uninventive and surprisingly square (the big set-piece scene, a takeoff on the Odessa Steps sequence from *Potemkin* staged in Chicago's cavernous train depot, stopped short of the DePalma black-comic jab you expected to be the culminating flourish). But it was impressively staged and shot, and it won him back the approval of both audiences and critics. By the time the grosses were in, DePalma found himself possessed of the hottest literary–movie deal in town (the film version of Tom Wolfe's *Bonfire of the Vanities*)—and all set to roll on *Casualties of War*, an adaptation of a 1969 *New Yorker* article by Daniel Lang so disturbing that, despite several passes at it, no one had managed to get it filmed in all those years.

Lang chronicled a true Vietnam atrocity story, altering only the names. Four grunts are sent out on a scouting mission with their sergeant (Meserve). On the way, acting on his orders, they kidnap a seventeen-or eighteen-year-old Vietnamese woman from her family hooch in the middle of the night, gang-rape her, and eventually kill her. The one soldier who refuses to take part (Eriksson) is immediately branded a homosexual and a traitor. When they return to camp, he reports the incident. The army brass is reluctant to bring the men to court-martial, however—to turn on their own, to expose behavior they must know is more than just an isolated case—and Eriksson, whose life has been in danger since he divorced himself from the actions of his buddies, begins to despair of *ever* bringing them to justice. And then, unexpectedly, a chaplain he confides in is sufficiently shocked and outraged to force the hand of the military higher-ups. The men come to trial, where Meserve stands on his excellent record and claims the victim was a VC spy, and even the most inexperienced of the four, Diaz, explains the importance of maintaining a unified front in the jungle. They all end up with stiff sentences.

If you've seen *Blow Out*, you can understand exactly what drew DePalma to this material. It's rich in his themes: the drive to expose the truth, even when everyone else wants to pretend it doesn't exist; the kind of horror that alters your life forever; the agony of a man who tries to save a woman in trouble and fails. You can see, too, why the playwright David Rabe was interested in writing the adaptation. Rabe, a moralist who chronicles the male condition in contemporary American culture, is famous for a trilogy of plays about Vietnam: *Sticks and Bones, The Basic Training of Pavlo Hummel,* and *Streamers*.

I spotted several ideas and images from *Pavlo Hummel*—by far the best thing Rabe's ever done—in *Casualties of War*, but he serves Lang's material honestly, and he's written a shrewd, smart, beautifully structured screenplay. It's framed (like Lang's account) by a scene in which Eriksson sees an Asian woman on a bus, stirring memories of his Vietnam nightmare. But it also includes an invented section (the first twenty minutes of the movie) where Eriksson (Michael J. Fox), stuck up to his waist in a tunnel, is pulled out by Meserve (Sean Penn) seconds before a VC can knife him from below, and Meserve's buddy, Brownie (Erik King), is cut down by a sniper in full view of Meserve's unit—Eriksson; vengeful, on-the-edge Clark (Don Harvey); and the dumb, eager initiate Hatcher (John C. Reilly). This section enables Rabe and DePalma to set up a number of essentials: to establish the group's dependence, in this sudden, terrifying world, on the cool, knowing sergeant (it's Meserve whom the obviously dying Brownie turns to for reassurance that he's going to be alright); to explain what happens to Meserve and get at the heart of the kind of xenophobic fury that permits him and Clark to rationalize their treatment of their Vietnamese captive; and to raise the stakes for Eriksson, who'll not only be siding with a Vietnamese against his American buddies but will be turning on the man who saved his life.

As Fox plays him, Eriksson has an almost country-bumpkin sweetness and naiveté from the start. It endears us to him when his openness to the Vietnamese children he gives chocolate to, and to the Vietnamese farmer he helps to plough his field, counters the hipsterism of Meserve and Brownie—veterans of months in combat, as opposed to Eriksson's meager three weeks. (With a mixture of condescension and head-shaking disdain, the veterans call recruits like Eriksson, not yet seasoned by war, "cherries.") Of course, Eriksson's lack of cynicism is a little embarrassing, too, and potentially dangerous. We admire Meserve's self-possession, his concern for his men, the quickness of his impulses in crisis. And so does Eriksson, who, still under the spell of the moment when this cooled-out big daddy calmly saved his ass from the Viet Cong, tries to emulate him in their first firefight together, screaming obscenities as he rips bullet after bullet at their attackers, working to get high off battle like Meserve does. But his exhilaration isn't riproaring like Meserve's; it's tentative—he holds something in abeyance.

I've liked Michael J. Fox as a debonair farceur in *Back to the Future* and *The Secret of My Success*; as the voice of the doomed boy in *Dear America: Letters Home from Vietnam*, who writes that he's got to make it in Nam because "I'm lucky, I hope"; even in *Bright Lights, Big City*, where he did as much as any actor could have with the dumb, slick material and an essentially insufferable character. In the difficult role of the young rocker in Paul Schrader's *Light of Day* who's pulled between tenderness for his mother and loyalty to his selfish, rebellious sister, he showed a remarkable emotional clarity, and that's what he brings to *Casualties of War*. Fox ensures that we always know what Eriksson is thinking and feeling; he's our touch with emotional and moral sanity as the world of the movie becomes increasingly psychotic. Critics of the movie who complain that Eriksson's too "good" miss the fact that we experience the film through his skin, just as we experience *Blow Out* through Travolta's. What happens to Eriksson happens to us, too.

The most fascinating character in the picture is Sean Penn's Tony Meserve. He's not a malevolent figure with advanced warrior's skills, like Tom Berenger's Sergeant Barnes in *Platoon*. De-Palma takes pains to show us his love for Brownie, and we can believe that his way of distancing himself—the unemotional way in which he confirms Brownie's death to the recruits—is a necessary guard against combat breakdown, though in practice it doesn't work: We can see by his actions on the scouting mission that he *has* broken down. But Penn's Meserve doesn't tip his hand in any of the usual ways. It's as important to Penn's performance that he conceal the workings of Meserve's mind from us as it's important to Fox's that he reveal everything, because we're seeing Meserve from Eriksson's point of view, and Eriksson doesn't know how to read him. While the recruits discuss the day's events, Meserve, on the other side of the screen and in the foreground, shaves himself silently and meticulously. The staging and the position of the camera tell us there's an invisible barrier between Meserve and the others, but we can't tell what Meserve's response is to the chatter of these still untried soldiers: Does he find them ridiculous? touching? wrongheaded?

It isn't until he learns that he and his men can't leave camp on their promised R&R, and blows a gasket, that we can trace Meserve's behavior back to Brownie's death (and understand that what he was probably thinking while he shaved was, "How the hell am I going to tell them Brownie's dead?"). And when he's out alone with his unit (with Diaz, played by John Leguizamo, replacing

Brownie) and Eriksson, responding to his orders about taking turns raping the Vietnamese woman they've kidnaped, goes through a cycle of shock, confusion, and rebellion, threatening his command, Penn allows us to see what this new, war-ravaged Meserve is capable of: the depth of his rage when his authority is questioned, the range and venom of the attacks he can level against a soldier who won't commit himself to the unity of the group, and a kind of impotence underneath his macho swagger. He'll initiate the rape, but he won't kill the woman himself. He orders it done by others, making it a test of the loyalty and commitment of his recruits, and the order acquires a certain hysteria when they either refuse or botch the job. Penn gives a brilliant performance. It takes a while to get used to the studied deep-Brooklyn accent, the bulky walk, the gum-chewing—Method mannerisms he relies on to work his way through to the character. They're not what his acting is really about here, though, as they have been in other films (like *At Close Range*). Listen and you'll hear some of the most amazing line readings in recent movies.

The battle sequences in this film have a devastating immediacy. DePalma uses his phenomenal timing—the driving suspense of his probing camera, the jolts in the editing that always catch us off guard—to suggest the unpredictability of guerrilla warfare. (*Casualties* was edited by Bill Pankow.) The felling of Brownie has the out-of-nowhere punch of scenes in *Carrie* and *The Fury* and *Dressed to Kill*, and I don't think there's anything morally questionable in that: To DePalma, war is a horror show, and who would seriously challenge him on that point? It's not as though he employed his chiller techniques just to give us a quick rush: Erik King has such warmth and boogying high style that we build up a relationship with Brownie in just a few scenes, and we're left unnerved and aching at his loss. The rapidity with which he's replaced by Diaz and forgotten—except as the unspoken impetus for Meserve's psychotic behavior and finally an excuse to propel Clark's hatred of "gooks"—is unnerving, too: What is this alien place where experience is in speeded-up motion, where the mourning period for dead men is only minutes long and battle ages you so fast that a generation seems to separate a twenty-year-old sergeant like Meserve from his raw recruits? When Fox's Eriksson returns from his ordeal, you'd swear by the wised-up tone of his exchanges with his buddy Rowan

(Jack Gwaltney) and the way he talks to a frightened "cherry" who hangs around him that he'd been gone ten years.

The nightmare of *Casualties of War* really begins when Meserve and Clark kidnap Oahn (Thuy Tu Le), and from then on, the experience of the movie takes on a De Sica–like intensity. The horrors come thick and fast, and each one is so much worse than the last that you get the feeling DePalma's leading you through the circles of hell. (It's more horrifying, too, because photographer Stephen J. Burum—who does his best work to date—shoots so much of it in daylight, so you can't delude yourself into thinking it's all a bad dream.) First the abduction, where Oahn's weeping mother, in a pitiful, desperate gesture, insists that her daughter be permitted to take a scarf along, and Clark uses it to gag her. (Don Harvey, with his closed face, has some truly frightening moments in this role. In one, he hovers over Oahn as they trek along, his rifle in his hands, chanting the words to The Doors song "Hello, I Love You" in a husky half-whisper.) Then the rape, where even Diaz, who's told Eriksson he wouldn't take part, acquiesces—the moment when this spooked boy (John Leguizamo is terrific) reluctantly loosens his fatigues and climbs on top of the writhing girl is as horrendous a loss of innocence as movies have ever given us. (The title of the movie resounds loudest at this moment; *everyone's* a casualty in this war.) Then the scene in which Eriksson, alone with Oahn while the others are higher up on the hill, on the lookout for VC, tries to help her. She cowers against a tree, and for the first time since before the rape we see Thuy Tu Le's face—and it's worse than we could ever have imagined. And finally the murder.

When DePalma pulls Meserve into the foreground while he's shaving, early on, distancing him from the recruits, he's initiating a motif you can trace through the movie. From the point at which the unit takes on their unwilling sixth traveling companion, however, it's always Eriksson who's separated from the other men (except, briefly, when Diaz allies himself with Eriksson); they form a unit that inevitably views him, the one outstanding soldier, as a menace. When Oahn is dragged away, Eriksson is left standing with her mother and sister, dazed by what he's witnessed, ineffectually muttering an apology they can't understand (and which, even if they could, would mean nothing to them).

When Eriksson begins to question Meserve (to suggest that

what they're doing comes under the heading of kidnaping), Meserve, astonished by his stance, calls him out and orders him to replace Hatcher on point. When Eriksson persists, Meserve makes a speech—using the others as props to illustrate his argument—that divides the group into two parts, VC and non-VC, and leaves it up in the air which side Eriksson's on. When Eriksson refuses to participate in the rape, Meserve sends him out in the rain on sentry duty, where he stands in the foreground, at the side of the frame, facing the camera, while the rape is played out in the background.

There's a phenomenal shot of Fox in the flickering blue slow-motion rain; it looks like an electric current. Time stops while Oahn's rape is branded on Eriksson's brain. He doesn't watch while his comrades violate the girl, but his presence is literally the frame through which *we* see it—that is, we view it through his horror and outrage. Yet he doesn't prevent it, or can't: It literally takes place behind his back. Later, he's on his stomach at the edge of a cliff, engaged in a firefight he started in the hopes of delaying Oahn's murder, when Clark, in the background, knifes her. Once again he's powerless to save her, like teenage Peter pounding his fist on that window in *Dressed to Kill* or Jack Terry driving through the streets of Philadelphia, screaming Sally's name helplessly while she's alone, trying to fend off a psychopath.

The two scenes between Michael J. Fox and Thuy Thu Le—before and after the rape—are the core of this movie, and they have a startling purity and directness; except for the final image of Travolta in *Blow Out*, DePalma has never been this emotionally open before. To use an acting-class term, Fox and Le attain a level of connection that actors seldom reach, where nothing is held back and every feeling seems etched in lightning. They're both magnificent. Instinctively pitying and humane, Eriksson seeks to gain Oahn's trust. When the unit stops at a clearing, he gently tends to her wounds and tries to tell her he's her friend. His tenderness toward her in this scene, and his proffered assistance, make his inability to prevent what happens to her a betrayal of that trust—that's the truth Eriksson has to start living with once Meserve initiates the rape.

The next morning, Eriksson's left alone with Oahn while the others are on the mountain, and he has to fight against her terror that he too means her harm. She's feverish, hysterical, little more than a wounded child; and once she's convinced that he wants to help her, she sees him as her only protection, clings to him, and tries to persuade him to run away with her. Unable to reason with her in language they can both understand, torn between his official loyalty to his unit and his emotional loyalty to this victim of his comrades' brutality, he finds himself pulled (like another helpless child) along with her. But before they can get away, Clark shows up and drags them both back to the unit.

Rabe and DePalma don't make anything easy. Far from battle, we can moralize about how soldiers ought to behave, and we can make judgments about who conducted himself well or badly. But when we see Eriksson forced to choose between an act of compassion (escaping with Oahn) that's inherently treasonable, and fidelity to his military duty, and so hung up by the dilemma that he wrecks their chances to escape, we can understand why he's haunted by what happens to her and can't forgive himself. Oahn's death is agonizing: Staggering from Clark's stab wounds, she stumbles across the tracks like a bleeding ghost out of Shakespeare—the walking embodiment of Eriksson's helplessness and guilt, whom he can't reach (Meserve blocks his path) before Clark's machine gun cuts her down. De Palma needs to take as long as he does with this sequence so we'll feel Eriksson's shock and impotence, so we'll understand his question to Rowan when they get back to camp—"What would you have done?"—and his tortured, drunken confession to the chaplain (Sam Robards): "I failed." The movie comes down to each of us; it puts us all in Eriksson's boots.

Oahn's murder occurs in the midst of an exchange of gunfire between the unit and the VC. When she falls, the world explodes around Eriksson—but the last thing he sees is her broken body on the rocks below him. Before he passes out, he separates that image out from the gunfire and the enemy corpses and the flaming landscape. And when he awakes in the camp hospital, amid wounded Americans screaming in pain, he realizes he needs to keep Oahn's cries (and his own) clear in his head. He rushes out of the tent to separate them out from the other sounds around him.

The last section of *Casualties of War*, where Eriksson combats the opposition and studied indifference of the officers he reports the incident to, as well as Clark and Meserve (who want him dead), is a culmination of the images of division we've seen through the Oahn scenes. Now Eriksson, whose decency and sensitivity have alienated him from his buddies, fights to isolate Oahn's fate from the rest of the noise and bloodshed, to give it the status of an atrocity and see that it isn't forgotten.

There are a few late scenes in *Casualties of War* that don't work. One, where the dreadful death of a young recruit provokes a spiritual revelation in Eriksson, is a miscalculation, because no violence can affect us more than what we've already seen perpetrated on Oahn. And we know how it's changed Eriksson—the movie doesn't need to supply him with any further self-discoveries. Another, where he tells his story to a black officer, Reilly (Ving Rhames), who counters with his own tale of racial injustice (he's cautioning Eriksson that anger and indignation seldom get you anywhere), is stagy and awkward; it stops the film cold for a minute, and I think that's because Reilly's monologue is full of the theatrical self-consciousness you can always hear in Rabe's stage dialogue. Other actors get saddled with that, too—Penn, and John C. Reilly as Hatcher (he's stuck with most of the male bonding speeches)— but the superb ensemble work in the unit scenes counteracts it. And DePalma's direction has a softening, humanizing effect on Rabe's inflated diction and pedantry in every other instance.

The ending is a thornier issue. When Eriksson returns to himself on the train, he sees that the Asian woman (also played by Thuy Thu Le) who's brought on his recollection has departed, leaving behind her scarf. (This delicate reminder of the scarf Oahn's mother pressed on her during her kidnapping is an exquisite, poetic touch.) He runs after her to return it, and she interprets his haunted look: "I remind you of someone, don't I?" Then she tells him he's had a bad dream, but it's over now, and as she walks away a choir begins to sing on the soundtrack. The choir is definitely a mistake (the *only* mistake in Ennio Morricone's plaintively beautiful score); as for the rest of the ending, I'm not sure. Since DePalma's other endings are, famously, reaffirmations of horror, I don't think we can take the young woman's line at face value—certainly not after what De-Palma has put us through (and the remnants of the horror that Eriksson's endured are still on Michael J. Fox's face). But I couldn't help thinking about what De Sica achieved in the last moments of *Umberto D.*, where the despairing old man, having failed at suicide, rediscovers the world. That ending doesn't devalue the sadness that's preceded it—it doesn't pretend that Umberto D.'s troubles are over, or that the world has become an easier place for him to live in—but it opens another door. That may be what DePalma wishes to do at the end of *Casualties of War*.

Casualties of War is a great, searing movie experience—but, despite Columbia's solid publicity campaign, audiences didn't come out for it. And though it inspired a handful of critics (like Pauline Kael and *The San Francisco Examiner*'s Michael Sragow) to passionate eloquence, there were some mighty strange reviews: tepid, reluctant, even (as in Frances FitzGerald's case) hostile. No matter what he does, DePalma can't seem to shake his unfounded reputation for enjoying cruelty to women—even here, where he demonstrates a wracked, heartbroken empathy for the victimized Oahn.

I think the main obstacle to *Casualties of War*'s success at the box office, though, was that people weren't anxious for the kind of intensity they knew DePalma would bring to a film about Vietnam. DePalma's messy, morally booby-trapped world is as true a portrait of America as any filmmaker put on the screen in the eighties, but it's a very bad time for an artist who works in the personal, direct, emotional way he does here, applying a phenomenally sophisticated technique to raw nerves. DePalma's Vietnam isn't the mysterious, acid-trip, rock 'n' roll war you couldn't understand if you weren't there. It's the war Fussell writes about in *Wartime*, the one we all know too well—from *All Quiet on the Western Front* and *The Red Badge of Courage*, from Picasso's *Guernica*, from Shakespeare's *Henry IV* and the opening scenes of *Macbeth*, from Euripides's *The Trojan Women*. It's the one you can't pretend is glorious or heroic, the one you can't escape. No wonder audiences would rather see *Field of Dreams*.

October 1989

BLACK AND WHITE

• • •

The problem with most eighties movies that cover racial topics is that they're strictly in black and white: simple-minded, like Steven Spielberg's *The Color Purple* or John G. Avildsen's *Lean on Me*. It was a sign of the desperation of audiences—black and white alike—for some genuine glimpse of black culture in our movies that Spike Lee's *Do the Right Thing* won such phenomenal success, popular and critical, at the end of the decade. You certainly couldn't blame black filmgoers for responding to a movie that put something of their experience up on the screen, and you probably couldn't blame white filmgoers for the ways in which they misread the movie as a fair-minded exploration of the causes of racism, an even-handed indictment of racial violence, a depiction of different kinds of anger (the movie's defenders came up with some fairly elaborate interpretations of Lee's motives), and so on. After all, what the reviewers said *Do the Right Thing* was—they treated it like *Native Son* or *The Invisible Man* or the combined output of Charlie Parker and John Coltrane—was what *we* wanted it, or *something*, to be. After the travesties of *The Cotton Club* and *The Color Purple* and *Cry Freedom*, alleged efforts to capture the black experience that turned it into mush (or Walt Disney or *The Sound of Music*), a movie with a pipeline into black urban anger was bound to cause a sensation.

But if anything makes Spike Lee a filmmaker for his era, it's his shrewdness at PR. *Do the Right Thing* is carefully layered so that it gives off different sets of signals to white and black audiences. White audiences get distracted by Danny Aiello's sweetness in the role of Sal, the Italian pizzeria owner; they don't see that his generosity and his concern for the neighborhood count for nothing in the scheme of the picture once he calls Radio Raheem (Bill Nunn) a nigger. At that point *Do the Right Thing* strips down to its real purpose: not to catalogue the horrors of racial intolerance but to demonstrate to blacks that if they pushed any white man far enough, even one who seemed to be a nice guy, he'd revert to type, and thus to racial epithets. (Since Aiello refused to play the role as Lee originally wrote it, Lee simply used the actor's qualities *against* the character.) White audiences concentrate on the reasonable way Lee sets up Sal's explosion: The oppressive heat, the long, hard day at work, the nail-on-slate irritation of Radio Raheem's ghetto blaster. They miss the fact that the director presents it, not as words spoken carelessly in anger but as a revelation of the kind of racial hatred the character has been harboring inside him all these years— which is a little like filming a scene in which a frustrated child tells his parents that he wishes they were dead and then suggesting the kid really is a psychopath.

White audiences see Mookie, the delivery boy played by Lee himself, as a mixed proposition at best: funny and smart, but lazy and irresponsible, a lousy employee; and a flop not only as a father, but as a partner to the woman who is raising his child with her mother's help. Black audiences (like the one I saw the movie with) recognize Mookie as belonging to a folk tradition—he's the shiftless charmer, the quick-talking scam artist who cheerfully gets away with murder—and respond with audible pleasure whenever he turns up on screen. They're willing to go all the way with him, which is why it's a calculated move on Lee's part to have Mookie start the riot that destroys Sal's store by heaving a garbage pail through his window. For a black audience, that's the equivalent of placing that pail in the hands of the Little Tramp. Nigger-calling Sal doesn't have a chance against this ballsy little man of the people; Lee is insuring that a black audience—the audience *Do the Right Thing* was made for—will be on the side of the destruction. So of course Mookie escapes judgment—when he comes back to Sal the next day and demands his back pay, pointing out that he's got a baby son to feed, the movie's solidly on his side. Any irony in this scene has to be supplied by white moviegoers who, naturally, feel queasy about what happens to Sal's Pizzeria and assume, wrongly, that Lee shares their feelings. Spike Lee, heating up his racist rabble-rouser of a movie, plays both black *and* white audiences for suckers.

Do the Right Thing is coded, and it's hard to decipher the code if you see the movie with an all-white audience. When Sal lays out the red carpet for Mookie's sister Jade (Joie Lee), and Mookie pulls her into the alley behind the pizzeria to warn her to stay away from Sal (because he's a dirty old man), it's easy to believe Lee wants us to think Mookie's out of line—unless we notice the words "Tawana told the truth" scrawled on the wall behind them. (The subtext of the scene, supplied by that graffito: We know what white men do to little black girls, and how the world judges their stories later.) When Lee ends the film with two contradictory quotes about violence, one from Martin Luther King and one from Malcolm X, the juxtaposition only *seems* fair-minded: In the context of the preceding riot, which he's set up to win their approval, a black audience stays silent during the first quote and cheers loudly for the second.

Lee, who's made some scandalously offensive public remarks (especially about Jews), is a lot like Mookie. He gets away with murder. In his movies he gets away with old-fashioned melodrama laid on with a trowel; the attack in *Do the Right Thing*, as in *School Daze* (which came out earlier) and *Jungle Fever* (which came out later), is broad, loud, and flat—as if the director were slapping you across the face with the back of his hand. He must be the greatest repository for white liberal guilt this country has ever known, and God, does he know how to milk that guilt. If you praise a complex movie like *A World Apart* or a deeply satisfying one like *Glory*, both antidotes to the idiot movies about racial relations, he hauls out the old nonsense about the inauthenticity of any work about a black

subject that isn't made by blacks—and current PC attitudes back
him up. Or he points out that the protagonists of these movies are
white, not black, and aren't black audiences sick and tired of having
their experiences filtered through the consciousness of white liberals?

Though *Glory* most assuredly *is* built around the story of Robert Shaw, the young white commander of the black 54th Massachusetts Volunteer Infantry in the Civil War, and though Matthew
Broderick's beautifully muted performance in the role *is* part of the
film's success, its heart and soul is in fact the great *black* actors in
it—Denzel Washington, Morgan Freeman, and André Braugher.
And have we become so doctrinaire that we can't see apartheid, the
subject of *A World Apart*, as a tragedy for *all* human beings? *A
World Apart* is the story of Ruth First, the first white woman to be
jailed under the Ninety Days Act (for her actions in opposition to
apartheid), and the screenwriter, Shawn Slovo, is First's daughter.
The movie certainly *feels* authentic. It used to be understood that
good writers didn't write polemics; they found more imaginative
strategies, subtler and more expansive ways of making their points.
That's the strength of *A World Apart*, which is the equivalent of a
fine short novel about growing up in South Africa.

Hollywood is currently supporting (for a while, at least) more
black filmmakers than ever. (We're all waiting for the black director who can transform the experience of black Americans into great
moviemaking.) Recently both Bill Duke, who worked lovingly with
his superb all-black cast in *A Rage in Harlem*, and John Singleton,
whose *Boyz n the Hood* makes a legitimate connection with black
urban experience, have shown talent and promise—whatever the
limitations of these particular movies. I don't think we can afford
to dismiss pictures like *A World Apart* or *Glory*, or to accept whatever Spike Lee's handing out just because he says he's the great black
hope and a lot of people, responding to the buttons he pushes, seem
to believe him.

Trashing Black Culture, Part I:
The Director as Superstar

• • •

In 1920 the first black heavyweight champ, Jack Johnson, acquired a new building on the corner of Lenox and 142nd Street in New York City and turned it into an establishment called the Club Deluxe. When he failed to make a success of it, the syndicate under the control of gangster Owen "Owney" Madden, who was then serving time in Sing Sing for murder, took it over from Johnson. Renaming it the Cotton Club, they sank a good amount of bootleg money into it and staged a grand opening in the fall of 1923, some months after Madden's release. For the next seventeen years—during the period of the Harlem Renaissance, when white socialites and intellectuals "discovered" the black man—the Cotton Club occupied the key spot in Harlem night life. It came to occupy a significant place in the history of black culture in this country.

The Cotton Club represented the highest plane to which black performers of the twenties and thirties could aspire, in terms of recognition, yet everyone associated with the production end of its shows was white, all the chorus girls were "high yaller" (light-skinned), at least until an insistent young black woman named Lucille Wilson broke the "color bar," and the clientele was exclusively white. Under the management of Herman Stark and a genial gambler named George "Big Frenchy" DeMange, Don Healy staged a series of elaborately designed, elegantly costumed revues that capitalized on the Negro stereotypes that white audiences had suddenly begun to delight in—the plantation darky, the jazz baby, the grinning, loudly dressed Harlem dandy. But however fake and deleterious the image of the Negro propounded by these shows, the talent they offered up was anything but counterfeit. Bandleaders Duke Ellington, Jimmie Lunceford, and Cab Calloway, dancers Bill "Bojangles" Robinson, Avon Long, and the Nicholas Brothers, singers Ethel Waters and Lena Horne, all were among the entertainers featured, often in numbers built around the music of Harold Arlen, whom Waters dubbed "the Negro-ist white man" she ever knew.

The Cotton Club's unique location at the crossroads of white society and black culture (which met on the whim of white savants), of gangland and the New York aristocracy (which met as a result of Prohibition), makes it a great subject for the movies. When you read Jim Haskins's scattered but still tantalizing account (*The Cotton Club: A Pictorial and Social History of the Most Famous Symbol of the Jazz Era*), you imagine a sumptuous, provocative, deliriously entertaining musical drama, filled with fabulous numbers and scintillating personalities and amazing incidents—like the one about how Madden's boys "arranged" the termination of Ellington's Philadelphia contract in order to get him to New York sooner, or the story of Lena Horne's having to smuggle herself out of the club in a crowd of chorus girls when she quit, because *no one* walked out on the Cotton Club.

But when Francis Ford Coppola directed the movie *The Cotton Club*, he had a different idea: to star himself, in the form of his technical razzle-dazzle and his spendthrift virtuosity—nearly fifty million dollars' worth. Squandering money, squandering the talents of his sizable cast, Coppola let a wealth of wonderful, rich material slip through his fingers. Because Coppola's movie isn't *about* the Cotton Club, any more than *Apocalypse Now* was about Vietnam or *The Outsiders* and *Rumble Fish* were about teenagers. The script that Coppola and Pulitzer Prize winner William Kennedy came up with (after God knows how many revisions) has three separate plots, two of them intertwined. There's the *gangster story*, centering on madman "Dutch" Schultz (James Remar) and his inability to keep out of gang wars, despite Madden's repeated attempts to play peacemaker. (In actuality Schultz had only the most tenuous links to Owney Madden's club; he used to hang out at Connie's Inn, a rival night spot farther downtown and closer to the Harlem River.) There's the *oddball love story*, in which a white cornettist named "Dixie" Dwyer (Richard Gere), adopted by Schultz when Dwyer saves him from a bomb, infringes on the gangster's territory by romancing his mistress, a hard-boiled nineteen-year-old named Vera (Diane Lane) whom Schultz has set up in her own nightclub. Dwyer's brother Vince (Nicolas Cage), making the most of his connections, becomes first one of Schultz's henchmen and then, greedy for some of his boss's wealth, one of his enemies. Finally there's the *other love story*, with a pair of ambitious black entertainers—tap dancer "Sandman" Williams (Gregory Hines), who promotes his black identity, and light-skinned torch singer Lila Rose (Lonette McKee), who disguises hers—as the hero and heroine.

Having made the idiotic decision to bypass the *real* story of the Cotton Club, Coppola and Kennedy might at least have concentrated on Sandman and Lila Rose, who are more or less concocted of bits and pieces of half a dozen true-life entertainers (Harold Nicholas, Lena Horne, and Dorothy Dandridge among them), and on the music and dancing. But the filmmakers handle this affair so haphazardly (and Coppola obviously did so much heavy cutting on this part of the picture) that we don't understand what's keeping them apart, or why the state of their relationship is never the same at the outset of one scene as it was at the conclusion of the previous one. Worse—unbelievably—Coppola shows so little interest in Hines's and McKee's musical-comedy gifts, which presumably prompted him to sign them for these roles, that he keeps shoving them, along with the other singers and dancers, into the background. McKee does a feverish rendition of "Ill Wind" (written by Arlen and Ted Koehler), but that's her only major number. And does Coppola really think that when you've got a dancer like Gregory Hines on screen, there's something *more interesting* to cut away to? Hines hoofs happily with his brother Maurice (as Sandman's brother Clay), and does some of the most glistening solo tapping seen in movies since the golden age of M-G-M musicals, but Coppola has other things on that entrepreneurial mind of his: He uses Hines's dancing as a point of contrast for the underworld violence transpiring outside—and on one occasion inside—the club. In fact, no violence ever disturbed the patrons of the Cotton Club in the two decades of its existence.

When Hines does his most prodigious dance, *a cappella*, Coppola turns it into *his* big number, intercutting Hines's feet with a series of killings, the way he intercut Anthony Corleone's baptism with the revenge murders in *The Godfather*. He seems to want to remind us that he's still the Godfather of Hollywood, commanding all the action from his director's chair, and to illustrate his (highly dubious) thesis: that whites express their anger through violence while blacks release theirs through popular art. He must be proud of this deduction—it's the only idea in the whole two-and-a-half-hour movie. But by calling attention to his own cleverness in this way, he minimizes our enjoyment of the performers (our chief reason for going to see this picture in the first place). He comes close to spoiling a joyous, spontaneous-looking display of classical tap by Charles "Honi" Coles and others, too, by trying to top it with his own flashy demonstration of directing and editing: He throws every shot in our faces.

The gangster story is old hat, and it has the unpleasant flavor of self-indulgence, both for the maker of the *Godfather* pictures and for the writer whose *Albany Trilogy* abounds with mobsters. (One scene, in which Schultz's wife catches him squiring Vera, reworks the central triangle of Kennedy's first novel, *Legs*.) Reprising *The Godfather* here wouldn't be quite so painful if Coppola still made movies the way he did in the early seventies, in the style of Renoir, honoring his actors and respecting his audience by keeping his camera at a distance so that we could take in an entire room at a glance and choose where to cast our eyes first. But when he got lost in that jungle in *Apocalypse Now*, the first piece of luggage Coppola threw away was the long shot. Since then, his prime medium has been the close-up, which he uses in tandem with a quantity of loud, undisciplined, overlapping improvisation. He may think he serves his actors by letting them overact in overlong, unshaped group scenes, but he isn't doing Nicolas Cage or James Remar (both of whom have turned in creditable work under other directors) any favors.

Luckily, not everyone in the film seems to be vulnerable to Coppola's intemperance. As Frenchy DeMange, Fred Gwynne uses that hanging-sausage face to superb comic effect: With his thinning hair slicked down and parted in the middle, he's an art-deco caricature. And when Bob Hoskins (as Owney Madden) and the Living Theatre's Julian Beck (as Dutch Schultz's top underling, Saul) overact, they do it with panache. Gwynne and Hoskins share one of the two scenes in *The Cotton Club* that we can get close to, a humorous reaffirmation of their friendship after DeMange, kidnaped by Vince and held for ransom, returns unharmed. The other is the Williams brothers' reunion after Sandman's aggressiveness and ego have split them up. (Hines reports that he and his brother Maurice experienced a similar rift in their relationship, which may account in part for the rightness of this moment on screen.)

The Dixie–Vera plot is the movie's great unsolved riddle. Since no white musician ever played at the Cotton Club, what the hell is a white horn player doing *in the leading role* of a film set there? Coppola and Kennedy don't violate history much in this case (Dixie sits in with the band only once, on a special occasion), so *wherever* they place him, in Dutch's entourage or in Hollywood starring in Cagney-type roles, they can't really explain his presence. As usual, Richard Gere's self-consciousness, all-licensed by Coppola's direction, doesn't help clarify things: When Gere tries to play hip, he's so mannered that he seems to have come off another planet. And Diane Lane's character is so misplaced in this movie that the filmmakers move her to another club altogether. Saddled with a couple of wigs (Louise Brooks brunette and plantinum blonde) that don't flatter her, and the worst lines in the movie (she actually calls Gere "my very, very lover"), Lane comes off even worse here than she did as the abducted rock star who sang those boring songs in *Streets of Fire*. These two noncharacters have a nonlove scene that ranks with the greatest of Coppola's follies (like the red and blue fish sitting in the middle of the black and white frame in *Rumble Fish*): They have sex under what appears to be an enormous mesh stocking.

If I sound angry about this movie, it's because it's such a horrendous waste: No one's going to make *another* movie about the Cotton Club, at least not for a long while. With the resources Coppola had at his disposal, there was no reason for reducing the material to self-reflexive banalities. From the glimpses we get of the production numbers, he or his choreographers (Michael Smuin of the San Francisco Ballet heads the list in the credits) seem to have understood the period and the style of those revues, and some strong jazz voices—Priscilla Baskerville on Ellington's "Creole Love Call" and Sydney Goldsmith on "Barbecue"—soar triumphantly above the gunshots. Probably Coppola was trying to be "mythic" again (as he was in his last musical, *One from the Heart*) by reverting to the Hollywood pictures of an earlier epoch and then enlarging them, in this case the gangster-melodrama/jazz-musical melees Warner Brothers made a fairly entertaining stab at in the forties (*Blues in the Night, The Man I Love*). Simply changing the size of a genre without rethinking its meaning leaves it stranded in no-man's land, though. Too outsize to be modestly enjoyable, too shallow to be memorable, *The Cotton Club* is a tinselly tribute to a time that never existed.

January 1984

Trashing Black Culture, Part II: Steven Spielberg Directs a Disney Picture

• • •

At the start of Steven Spielberg's *The Color Purple*, two black teenage girls dance through a field covered with pink–purple flowers. Wide-eyed, pigtails flying, they swing linked arms and tramp through the high grass in a spirited game of Follow the Leader and vow their eternal devotion in a pattycake jingle. Then the whirling camera rests at an angle sufficient to take in a full profile of the girls, and we see that one of them, Celie (Desreta Jackson), is pregnant. In the next scene, Nettie (Akosua Busia), her sister and playmate, helps her give birth to their father's child, and the grim-faced old reprobate shows up out of a raging snowstorm to seize the baby from its mother and discard it. This sequence, like the joy-of-childhood dance through the fields that preceded it, is shot in a deep, otherworldly glow; the snow outside Pa's cabin door is a childhood memory of snow, like the snow under glass at the opening of *Citizen Kane,*

The source of *The Color Purple*, Alice Walker's phenomenally successful novel, incorporated these events into the first and second of Celie's letters to God. Celie's and Nettie's Pa (known by no other name) has instructed this pitiful, uneducated victim of his lechery to take her troubles to God, and so the first hundred pages or so of the novel, which is entirely epistolary, are directed to an unanswering deity. All the virtues of the book—its gumption and directness and the potency of its private, vernacular vision of anguish—are evident in the first half of this section. Walker hauls you in by serving up rape, incest, and infanticide on the first two pages, reported by a fourteen-year-old girl who doesn't know what's happening to her. It's a shock the reader doesn't recover from until, sixty or seventy pages later, the bells of sisterhood begin to peal so loudly that they drown out everything else in the book.

In the movie, Spielberg doesn't just modify the shock of these early events—he insulates it by throwing the narrative into a Walt Disney fairy-tale context. Using rich, warm colors (the photographer, Allen Daviau, worked with him on *E.T.* and the old-folks'-home segment of *The Twilight Zone*), and period detail with a storybook hyperrealistic look (J. Michael Riva did the production design), Spielberg suggests the world of the Disney full-length cartoons, especially *Snow White* and *Pinocchio*—which are, of course, dedicated to the proposition that a hero or heroine is someone who has a rough time of it for a while but, inevitably, finds deserved happiness. When Pa takes Celie's baby off into that pictorially perfect storm, we know she's going to get the best of the bad man and—one day—be reunited with her child. Real-life tragedy doesn't reside in this setting. Walker's Celie goes through hell when Pa marries her off at fourteen to a widower ("Mr.") whose real itch is for her prettier sister, but Spielberg's Celie quickly manages to turn her sad life into a celebration of simple domestic bliss. When she walks into Mr.'s filthy kitchen for the first time and begins to make the grimy, encrusted walls shine, we can guess that the next shot will be of a cozy fire in the hearth and a pot boiling merrily on the stove. (This scene is actually a quotation from *Snow White*. Remember "Whistle While You Work"?)

How could Spielberg have read Walker's book and arrived at *this* vision of it? This story of the personal triumph of a downtrodden black woman is so far from the kind of experience (white suburban) he's a genius at getting on the screen that he must have reimagined the whole thing, through the haze of the movies he grew up on. And, bizarre as that approach seems, it *could* work—*if* he played against it, the way Martin Scorsese played against the M-G-M Technicolor and the back-lot fakery in *New York, New York*. That is, Spielberg's *The Color Purple* could *look* like a white

Hollywood director's interpretation of black rural experience, circa 1945, and then sting the audience by introducing genuine characters incongruously into the cheery–phony warmth of the wide-screen green fields and the wood-slat country churches and the whitewashed porches with their rockers and glasses of homemade lemonade. But Spielberg is no ironist. Though he has the technological sophistication to recreate an earlier period of film and then lend it an overpowering intensity (visually, what he gives us is the apotheosis of the Technicolor film of the late forties and early fifties), he still has a child's sensibility. *The Color Purple is* a white man's movie from the postwar period; it's *Song of the South.*

The creatures in the Disney animated features were always anthropomorphic; what made the live-action musicals so ludicrous was that the human actors, especially the children, were made into cute pets, so a movie like *Song of the South* cartooned human experience. And because the subject matter in this case was *black* experience, which already had a sad history of being melted down into cartoon for the amusement of white audiences, the result was unintentionally racist. Spielberg makes the same mistake here. (The way Menno Meyjes has written the script, minus a real screenwriter's understanding of the process of adaptation, Spielberg can really take off in any direction he pleases.) He employs the children's expressive huge eyes, and later Whoopi Goldberg's new-moon smile as the grown-up Celie, the way Norman Rockwell used faces for his magazine-cover art—as objects to be cooed over. And the comedy is Disney comedy: broad, repetitive, leaden-footed. When Mr. (Danny Glover) prepares to meet his long-absent mistress, a blues singer named Shug Avery (Margaret Avery), he slips and slides around the house in a nerve-racked effort to make himself presentable. Fixing her breakfast, he's so inept in the kitchen that he has to blow out the flame on the toast as he hustles it up the stairs to her bedroom. His son Harpo (Willard Pugh) falls through the roof every time he tries to repair it. When Harpo tries to control his wife Sofia (Oprah Winfrey), by beating her up, it's *he* who shows up with a black eye. Celie leaps when she bumps into a dressmaker's dummy and thinks it's Mr. spying on her.

Spielberg's conception doesn't allow room for most of the actors to give full-scale performances. Adolph Caesar, who plays Old Mr., Mr.'s clucking, disapproving father, with the same nineteenth-century overstatement he brought to *A Soldier's Story*, is probably just about right for what Spielberg had in mind. (Caesar sneers out of the left side of his mouth; it seems to be his only trick.) Surprisingly, though, almost everyone else manages at least a few moments when *something* authentic comes through. Whoopi Goldberg's craggy deep voice has traces of worldliness, so that even though she has to mimic the pitiful Keane stares that Spielberg gets out of her younger counterpart, Desreta Jackson, and stand with her arms dangling from the wrist, her legs turned out, her body folded inwards to emphasize how self-deprecating Celie is, still she suggests a truly resilient spirit. She holds her ground; the longer we look at her, the more she pulls us down through the cartoon face into Celie's stored-up anger. And she shows us how Celie blossoms as Shug's friendship ameliorates her self-image.

Danny Glover has a handsome shine in the nearly impossible role of Mr., and his mock-courtship of Nettie includes a few high-stepping comic moments. In two or three brief scenes, Rae Dawn Chong makes Squeak, Harpo's squirrelly girl friend, memorable. And there's one performance that's worth seeing the picture for: the one Oprah Winfrey gives as Sofia. Winfrey, who has an intimidating frame and a barrel-chested speaking voice like some of the singers in *Say Amen, Somebody* and *Gospel*, wakes the movie up when she marches into Mr.'s parlor, carrying his son's child, to find out what's what. Winfrey's comic punch in her early scenes has the depth of real experience behind it. But then, when quick-tempered Sofia knocks a white man down for slapping her when she refuses his offer of employment, and is laid low by eight years' beatings in jail and a life sentence as a maid in a white household (the very job she turned down in the first place), Winfrey acquires a tragic calm. We get a sense of something great lost when Winfrey stumbles out of jail after those eight years. This actress is Spielberg's one connection with the reality of black life that his movie defuses and romanticizes the rest of the time.

Margaret Avery's Shug is the major disappointment in the cast, and perhaps an inevitable one, given Spielberg's treatment of her character. In the novel, hard-drinking, sexy Shug rouses Celie out of her subservient shell. Mr. drove Nettie, Celie's soulmate, out of the house years ago for refusing his advances and, out of spite, has prevented any communication between the sisters all these years.

Shug responds to Celie's little-girl starved affections by becoming first her friend, then her lover, and finally her ally—against Mr., and thus, in the book's terms, against the oppression of the male sex. In Walker's scheme, all men are such self-concerned sexual tyrants and all women such benevolent primal creatures that women with any sense just naturally turn to each other. Celie's sexual awakening can only be accomplished at the sensitive hands of another woman, and thus the awakening is, inevitably, a political one as well.

This outrageous feminist flag-waving may make you choke when you read the novel, but there's no easy way around it if you're going to adapt it to the screen. Spielberg makes no attempt to downplay the sexual politics, but he touches so lightly on the relationship between Celie and Shug that it doesn't make a great deal of sense. They do sleep together (presumably—all we see is a kiss that consciously echoes the kisses Celie and Nettie shared as children), but since the movie doesn't make it clear, as the book does, that they remain lovers for years, we wonder why Celie's sexual liberation doesn't lead to a more satisfying romantic life. (Sisterhood seems to be enough for her; she doesn't need sex.) And there are other examples of Spielberg's peculiar reticence when it comes to sexual matters: Walker explains, graphically, that Pa's repeated rape of Celie causes her to menopause before she marries Mr., but in the movie we're given no clue as to why she never bears him children.

You need someone like Lena Horne in her thirties for a role like Shug, who wears a beaded headband and peacock feathers to sing the blues at Harpo's juke joint. What you get instead is an attractively maternal-looking actress without much soul. (Tata Vega, who sings for Margaret Avery, isn't what the soul doctor ordered, either.) And Spielberg and Meyjes have saddled the actress with an unplayable subplot about Shug's longing for reconciliation with the preacher daddy who disowned her. Walker's feminism is her religion; Celie stops writing to God when she begins to express her anger at male oppression, and starts again when her newly-won female identity brings her peace. But the filmmakers must have figured (not unreasonably) that they needed more of a dramatic device to move religion into the movie, so they whipped up a scene—a real antique—in which Shug drags her jazz band into her father's church to join in the hymn singing. (For one dreadful moment, you wonder if Spielberg could have thought *Footloose* made a significant statement.)

After Celie has found her voice, *The Color Purple* acquires more big emotional numbers than *Gone with the Wind*: Celie mouthing off to Mr., Celie's farewell speech when she goes away with Shug, Celie throwing coins to a little black girl running along a railroad track (Spielberg stages this moment as if it were terribly important, though who this kid is and why Celie should be tossing coins to her are questions left unanswered); Shug's reconciliation with her father; and the Dickens-scale finale, in which everyone is reunited. And throughout, Quincy Jones's shamelessly slurpy Hollywood-epic music keeps plugging away at your emotions.

I've never been among Steven Spielberg's detractors; I don't think *E. T.* is mere commercial manipulation. But that's because he understands something about what white kids go through in the suburbs of northern California, and he can access his own experiences—that's what makes his best movies such a joy. *The Color Purple* needs an emotional purity, like the last episode of "Roots II" on television had; it needs to be grounded in *somebody's* experience. Spielberg has to substitute—and what he falls back on are old movies.

January 1986

Trashing Black Culture, Part III:
Genteel Fakery

• • •

The kindest thing you can say about *Cry Freedom*, the film about the martyred South African revolutionary Steve Biko and his effect on the white journalist Donald Woods (who ended up writing Biko's story), is that it's better than the HBO movie *Mandela*. *Mandela* was a combination of a Landmark children's bio, an inflated sitcom (the scenes of Nelson Mandela's whirlwind courtship of Winnie), and a simple-minded political melodrama: The evil police chief who made it his life's work to get Mandela behind bars was shot in close-ups so enormous I found myself pulling my chair farther and farther away from the television set. *Cry Freedom* also has its meanie cops with one-track minds (they even sneer in unison). But the approach of the screenwriter, John Briley (working from Woods's books, *Biko* and *Asking for Trouble*), and the director, Richard Attenborough—the pair responsible for the 1982 *Gandhi*—is lethal in an entirely different way.

When Woods (Kevin Kline), the editor of *The Daily Dispatch* (the single liberal paper in East London, South Africa), condemns Biko, the founder of the Black Consciousness Movement, as a black racist, Biko's friend Dr. Ramphele (Josette Simon) marches into Woods's office and challenges him to meet Biko on his own turf—King William's Town, where, as an officially "banned person," Biko is forced to remain—and allow Biko to present his side of the argument. From the moment that Biko (Denzel Washington) appears, illuminated by the glimmering sunlight, and takes Woods on an odyssey through the shanties and bars of the black settlement in King William's Town, the movie becomes a round of lectures on apartheid. Every black man or woman Woods is introduced to gives him a little prepared speech; articulate but lifeless, these characters are like meticulously rehearsed children in a pageant, and the movie keeps stopping politely for each to speak his or her piece. And when Woods, converted to Biko's cause, appeals to the consciences of his white compatriots (including the minister of police), they make speeches, too.

Mandela did have Danny Glover in the title role, and the amazing actress Alfre Woodard as Winnie; *Cry Freedom* has Denzel Washington. Attenborough is stupid about a lot of things, but he basically stays out of the way of Washington's performance—he gives him a chance to breathe with the role and bring it a cool, elusive wit and a cautious intelligence. The filmmakers stick in scenes of Biko playing football with the guys and dancing with the women so we'll understand he's a man of the people, and these bits are inadvertently condescending. But Washington keeps Biko at a canny distance from everyone else (including his wife), and we register his smiling remoteness as part of the subversive equipment that allows him to slip the net of the police as long as he does, while breaking his ban and roaming freely through the country. (By South African law a banned person is required to stay put, and is denied the society of more than one visitor at a time. He's also kept, of course, under constant surveillance.) The problem is that, halfway through *Cry Freedom*, Biko is thrown in prison and beaten to death—and at that point, when the only reason for watching the movie has vanished, what we're left with is the monumentally uninteresting Woods family and the banal story of how (once Woods himself becomes a banned person for openly supporting Biko) they escape from South Africa.

Why did the filmmakers insist on such a disastrous structure? Blame Richard Attenborough's unhappy mix of liberal sincerity, big-moviemaker ambitions, and ineptitude. Attenborough must have thought that the way to get people in to see a movie on apartheid would be to give equal weight to the escape story. But he was counting on two things, commercial instincts and the finesse to carry off a large-scale adventure tale, neither of which he possesses. Wan, bespectacled Donald (a humorless, inexpressive performance by Kevin Kline) and his tense wife Wendy (played by the aptly named Penelope Wilton, she of the care-creased brow) are the blandest, pastiest couple this side of a Disney domestic comedy. They're aggravating enough characters while Biko's still alive, when they seem to function as a kind of adoptive uncle and aunt, counseling him and fretting over him. Once their problems move into the foreground in the second half of the movie, they become offensive—

just as Sidney Schanberg became offensive when *The Killing Fields* began to insist that we should care about his friendship with a Cambodian while the whole country was falling to pieces around them.

All of the Woodses' troubles seem manufactured, anyway. When Donald decides to write a book about Biko, Wendy's ferocious response ("I know you. You're willing to tear our lives apart just to see Donald Woods's name on a book cover. And you're willing to use Steve's death as an excuse") comes out of thin air. Then, just as suddenly, she drops her objections and becomes loyal and supportive. Does anyone really care what happens to these people? The escape sequence is complicated—Donald and the rest of the family have to leave separately—but utterly lacking in excitement; Attenborough substitutes cutesy details (a river Woods is afraid to wade across, an ally's broken-down wreck of a car) for suspense. And he cranks up the sentimentality. There are interminable close-ups of the Woods daughter blinking back tears as her father heads out the door, and for a good five minutes Attenborough focuses on the question of whether to take the family dog on the picnic Wendy and the kids will use to cover their tracks. By the time these clowns make it to safety, you're ready to kill them. And then Attenborough cuts to a reenactment of the slaughter of Soweto schoolchildren marching in protest in 1976 (a year earlier than the Woods family's escape). Even if you can see that he's trying for a Brechtian effect here—shattering the happy ending by interjecting a horror show that he hopes will prick the consciences of the audience and arouse us to political action—the previous hour has been so limply benign that it's hard not to take issue with the sudden manipulation. Watching *Cry Freedom*, you'd really like to pin a medal on Richard Attenborough's liberal heart and then suggest he try another profession.

January 1988

Portrait of the Liberal as a Young Woman
• • •

Chris Menges, who began as a documentary filmmaker and then became one of the world's great cinematographers (he shot *Local Hero, Comfort and Joy, The Killing Fields,* and *High Season*), has made a first-rate film about apartheid: *A World Apart,* starring Barbara Hershey as Diana Roth, who's based on South African journalist Ruth First, the first white to be arrested (in 1963) under the Ninety Days Act. (This infamous act states that anyone may be held without trial for ninety days at a stretch.) Apartheid is a booby-trapped movie subject; anyone who tries to depict the struggles of blacks in South Africa ends up romanticizing their plight and reducing the pro-apartheid whites to heartless villains, because (for Western art-house audiences at least) there's no counterargument you could make convincing. Wisely, Menges has looked for complexity in other corners. Working from a superb screenplay by First's daughter, Shawn Slovo, that focuses on how the political activity of parents affects their children (the subject of the botched *Daniel*), Menges has framed Diana Roth's story as a coming-of-age film in which the central character is her eldest daughter, Molly, who is just entering adolescence when her father, Gus (Jeroen Krabbé), is forced to seek shelter in exile and her mother is thrown in jail. (Ruth First was assassinated by means of a letter bomb in 1982, but the movie restricts itself to the events of 1963.)

As played by the remarkable young actress Jodhi May, Molly is at the tail end of her in-between stage. She's taller than her classmates, a little like Frankie Addams in *The Member of the Wedding,* but she's already acquired a teenage litheness and gracefulness, and her schoolgirlish giggling sessions with her best friend Yvonne (Nadine Chalmers) are touched with a self-conscious femininity. We can see from the outset that this kid is different from her peers: Riding home after school with Yvonne and her mother (Kate Fitzpatrick), she sees a black man injured in a hit-and-run accident, and without hesitation she suggests they give the victim a lift to the hospital. Yvonne's mother, who has a sloppy aristocratic mien but exudes a kind of clumsy charm, backs off, explaining it's best not to get involved. (This scene, which communicates an amazing amount about the South Africa of the early sixties in an understated dramatic shorthand, pulls us into the movie immediately.) This is hard for Molly to fathom. She's used to her mother's racially mixed parties, where the guests are trained to dump their glasses of liquor as soon as a cop car is spotted, because Diana could be arrested for serving alcohol to blacks. Molly has an intimate relationship with Elsie (Linda Mvusi), the Roths' housekeeper, who teaches her the African national anthem in her room at night, and whose brother, Solomon (Albee Lesotho, in a joyously expressive performance), is a revolutionary just released from prison. Invited to a party given by Yvonne's parents, she balks when her friend calls a black servant "boy" and retreats to the kitchen, where the faces are familiar and she feels more at home.

The filmmakers establish Molly's liberal impulses—the legacy of her parents—very early, and then set up her difficult relationship with Diana in opposition to it. Diana's professional and private commitment to the oppressed blacks leaves her less time for Molly and her two younger sisters (Carolyn Clayton-Cragg and Merav Gruer) than they need, especially after her husband's departure; she counts on her mother, Bertha (Yvonne Bryceland), to fill in, and she counts on Molly to act grown-up and accept her priorities. But Molly's still a child, and anyway Diana isn't consistent in her treatment of the girl—Molly's curious about her political life, but Diana excludes her, growing angry when Molly walks into her study without knocking and discovers a hiding place for secret documents.

You can certainly understand Diana's reticence to let Molly in on such dangerous secrets, or to bring her along when she covers strikes and protest marches, but you can sympathize with Molly's frustration, too: If Diana doesn't have time to tune in on her life (when Molly tries to tell her about the hit-and-run, Diana isn't listening—her attention is elsewhere), it doesn't seem fair that *she* can't share *Diana's* life either. The scenes between Molly and Diana are the most trenchant depiction of a mother–daughter relationship in recent memory, with the sole exception of *High Tide*: Slovo and Menges get into issues that movies about domestic tensions almost never go near. When Molly tells her mother she misses Gus, Diana's reply, "So do I," has an unexpected sharpness. The subtext seems to be "Don't you think *I* do?" or even "What makes you think your feelings are as important as mine?"

Menges and Slovo chronicle Molly's struggle between her instinctive humanity and empathy for her black countrymen, and her anger at being abandoned by her parents. She learns the lessons of integrity and faithfulness years before she ought to have them thrust upon her, and they're like thorns slashing across her open face. She's increasingly isolated from her schoolmates, who—like cruel, absurd miniatures of their parents—scrawl "Traitor" across scraps of paper and leave them in her locker, or demand to know why her father doesn't come back to South Africa and "take his punishment like a man." At first, Yvonne sides with Molly, but when Molly is out of school for a few weeks, in mourning for her mother's departure, Yvonne grows naturally close to some of the other girls. And then Molly figures out that Yvonne's parents have instructed her to stay away from this subversives' child. (In one shocking scene, Molly shows up at Yvonne's gate after she's been told on the telephone that her friend's not at home, and Yvonne's father chases after her, dragging her into his car to drive her back.)

Jodhi May keeps us in close touch with Molly's hurt and her ambivalence. Molly feels the same injustices her mother feels, but she can't help a childish wish that her parents were like the parents of her classmates, leaving the woes of the world to be attended to by other hands. She's not comfortable singing the white South Africans' anthem—the official one—with her classmates (she keeps her mouth closed, mumbling only a few of the words), but when Elsie takes her to a church meeting and the black men and women all around her burst into a spirited chorus of the black anthem Elsie's been teaching her, she doesn't want to sing along then, either. She doesn't feel part of that community—not in her mother's absence. (Menges resolves this motif at the end, triumphantly, when Diana stands beside Molly at the funeral of a black friend, and they do sing the black anthem together.) The film keeps reminding us that Molly is, after all, still a child. In fact, crying over and over, "Mummy, don't go!" when Diana is taken away—as if Mummy had any control over the situation—she seems little more than a baby.

The reason I loved *High Tide* so much was that I felt drawn into a realm of female relationships, a realm men are seldom privy to. *A World Apart*, which has only a handful of male characters

(Solomon; Diana's photographer, Harold; her interrogator; Yvonne's father; and—very briefly—Gus Roth) but a great many girls and women, drew me in the same way. A female screenwriter and a male director do a splendid job of evoking the delicately piercing mood of feminine domesticity. The mainstays that allow Menges to accomplish this are four wonderful actresses: Jodhi May, Barbara Hershey (whose unflinching, masterfully controlled performance is beyond anything we might have anticipated from her), Linda Mvusi (whose expressions of grief when she receives bad news about Solomon are worthy to stand beside the purest expressions of emotion in Cicely Tyson's performances), and—in a less flamboyant role—the South African stage actress Yvonne Bryceland. There's a scene where Bertha takes her granddaughters to visit Diana in jail, only to learn that she's been transferred to another city; a tightness in the jaw, an unsettling inner focus, and the actress has told us how deeply the disappointment has affected Bertha. (Bertha knows what Diana later conveys to Molly: that prison is the fortress of the enemy, and you don't ever display your pain in front of the enemy.) When we're told, a couple of scenes later, that Bertha is no longer taking care of the girls because she's had a minor breakdown, we're not surprised.

Beautifully shot (by Peter Biziou) and edited (by Nicolas Gaster), *A World Apart* is a stunning feature film debut for Menges. You can see what he picked up from his experience as a documentarian, and from Roland Joffé on *The Killing Fields*—a willingess to let the power of images make the political points—and, much more, what he got from Bill Forsyth: a sense for the telling human detail. When Diana, thrown into a cell, is denied reading matter or writing implements, she hoists herself up to look out the barred window. Across the street, a newspaper headline is printed on a pole, and she struggles to put it together from the letters she can see. In this brief, silent scene, Menges tells us what it must be like for a woman whose life is defined by the acts of reading and writing to be suddenly deprived of them. When her ninety days are up and she finds herself clapped in jail again for a second term the moment she steps outside, she throws a tantrum, smashing the furniture in her cell, and Menges shows us two female guards peering through the keyhole of her cell, in wonder and awe, unable to do anything but watch—

because, though they may be sympathetic to her pain, they can't begin to comprehend what she's going through.

Sensitive and unsensational as they are, the prison scenes (featuring David Suchet as Diana's chief interrogator) don't stay in the memory the way the domestic scenes do, because Jodhi May isn't in them. And Menges errs, I think, in providing a final image that shifts away from Molly and Diana—especially since, five minutes earlier, we got the scene the movie had been working toward and needed so badly, the confrontation between mother and daughter during which Molly breaks through to Diana and makes her understand what she's been feeling. (This scene is enough to break your heart.) But these are quibbles. A friend of mine who was tremendously moved by the film told me she thought the whole picture was summed up in the moment near the end when Molly cries "It's not fair!" to her mother, and Diana offers the only consolation she can: She agrees with her. *A World Apart* travels from the separate agonies of mother and daughter to a shared agony, offering it up as the only possible salvation. Chris Menges works with an instinctual honesty most filmmakers can't even conceive of.

September 1988

The Fighting 54th

• • •

War was so cruelly and publicly deglamorized for us during the Vietnam era that audiences stopped being able to watch the harmless jingoistic movies of earlier decades—like the Errol Flynn *Charge of the Light Brigade* or *Gunga Din*—without jeering at the sentiments and feeling a moral obligation to resist the pull of the action, which in both these films had a primal exhilaration. The sensibility behind those pictures—that war ennobles—*was* offensive, but it was defused by the boys'-adventure-tale preposterousness of the presentation; getting exercised over these displays of juvenile bravado was as much a case of misplaced liberal values as taking a fervent stand against war toys. (It's amusing to think of the movies popular among liberals that relied on slightly distorted versions of the all-comrades-together appeal of boys' fiction: *The Deer Hunter, Gallipoli, The Year of Living Dangerously.*)

Still, though it's fine to watch something like *The Charge of the Light Brigade* at a cozy distance of half a century, there's something queasy-making about watching the warmongering thinking that it's heaped on top of stage a comeback. That's why you want to bang your head against a wall when you see *Top Gun* or *Rambo*. But the Civil War film *Glory*, written by Kevin Jarre and directed by Edward Zwick, is a strange kind of test case. Despite the carnage in the war scenes, the movie is certainly in a prowar mode; Zwick doesn't undercut the excitement of the battle scenes, and it's clear—even explicitly stated—that we're meant to see the savagery of the men in action as evidence of their best (i.e., most courageous) impulses coming to the fore. The filmmakers are very much aware of the values inherent in the genre, and they make no attempt to subvert them, the way Brian DePalma does in *Casualties of War* or Oliver Stone does in *Platoon*.

But the men of the 54th Massachusetts Volunteer Infantry, who are the subject of *Glory*, are black, and that makes all the difference in the world. For these men, who are freed slaves, or sons or grandsons of slaves, or slaves who have made themselves free by slipping the borders of the southern states, fighting for the North is less a gesture of solidarity with the abolitionist doctrine (though it's undeniably that, too) than a testing of the implications of that doctrine—an affirmation of the fact of their equality. And that's why the sight of these foot soldiers marching down the street in their new uniforms, with their families waving proudly from the sidelines, is so cheering. You've seen this scene hundreds of times, but the fact that almost all the faces in the street are black freshens the platitude, even alters its meaning.

I wouldn't call *Glory* a great piece of filmmaking. Most of the first half hour is clodhopping, stiff in the familiar style of bad Hollywood period epics; the James Horner score (some of it intoned by the Boys' Choir of Harlem) is drilled into you like "Taps"; and most of the scenes involving the struggles of the 54th's Quaker commander, Col Robert Gould Shaw (Matthew Broderick), to contend with other white officers whose racism is ill-disguised are so bald they make you wince. (The scenes where Shaw quarrels with his college friend and immediate subordinate, Cabot Forbes—a lousy role for Cary Elwes—aren't much better.) But the picture's stress is on his interaction with the black enlisted men, and on their sometimes uneasy contact with each other, and you may not realize what a revelation that is until the towering black actors in the cast make their way onto the screen.

Morgan Freeman plays John Rawlins, who becomes Robert's unofficial representative among the men, and the first black officer (noncommissioned, of course—the army has stipulated that blacks can't rise any higher). Shaw's first glimpse of Rawlins was at Antietam, where he was wounded and Rawlins was one of the gravediggers he saw combing the fields for corpses. With his sober, level gaze and his un-self-conscious regal bearing, Freeman's Rawlins is a natural leader among the black soldiers. Denzel Washington plays Trip, the field slave who brings a full battery of hatred for the white man to his service in the Union army. Cynical and quick-witted, he braces and entertains the other men—and puts them on their guard; his experience is brutal, hand-to-mouth (a runaway, he's been through so much he's way past fear). And his presence among northern blacks, some of them free for generations back, is the equivalent of having an escaped convict in their company. That's especially true for Thomas (the gifted young André Braugher, sensationally charming as "Kojak"'s partner on TV), who is college-educated— he's a classmate of Shaw's and Forbes's—and has never encountered anyone quite like Trip before. Trip spots him straight off as a "white nigger," a black man who (in his view) pretends he's a white man, and has nothing but disdain for Thomas's well-meaning efforts to teach some of the other men to read. (Denzel Washington's Trip looks across at Thomas with a sardonic gleam in his eye, a look of incredulous amusement, and you can see he's thinking, "Teaching the darkies, uh-huh—the white man's burden.")

Thomas has his own problems: Ill fitted for the constant grind of soldiering, he feels picked on by Mulcahy (Jonathan Finn), the hard-ass sergeant Shaw brings in to toughen up the men, an Irishman who incorporates his evident disdain for his Negro charges into his professional treatment of them. (There's a give-away moment, though—a soft moment the filmmakers didn't need to put in— when Mulcahy's sudden kindness to Thomas indicates that his contemptuous attitude is mostly show.) And Robert, conscious that he can't carry his long-time friendship for Thomas into this military context, and concerned that, incompletely trained, these raw recruits don't have a chance in battle, keeps shying away from Thomas's efforts to draw comfort and support from him. Shaw is under special constraints: Not only does he feel the need to prove his men are the equal of any white soldiers, since his fellow officers take a snickering, cavalier attitude toward his regiment (the supply officer denies them the boots Shaw has ordered; the salary they draw on their first payday turns out to be two-thirds of what white enlisted men are getting), but the Confederate Army has issued a declaration that any black soldier captured in battle will be put to death.

If you saw the black roles on paper, you'd probably dismiss them as clichés hauled out by a screenwriter with more white-liberal credentials than dramatic imagination. (The stuttering, sweet-souled Bible-thumper played by Jimhi Kennedy is the worst of them.) And they are; almost every idea in the picture is a cliché. But, energized by the actors, whom Zwick directs with infinitely more sensitivity than he showed in *About Last Night . . .* , they play like nothing you've seen before. Scenes that could be stale and impossibly high-minded become iconic. In one, Mulcahy drags Trip back to camp as a deserter and Shaw, feeling he has no choice, assents to Trip's being flogged (by Mulcahy) in full view of the other men. (Robert later learns from Rawlins that Trip, his feet badly cut up, was simply off hunting for a new pair of shoes.) When Mulcahy strips off Trip's shirt, we see he wears the scars of countless whippings from some slavemaster. Trip is hardened to the ritual—he resolutely refuses to cry out. Zwick is smart enough to shoot almost the entire scene as a close-up of Trip's face, which is turned relentlessly on Robert during the ordeal. Denzel Washington was the main reason to see *A Soldier's Story*, and he was so powerful as Steve Biko in *Cry Freedom* that you could feel the terrible movie sag like a punctured balloon after the filmmakers killed him off halfway through. As Trip he approaches greatness, and this is his most phenomenal scene. His emotional control is staggering. The pain drives him to tears but he still won't crack; you can feel him cursing his body silently for turning traitor as he stands there, every muscle in his face clenched.

In another scene, Trip provokes some retreating (white) Union soldiers; then, still full of hell, he insults Thomas and challenges him to a fight. Rawlins intervenes, reminding Trip he owes something to the whites who've been fighting the war since long before there was a 54th Regiment to enlist in. Freeman, an actor's actor, braces Rawlins's modesty—his impulse (natural or learned, or perhaps a little of both) to efface himself—with an innate balance, what you might call a spiritual self-confidence. Yes, this is the wise, soulful Negro role, or at least it was when Freeman picked it up. It's always a mistake to reduce a Morgan Freeman performance to the familiar old notion it might have been before he filled it up with his warmth and charm and some of the most astounding actor's resources contemporary movie acting has to offer.

The pride of performers like Freeman and Washington and Braugher in the work they're able to do here—and in the great story *Glory* tells—gets all mixed up with the pride of the black soldiers in the 54th, and together they make a heady, potent brew. And something similar happens to Matthew Broderick in the role of Robert Gould Shaw (whose letters are one of the three sources for Jarre's screenplay). Broderick isn't really right for the role of the young Quaker colonel, but his struggles to stretch himself toward it are touching. They parallel Shaw's efforts to overcome his natural reticence and act the role of the iron-willed commander he clearly doesn't believe he has it in him to play. Finally Shaw triumphs, and so does Broderick. As he's portrayed here, Robert Shaw becomes a hero despite himself. Shaw is by far the most interestingly drawn character in the picture; perhaps he's the only one of the major figures Jarre felt he could get close to. Jarre has said his lifelong interest in Shaw led him to write the script, yet the intended focus of the picture gets away from both him and Zwick—despite Matthew Broderick, the movie dies whenever the black performers are off camera.

The climax of the film is the July 1863 attack on Fort Wagner, which Robert volunteers his regiment to lead. Zwick takes far too long setting up the sequence: He's too conscious of its symbolic significance. But once it gets rolling, he manages to keep the action clear (no mean feat in a battle scene), and the photographer, the great Freddie Francis, gives it a glow. The filmmakers can't help racking up obvious dramatic points here—they want to tie everything up, to give each of the characters we've gotten to know an emblematic moment—but by then you're too involved with them, and too moved, to grouse about the pedestrian dramaturgy. In a lot of ways *Glory* isn't a very good movie. But it's just wonderful.

January 1990

LETTING THE REAL WORLD IN

• • •

For many of us, the Reagan eighties recalled the Eisenhower fifties, and nowhere was that comparison more strongly felt than
in our movies, which seemed largely dedicated to the proposition of
keeping the real world out. When you watch a picture like *When
Harry Met Sally . . .* , you may feel you've stepped into a parallel
universe. It's not just that the ostensible subject of the film (male–
female relationships) is trivialized by the coy exchanges between the
characters—lines of an incredible smugness, each asking us to admire it for its wit and wisdom about the human condition, with
space around the punchlines for us to react (a kind of silent laugh
track). The very conflict the film sold itself on broaching—can men
and women really be just friends?—is manufactured: Do *you* know
anyone for whom male–female friendship is actually an issue? But
then, *When Harry Met Sally . . .* isn't a film that presents women
and men in a way that's consistent with any experience we're likely
to bring into the theater. When prim Sally (Meg Ryan, playing the

113

Diane Keaton role in this second-generation Woody Allen farce) wants to embarrass Harry (Billy Crystal), she fakes an orgasm in a crowded New York delicatessen. It's a funny bit; it brings down the house. But Sally is about as likely to pull a stunt like that in public as Katharine Hepburn's Tracy Lord would have in *The Philadelphia Story*.

There was no surer way for a movie in the eighties to court box-office failure than by introducing the social and political realities of the world outside the moviehouse. Brian DePalma got slammed for directing *Blow Out*, though, ironically, few people actually picked up on the political themes and motifs. (As late as 1988, when I sold a review on another political movie to a film magazine, the editorial board asked me to excise a reference to *Blow Out* because they thought it was misplaced in a discussion of films and politics.) Roger Spottiswoode's *Under Fire*, set in Nicaragua during the Sandinista revolution, was a flop; so was Philip Kaufman's *The Right Stuff*, about the NASA space program, because it smacked of politics. (Everyone knew it had come from a book by the social commentator and satirist Tom Wolfe, and it didn't help that John Glenn, one of the main figures in the movie, had just thrown his hat into the 1984 Democratic presidential-candidacy race, and his face had appeared on the covers of several national magazines.)

And yet, despite the obstacles, the decade produced a stack of provocative movies on social and political subjects, three of which are examined in this section: the Brazilian *Pixote* (by Hector Babenco, about street kids in São Paulo), the British documentary *Thy Kingdom Come, Thy Will Be Done* (by Antony Thomas, about the "born again" Christian movement in America), and the Australian *A Cry in the Dark* (by Fred Schepisi, about the Lindy Chamberlain child murder trial). Michael Moore's *Roger and Me* claims to bring the real world onto the screen in responding to some of the social ills that are crippling it. Moore is as much a peacock of the left wing as Clint Eastwood is of the right; mostly he parades his feathers. Yet, incredibly, *Roger and Me* was taken very seriously. I thought it might be helpful to lay his movie side-by-side with Babenco's, Thomas's, and Schepisi's.

The Power of Despair

● ● ●

Hector Babenco's powerful *Pixote* relates the story of a ten-year-old child from São Paulo. Babenco grinds a heavy political axe. By law, minors are immune from prison sentences in Brazil, but politicians seeking reelection want to appear effective in controlling city crime, so they pressure police officials. Resentful cops round up street gangs as a matter of course when a murder is committed— particularly, as in the case the movie takes up, when the victim is a citizen of some distinction. The kids are beaten and thrown into detention centers that are as horrible as prisons; when some die, the blame is officially laid on other kids so that the muckraking press can be led away from the truth. So the children are caught between the bosses and the do-gooders. Nobody wins, and the children, with no political clout except a useless law that many Brazilians naively believe is in their favor, are doomed: If they survive the institution, they'll almost definitely resurface as thieves and murderers, pimps, dope dealers.

The youth crime statistics in our country and other countries are horrifying. *Pixote* is the first movie that attempts to understand the conditions that trigger the mechanism of the new wave of juvenile delinquency. The children in this film aren't the faceless, numb punks of the *Time* cover stories; they're baby-faced nomads wearing grown-up clothes, trying to play by grown-up rules—which means internalizing their horror and disgust at situations they're much too young to be asked to comprehend. They're innocents in hell (like the twelve-year-old hooker Jodie Foster played in *Taxi Driver*), clinging to each other or to whichever adults they feel can give them direction or consolation—like the alcoholic whore Sueli (Marília Pera, in a wild, phenomenal performance), who is more adolescent and less capable of coping than they are. They're innocents even when they kill.

"Lord save little children! They abide and they endure," says the benevolent godmother figure (Lillian Gish) at the end of *The Night of the Hunter*. We're so inured to the fiction that a special

115

providence watches over youngsters that the brutality of the world Pixote and his friends inhabit delivers a more severe shock than any other movie within miles. It's the shock of *Shoeshine*, the great Vittorio De Sica picture about two boys led by the alleged rehabilitative arm of a society to turn against each other—except that *Pixote* is sour and hard-edged, rather than bittersweet like *Shoeshine*. Babenco doesn't really work like an artist: He doesn't refine his observations, or keep the narrative line clear (he and Jorge Duran wrote the screenplay), and he's not above staging a big scene for sensationalism. In the second half of the movie, after Pixote and three of his companions have escaped from the detention center, the claustrophobic, concentration-camp atmosphere and the unending string of beatings and framings give way to the more leisurely world of the streets, and the film dissipates somewhat; so Babenco shoots it up with aborted fetuses in garbage pails and close-ups of vomiting and bleeding. There's something of the yellow journalist in Babenco. But if his methods are occasionally suspect, his motives aren't.

In one way, the plot confusion in the detention-center scenes works to the film's advantage: When we don't know who's responsible for the murders of some of the children, we feel as disoriented as their friends must. This section of the movie, in which the boys play-act robberies and police interrogations with frightening seriousness, has extraordinary energy, and it culminates in a scene of operatic intensity: The homosexual Lilica (Jorge Julião) cradles his lover, who's been beaten to death, in his arms. Lilica is the only one of the kids who conveys real passion in this movie; his chosen role—drag queen—allows him to be flamboyantly expressive. And his mourning cries serve as a sort of anthem for all the children who are mute in the face of violence and terror.

Pixote is so grim and relentless in its representation of a dead-ended lifestyle that you may have difficulty resolving your feelings about it. Babenco leaves us with no hope for the salvation of the main character, Pixote (played by Fernando Ramos da Silva), and—despite the fact that the film, a cry for help, is clearly dedicated to illuminating the horrifying state of affairs in São Paulo—no expectation that conditions for children there can be improved. Babenco works on your emotions enough to make you want to fight back; I had to struggle against my anger at that kind of manipulation (anger that's almost a reflex) to find an appropriate response to the movie. But *Pixote* doesn't leave you alone. Days after seeing it, you can't get it out of your head.

In the most amazing series of scenes in the picture, Pixote accidentally shoots one of his friends, the gently commanding Dito (Gilberto Maura), and then one of Sueli's johns, who was his intended target. It's the second time he's killed, and once more his failure to have an emotional reaction to what he's done unsettles and alienates us. For a moment he turns from a child, the object of our pity, into a monster. Then our perceptions are scrambled again: Sueli begins to suckle him, and we think, "My God, he's just a baby!" And suddenly she pulls him off her breast and throws him out into the street. Babenco's refusal to allow us a single untainted moment of beauty isolates him from other filmmakers who have created brilliant portraits of a harrowing childhood—Julien Duvivier in *Poil de Carotte*, De Sica in *Shoeshine*, Truffaut in *The 400 Blows*. *Pixote* enrages us even as it breaks our hearts.

November 1981

Rich Man's Spiritual
• • •

The style of the British documentary filmmaker Antony Thomas is passionate and committed. He has a gentleman's *politesse*, but he's a good old-fashioned muckraker at heart; he's not afraid to ask embarrassing questions (and he's skillful enough to get away with it), or to let his own views filter into his interviews—to put himself on the line. And maybe, treating the explosion of the "born again" Christian movement in this country since the watershed Baptist convention in Dallas in 1980, he's dug deeper than an American might have been able to. Thomas's riveting two-part documentary,

Thy Kingdom Come, Thy Will Be Done, could be subtitled *The Greening of Christian America*. He lays out the issues with tremendous clarity; despite the amount of information the movie asks you to assimilate, you feel your head is being cleared out while you watch.

The movement is an outgrowth of Baptist Christianity, which refocused the basic Protestant impulse—the desire for a potential link between man and God—on the moment when a Christian receives God into his/her heart. This "personal salvation," known in contemporary religious jargon as being "born again," is the crucial step that guarantees today's churchgoers entrance to the kingdom of heaven—with no strings attached, if you listen to men of the cloth like Dr. W. A. Criswell, the minister of the First Baptist Church of Dallas (the largest Evangelical church in the country, with 26,000 members), or Dr. Paige Patterson, the president of Criswell's college, the Criswell Center for Biblical Studies (which turns out preachers). According to these men, heaven is the most exclusive of country clubs: There are no exceptions to the "born again" entrance rule. (Patterson tells Thomas that even Mother Teresa is damned if she never has the "conversion experience.") Listening to Criswell and Patterson talk, you feel as if you'd fallen down a rabbit hole and ended up in a land where the Crusades are still being fought. And the new pagans are the liberals (or "secular humanists"), and especially the Communists.

Thomas shows us a sampler of people attracted by the movement. Some of the Christians he interviews have dreadful stories to tell, of alcoholism and dope addiction, incest and child rape, and you don't wonder that, finding God, they "felt clean for the first time" (as one woman explains, gripping her husband's hand, in a particularly touching interview). You marvel, in some cases, that they were able to resurface at all and get their lives together. Thomas doesn't have it in for these people; he validates their need for some kind of affirmation, and the need of women and men in far less desperate straits for respite, solace, and easy answers in the confusing world of the late twentieth century.

Thomas's righteous quarrel is with those who rush into the void to supply these things: Pat Robertson, Jerry Falwell, Jim and Tammy Faye Bakker, and less-well-known religious politicos like Morton Blackwell, who heads the Leadership Institute (the link between President Reagan and the "born again" community, which, he claims, contributed over one billion dollars to conservative religious leaders in 1986 alone), and Gary Jarmin (whose publication, *The Christian Voice*, claims to be "at the cutting edge of bringing the political technology" to this community). He exposes not only their mean private greeds—we see the appalling spectacle of the Bakkers' Heritage, U.S.A.; Falwell's argument that God brought the Bakkers down prefaces the announcement that he's replaced them himself as the head of the PTL television network—but also their more alarming political agendas. Falwell says that God will destroy Russia; Richard Viguerie, who publishes *Conservative Digest*, explains the necessity of "bypassing" the leftists who have been controlling the airwaves until now. *The Christian Voice* issues "report cards" summing up the platforms of politicians who run against the representatives of the "born again" community, simplifying their stands on complex issues to label them as, say, pro-pornography or pro-gay. (Jarmin has succeeded in turning nuclear armament and capital punishment into religious issues.)

Thomas's curiosity and intelligence, and his filmmaker's instincts, which are given a boost by the classical, muted beauty of Curtis Clark's cinematography, keep your eyes and mouth wide open and your brain active. When you hear Pat Robertson warning listeners that they are committing "racial suicide" because in a hundred years "Western peoples" will make up only four per cent of the world, or when an evangelist preacher says he's tired of perverts and Communists coming out of the closet ("It's time God's people came out of the closet"), you can almost hear Joe McCarthy screaming about the Reds in the Senate, and the hysterical voices of the early-sixties segregationists defending the purity of the white race. After waffling for a year, PBS finally showed *Thy Kingdom Come, Thy Will Be Done* in April 1988, not long after rerunning the superb *Eyes on the Prize* series about civil rights. The juxtaposition was frightening—you'd thought those paranoid crackers were dead and gone, but here they were again, still waving the american flag. (Criswell used to call integrationists "infidels" from his pulpit.)

You still don't see many nonwhites in the Dallas churches Thomas uses as his focus—Dallas being "the buckle on the belt of the Bible," the seat of the largest cluster of born-againers anywhere. You don't see many poor or homeless, either, except in Criswell's downtown revival church, which locks them out at night to sleep on the streets. In fact, Dallas evangelists preach what can only be-called the rich man's gospel. "There's no virtue in being poor," says Criswell, and one of his colleagues, "Zieg" Ziegler, goes farther: He claims that prosperity is a sign of God's approval. We hear from Roberts Williams, a young preacher who was forced to resign from Criswell's organization when he submitted a paper suggesting that the rich have a responsibility to the poor: Fundamentalists like Criswell, he explains, don't want to pass on any news that might unsettle their congregation and cut down the (impressive) numbers. "You have a wrong idea of the gospel" is Criswell's reply when Thomas challenges him with the poverty of Christ's disciples.

This isn't just feel-good religion; it's religion that stuffs up the ears of the faithful so they won't hear the suffering right outside the church walls. (Dallas's poverty and crime rates are astronomical.) It marks the poor and destitute of this country (and others) as unworthy of attention, and encourages intolerance and callousness. It's hardly a surprise to learn that all "born again" paths lead to the White House. Reagan's appearance at the 1980 convention in Dallas provided the presidential seal of approval that sent the movement into the stratosphere. And, after all, Reagan's cutbacks of funds to the poor and sick and dispossessed were the secular embodiment of religious elitism—Criswell's word made flesh.

Thy Kingdom Come offers a few glimpses of the ridiculous extremes of its subject. There's the amazing Jim-and-Tammy national soap opera, with Tammy weeping her eye liner into charcoal blotches as she moans that too many in the TV audience aren't following through on their pledges. ("Sometimes I get so tired of the worry of it," she cries, like the lyric of some country–western ballad.) There's Ruth Hunt, the dotty widow of H. L. Hunt, who leads Bible classes in her Mount Vernon mansion; and North Carolina's *Saturday Evening Post* small town, Heritage, U.S.A., as defeating in its way as the electric parade on Disneyland's Main Street—it's so overwhelmingly kitschy you don't know how to *begin* to respond to it.

The movie's creepiest moment comes in an interview with a disabled boy named Kevin Whittum (he's eighteen but, due to a bone disease, he looks about eight), in whose honor Jim Bakker built Kevin's House in Heritage, U.S.A., for handicapped children. No one except Kevin has ever lived there; his residence is his pay for doing PTL spots whenever he's asked. He tells Thomas that Kevin's House was built in thirty-two days—so there could be a dedication on the Fourth of July, and, he adds, because the Bakker regime was afraid he might die if they waited too long. When Thomas asks him which he believes was more important to his benefactors—the holiday or his health—Kevin answers in a tiny voice, "The Fourth of July, I guess." I can't remember another documentary that has engaged such a sensational topic on so many levels.

June 1988

A Jury of One's Peers

• • •

In 1980 Michael Chamberlain, a Seventh-Day Adventist minister in the Queensland region of Australia, and his wife, Lindy, took their two young sons and their baby daughter, Azaria, on a camping trip through the outback to a popular tourist attraction called Ayers Rock. That night, while Lindy was preparing dinner, she saw a dingo—a wild dog, not unlike a coyote—scurrying out of the tent where she'd put Azaria to sleep. When she opened the flap she found the baby was gone, and a search party consisting largely of other campers failed to turn up a body. (None was ever discovered, but articles of Azaria's clothing, located the next day, figured significantly in the case.) Over the next five and a half years, while Lindy was put on trial for murder and Michael for being an accessory after the fact, while she served two years of a life sentence before new evidence confirmed her story, the Chamberlain case was hotly debated in every bar and at every dinner table in Australia. According to John Bryson, who wrote about it in the 1985 *Evil Angels*, the couple was effectively tried and convicted not by due process (the judge practically instructed the jury to acquit them) but by public opinion. And that's the point of view of Fred Schepisi's remarkable film of the story, A Cry in the Dark, starring Meryl Streep and Sam Neill.

In the movie, what triggers the protest against the Chamberlains is the general skepticism that greets Lindy's story: How could a creature the size of a dingo have carried off a ten-pound baby? (Schepisi shows us the comic spectacle of middle-aged newspapermen conducting experiments with ten-pound buckets in their mouths.) The judge at the preliminary hearing rules that no criminal act has been perpetrated, but the police locate forensics experts who claim the baby's clothing shows no saliva or teeth marks, and the case is reopened. Even before that, though, it's clear that Australia doesn't believe the Chamberlains because it just doesn't like them. Their air of calm in the face of their loss strikes people as callous; they're thrown by the meticulousness and straightforwardness with which Lindy sets out to correct the errors in the news stories, and by her lack of squeamishness when she talks about the violence dingos are capable of; they're turned off by Michael's evangelical speeches to the press, and misconstrue his faith in a Second Coming as an absence of grief. Wild rumors circulate about child sacrifices—at one point, it seems half of the country is sure that the name Azaria means "sacrifice in the wilderness." When Lindy shows up in court looking very pregnant (she'd intended to have another baby after the ordeal was over, but then the trial was suddenly postponed more than half a year), she's seen as creepier than ever: One prosecution witness tells her friends she could feel Lindy's eyes burning into her back as she sat in court after her testimony. "She's a witch, you know," the witness confides, as if it were a documented fact.

In the late seventies and early eighties, when critics were discovering the Australian cinema and going gaga over such bloodless exercises as Picnic at Hanging Rock, Breaker Morant, and Gallipoli, Fred Schepisi made the one Australian film that really deserves to be called a masterpiece—the shocking, incendiary The Chant of Jimmie Blacksmith—out of Thomas Keneally's novel. (He also made The Devil's Playground, a fine, wry comedy about life in a Catholic boys' school.) Jimmie Blacksmith is about a half-Aboriginal, taught by whites to reject his tribal origins, whose drive to be accepted into white society meets with racist scorn and worse. He takes his revenge by striking at the soft center of the white man's existence—his fire-warmed, fleshy women and his children. This violent movie is as crucially about the Australian experience as, say, *The Godfather* is about Americans, though it rarely gets talked about. And now, after a sojourn in Hollywood that produced three of the most lyrical films of the decade (*Barbarosa, Iceman,* and *Roxanne*), Schepisi returns to his homeland to make another incisive movie about the Australian temperament.

For in *A Cry in the Dark* the whole country is on trial. Working from a script he wrote with Robert Caswell that's a model of narrative economy and clarity, Schepisi focuses as much on how the case is presented in the press and viewed by the public as on the actual courtroom proceedings. We see how TV news teams edit interviews with the Chamberlains for maximum dramatic effect, and then, when Lindy struggles to set the record straight, how viewers perceive her and Michael as celebrity-mongers. The case gives rise to a fresh batch of dingo-and-baby jokes; on a matinee talk show the host polls his audience on Lindy's guilt; a young man argues passionately on behalf of the maligned dingo, and animal societies solemnly picket against the Chamberlains. At the end of the film, Lindy says that her and Michael's battle to clear their names was a fight for all Australians, so nothing like this could ever happen again. It's the one time this pragmatic, matter-of-fact woman seems to be pipe-dreaming. The country that begins to emerge in *A Cry in the Dark* is a fascinating mix of the laid-back and the feisty, blithely judgmental and frequently deluded, most confident when it's most in the dark. It's a lot like our own.

The first section of the movie, in the outback, has some of the expansive beauty Schepisi and his constant collaborator, photographer Ian Baker, brought to *Barbarosa* and the exterior sequences in *Iceman*. Schepisi zooms into magnificent Ayers Rock—immense, coppery, crab-like—while Baker uses an exotic, pastel palette to convey the mystery of the region. The scene where the baby is lost is a brilliant depiction of chaos: Responding to Lindy's cries, Michael leaps into the dark, then whirls about in confusion like a dog chasing its tail, and when the search party heads out, silhouettes with torches aloft, you can see they haven't a chance in that preternatural blackness. For the rest of the film Schepisi adopts a densely edited, throwaway style; the public-opinion segments are collages of quick revue sketches, reminiscent of the lopsided naturalism in Bill Forsyth's comedies. Schepisi's honest—he's not interested in scoring individual points against these case followers. What he wants us to see is how casually, almost innocently, the whole country pronounces sentence on the Chamberlains.

Meryl Streep was miserably miscast in *Plenty*, her first picture with Schepisi, and you may cringe when you see her for the first time here in a helmet of straight, slick black hair. But for once she seems completely subsumed by the role; it's her only performance since *Sophie's Choice* that I have no reservations about. The very qualities that turn some of us off about Streep—the stiff-neckedness, the cold, technical proficiency, the obstinate, unyielding distance— are perfectly in character for Lindy Chamberlain, and Streep uses them unhesitatingly in the service of the role; she doesn't try to make herself look good, and she's dropped the great-lady attitude. She has a virtuoso scene on the stand where she's cross-examined by the prosecutor (Bruce Myles), a master obfuscator. We don't feel close to this woman, but when we see her fighting tears of frustration, biting back her anger at what she's being put through, and incapable of either perverting the truth or giving easy satisfaction, her integrity is somehow inspiring. Sam Neill, who gives a superb performance as Michael, has a scene on the stand that's equally amazing; it's the only time I've ever fully understood how an intelligent witness can be reduced to a blithering idiot by a shrewd lawyer. (The filmmakers also refuse to simplify the bewildering mass of evidence, pro and con, because they want us to see how, inevitably, evidence becomes an irrelevancy in this trial.)

When I came out of the movie my first response was "This is a terrific movie, but it has no emotional center"—even though I could see exactly why the nature of the material precludes the usual warm treatment of the victimized protagonist. (If we aren't made to feel some of what the public feels, the film's too easy an indictment.) I was wrong, though. *A Cry in the Dark* isn't about Lindy Chamberlain; it's about the arbitrariness of public opinion and the obscuring of justice, about Australia and human nature. And there's a keen, dry-eyed anger at the bottom of it, under the black comedy—the filmmakers' anger. At the end, we're told that the Chamberlains didn't receive official exoneration until two months before the movie's release, eight and a half years after Azaria's disappearance. The final title reads, "The fight to restore their lives continues."

November 1988

Con Job
• • •

In his article in *Film Comment* on *Roger and Me*, Michael Moore's comic indictment of General Motors and its chairman, Roger Smith, for closing plants and laying off workers in Flint, Michigan, Harlan Jacobson documented several instances of Moore's falsification, deliberate reordering and willful misinterpretation of the facts. A number of reviewers and reporters have subsequently made direct reference to Jacobson's findings, yet the country continues its love affair with Moore's brand of snake-oil salesmanship, as if misleading audiences were something to be applauded—a clever trick slyly turned.

The fact is, *everything* about *Roger and Me* is misleading. Using as his structure a two-and-a-half year quest for Smith (allegedly to drag him back to Flint to take public responsibility for the wrongs he's committed), Moore claims to be making a left-leaning exposé of GM's cavalier treatment of poor working-class stiffs in Flint. But he doesn't show a shred of genuine compassion for them. At worst, he makes them look dumb or ignorant; at best, they're irrelevant (as human beings) to his picture. His condescension toward them is apparent in the opening sequences, when he uses footage of fifties middle-American pop culture mockingly, to damn the people who bought into it. Moore's voice-over narration tells us that this benign, cheerleader's America is what he grew up believing in (his father worked at GM), and what GM's heartlessness somehow violates. But his ironic tone, and the distance he knows he can count on between his audience and the dated footage, tell us subtextually that nobody with half a brain would believe this crap.

As he moves through Flint, and across the country on an alleged hunt for the elusive Roger, Moore makes joke after joke, and always at the expense of the subjects of his interviews. The audience feels no qualms about laughing, because Moore makes it look as though what he's lampooning is the selfish corporate spirit that led GM to act as it did. Yet few of the people he picks on have a significant connection to GM: a pair of matrons at a golf club who surmise that the unemployed workers are probably lazy; local monied citizens at a costume ball or paying (as part of a community drive) to stay overnight in Flint's jail; a black sheriff who has the unfortunate job of evicting families behind on their rent; the manager of Flint's one live theater, who has a groupie mentality; an uneducated young woman who raises rabbits, selling some for pets and others for meat; Anita Bryant (an easy target for politically correct audiences); Pat Boone, who used to sell Chevies on TV on his weekly variety show.

Are these really the villains of Flint's economic plunge—assuming there are villains at all? Boone gets the worst deal: Moore catches him saying that, as part of his contract, he got to drive a new Chevy every year. You can see Moore wants us to think Boone's a sleaze for accepting the cars, though there was no moral reason for him not to—it was part of his salary. But we all know how *immoral* GM is, right? *Roger and Me* has been "proving" it to us all along. So anyone who'll accept their tainted product as pay (even decades before the taint) *must* be corrupt. Moore also counts on our misunderstanding Boone's awkwardly worded statement about how good he felt about the cars he sold. That's meant to incriminate him, too (as if he'd been bribed to like Chevies), when what he *seems* to be saying is that his experience behind the wheel of a Chevy convinced him he was advertising a solid product.

Even if you don't know how Moore has played with the facts, it's not hard to spot his maneuvering; there's almost always an alternative story going on behind the one he wants us to buy. He interviews a young man (perhaps twenty-one or twenty-two) outside a blood clinic who talks about how often he can get away with selling his blood. The implication is that things are so bad in Flint that the youth of the city are reduced to this. But we don't know whether the kid ever worked for GM, or would have done so if the plants hadn't closed. We also don't know whether the poor families we see being evicted are laid-off GM employees: Moore wants us to take it on faith that *all* of Flint's poverty and destitution can be laid at Roger Smith's door. Moore eventually tracks Smith down at a stockholders' meeting, which he manages to infiltrate (he says) by pretending to be one of them; then he's outraged/amused (his usual response to Smith's exclusiveness) when the meeting shuts down just as he steps up to the microphone to ask his question. But Moore has shown up with a camera crew in tow, so his claim that he's passing as a stockholder is utterly implausible. How does he *expect* the GM executives to respond to an aggressive filmmaker who bulls his way uninvited into their meeting? With open arms?

That's the big question the movie refuses to ask: What does Moore expect? When he and his crew appear at Smith's club, he treats the manager's insistence on removing him as intolerable snobbishness; when the PR person at one of the Flint plants won't let him through the door on closing day, and refuses to give him an interview, he's appalled. It doesn't occur to Moore—at least he doesn't *let on* that it ever occurred to him—that forcing yourself on people in this way, even official people, is intrusive; or that when he demands social and political responses from Miss Michigan moments after a parade, or from those women on the golf course, he puts them on the defensive. He wants us to think *they're* at fault, that they're stupid or thoughtless or rude or inept or hiding something.

Moore sets up the movie as a hipster's contemporary version of a Frank Capra movie and casts himself, a chubby independent moviemaker with unruly long hair and a baseball cap, in the Jimmy Stewart role. His unprepossessing appearance is as much part of the ploy as his claim that he offered an official at GM his Chucky Cheese discount card as ID. (We're supposed to register Moore as a regular guy who isn't pretentious enough to dress in a tie and jacket for interviews, or carry a credit card.) Moore wants us to see him as Flint's sole chance to make itself whole again: There's actually a sequence where he cuts from yet another failure to pin down Roger Smith, to shots of a dilapidated neighborhood, and tells us, "Meanwhile, in Flint, things were getting worse"—as if he, Michael Moore, were racing against time to save the town. Everyone he meets is either an obstacle, or proof that there's corruption as far as his sharp eye can see.

My favorite Moore story appeared in an article in the January 19th, 1990 edition of *The New York Times* about Ralph Nader's attempt to get the filmmaker to pay him back $30,000 "for financial and material support contributed to projects of Mr. Moore." James Musselman, a Philly lawyer who's one of Nader's associates, suggests that the idea for *Roger and Me* was lifted from Nader's book *The Big Boys*, and then he makes this astounding claim:

> Mr. Musselman also said the comedic premise of the movie— that it was impossible to pin down Mr. Smith for an interview— was bogus. He said he had watched Mr. Moore interview Mr. Smith at a January 1988 exposition of G.M. technology at the Waldorf–Astoria Hotel in New York.

Perfect.

January 1990

SEX IN THE NEW PURITAN AGE

• • •

In the thirties and forties the censorship strategy that a terrified Hollywood imposed on itself, known officially as the Production Code and popularly as the Hays Code (after Will B. Hays, who framed it), kept American movies repressed. At least that's how they were on the surface: Bathroom sets were built without toilets, married couples slept in twin beds, homosexuality was never mentioned, and adulteresses were always punished (usually by death) in the final reel. Some Hollywood moviemakers subverted these rules as best they could; the sexy screwball comedies of the Depression, fashioned around the delay of sexual gratification, were perhaps the most creative and enjoyable of these subversions. Others put up shrines to the Code, some of which are pretty famous. At the end of 1942's *Now, Voyager*, Bette Davis chooses to preserve the sanctity of her lover Paul Henreid's miserable marriage and convey her passion for him indirectly—through his daughter, whom she's ensconced in her home and restored to self-worth and happiness.

"Don't let's ask for the moon," she counsels the impatient, impetuous Henreid, "when we have the stars."

It's not clear what would have happened if Hollywood had thrown the Production Code out the window rather than allowing the changing times to erode it. By the mid-sixties it had become a joke. But in the eighties, amazingly enough, we returned to something like it. Suddenly a Puritanism ran rampant through our movies once again. Hollywood has always been the repository of our greatest fears, as well as the constant reflection of our preferred self-image of the moment. So it's not difficult to see where this current trend derives from: a combination of the return-to-homespun-values pronouncements of the Reagan regime, which struck a chord in millions of Americans; and the AIDS crisis, our response to which was very much linked to our wholesale embrace of those values.

The new sexual moralism is evident not only in a hysterical thriller like *Fatal Attraction* or the more somber *Presumed Innocent*, and in the sex–procreation, sex–marriage comedy specials like *Parenthood* and *When Harry Met Sally . . .* , but in the structure and tone of a weird movie like 1989's hands-down art-house favorite, Steven Soderbergh's *sex, lies, and videotape*. Here's the plot: A successful Baton Rouge attorney, John (Peter Gallagher), is married to a beautiful analysand, Ann (Andie McDowell), who doesn't much care for sex. So he gets it off regularly with her sister, Cynthia (Laura San Giacomo), a hot number who finds the added twist that she's cuckolding her own flesh and blood an irresistible turn-on. Enter the lawyer's long-gone fraternity pal, Graham (James Spader), who's impotent—except when, alone in his apartment, he runs the videotapes he's made (he's amassed dozens) of attractive women he's interviewed about sex. All of this sounds like a clever idea for a whacked-out farce, a southern–Gothic chamber-play conceived by Almodóvar. But Soderbergh isn't a farceur; the movie is deadly serious.

In Soderbergh's scheme, the video-viewing intruder is a reticent Christ figure whose cross is his saintly honesty and his sensitivity to lies in the tainted (i.e., sexual) world he's withdrawn from. He explains to Ann that he used to be a pathological liar, and it's the guilt over his last relationship that has made him impotent. He also admits that he doesn't care for John, because *he's* a liar. Both women (Ann, who intuitively backs away from John's sexual desire, and restless Cynthia, who at heart wants something better) are attracted to the asexual Graham. The movie treats him less as a psychological drifter who can't function in the world than as the superior of every character in this underpopulated film except Ann, whom Soderbergh entrusts with the task of saving Graham—bringing him back into the world he's forsaken by touching him with the power of her love.

When Ann revives Graham by making love to him, and he turns off his video camera for good, the solemn movie hobbles to its close. Love is good; sex without love is bad, and spiritually and emotionally crippling. Soderbergh's cautionary, AIDS-era fable—*Teorema* without mystery or sex—received the kiss of approval from critics all over the country and ran away with the grand prize at Cannes. The movie didn't have any trouble finding a receptive audience here because Soderbergh consoles our fears and makes us feel virtuous for championing monogamy and fidelity and sexual honesty. He's made an art-house/feel-good movie. What's alarming about it is the morality play underneath. Neither of the two characters we're meant to find appealing—radiant, delicately flaky Ann or the damaged holy man Graham—has sex until the end, when they share some vague, spiritual, off-camera kind of union. The villain of the piece is John, who loses not only his wife and his mistress by the fade-out, but his clients as well; presumably they smelled the whiff of moral decrepitude on him and simply backed away.

Though the movie makes Ann frigid, it takes pains not to let that frigidity serve as a justification for John's behavior. But Peter Gallagher's expectant-satyr smile as he lies nude on his bed, a birthday gift (a plant) for his lover resting squarely on his crotch, is the only sign of life in *sex, lies, and videotape*. Soderbergh is doing unconsciously what shrewd Hays Code–era filmmakers did deliberately and out of very different motives: giving us a sexy "bad" character to revel in—John wears his permanent hard-on like a villain's black hat—and then piously doling out the wages of his lust at the end. In another era—say, the one in which Fielding wrote *Tom Jones*—John's erection would be the source of hilarity rather than moral outrage.

When viewers refuse to accept Tomas's happy resignation to being in love with his wife, in the final scenes of Philip Kaufman's

The Unbearable Lightness of Being (one of the great movies of the eighties), because they say they still can't forgive him for his earlier infidelities, it's really *Kaufman* they won't forgive—for refusing either to pass judgment on Tomas or to punish him, the way adultery used to be punished in the Production Code days. That's the way the culture guides us to think now. And, faced with the less rigorous sexual codes of other cultures' films, moviegoers may be as confused now as many Americans were when the first waves of English and French imports hit this country in the fifties and sixties. All the movies in this section deal frankly and inventively with sexual relationships, and only one was made by an American: Paul Mazursky's *Enemies, A Love Story*, whose main character is a bigamist. The others came to us from England (Stephen Frears's *My Beautiful Laundrette*; *Rita, Sue and Bob Too*; and the David Leland pictures), France (*Ménage*), and Spain (the films of Pedro Almodóvar). Mazursky, like Kaufman, still makes the movies the way he did in the early seventies, when Americans embraced the nonjudgmental attitudes of *M*A*S*H* and *Murmur of the Heart* and *Sunday, Bloody, Sunday*, and the climate was loose and liberal enough to allow Bertolucci to release *Last Tango in Paris*.

Another Country

• • •

There is hardly a sequence in *My Beautiful Laundrette* that I recognized from any other movie I'd ever seen. This disarming film
by the young English director Stephen Frears, written by a twenty-
nine-year-old Anglo–Pakistani playwright named Hanif Kureishi, is
about how an immigrant culture gains a foothold in London by
beating the British at their own game, and about the implications
of that kind of assimilation for the culture, for the country, and for
the emotional and moral development of individuals involved in the
process. Omar (Gordon Warnecke) is a bright-eyed young Pakistani
who, having dropped out of university after failing his exams twice,
hangs around the apartment he shares with his father Hassim, a
one-time journalist laid low by liquor and his wife's suicide. Hassim
feels that if the boy is not receiving an education he ought to be
gainfully employed, so he farms him out to Omar's Uncle Nasser
(Saeed Jaffrey), who runs a successful parking garage and has a
number of smaller businesses on the side. Omar's new job—washing
cars—wins him an introduction into an extended family that includes Nasser's bored, lusty daughter Tania (Rita Wolf) and his
shrewd partner Salim (Derrick Branche). Before long Omar has
been offered the management of a laundrette Nasser owns in a
tough section of town.

Kureishi has a complex understanding of the interaction between the Pakistanis and the native whites; his vision is as broad
and intricate as that of Satyajit Ray's modern-day Indian films dealing with a clash of old and new lifestyles (such as *The Adversary*
and *The Middleman*), but his sensibility is much different—funnier,
earthier, more bristling, less classical and reflective. Hassim, played
by the splendid Roshan Seth (he was Nehru in *Gandhi*) with the
sublime snobbery of a dissolute, displaced Eastern prince, can't forgive his adopted country for the ways in which it has attacked his
people; he's never recovered from the shock of seeing neighbors
(friends, he had once believed) marching in the National Front protests against the influx of immigrants. "This country has done me

in," he tells his brother; and in his less despairing moments, when
the old muckraking-journalist impulse sneaks in, he sermonizes on
the importance of education for young Anglicized Pakistanis like his
son: "We all must have knowledge to see what is being done to
whom in this country." Nasser has another perspective. Pakistan, he
reminds Hassim, has been "sodomized by religion" which has "begun to interfere with the making of money," but in England money
is still a god everyone can worship, native and immigrant alike. He
tells Omar, on his first day at work: "In this damn country, which
we hate and love, you can get anything you want . . . but you have
to learn to squeeze the tits of the system."

Nasser is an expert squeezer. He straddles the English–Pakistani
line with superb comic grace (and Saeed Jaffrey gives a superb
comic performance): At home his wife, draped in a sari, entertains
members of the community on Sunday evenings, while his white
mistress, Rachel (Shirley Anne Field), drops in on him at work.
Each of the women is aware of the other, but they keep each other
at a distance, like twin satellites orbiting around Nasser's life, until
his wife grows so furious at his mistress that she hauls out ancient
Eastern charms to bring Rachel discomfort. (Kureishi displays his
sly, wild-card humor and his broad-eyed grasp of the comic richness
of his subject when he shows us Tania, the alienated daughter who
schemes to leave her father's home and strike out on her own, actually aiding her mother in casting these spells—and when Rachel
gives Nasser evidence that they've actually had some effect.)

Omar seems to be less Hassim's son than Nasser's: The moment
he's exposed to Nasser's way of life, his indolence metamorphoses
into go-getter energy, and he leaps at the chance to enter the capi-
talist world his uncle and Salim are such masters at. As played by
Gordon Warnecke, a fresh young actor with an appealing physical
restlessness, Omar isn't easy to read at first; there doesn't appear to
be much underneath his smiling opportunism and recessive charm.
In his polite, boyish manner, he takes in the atmosphere of patriar-
chal ease at Nasser's Sunday gatherings, where the men belly-laugh
over politics and sex in one room and the women gossip in another,
and he's just as passive and noncommittal when Tania parades outside the window, baring her breasts for his view alone, to entice
him to offer her a little diversion in the garden pavilion. Later that
night Salim's car, with his family and Omar in it, is attacked by a

gang of young "Paki-bashers" and, seeing an old school chum, Johnny (Daniel Day-Lewis), in the second (nonactive) ranks of the punk troops, Omar rushes up to him to renew their acquaintance—as if he were unaware of the offense being perpetrated against him and his friends. And we wonder if that could really be true. It's only as the movie develops his relationship with Johnny that we begin to comprehend Omar. Hassim refers disdainfully to his son as "a little Britisher," and indeed when he calls Johnny up to offer him a job at the laundrette, as a sort of physical jack-of-all-trades (including bouncer), Omar Anglicizes his own name—he pronounces it "Omer." He's drawn to Johnny, a working-class white kid who's been in and out of jail, just as his uncle is drawn to Rachel, and when they become lovers everything we haven't been able to fit together about Omar suddenly makes sense.

If this beautifully balanced film has a strong suit, it's the Omar–Johnny relationship. And much of the credit for these scenes belongs to Daniel Day-Lewis, whose Johnny is full of surprises. Day-Lewis makes a stunning first impression, standing aloof from his destructive pals, a patch of dyed blond hair at war with the dark brown pressed down under his workingman's cap. When he accepts Omar's job, his other friends rag on him for turning his back on his countrymen, but he holds their taunts at bay with such grinning expertise that, in an understated comic moment, one of them actually lends him a hand in putting up the laundrette's neon sign. We don't expect the length of the fuse Day-Lewis and the filmmakers have planted in Johnny, and we don't expect his fidelity, either, or the sincerity of his respect for Omar's father—or the injured look on his face when Hassim, who felt his parental affection for Johnny betrayed when he saw him in the National Front demonstrations, asks him if he's still a Fascist.

Johnny is turned on by the hum of constant activity beneath Omar's quiet surface—the sound that the gleaming alertness in Omar's eyes cues you to listen for. And when they're alone Johnny's wry, playful sexual energy brings out Omar's sensuous side. The love scenes between these two young men are erotic and enjoyable, unlike the (off-camera) clinch between William Hurt and Raul Julia in *Kiss of the Spider Woman*, because they aren't as painfully pointed; they convey the exploratory adventurousness of genuine adolescent sex. (Their real connection is to the sexual interludes in Robert

Towne's *Personal Best*.) In one sequence, Johnny walks past his
punk hangers-on and, just out of their sight, licks Omar's neck; it's
a private show for Omar, like Tania's breast-baring earlier in the
picture. And there's a glorious scene in which he makes love to
Omar in the back room of the about-to-open laundrette while the
other racially mixed couple, Nasser and Rachel, dance seductively
out front. (The filmmakers are making a point here, but it doesn't
detract from the pleasure of the scene; in *My Beautiful Laundrette*,
sex is permitted to be both political *and* fun.)

The laundrette is an emblem of Omar's two-fisted ascension
into the world of "little Britishers." Using money they've made by
filching cocaine from Salim, who deals on the side, he and Johnny
dress the place up in a sort of op kitsch decor, with waves painted
on the walls and real plants in every corner, and serve champagne
at the grand opening. When Johnny wanders away from the laundrette during the night to drink with his other buddies, Omar comes
after him, hurt by what he perceives as his friend's desertion, and
pulls rank on him, threatening to fire him if he doesn't return to
work. He tells his lover he likes the idea that a white punk who used
to beat up Pakistanis is now washing their floors, and we wonder if
we're seeing the anger Omar absorbed when we thought he was
looking the other way—during the National Front marches, or
when the hoodlums attacked Salim's car. But this is a moment of
private fury at a private betrayal, not a political eruption. Omar,
who doesn't identify with the Pakistanis, isn't the one who was hurt
by Johnny's identification with the xenophobic National Front:
That was his idealistic father. Omar is hurt because his lover took
off on the night of their triumph to party with his other friends.
And it's to *that* injury that Johnny responds by returning to the
laundrette.

When so few movies have a sophisticated political text, *My
Beautiful Laundrette* is practically a revelation, but for Kureishi,
as for Satyajit Ray, political concerns always take second place to
humanistic ones. Salim, who is this movie's equivalent to the slick,
razor-sharp, second-generation hoods in *The Godfather, Part II*,
gives Johnny a job "unscrewing"—i.e., removing the apartment
doors of "undesirable" (black) tenants. We can chart Johnny's
growth into moral adulthood partly by his eventual rejection of this

job (offered to him by a man who suggests with sublime condescension that a social outcast like ex-con Johnny no longer has a place in the British caste system and had better bond with the Pakistanis).

This sequence is actually foreshadowed in the opening moments of the film; *My Beautiful Laundrette* has such a lively, spontaneous surface that you may not notice at first what fine craftsmen Kureishi and Frears are. And the cast helps to bring out the virtues of their work. All the main characters have distinctive, complicated personalities, and the performers, including Rita Wolf as Tania and Derrick Branche as Salim, rise to the occasion. Salim's wife (Souad Faress) calls Omar an "in-between" because he has never seen Karachi, but it is Salim who is the true "in-between": He preserves his ties to the Pakistani community while acting with the swift vengefulness of a new-world gangster, and so he's unpredictable. His ability to shift from familial warmth to attacks of malice disproportionate to what provoked them keeps us on our guard when he's around.

My Beautiful Laundrette moves at a clip. Frears and Kureishi don't go in for filler (Omar's initial efforts to make the laundrette pay off flop in what seems like just a few hours), so sometimes the narrative fails to ring in and we have to catch up to it. Considering what the movie achieves, though—a fresh, buzzing portrait of people responding to a real-life context—this complaint seems minor. Occasionally scenes don't come off, like the punks' attack on Salim's car, which the photographer, Oliver Stapleton, has shot in an expressionistic neon glow that (perhaps because it is a one-of-a-kind sequence) isn't evocative in the way Frears probably intended it to be. But it's easy to forgive an experiment that doesn't work in a fabulous movie like this one, which is in a larger sense an experiment—trying on new material, a new setting, a new tone. Possibly the shoestring budget ($850,000) helped to keep Frears honest; the only scene I can recall that sounded false to me was the inevitable confrontation between Tania and Rachel, which he shot in close-up. The rest of the movie is delightfully new. When Hassim stumbles drunkenly into his son's laundrette late on opening night and sees Johnny for the first time in years, he calls him, with superlative disdain, an "underpants cleaner"—and then, on an immense sigh, confesses "Oh, the working class is such a disappointment to me." Like so many other details in *My Beautiful Laundrette*, this prize scrap of comic irony ricochets off the edges of the movie and hits you after you think you've left it far behind.

June 1986

Sexual Bohemia

• • •

The trio that makes up Bertrand Blier's *Ménage* consists of Antoine (Michel Blanc) and Monique (Miou-Miou), whose marriage has begun to dissipate under the pressure of hard times, and Bob (Gérard Depardieu), an expert burglar who leads them into prosperity and turns their lives around. Their first encounter with Bob is like the startling *in medias res* opening of Blier's *Get Out Your Handkerchiefs*, where Depardieu played a frustrated husband who procures a lover for his wife from among the patrons in a restaurant. *Ménage* begins with a public squabble between Antoine and Monique: She's fed up with their poverty, with his lack of ambition, even with his puppy-dog adoration of her, and she wants to leave him. But before she can take that walk Bob saunters over to their table, holding a cocktail glass aloft like a standard, and enters the argument. First he castigates Antoine for allowing his wife to treat him so shabbily, and then, with a princely flourish, a perfect mockery of *noblesse oblige*, he tosses her a thick bundle of francs to appease her. This seductive act of generosity initiates their partnership. By morning Monique has determined to upgrade their lifestyle by joining forces with this wealthy thief, and Antoine, puzzled and reluctant but helplessly bound by his wife's whims, trails along behind her.

Bob is a gifted outlaw (he describes his penchant for thievery as a "state of grace"), and Monique falls in love with him. It's Antoine he's after, though. The first time Bob flirts with him, Monique quiets Antoine's fears by making a move on Bob herself, ostensibly to prove he can respond to a woman's advances; the second time, Bob is so bold and forthright and funny that you can't believe he's serious. Michel Blanc, with his tiny, immaculate moustache, his soft features, and his slightly effeminate vocal rhythms, fits the homosexual stereotype far more easily than the burly, tattooed, aggressively masculine Depardieu. So when Bob starts to chase Antoine, courting him with the romantic ardor of an Italian tenor (and, in one hilarious scene, slipping into his room in a pair of leopard-skin briefs and cornering him in bed), you laugh at both the humor of the reversal and the way Blier has caught you in thrall to that stereotype. It's a wicked joke on the audience, and Blier keeps playing variations on it.

Ménage suggests *No Exit* rewritten as a comedy of manners. Blier starts with a Sartrean dramatic conflict—each character has a sexual longing that can't be answered by either of the others—but the combination of frivolity and seriousness of purpose (which S. J. Perelman cited as one of the rules of high comedy in his famous essay, "What Makes Comedy High?"), along with the *ménage à trois* setting, recalls Noel Coward's scandalous 1932 play *Design for Living*, in which a pair of amorously befuddled gentlemen share an independent-minded young woman. Blier's sexual bohemia goes much farther than Coward's, however. Monique is so frantic to hold onto Bob and the upward mobility he represents for them that she drives her husband into his arms, promising to compensate him for his erotic exertions with Bob by servicing him when he returns. Her plan backfires: When Bob finally gets Antoine into bed, Antoine discovers he enjoys what he finds, and he transfers his moon-eyed devotion from Monique to Bob. She's reduced to lying at the foot of Bob's bed, listening to the lovers' moans of pleasure and begging them to let her in—and then bringing them breakfast in bed after their bouts of lovemaking.

Gérard Depardieu is one of the most prolific movie actors in the world, but Blier throws him curves no other director does, and in fielding them he rediscovers his instincts. He's not just robust and energetic and witty in this picture; he's also more uninhibited than he's been since the great days of *Going Places* and *The Last Woman*: His love scenes with Michel Blanc have a blazing comic intensity.

And Blanc does something remarkable—the more skewed and difficult his role becomes, the more touching he gets. As Monique,
Miou-Miou employs her blurry, soft-tough quality with an authority lacking in the straight performances that have won her so much
acclaim in France (in movies like *La Dérobade* and *Entre Nous*).
She gets some terrific effects here. In one scene she goes to work on
Depardieu, struggling to rouse him to heterosexual passion, and
when her husband wanders into the room he can't break her un-
comprehending gaze—she's under sexual anesthesia.

Unlike *Design for Living*, *Ménage* is less a coherent situation
comedy than a series of burlesque sketches, each a new twist on the
notion of the romantic triangle as well as a fresh assault on the ves-
tiges of old-fashioned bourgeois sensibility. There's a decidedly juvenile pleasure to be had in this kind of calculated outrageousness—
a pleasure akin to what you feel at a Buñuel picture when he's being
naughty about the church. (One sequence might have been devised
by the Buñuel of *The Discreet Charm of the Bourgeoisie*: Jean-
Pierre Marielle and Caroline Sihol play, with deadpan expertise, a
couple whose general boredom has turned them into walking ici-
cles.) The style and structure link *Ménage* to Blier's comic fantasy,
Femmes Fatales, which took the metaphor of the war between the
sexes to new extremes, but—unlike that movie or *Going Places* or
his masterpiece, *Get Out Your Handkerchiefs—Ménage* lacks a personal vision. Those earlier comedies introduced a frankness about
men's bewildered responses to women that seemed like a revelation
in the wake of cautious, respectful postfeminist pictures like *An Unmarried Woman*. Blier insisted that, underneath all that good-
liberal sensitivity, the war was still going on, and his movies made
you feel you were getting reports from the front. You can't find any
evidence in *Ménage* that Blier had a real stake in making it; all you
can see of him in it are his daring and his technique. That doesn't
prevent it from being a very funny movie, though, for the first two-
thirds.

It's in the last half hour that Blier makes his fatal mistake: He
shifts tones, heading into a melodrama full of violence and betrayal.
Here *Ménage* doesn't just stop being funny, it becomes utterly baffling—and when you can't unscramble Blier's signals, you start to
feel cheated. At that point only the good will built up in the first
hour, and the new wrinkles in Michel Blanc's performance (when

the plot requires him to appear in drag), save the movie from total collapse. It's possible that Blier intended these final sequences to resonate in ways that aren't clear because they've been insufficiently prepared for, but you can't even find the remnants of a strategy in what ended up on the screen. Instead you get the sense that he just ran out of steam—and ideas. *Ménage* has more life than any Blier picture since *Get Out Your Handkerchiefs*, but it's ultimately unsatisfying; you wish it were powered by a more obsessional drive than just the will to shock the conventional. Maybe he couldn't finish it because it just didn't mean enough to him.

October 1986

The Old In-Out

• • •

A cocky, purposeful walk—the walk of indomitable people impatient to get where they're going—is the emblem of the sex farce *Rita, Sue and Bob Too*, from England's Channel Four. Blonde Sue (Michelle Holmes) and Rita (Siobhan Finneran), a brunette, walk all the way from their bleak ghetto neighborhood in a northern industrial city to the equally undifferentiated upper-middle-class suburb where they babysit once a week. Their energetic, headstrong, lopsided waddle, which is great fun to watch, is meant to contrast with the aimless meandering of Sue's permanently besotted dad (Willie Ross), which opens the film, and it squares nicely with the queerly angled movement of their employer, Bob (George Costigan), who takes the earliest possible opportunity to get into the girls' pants. Bob's body follows his delighted leer: Slim and tall and slick, he's like an arrow constantly on its way to a target—not a bad physicalization for a character who behaves like a self-propelled erection. (There's even a freeze frame of Costigan in mid-leap into bed with the girls, his trousers slipping off him—a perfect summary of this character.) And the movie's best gag is that when Bob's wife, Michelle (Lesley Sharp), learns what her husband's been up to, she strides out of their bungalow in the direction of the girls' slum to confront them, and we see she's got their determined walk down perfectly.

Actually, this moment is part of the larger joke of *Rita, Sue and Bob Too*: Except for money, there's no significant shift between the screaming and pounding in Sue's digs (Rita doesn't appear to have a family) and what goes on between Bob and Michelle, who have an embattled marriage. Judging from their accents, Bob and Michelle are a couple of working-class folk who've made good, and they haven't lost their lowdown, scrapping energy. In the vision of writer Andrea Dunbar and director Alan Clarke (which is borne out by Ivan Strasburg's photography), the two environments are equally sterile and dead-ended, but as long as the people who reside in them can keep kicking, life isn't over yet. There are earthy pleasures to be squeezed out of it.

In the song "The Miller's Son" from the Stephen Sondheim musical *A Little Night Music*, one of the characters describes sex as "a wink and a wiggle / And a giggle on the grass . . . / A pinch and a diddle / In the middle of what passes by." That's what it's like for the three central figures in this movie—messy and fun, and without the downer of postcoital guilt. (In the aftermath of sex, what they want most is to start all over again.) Lesley Sharp's Michelle has smeary lips and an insinuating, tarty way with a line, and she sticks out her swishy bottom when she walks; but she doesn't really enjoy sex, so Bob goes after the babysitters (Rita and Sue aren't his first teen conquests). And they're only too eager to dispose of their virginity. Driving them home, he produces a condom and passes it around for their inspection. Sue twists it around her finger, Rita snaps it like a slingshot, and in a matter of seconds (the condom having served as a convenient aphrodisiac) Bob's having it off with Sue on the reclining driver's seat while, in the throes of orgasm, she keeps pumping the horn. Meanwhile Rita, in a foul temper, stands outside the car with her arms folded on her chest; she doesn't disapprove—she's just annoyed that Sue gets to go first. When it's Rita's turn, Sue yells encouragement like a cheerleader while, scrunched into the only remaining area of the back seat, she pulls up her panties.

It's refreshing to watch people who get such a kick out of sex; this movie's lewdness is its trump card. (In one scene, Bob takes the girls to a local club where the band plays a crowd-pleaser called "We're Having a Gangbang," and everyone sings along, joining in a group dance that's like a dirty-minded version of the Bunny Hop.) And if the filmmakers' message is that life in the north of England is so cruddy that only sex can salvage it, it's a far saner view than the one put forth by the fuzzy-left romantics who assembled *Letter to Brezhnev*, which also deals with forms of escape from urban rot. *Rita, Sue* aims low, but it's pretty successful on its level. Dunbar has a fine ear for proletarian speech rhythms, and Clarke sets a slightly hyperbolic style for the performances that he gets everyone in the cast to conform to (except for Willie Ross, who repeats the same impossibly broad drunk routine every time he's on camera).

George Costigan has an up-and-at-'em buoyancy that's pure music hall, and a great lumbered-knave expression when he's horn-swoggled by his own inability to stay faithful to his wife. And Finneran and Holmes are especially sharp as Rita and Sue, the kind of high-schoolers who sneak a smoke on a field trip and get into fist-fights in the schoolyard. Sue is a compulsive loudmouth, but she derives such obvious enjoyment out of invective and backtalk—she takes a big bite out of it, as if it were a juicy apple—that even her teacher seems to be entertained when she cracks wise. (He knows she's no fool: She gets her homework handed in, even though she has to wrestle it back from her brothers, who use it to scribble racing bets on.) Holmes gives a feisty, acting-out performance. In one scene, Bob interrupts P.E. class to score with the girls, and though Rita slips out of class unnoticed, Sue can't make it past the hassling teacher. Returning, disgruntled, to tennis practice, she slams the ball across the court with hilarious sour force, making her poor partner pay for her missed chance at a midday "jump." Rita is dumpier than her pal, but almost as lively in her way—as Finneran plays her, she has a charged slovenliness. In one scene, waiting for Bob and Michelle to come home so they can get their customary evening's-end treat, the girls gorge themselves on napoleons and potato chips and strawberry milk shakes. You can see where all this heavy food goes when you look at them, but it doesn't appear to slow them down.

The script includes a fairly banal exchange between Bob and Michelle when she figures out he's been sleeping around, and a full-scale argument involving all the characters (including Patti Nicholls, who has a terrific battleaxe-in-repose quality as Sue's mother) starts high but fades to a drizzle before the end. And though the filmmakers make good use of the other tenants in Sue's building as a chorus of jeering onlookers in this sequence (family arguments as an irresistible spectator sport), there are about five too many shots of Bob's paunchy neighbor, watering his lawn silently as he gobbles up the scandal next door. (The obvious parallel Clarke is drawing here between the two environments is not a satirical point worth making.)

The picture almost runs out of steam in the last half hour, when Sue hooks up with a Pakistani (Kulvinder Ghir). Their scenes together are well enough written and played, but in the scheme of the movie they feel too much like an extended digression. Fortunately, though the film threatens to slip away from Dunbar and Clarke, they manage to get it back in time for the final fadeout. It would be an exaggeration to call the end a resolution, exactly, but it's very agreeable, and it restores *Rita, Sue*'s randy, pinprick mood. This is a domestic comic strip of a movie: an English *Dagwood Meets Little Annie Fanny.*

August 1987

David Leland's Fictions

• • •

The tough–tender heroines of David Leland's movies may be the most complex female characters on the screen in the late eighties. You don't notice that at first; his elliptical style, with its scabrous bursts of blackout-sketch humor and its sudden glimpses of intensity, contains its own abundance of mysteries to uncover. Besides, since both Simone (Cathy Tyson) in *Mona Lisa* and Christine (Julie Walters) in *Personal Services* are variations on the movies' oldest type, the whore with a heart of gold, you aren't prepared for their depth, their contradictions. It takes a while to make the connections between them, too, because the two pictures have sharply contrasting tones that are largely accountable, one would guess, to the two directors.

Neil Jordan, who directed and co-wrote *Mona Lisa*, has a doomed-romantic, *film noir* sensibility. The movie focuses on George (Bob Hoskins), a decent, unimaginative con. Applying to his old boss (Michael Caine), for whom he took a seven-year prison rap, he lands a job as Simone's driver. Terry Jones, the director of *Personal Services*, is a Monty Python alumnus; his frontal burlesque style boomerangs off Leland's jump-cut narrative, and the result is a kind of knockabout wigginess. The central character is based on the notorious London madam Cynthia Payne, and though *Wish You Were Here*, which Leland directed himself, isn't about a prostitute, Payne supplies the link to *Personal Services*: The teenage protagonist of *Wish You Were Here*, Lynda (Emily Lloyd), is a fictional version of Payne as a girl. Not surprisingly, it's Lynda's burgeoning sexuality that provides the emotional setting for the movie.

Nat King Cole's toasted-velvet rendition of the old standard "Mona Lisa" is the key to the movie of the same name. (You hear his recording over the credits.) The song, which Jay Livingston and Ray Evans wrote for the picture *Captain Carey, U.S.A.*—they took the 1950 Oscar for it—is a silver-plated sham, an irresistible romantic bauble with a cheap heart, but Cole breathes so much feeling into it that you'd swear you were listening to Gershwin or Rodgers and Hart. And finally it doesn't matter that you're not, because Cole transforms it.

Jordan and Leland accomplish the same sleight-of-hand with *their Mona Lisa.* Simone is the elusive heroine to whom the title refers. The movie is structured as a suspense thriller in which George picks his way through the spider webs of the city's underground in search of Cathy (Kate Hardie), a teenage hooker Simone has undertaken to save from the tentacles of a sadistic pimp (Clarke Peters); but it's Simone herself whose mystery is uncovered as the movie winds down. The solution to that mystery is, inevitably, a disappointment: It's in the nature of the kind of story Jordan and Leland set out to tell that the ending be a reduction of characters and relationships. (When you set out to find the single missing piece that will explain a human being, you end up with what Orson Welles, dismissing the ending of *Citizen Kane,* called "primer Freud.")

What's unusual about *Mona Lisa* is how the filmmakers transcend the boundaries of their own character puzzle. This has partly to do with the depths the filmmakers suggest in Simone right from the beginning, and partly to do with the casting of the role. Cathy Tyson is tall and slender, and her elegance is exotic: She has wary, coal-burning eyes, and cocoa skin so smooth it has a tactile appeal to a viewer; above her Nefertiti face she wears her hair like a soft crown. She's so exquisite that she elevates the chintzy pop outfits she sometimes wears, and even (in one scene) the frilly Victorian underwear beneath her trenchcoat. And when she strolls through a department store in sweater and pants, off duty and relaxed, she looks fantastic.

We're first introduced to Simone's harsh, scrapping side, but soon we're exposed to her warmth and her graceful melancholy, all floating in a coffee-and-rum voice that doesn't sound like anyone else's. Her erotic incandescence comes from the tension between her sexual knowingness—her experience—and her ladylike recessiveness. That's her true mystery, the one the movie doesn't set out to solve: We wonder how such an aristocrat got into this profession. (It's no surprise that her services seem in constant demand, or that she gives the impression of queening it over her underworld bosses; she has no pimp, and she conducts herself as if she were working in complete independence.)

Paul Mazursky engages so many emotional tracks at once that you can't analyze exactly which element is having the strongest effect on you: Cleavant Derricks and Robin Williams in *Moscow on the Hudson* (1984). © Columbia Pictures

Employing the precision and clearheadness of a child's observations to debunk a sacred myth: Sebastian Rice-Edwards as Billy and Geraldine Muir as Sue in John Boorman's *Hope and Glory* (1987). © Columbia Pictures

"How could you do those things? How could you do this to us?" Jessica Lange with Armin Mueller-Stahl in Costa-Gavras's *Music Box* (1989), an illustration of how mysterious and unknowable evil can be. © Tri Star Pictures

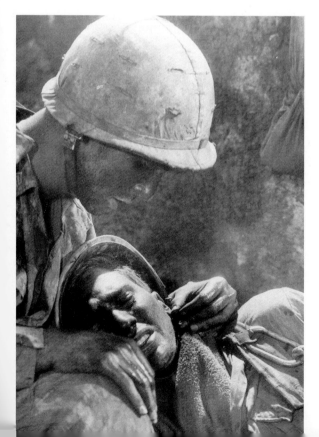

Hamburger Hill (John Irvin, 1987), with Dylan McDermott and Anthony Barrile: some of the images have a ferocious, visionary beauty. © Paramount Pictures

"What would you have done?" Brian DePalma puts us all in Eriksson's boots:
Michael J. Fox as Eriksson and Sean Penn as Meserve in *Casualties of War* (1989).
This scene is one example of the "separation" motif DePalma uses in the movie.
© Columbia Pictures

A World Apart travels from the separate agonies of mother and daughter to a shared agony, offering it up as the only possible salvation. Barbara Hershey and Jodhi May star in Chris Menges's film (1988). © Atlantic Releasing Corporation

Hector Babenco, the director of *Pixote* (1981), refuses to allow us a single untainted moment of beauty: Fernando Ramos da Silva at Marilia Pera's breast. © Unifilm/Embrafilme

The sequence at the heart of Neil Jordan and David Leland's *Mona Lisa* (1986): George (Bob Hoskins) wanders through London's porn shops and strip clubs, and his employer, Mortwell (Michael Caine), is the face he finds behind every filthy door. © Island Pictures

David Leland's *Wish You Were Here* (1987): Lynda (Emily Lloyd) wants so much and expects so little that she's often angry, always hurting. © Atlantic Releasing Corporation

Carmen Maura as Pepa in Pedro Almodovar's *Women on the Verge of a Nervous Breakdown* (1988). Almodovar has a capacity for visualizing metaphors that suggests a trippy, post-surreal Dickens: is there a funnier image than this one for the end of a love affair? © Orion Pictures

Paul Mazursky's *Enemies, A Love Story* (1989) gives a complete picture of what it meant to be a Jew in New York after the war: Anjelica Huston as Tamara and Ron Silver as Herman. © Twentieth Century Fox

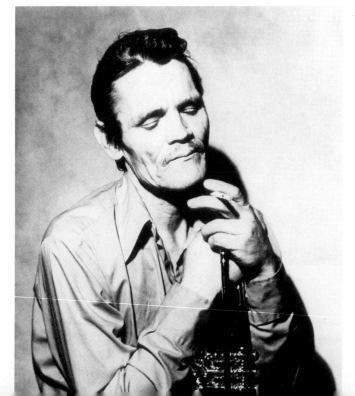

Chet Baker was the most appealing kind of narcissist—the gifted-artist kind, the hurting-bad-boy kind. Bruce Weber's *Let's Get Lost* (1989) explores the appeal of that narcissism. © Zeitgeist Pictures

Michelle Pfeiffer and Jeff Bridges in Steve Kloves's *The Fabulous Baker Boys* (1989): pushing the inside of the conventions of romantic melodrama so they reveal something genuine. © Twentieth Century Fox

Marco Bellochio's *The Eyes, the Mouth* (1983): Lou Castel plays Giovanni, a renegade who became a movie star for a brief period in the sixties. In a suggestive example of self-reflexive moviemaking, Bellochio uses Castel's performance in his own 1966 *Fists in the Pocket* as an example of Giovanni's youthful appeal. © Columbia Pictures

In *Hour of the Star* (1985), the director, Suzana Amaral, and the leading actress, Marcelia Cartaxo, remove all the usual obstacles between the audience and the character so that we have direct access to Macabea's feelings. © Kino International

Like Mick Jagger and Bette Midler, David Byrne in *Stop Making Sense* (Jonathan Demme, 1984) never stops mocking himself; if he did, his fierce physical commitment to every number would be frightening. © Cinecom International Films

Cecilia crosses over into the land of Hollywood movies, and everyone responds to the preposterousness of these new circumstances with typical Woody Allen casualness: *The Purple Rose of Cairo* (1985), with Mia Farrow as Cecilia, and John Wood, Van Johnson, Jeff Daniels, Zoe Caldwell, Milo O'Shea, Edward Herrmann, and Deborah Rush. © Orion Pictures

Akira Kurosawa takes *King Lear* out of the nihilistic world many critics and directors have placed it in: his resetting of the play is profoundly humanistic, though his tone is pessimistic. Peter as Kyoami (the Fool) and Tatsuya Nakadai as Lord Hidetora (Lear) in *Ran* (1985). © Orion Pictures

John Huston's *The Dead* (1987): Donal McCann (as Gabriel Conroy) shows us the fine distinctions among the character's emotions by the degree of warmth in his face, and Anjelica Huston (as Gretta Conroy) effects the kind of physical transformation through acting you associate with only a handful of actresses. © Vestron Pictures

An unfamiliar weight on Tomas's life: Tereza's conviction is something he's never experienced before, and he falls in love with her, becoming a traitor to his own "light" nature. Philip Kaufman's adaptation of Milan Kundera's *The Unbearable Lightness of Being* (1988), with Daniel Day-Lewis and Juliette Binoche, is a series of variations on Kundera's light/heavy theme. © The Saul Zaentz Company

Kyle MacLachlan as Jeffrey and Dennis Hopper as Frank in David Lynch's *Blue Velvet* (1986): images that are startlingly sharp and close, but emotionally have a faraway, half-submerged quality, like something stirred out of childhood memories. © De Laurentiis Entertainment Group

Locating an emotional depth at the core of a screwball comedy: the reunion scene in Jonathan Demme's *Something Wild* (1986) that completes the metamorphosis of Charles Driggs, with Jeff Daniels as Charlie and Melanie Griffith as Lulu/Audrey. © Orion Pictures

Judy Davis's most stunning creation: Lilli in Gillian Armstrong's *High Tide* (1987), who's lived in constant flight, but is too smart and too sensitive to deny the primacy of the instincts that lead her back to the daughter she left behind. © Tri Star Pictures

The best scene in Jonathan Demme's *Swing Shift* (1984), cut from the release print: the walk on the beach, where Kay (Goldie Hawn), her back to the tide, confesses: "Jack, there's another guy."

Perhaps the greatest American film of the eighties: *Shoot the Moon* (1982), written by Bo Goldman and directed by Alan Parker. Diane Keaton's performance as Faith Dunlap has the nonreductive clarity of great acting; she manages to look blurred and jagged at the same time. © MGM Entertainment

Jordan shows us Simone, and everything else in the picture, from George's perspective, and it's his depth of feeling that really carries the movie—he's Jordan's Nat King Cole. At first Bob Hoskins's scenes with Cathy Tyson have a cat-and-dog energy. She thinks he's a stooge, and then when she doles out money and orders him to buy some new clothes and he shows up to work in a flower-print shirt and a tan fake-leather jacket, a gold medallion around his neck, she berates him for having no class. Bob Hoskins is one of the few actors around who can make a scene like this supremely funny without losing our sympathy: He stands in that screamingly loud get-up, puffed up like a peacock, waiting for a compliment, and when she puts him down he sputters and explodes, giving us an indication of his capacity for being hurt. (Early as it is, it's already our second glimpse. When George gets out of stir he shows up at his wife's door, where his teenage daughter doesn't know who he is and her mother, played by Pauline Melville, turns him away in fury, screaming through a big, expressive horse's jaw that he's been away too long.) He throws Simone out of his car for her insults, but then, feeling rotten about his behavior, he doubles back and coaxes her inside, and from then on they're friends. More than friends, in fact—at least from *his* point of view. He quickly grows to adore her, seeing in her cultivated grace and her faraway sadness the mark of a finer sensibility. When she takes him to the rowdy, brightly lit bridge where she once peddled herself to passing drivers, searching for the girl whose fate echoes her own, he joins her cause, becoming her emissary in porno hell.

Jordan and his gifted photographer, Roger Pratt, shoot the scene on the bridge beautifully, lending it the alluring grotesquerie of a *demimonde* carnival. But the sequence at the heart of the movie is the one where George wanders through London's porn shops and strip clubs looking for Cathy and ends up with another girl, May (the lively young actress Sammi Davis), whom the pimp and his associates have fobbed off on him to put him off the scent. Jordan and Leland may have been thinking of Paul Schrader's *Hardcore* here, and certainly they had their minds on Schrader's and Martin Scorsese's *Taxi Driver*—especially in the dialogue between May and George, who tries to pull her out of the swamp of her street life, and in the ending. But the tone isn't primly shocked (*Hardcore*) or primal–seductive (*Taxi Driver*); it's one of sustained horror mingled with pain. Phil Collins sings the plaintive ballad "In Too Deep" on the soundtrack, and as Hoskins's eyes take in one outrage after another, you can see that George never realized it was this bad. Nor did he realize that his employer, Denny Mortwell (Michael Caine), was the face he'd find behind each filthy door.

Bob Hoskins is in every scene of *Mona Lisa*, acting (as usual) with every nerve in his body; he gives a phenomenal performance. Michael Caine, who is in only three or four scenes, does comparable work on a smaller scale. Mortwell is a truly frightening character. At first he seems like just another seedy crook, and you can't put your finger on what it is about him that so unsettles you; then you realize there's no spark of life inside that large frame. As Caine plays him, this porn king is the undead.

Neil Jordan's previous feature, *The Company of Wolves*, was an almost incoherent, baroque mess, but *Mona Lisa* is an amazing piece of direction. It has moments of astonishing deftness, like a startling scene in which the pimp tries to attack George and Simone through the metal grate of an old-fashioned elevator—a tribute, possibly, to *Last Tango in Paris*. It has moments of odd, plucky humor: When George and Mortwell talk for the first time, at one of Mortwell's clubs during daytime hours, a row of chorus girls in rehearsal spin around them as though they'd landed in the middle of a Busby Berkeley number (though the setting is chiefly reminiscent of *The Blue Angel* or the early Helen Morgan talkie *Applause*). And it has moments of sheer magic. I don't know how to explain the emotional effect of the George in Nighttown sequence. Robert Altman has directed scenes this mysteriously affecting, and there's one in an antique shop in Nicolas Roeg's *The Man Who Fell to Earth*, with Louis Armstrong's "Blueberry Hill" playing on an old Victrola—but otherwise they're few and far between.

The filmmakers err, I think, in having Hoskins and Cathy Tyson play their climactic encounter on a Brighton pier with joke sunglasses on. Hoskins is terrific, but the attempt at something extravagantly theatrical in this scene—something *Lady from Shanghai*-ish—diminishes it. Nevertheless, the movie's a wonderful, heady experience, and it's full of character grace notes for George, like his sheepishness around his daughter, played by Zoe Nathenson (her relationship to him neatly parallels May's—and explains it), and his comic rapport with his friend Thomas (Robbie Coltrane, who has a dumbstruck, dropped-jaw delivery in his thick Yorkshire accent that's a show in itself). It's full of warmth, too—George's warmth, Bob Hoskins's warmth. That's the crucial difference. Jordan and Leland started from the same place Alan Rudolph did in *Trouble in Mind*, and other Americans have in various self-conscious melodramas over the past several years: *film noir*. But in *Mona Lisa* all the affectation is on the outside.

It takes a while to get your bearings in *Personal Services*—to get the relationships between characters straight, and to latch onto the combination of Leland's narrative technique and director Terry Jones's style (which is offhand but very bold). Without Neil Jordan's dark-romantic ambiance, which lingers over details, Leland's quick-sketch scenes, containing exposition in snippets, seem abrupt, and at first you don't think you're being told everything you need to know. (But you are: As the movie goes on, you become more and more expert at reading plot information at a glance.)

Julie Walters plays Christine Painter, a waitress who's struggling to put her young, fatherless son through school. She sublets a flat to a greasy, ill-tempered whore who can't seem to make the rent, and when the landlord (Leon Lissek) comes round, a strapped Christine agrees to masturbate him in return for a rent break. Christine, who has never done such a thing before, is both startled and amused at how easy it is to service a man as a business proposition, so when she has a falling out with the hooker in her rooms, she decides without much fuss to take over her clients. Her best friend, Shirley (Shirley Stelfox), is already "on the game," so they go into business together, sharing a maid–receptionist, their pal Dolly (Danny Schiller, who plays the part in drag).

I didn't care for Julie Walters as Michael Caine's working-class student in *Educating Rita*, because she seemed to have worked out every line reading beforehand (on the West End stage, where she'd originated the role). But she's marvelous in *Personal Services*. Christine is brassy and hilariously down-to-earth: She thinks nothing of dashing out of the restaurant where she's employed, to scream for her rent in the street, when she sees her tenant scurrying by, and when she's busted for soliciting, she delights in taunting one young cop because he looks like a virgin, and snickering with Shirley and Dolly about the likely measurements of another one's penis. She has a habit of answering the telephone in a broad upper-crust accent; and, gathering up her father and son for a family wedding, she's got the cheerful, no-nonsense bounce of a WAC. She's as thoroughly, indomitably, and eccentrically English as Margaret Rutherford's Miss Marple, or Joan Greenwood in *Kind Hearts and Coronets*.

But when Christine goes into prostitution, she doesn't know the first thing about it. She advertises that she specializes in "French polishing" because that's what the previous occupant of these rooms did, but she doesn't realize it means fellatio. When her first john shows up—a soft-spoken gentlemen with an invalid wife he hasn't slept with in twenty-three years—she gets so confused that he has to spell out what he wants, and by that time she's addled enough to continue insisting he use a condom. (She calls it a "contraventive.") It's Shirley who eventually shows her the ropes, in a series of wittily costumed brothel bits: Genet's *The Balcony* played for laughs.

This comedy is so consistently rambunctious and ballsy and so expertly played that you can forgive its disjointed passages (which seem much less jarring when you think back on them afterwards— this is a movie that requires rapid, alert responses). You can forgive, too, the scenes that fall flat, like the confrontation in which Christine tells her father about her new vocation; or her hazy summer's-night reverie about a naked man on a balcony. Perhaps these sequences are incongruous in the racy, burlesque context of the movie; perhaps Jones doesn't feel comfortable with the serious tone they call for. But he's breezily at home with the humor—much of which is in fact a variation on the running gag in *Mona Lisa* about creating fictions.

In *Mona Lisa*, George's buddy Thomas adores murder mysteries and shares them with George, so when George starts to drive for Simone, he turns his "adventure" into a mystery for Thomas's amusement. (Thomas refers to it at one point as "the tall, thin, black story," building on George's description of Simone.) The gag becomes serious when we realize that George is actually creating a fiction for himself around Simone; that his feelings for her prevent him from seeing her clearly. (It's the movie's conceit that *we* don't see her clearly, either. The filmmakers shape her story as a thriller, with Cathy as the missing "corpse"—a dope addict, abused by sadistic johns, she's *practically* dead—and a violent climax in the final reel.) At the end of the movie, George employs the device of finishing off the "story" for Thomas, in order to free himself from the feelings that Simone has generated in him. Though there's more to it than this, on one level she's been manipulating him for her own ends, like a whore who controls her clients' fantasies. In *Personal Services* the act of creating fiction has become a splendid joke, a game that Christine's clients engage in gleefully when they enter her rooms to dress up. Julie Walters's permanent expression during these scenes—a combination of shocked primness and genuine amusement—gives them an air of comic detachment that assures us we're in a different world from the haunted, dangerous *noir* streets of *Mona Lisa*.

Stelfox and Schiller are excellent foils for Walters; with the help of a series of bit actors with impeccable timing, they carry off some outrageous scenes. In one, Christine and Shirley entertain a distinguished barrister by playing lesbian schoolgirls. In another, Christine discovers that Dolly is a hermaphrodite. The most colorful supporting performance is given by Alec McCowen as retired RAF Wing Commander Morton, who boasts of the 207 missions he flew during the war, attired for every one of them in bra and panties. He takes such a friendly interest in Christine's venture that he offers to put her and her friends up in a full-scale house in the suburbs, and that's when Christine's deep-seated yearning for domestic stability emerges. The house she establishes acquires its own "family," who gather for sex parties at Christmas. And one day Christine's estranged father comes knocking at the door—not to start another argument with her, as it turns out, but because he wants to get laid. This ruffle on the plot tops it off perfectly. *Personal Services* is the funniest unhinged English comedy since *A Private Function*.

Wish You Were Here is a prequel to *Personal Services* that tells us how Christine's personality was formed. Like *Mona Lisa* it's a movie about the end of innocence. But in tone and look it's as different from each of these earlier pictures as they are from each other. *Wish You Were Here* is a double astonishment: Emily Lloyd's performance as sixteen-year-old Lynda is one of the most remarkable debuts an actress of *any* age can have made in the history of movies, and much the same might be said for David Leland as a director. What this film reveals is a fully rounded writer–director's sensibility: Leland thinks in terms of word *and* image, simultaneously, and, cut loose from collaborators, he turns out to have a style all his own—he's a lyrical impressionist with a taste for vaudevillian kicks. Imagine Shelagh Delaney's script for *A Taste of Honey* with someone like the Louis Malle of *Murmur of the Heart* behind the camera, and you've got *Wish You Were Here*.

Visually, Leland works sparely, isolating objects or returning again and again to certain evocative locations so that they take on an emblematic power. The bike Lynda rides through the narrow, suffocating seaside town she grew up in becomes a quirky symbol of her resilience; a lonely stretch of beach, leading out to a washed-out horizon, begins to represent the context for her rebellion—both the dead-ended existence she sees all around her and the dull pain of her own restless, love-hungry adolescence. The movie's major recurring image is of Lynda with her back to the camera, sitting alone in a room, looking out a window, as if she were trying to find a focus outside herself.

Wish You Were Here is about the search for that focus, and, seen congruently, the four shots depicting her in the same position define both the source and the parameters of the search. *First:* Banished—for swearing—from the parlor by her fidgety, tensely conventional father, Hubert (Geoffrey Hutchings), just back from a wartime navy stint, the child Lynda (Charlotte Ball) sits, in silent tears, until her mother (Susan Skipper) comes in to comfort her. *Second:* Eleven years old, she sits, staring ahead, until her aunt (the marvelous actress Pat Heywood, too long absent from movies) fetches her for her mother's funeral. *Third:* She peers through the window at her father's pal Eric (Tom Bell), who loiters in the alley behind her house, waiting for her to meet him for some quick sex. *Fourth:* Having walked out on her father and presented herself at Eric's flat (undemonstrative, middle-aged, gone to seed, he's nonetheless become her lover), an older Lynda sits on his rumpled bed and weeps for the inadequacy of the affair she's slipped into: Eric's the projectionist at the local moviehouse.

Leland uses these images not only as a way of getting into flashbacks but also as a psychological hinge for his character: Taken together, they sum up both Lynda and the concerns of the movie. And they're poetic, suggestions of Proust and Joyce mottled onto the landscape of this English coming-of-age story. (There are other signs

of a poet at work. The cinema, with its immense cardboard cutout
of Betty Grable, is an emblem of Lynda's romantic, sexy dreams.
At one point she lifts her skirt and kicks out her leg, in tribute to
the pin-up queen. This moviehouse, where several significant scenes
take place, is part of the pop texture of the film, which Leland
punctures with a sad-sack irony—like the cheery postcard title that
refers to the gap Lynda's mother's death has left in her life.)

The movie opens and closes with an aging tap dancer (Trudy
Cavanagh) performing on a stand she's set up on the beach. The
song she plays on her Victrola, a wistful ballad called "I'm Just Lost
in a Dream," recurs several times in the film. As far as we know,
she's dancing for her own pleasure—there are no spectators, and at
the end she packs up and strolls off without complaint. *Wish You
Were Here* is a spirited defense of eccentricity, like *Personal Services*, but with an undercurrent of melancholy. Growing up in the
dim days after World War II, Lynda has a horror of conventional-
ity: She's repulsed by her kid sister, Margaret (Chloe Leland), who
trails around in a Girl Scout uniform, carrying a flag; and she
doesn't want to turn out like her father. She has good reason—he's
emotionally constipated. As Geoffrey Hutchings plays him, he see-
saws when he walks, and he's awkward and helpless with his
daughter, and constantly embarrassed by her. There's a heartbreaking moment during the preparations for her mother's funeral
when, unable to handle her tears, he throws her the same distasteful
look he gave her when she swore in front of company. Hutchings is
a fine actor: We're appalled by Hubert, yet his inability to communicate with his daughter because of his own private constraints
touches us.

So Lynda's rebellion is a survivor's reflex, fueled by the pain
her father's coldness has caused her (especially since her mother's
death). She's like Pookie Adams, the character Liza Minnelli played
in *The Sterile Cuckoo*, but without Pookie's neurotic desperation.
Lynda's a healthy specimen, and though her bad temper can be
exasperating, we mostly delight in her expressions of contempt for
the community that keeps trying to confine her. When she swears,
we sense the life force behind the forbidden words. Clad only in her
nightgown, she does a little improvised dance in the yard behind
her father's house, singing "Up your bum! Up your bum!" over and
over like a nursery rhyme, and mooning a neighbor who stares

down in disapproving amazement. She's thrown out of beauty school for bad comportment, and fired from a bus-company job for entertaining the men by lifting her skirt and showing them her bloomers. Undone by her behavior, her father sends her to a shrink (played by the English poet Heathcote Williams) whose treatment she deftly undercuts. He tries to expose the childishness of her bad language by asking her to list alphabetically all the obscenities she knows; he doesn't understand that, for Lynda, swearing is an expression of freedom. She stymies him by hitting a blank when he asks her for a swear word that begins with "f."

What startles you at first about Emily Lloyd is the sour-ball pungency of her line readings, and how it plays against her soft, fuzzy almost-reticence. She gives Lynda a sexy adolescent bravado that reaches boldly out in front of her lack of experience; behind it she's quizzical, tentative—she can look out at the world with those level, bright eyes, recognize how crazy it is, and say so, but she's not so sure about herself. There's a wonderful scene in which a date (Lee Whitlock) puts his hand on her breast during a movie, and we see her struggle between fear and hopefulness as she tries to decide how she feels about what he's doing. (It's the funniest and most honest depiction of pubescent gropings since Molly Ringwald fell apart at the school dance in *16 Candles*. It also brings to mind the moment in *The More the Merrier* in which Jean Arthur discovers her sexuality while she's making out with Joel McCrea, and it scares the hell out of her.)

As Lloyd plays her, Lynda's sexiness is comically self-conscious; it's her way of kicking at the world and going out after what she thinks she wants. She has romantic longings, but she's too clear-headed not to notice how inadequate the returns are, and her sardonic responses to the constant disappointment are blissfully sane—they keep us in tune with her, and on her side. A bus-company beau (Jesse Birdsall) becomes her first lover. Appearing at her bedside in a pair of flashy pajamas, a cigarette holder stuck fatuously in his maw, he asks her, "D'you fancy me?" and she can't help replying, "Not half as much as you fancy yourself." He's breaking his back to act debonair, while she keeps up a giggling repartee. But when he gets on top of her, her amused ignorance of what she's supposed to do turns inevitably into letdown because he's too concerned with his own sensations to care about hers. "It was nice," she says politely when he's done, "but is it always so quick?"

Her affair with Eric has a fumbling, below-the-stairs cruddiness from the first. He follows her around, spying on her, and when he gets a moment alone with her, he makes a few sniggering comments and molests her. And then he starts hanging around her window at night. Her eventual assent to his advances—she lets him take her in the shed behind the house—is as much out of curiosity as anything else, since the official loss of her virginity hardly qualifies as a sexual experience. "Do you love me?" she asks him as she lies down on the mattress they've thrown hastily onto the floor. Eric, no romantic, answers in the negative. "Bloody hell," she mutters. "Come on."

Lloyd's performance deepens as the movie goes on; Leland has written some superb scenes for her. Leaving her father's house, she shows up in Eric's room, asking him to take her in. Begging him, "Cuddle me," she reveals more vulnerability than she's ever shown him. But she doesn't give him a chance to respond—she insults him, she packs up and departs while he's gone, and when he tracks her down at the high-toned tea room where she's gotten work as a waitress, she treats him shabbily. They fight afterwards, on the beach; that's the first time he hears that she's pregnant.

It's to Leland's credit, and Tom Bell's, that despite our intimacy with Lynda's feelings by this point in the movie, we can still sympathize with Eric, who is trying to reveal his generous side but keeps getting beaten down. Lynda can be merciless—she wants so much and expects so little that she's often angry, always hurting, and she doesn't let other people try to match up to her demands on them. (She walks away too fast.) That's the part of her that's most like those other adolescent sufferers—Pookie, and Holden Caulfield, and Jo in A Taste of Honey. What distinguishes her from them is her irrepressible spirit; and that's what triumphs, finally, in the gutsy, beautifully sustained, satisfying ending.

Wish You Were Here contains some terrific comic bits (one involving a dog and a condom is hilarious) and impressionistic details, like a group dance at a pub in which everyone participates with glum dutifulness. And there are scenes where the writing is so lucid and precise it seems to vibrate: Hubert catching Lynda sneaking back from the shed; a coffee-shop conversation between Lynda and her aunt in which the older woman advises her to have an abortion. As a writer, Leland seems to have inherited both the English spark for farce and the gift for bristling, incisive dialogue of the Angry Young Man playwrights. As a director, he's an anomaly, even among the constantly surprising new crop of British filmmakers. In the first flashback sequence, Lynda and Margaret sit uncomfortably in the parlor, listening to the adults exchange niceties (the occasion is Hubert's return from a stint in the army). Leland shoots the scene from Lynda's point of view: The grown-ups seem larger than life, and twice as foolish—their conversation is full of exaggerated enthusiasms—and Ian Wilson's beautiful photography has a faded, evanescent quality that makes it not quite real, like the episodes we remember from childhood. This sequence is similar to scenes in *The Magnificent Ambersons*, minus the jagged edges of Orson Welles' theatricality: In sensibility it's close to *Ambersons*, but in style and tone it's in another world entirely. *Wish You Were Here* is a breathtakingly accomplished piece of work. It's almost impossible to believe it's Leland's directing debut.

September 1987

Upholding the Law of Desire

• • •

The Spanish director Pedro Almodóvar's movies have more than just the tingle of forbidden fruit; they gorge on it and come up grinning. When you watch the 1986 *Matador* (not released in this country until early in 1988), *Law of Desire* (1987), and *Women on the Verge of a Nervous Breakdown*, which opened the 1988 New York Film Festival, you get the ridiculous feeling that when Franco died, Spain, her corsets loosened, turned magically into the Athens

wood from *A Midsummer Night's Dream*, where previously repressed citizens try out their follies. Almodóvar is the mischievous
Puck who takes a free hand in raveling up the madcap roundelay,
but he doesn't take a mocking, detached tone: He's a sweetly indul-
gent master of the revels who neither judges his guests nor laughs
at the way their lives have been screwed up. Women and men of
disparate inclinations stalk his pictures—heterosexuals and homo-
sexuals, heroin addicts and cocaine freaks, transsexuals and trans-
vestites, serial murderers and rapists, philanderers and pedo-
philes—but so long as they've sworn to uphold the law of desire,
Almodóvar doesn't care *what* vices they've enlisted in. His movies
throb with carmines and hot pinks and oranges, and wear a benevolent smile beneath cheeks flushed with passion.

The earliest of Almodóvr's films to obtain an American release
was *Dark Habits*, from 1983—though it didn't get here until 1988.
It's a comic "study" of the nuns of the Humble Redeemers convent,
a kicky bunch. Sister Manure (Marisa Paredes) sleeps on a bed of
nails and walks on glass, to mortify her flesh; she also drops acid
regularly, inducing religious hallucinations. Sister Damned (Carmen Maura, featured in each of Almodóvar's films from *Dark
Habits* through *Women on the Verge of a Nervous Breakdown*)
keeps a menagerie, serenading her prize beast, a passive tiger, on
the bongo drums. Sister Snake (Lina Canalejas) designs and sells
women's clothes—as shiny as Christmas tree ornaments, they're
prime kitsch—and seeks out the company of the chain-smoking
chaplain (Manuel Zarzo), to whom she declares her love in confessional. (They're a match made in heaven: She shares his passion for
Cecil Beaton.) Sister Rat of the Sewers (Chus Lampreave), under
a pseudonym, writes sensationally popular potboilers based on the
stories of the young women who've spent their time at the convent—whores, murderesses, junkies. They're the specialty of the lesbian Mother Superior (Julieta Serrano), who tries to keep them in
residence by supplying dope for them, and even indulges in it herself.
The movie is outrageous, but you can see Almodóvar hasn't
learned what to do with his wacky ideas. He hasn't yet fused into
a style the naughty-boy Catholicism, the Hollywood camp (the
walls of the Mother Superior's office are papered with pictures of

starlets—Monroe, Bardot, Loren, Raquel Welch—whom she refers
to as "some of the world's greatest sinners"), the sentimental pop
(the ballads of hopeless love that Yolanda, played by Cristina Pascual, performs), and the homoerotic imagery. *Dark Habits* is lively
but a trifle flat; if you've already seen the later Almodóvars, you sit
through it dutifully, knowing he'd get it all together three years
later. The picture does provide a few jolts—frissons of wit, like the
scene where the eternally penitent Sister Manure tries to show up a
fire swallower at a street fair by plunging a skewer through her
cheek, or the moment when Yolanda, newly arrived at the convent,
looks out her window and sees Sister Manure in a clinch with the
tiger. And though the movie's passes at melodrama generally don't
work, the final shot—in which one of the nuns, abandoned by her
lover, weeps inconsolably on another sister's shoulder while the
camera tracks all the way back through the window of the convent
cell—has a sudden operatic grandeur.

The film Almodóvar followed *Dark Habits* with, *What Have
I Done to Deserve This!*, was the first to show up in the U.S. It's a
burlesque, a series of sketches in the Buñuel manner: The wildness
of the material is brought into bizarre relief by the almost banal
straightforwardness of the presentation. (In *Dark Habits* the influence of Buñuel is *too* marked; it's like a tin can tied to the movie's
tail, though at least the can has a jagged edge.) Carmen Maura
plays Gloria, a put-upon housewife with two sons—one a dope
dealer, the other a gay teen who shrugs off his mother's disapproval
of the affairs he keeps having with his friends' fathers ("It's my
body," he tells her). She also has an abusive, insensitive husband she
finally beats to death with an oxbone, and a mother-in-law who
adopts a lizard she names "Dinero" ("Money"). Gloria's neighbors
include a whore named Cristal, who regularly drops by to borrow
props for her S/M encounters or to engage Gloria as a voyeur for
exhibitionistic clients, and a little girl with telekinetic powers. The
child is likely a nod to Brian DePalma, who shares Almodóvar's
comic appreciation of Hitchcock (you can catch allusions to *Rear
Window*, *Vertigo*, and *Marnie* in Almodóvar's films) and his penchant for taking crazy, sexy ideas right to the edge and then over it.

But *What Have I Done*, lively and entertaining as it is, doesn't
add up to much beyond Maura's brashly committed farce style. Its
upbeat ending—abandoned by everyone, Gloria is about to jump

off the balcony of her apartment when the gay son, who's been living with his dentist, returns ("I'm here to stay," he tells her. "This house needs a man")—doesn't take hold any more than the previous scenes did; it's only a blueprint for the more resonant affirmation of *Women on the Verge of a Nervous Breakdown*. But its dizzy, free-for-all style, which combines elements of Buñuel, Godard, Brecht, and the agit-prop theater of the sixties, gives you a buzz, and it's a fitting introduction to a director who sees no reason why he shouldn't shoot the works.

You don't have to get far into *Matador* to see that attitude in operation. The movie opens with a collage of porno-violent images of women—one is drowned and then her wrists are slashed, another is decapitated by a chainsaw, a third is smothered in cellophane, and a fourth hangs from a chandelier. It takes a few moments to grasp that these murders are segments of a video, that the TV playing them is clamped between the feet of the solitary watcher, and that he's masturbating to them; you can hear the sharp intake of breath as the audience realizes what's going on, and then (if you're in the right audience) an eruption of laughter. Almodóvar's being impish here; he knows how Buñuel's unholy mix of clerical and sexual motifs upset the pious, and how the turn-on killings in DePalma's thrillers branded him a pornographer in certain feminist cadres, and he's sending out shock waves ringed with humor in order to send up our capacity for being shocked. He's also making the connection between sex and violence laceratingly clear; it's the link upon which the whole nutsy narrative is built.

The man taking his pleasure in the extravagant deaths of women is Diego (Nacho Martínez), a legendary bullfighter who retired from the ring after an injury that left him with a limp; he now teaches the art of the matador to young men and women, who call him "maestro." When one of his students, Ángel (Antonio Banderas), confides that he's a virgin, Diego advises him, "Chicks are like bulls. You have to hem them in, then it's easy." When Diego wonders aloud if Ángel might be gay, the young man is sufficiently incensed to put Diego's advice into effect upon the maestro's own girl friend, Eva (Eva Cobo), an actress and model who happens to be a neighbor Ángel has spied on from his bedroom window. That night, Ángel shadows Eva, pins her up against a car, draws a penknife on her (he's so unglued he can't get his fingers to behave—the first blade he turns up is a corkscrew), and tries unsuccessfully to rape her. Eva finds his efforts pathetic, but Ángel, the product of a very severe religious upbringing (his mother, played by Julieta Serrano, is a member of Opus Dei, a fanatical right-wing religious group), is so devastated by what he's done that he immediately turns himself in to the cops. When the inspector, Del Valle (Eusebio Poncela), shows him photos of students of Diego's (female) and other youths (male) who have mysteriously disappeared in the last several months, Ángel confesses to their murders, all of which he asserts occurred on the brink of sex.

In fact, Ángel is innocent of these crimes: He's psychic, and his teeming brain is merely the medium onto which other people's homicides are projected. But the sex guilt instilled in him by his mother (who peers at his naked body through the bathroom door and then commands him to stop admiring his own body) has turned him into an all-purpose scapegoat, a martyr for the sins of others. Almodóvar may have been thinking of *Carrie* here, though Berta, the mama–monster, is also a distinctly Spanish creation; she's a cartoon of all the tyrant matriarchs in García Lorca's plays. She's so sure of her son's guilt that when Del Valle confronts her with evidence that seems to the contrary she replies, "The devil's paths are unfathomable—don't forget that." By easy implication, she also stands in for Franco's regime.

To make matters more complicated, the woman lawyer who shows up to defend Ángel, María Cardinal (Assumpta Serna), is the vampirical *femme fatale* of his nightmare visions: It's she who picked up the missing men, targeted them with scarlet-lipstick kisses on their necks, and then plunged in the lethal pin she'd removed from her hair. And it was Diego who offed the young women. When these two serial murderers finally meet, she tells him she's worshiped him since she first saw him in the ring (she was in the crowd when he was gored by the bull, too), that she's seen him in every man she's killed, and that she's tried to mimic his death stroke with each thrust of her hairpin. In a sense, Ángel is their reluctant pander; they link up in his head, and as they dance toward their inevitable *Liebestod*, his overactive mind records every step.

I realize that, in detailing the film in this way, I make it sound much more serious than it is. Certainly there's a pass made at serious themes here—Almodóvar takes on not only the Spanish matriarchal system but also its opposite number, machismo. Diego the limping bullfighter can't become erect without the thrill of the kill; Eva has to play dead before he can enter her. And the scene where Ángel confesses his inexperience has the mood of an unconsummated gay pickup, as does the moment when Del Valle makes eye contact with Ángel at the police station. And when the inspector visits Diego's class and watches the novice matadors in action, we see the spectacle from his point of view, which focuses on the crotches and buttocks of the young men. But Almodóvar stays on the vibrant, frictional surface of these erotic encounters, pretty much as Paul Verhoeven did in *The 4th Man*: What he seems to want is to make sexual fireworks, and to have (and provide) a great time.

Matador is funny almost straight through; the lush, swirling passion colors (Ángel Luis Fernandez, who gave *Dark Habits* its tantalizing, silky texture, photographed; Roman Arango, José Morales and Josep Rosell designed the production) and the whirling camera, eroticizing everything in a brazen stylistic lift from Ophuls and Bertolucci, are both ticklish and heady. (Almodóvar includes an *hommage* to Bertolucci—a sensuous, downswept shot of María descending from Diego's rooms in an old-fashioned grille elevator like the one in *Last Tango in Paris*.) If a movie like *Diva* is in love with the comic possibilities of chic, *Matador* (and indeed both of Almodóvar's subsequent pictures) is closer to the bright, pop-up world of the Jonathan Demme comedies and John Waters's *Hairspray*, even though the way he uses his camera, to create vertiginous effects—like a shot of Assumpta Serna, her head thrown back, enclosed in the yellow folds of her matador-style cape so she looks like an exotic flower in full bloom—may seem more continental. And *Matador* is as insistently, pleasurably superficial as *Diva*. In *Matador*, you get just as excited about Eva Cobo's gold hoop earrings, or the way Serna's lipstick, dropped accidentally into her lap, makes a perfect little blood-red pinpoint on her dress, as you do about the psychosexual complications. And you get the definite sense that that's how Almodóvar wants it.

Almodóvar unwraps the plot (he coauthored the script with Jesus Ferrero) in a deliberately puzzling way; until you've worked out the contact points between the characters, you have no way of knowing how much of what we see is in Ángel's head. It's a tantalizing approach. But there's an unfortunate side effect: Once you've straightened it out, the movie loses some of its kick. And though Assumpta Serna is a luscious icon, like Ava Gardner (whose picture Diego keeps on his desk, next to Eva's), Nacho Martínez is a trifle dull as the bullfighter. But Antonio Banderas brings a goofy desperation to Ángel; he's a little like Danny Kaye or Eddie Bracken in their nerve-shattered juvenile roles, but much softer, more tenderly vulnerable. Almodóvar has supplied this poor dupe, wracked by devils he mistakenly takes for his own, with a guardian angel— the psychiatrist Julia, played by Carmen Maura, who defends the essential goodness in him while everyone else is taking the evil for granted. Ángel, it turns out, faints at the sight of blood (that's Del Valle's tipoff that he's not the killer he swears he is); and Julia, who's fallen in love with him, wakes him with a kiss.

The plot of Pedro Almodóvar's tragicomedy *Law of Desire* is flamboyantly, hilariously melodramatic. Pablo (Eusebio Poncela), a director who specializes in homoerotic movies, is sleeping with a younger man, curly-haired, delicate-featured Juan (Miguel Molina), who swings both ways. When Juan goes on vacation, leaving their relationship in an uncertain phase, Pablo is approached by the son of a government minister, Antonio (Antonio Banderas). Antonio has never had sex with a man, but he was so turned on by Pablo's last movie that he's been shadowing the filmmaker, hoping for a snatch of conversation with him. Pablo finds him attractive and invites him home. Antonio goes—reluctantly at first, then so eagerly he practically drags Pablo by the wrist through the streets of Madrid. By the time Pablo wakes up the next morning, Antonio has moved into the role of possessive lover, jealous of his connection with Juan. Ironically, what sparks his jealousy, a romantic letter from Juan, is a fake; Pablo, ever the *auteur*, has written it himself and sent it to Juan to sign. Pablo plans a trip to visit Juan at the ocean, but Antonio gets there first and throws his rival off a cliff. Later, he tells Pablo he killed Juan "for the two of us," that Juan's death "will unite us forever."

The other major character in the film is Pablo's sister, Tina (Carmen Maura), an actress he is starring in his stage revival of Cocteau's *The Human Voice*. In a previous incarnation Tina was Pablo's brother, whom their father took as a lover; they ran away

together, father and son, and the boy underwent a sex change operation. Eventually her father abandoned Tina, and she swore off
men. Now her latest lesbian lover (Bibi Andersen, a true-life trans-
vestite who has a funny cameo in *Matador* as a palm-reading flower
vendor) has taken off, leaving her daughter Ada (Manuela Velasco)
in Tina's charge. To all intents and purposes Tina has adopted Ada
and made her a part of her own and Pablo's world: A hip little
offspring of the Madrid high life, Ada appears in Pablo's production
of *The Human Voice*, lip-synching a recording of the great, masochistic Jacques Brel ballad "Ne Me Quitte Pas (Don't Leave Me)."

The movie is gloriously entertaining gay camp, steeped in the
tainted pleasures of self-indulgence, but it's not a superficial treat
like *Matador*; there's passion bubbling up under its skin, at first
indistinguishable from the comedy. Almodóvar constantly distances
us from the picture and then, with no warning, brings us closer to
it; the appropriate response from an audience probably would be a
series of double takes. In the opening sequence a teenage boy is led
into a room and instructed, by off-camera male voices, to remove
his clothes and masturbate on the bed, while the voices, like ghostly
lovers, offer him encouragement. In the middle of the scene, Almodóvar pulls back and shows us who's speaking these words of love:
a couple of balding, middle-aged men at a podium, reading from a
script, while a camera crew films the boy's ecstasy. Remarkably,
even after this visual punch line, the scene continues to be a turn-
on; Almodóvar's gliding camera sexes it up. In another erotic sequence the comic distancing device is built right in; the scene plays
as farce while Almodóvar draws us into the love play. When Pablo
takes Antonio to bed for the first time, the younger man is so nervous and uncomfortable that he keeps interrupting the lovemaking
to ask questions ("Do you have any diseases?" "Do you really want
to screw me?")—and when the director, having succeeded in silenc-
ing his lover with a kiss, tries to mount him, the camera registers
Antonio's expression of quizzical discomfort.

In Carmen Maura's scenes, desperation and extreme emotional
risk underlie the wild, drag-show energy. Maura is *Law of Desire*'s
tragicomic emblem. She scurries through her scenes in tight skirts
and high heels (her legs always seem to be racing to catch up with
the rest of her body), but she isn't petite—she's all gyrating hips,
and she's plugged into some invisible power source with an appar-

ently bottomless source of juice. In one scene, Tina and Pablo and Ada promenade through the muggy streets after a performance and pass a man hosing down the sidewalk; the photographer (once again Ángel Luis Fernandez) has given the nighttime street a glistening, wet-canvas look, and when the city worker raises his hose, it forms a rainbow arc. Tina runs her hands down her body (which is encased in a luminous orange suit with a zipper in front that goes all the way down to her crotch) and begs him to turn the hose on her. Maura's delight in sensation has a Marilyn Monroe innocence here, but she doesn't suggest a drag performer imitating a Hollywood sex queen. Tina has assimilated her adopted identity in a way that the transsexual Karen Black played in *Come Back to the 5 & Dime, Jimmy Dean, Jimmy Dean* hadn't; she's plunged into it, and we feel exhilarated as we leap over the gender boundaries with Maura, a woman playing a man converted into a woman. The plunge is the key to Tina: You don't question the authenticity of her maternal role (with Ada), or her gutsy, all-out performance in Pablo's production of *The Human Voice*, in which she takes an ax to the wall of her lonely apartment when her lover tells her goodbye over the phone.

Cocteau's one-act can be nothing more than an elegantly masochistic monodrama; when it's played by a great, intuitive actress (like Anna Magnani in Rossellini's 1948 film version), it reveals itself as a work of operatic breadth. Of course, it's the perfect play-within-a-film for Almodóvar. *Law of Desire* is a movie in which everything that seems a conceit at first—the icons Tina purchases in a sudden burst of religious affirmation, the letter Pablo writes to himself and asks Juan to endorse, *The Human Voice*, "Ne Me Quitte Pas"—resonates. For Almodóvar, desire is a kind of religious devotion, and Pablo commits a sin when he doesn't desire fervently enough—when he stays medium cool, secure behind his typewriter, creating characters who have more passion than he really feels, or penning letters that formalize his emotions and detach him from them. Antonio, like transsexual Tina, makes a supreme commitment to the new role he's taken on. His seriousness first amuses Pablo, then annoys him, frightens him, and finally converts him. (Pablo's final action in the movie is to hurl his typewriter out the window of his apartment, where it bursts spontaneously into flame.) At the end of the picture Antonio sacrifices himself to the law of desire, while Pablo, with ineffable sadness, realizes he's been living outside it all his life.

Women on the Verge of a Nervous Breakdown is *The Human Voice* as it might have been rewritten by the team of Feydeau and John Guare. And it begins where Cocteau leaves off—the moment when the man the heroine is trying so desperately to keep on the line finally rings off. Maura gives a sensational performance as Pepa Marcos, the star of a popular Madrid TV show (she plays the mother of a psychotic killer), whose lover, Iván (Fernando Guillén), has walked out on her. He phones her from the studio both of them work at to ask her to pack his suitcase for a trip and leave it with the superintendent. (This role is played by the gifted comedienne Chus Lampreave, who plays the grandmother in *What Have I Done to Deserve This!* and Eva's trendily groomed stage mother in *Matador*.)

Pepa reaches the phone just as he's finished talking to her answering machine, and by the time she gets through to the front desk at the studio, he's gone. So she rushes off to the studio, where she finds a slip of paper in Iván's writing still on the receptionist's desk; it contains Pepa's phone number and another that, Pepa learns, belongs to his insane ex-wife Lucia (Julieta Serrano), who's never given up on him and assumes he's still attached to Pepa. Meanwhile, she returns home to find, rather than a fresh phone message from Iván, dozens of panic calls from her friend Candela (María Barranco), who's going through her own private crisis. (A guy Candela's slept with a couple of times is part of a group of Shiite terrorists who plan to bomb a plane that evening; she's petrified the cops will arrest her as an accessory.) Furious that Iván hasn't called, Pepa rips out the phone and pitches it through the window. So much for Cocteau.

Women on the Verge is a brilliantly constructed farce; no matter how many crazy subplots Almodóvar tosses into the mix, he figures out a way to criss-cross them so that every new development produces comic echoes on the other narrative planes. (You can practically hear him giggling as he piles the story impossibly higher and higher.) Pepa tracks down Lucia's apartment building and observes her from the street. When she steps into a phone booth beneath Lucia's balcony, she's bombarded by suitcases, and one falls open, dropping a photo of Iván practically into her hands. Iván's son Carlos (the ubiquitous Antonio Banderas, who proves his gentle deftness as a farceur), trying to avoid upsetting his unbalanced mother, is sneaking his belongings out of the apartment to the girl friend he's about to move in with, Marisa (Rossy de Palma, an actress with amazing Cubist features who appeared briefly as a TV interviewer in *Law of Desire*). They're on their way to check out an apartment—Pepa's, which she decided to sublet as soon as she and Iván broke up.

Even the suitcases, the phone booth, and the surprise attack from above turn out to be motifs. When Pepa learns that Iván, hoping to avoid a confrontation with her, has asked the super to enter the apartment and haul down his suitcase, she gets furious and deposits it in a dumpster; at that moment, in a phone booth a few feet away, Iván is leaving her a message (her phone's been repaired in the interim), while his *new* lover (Kiti Manver, from *What Have I Done to Deserve This!*) waits in his car. Once again Pepa reaches her phone only seconds too late to speak to Iván. Enraged, she rips the answering machine out of the socket and sends it crashing through that abused window—right into the side of the phone booth. That's a particularly outré example of Almodóvar's gleeful patchboard plotting, which goes hand-in-hand with the most expert staging and exhilarating timing in any comedy since *Tootsie*.

Farce is the ideal medium for Almodóvar because it implies a world of possibilities. In *Women on the Verge* he sees all sorts of potential paths for the characters, situations, settings, and props he's started out with, and he seems bent on trying them *all* out. The movie is both a Pandora's box and an immense Follow the Dots picture—and more. Almodóvar may count throbbing romantics like Nicholas Ray and King Vidor among his heroes (Pepa and Iván dub scenes from Ray's *Johnny Guitar*; in *Matador*, María and Diego meet in a movie theater where Vidor's hilariously overwrought *Duel in the Sun* is playing), but he has a capacity for visualizing metaphors that suggests a trippy, pop-surreal Dickens. Pepa imagines Iván as a hopeless philanderer, sauntering through the streets, throwing a different (hilarious) pickup line at every woman he passes—each one clad in her national costume. Pepa lights a cigarette as she decides what to pack in Iván's suitcase and tosses the matches onto her bed. When she turns around again the bed is on fire, and she stands before it in her nightshirt, mesmerized, like a mourner before a funeral pyre. Is there a better—or funnier—image for the end of a love affair?

Women on the Verge isn't as profound as *Law of Desire*, but it's far from shallow: The amazing, manic surface conceals a definite undercurrent of sadness and hysteria, just as *Private Lives* or *Design for Living* does—these women really *are* on the verge of nervous breakdowns. (In Lucia's case, the breakdown is happening as we watch.) And once again Carmen Maura is the key to the tragicomedy under the farce. Almodóvar reports that when she plays one of his heroines, Maura gets so deep into the pathos of the role that she can barely keep from weeping; and though what we get on screen is pure comedy—and dispensed with a technique so sharp you can cut film stock on it—it does have that Anna Magnani emotional fullness. (In this movie she's the center of a group of half a dozen superb comediennes, including Chus Lampreave as a Jehovah's Witness who wishes her religion allowed her to tell lies, and Julieta Serrano in hairstyles like headdresses that makes her look like a looped-out Geraldine Page.)

What's so satisfying about Maura's Pepa is that she climbs back down from the verge. Early in the film she mixes some gazpacho in the blender with a prescription load of downers. You assume she intends it for herself, but she puts it in the fridge and goes about her business, as if she'd forgotten she wanted to commit suicide. Later, when Candela tries to throw herself off Pepa's balcony, Pepa lectures her on the value of fighting, suffering, sticking it out. And when, inevitably, the gazpacho reenters the story, Pepa explains to the others that she didn't prepare it for herself, but for Iván—"to teach him a lesson." Pepa's a survivor, and the movie is a paean to survival. It says that you have to fight through to sanity.

In *What Have I Done to Deserve This!* one of Gloria's teenagers asks his grandmother to help him with his literature homework, which is to divide up the romantics and the realists. She gets them mixed up, classifying Goethe and Byron as realists and consigning Ibsen and Balzac to the romantic camp. There's a point to this joke: For Almodóvar, the romantic impulse—the ax taken to the furniture after a lover has left, the telephone or the typewriter hurled through the window, the death by orgasm, the bed set aflame—is the ultimate reality. This filmmaker, who got through the end of the Franco years to make the most deliriously enjoyable movies since Brian DePalma in the seventies, is what Pepa would be like if she were a director. He's off-the-wall passionate, and utterly sane.

December 1988

Hunger

• • •

In Paul Mazursky's magnificent tragicomedy *Enemies, A Love Story*, set among Holocaust survivors in the New York of 1949, Ron Silver plays Herman Broder, married to the Polish domestic Yadwiga (Margaret Sophie Stein), who kept him alive during the war by hiding him in a barn. Now, in their Coney Island apartment, he sits impassive in his bath, reading *The New York Times* while she scrubs him. Hawk-nosed, olive-skinned, he's like some exotic, transplanted monarch; and Yadwiga, who longs to convert to Judaism (she follows the traditions slavishly, like a well-trained servant) and have his child, worships him. She believes him when he tells her he's a book salesman who has to make frequent out-of-town trips—at least, until their Jewish neighbors, who've adopted her, put her wise. Actually, he's a ghost writer for a wealthy rabbi, Lembeck (Alan King), on Central Park West, and his overnights take him to the Bronx, where his mistress, Masha (Lena Olin), lives with her mother (Judith Malina)—both refugees from Auschwitz. Masha, pregnant by Herman, persuades him to marry her, too; by Jewish law, she reminds him, his union with the Gentile Yadwiga isn't valid. But his first marriage, in Poland, is: One day Tamara (Anjelica Huston) shows up on the Lower East Side, years after Herman heard she died—along with their chidren—at the hands of the Nazis. (She managed to escape to Russia.)

Mazursky and Roger L. Simon, who co-wrote the screenplay, lifted the farce structure, and much of the dialogue, intact from Isaac Bashevis Singer's wonderful 1966 novel, which has the aura of a folk fable. The material plays much funnier than it reads, but so does Chekhov; Mazursky hasn't altered Singer's tone. Like Singer, he and Simon use the comedy—the amorous convolutions of Herman's life—to get at the horrifying fact that the Holocaust has left him an emotionally starved man, gorging on all three women, running manically from one to the other because he's incapable of making up his mind. At night he has nightmares about the war, and even in broad daylight his fevered imagination turns strangers on the subway into Nazis. In permanent retreat from them, he tries to hide in these women's beds and in the lies he tells Yadwiga and Masha and Rabbi Lembeck. He carries his enemies around inside him; he doesn't realize he's made the women he loves, and is always running away from, his enemies, too. The back-and-forth movement of the film, its obsessive restlessness, comes right out of Herman's consciousness, just as the seesaw plotting in *Jules and Jim* (which *Enemies* sometimes recalls, especially in the second half) mirrors the neurosis of its Jeanne Moreau heroine.

Mazursky's movie is a phenomenal literary adaptation, like *The Dead* or *The Unbearable Lightness of Being*, and like them it has the cast of one's dreams. I've loved Ron Silver's work before—his too-brief caricatures in *Best Friends* and *Lovesick*, his work on Broadway in *Hurlyburly* and *Speed-the-Plow* and as Jerry Lewis's son in a five-part arc on the second "Wiseguy" season—but he's never had a role that tested his resourcefulness like this one. It's a down-under performance; he's buried so far inside Herman Broder (who is himself an expert at deep submersion) that you wouldn't know there was an actor there at all if it weren't for the amazing choices he keeps making. The script exerts frighteningly strenuous demands on him, and he's up to every one—farce shifts and takes one minute (twice he's caught with one wife by acquaintances who know him to be attached to another), and then, suddenly, a lonely moment of agony: After staunchly refusing to accompany Yadwiga to Yom Kippur service, he weeps over a photograph of his murdered children, *dovening* like an orthodox Jew reciting Kaddish for his dead. (God is one of those issues Herman can't resolve for himself.)

With curly auburn hair, Lena Olin looks fuller, more blooming than she did as Sabina in *The Unbearable Lightness of Being*. No actress in movies is as brilliant at expressing the kind of emotional duality Olin specializes in—her Masha is sensually aggressive yet sexually distanced (in bed with Herman she riddles him endlessly, testing the limits of his love); melancholy and private yet prone to crazy, jealous rages. She can't stop herself from flying off the deep end, but she watches herself in the act. Her sexual relationship with Herman is passionate and intense, but it has a strong combative element: When they make love, they seem to be working something out. Especially Herman—you get the sense that he's fighting something in himself, that his sexual drive comes from the same place as the impulse to knock his head against the pole on the pier in the Catskills when he imagines Nazis are chasing him.

In high black curls, Anjelica Huston brings her peerless irony to the role of Tamara. Her lip trembles with suppressed laughter when Herman, who can conceal nothing from her, admits he married the servant who saved his life. "Couldn't you have found any other way to repay her?" she asks. But her epiphany in bed with him, when she admits she took no lovers in Russia because she couldn't get the image of her lost children out of her head, is equal in intensity and power to her unforgettable monologue in the last scene of *The Dead*. Tamara becomes Herman's adviser, the woman he runs to when he feels he has to escape from Yadwiga and Masha—when life gets too complicated for him—because he feels safe with her. She's the one person he never lies to; she knows him too well. (She's his past; she bore his children.) And besides, in her own words, she's dead.

You can see why Herman is drawn to these women—to their wit, their intelligence, their cosmopolitanism—and why it's Yadwiga he lies to the most. Blonde Margaret Sophie Stein is marvelously funny as the clinging Yadwiga, who scolds him for turning on a lamp on the Sabbath, but instinctively crosses herself when Tamara, who she thought was dead, appears on her doorstep. But she, too, has a fine dramatic scene: When Herman, in a temper, slaps her, she's shocked into reminding him that she kept him alive in

Poland—and Stein shows you Yadwiga's surprise at her own temerity in saying it.

There isn't a performance in *Enemies* that doesn't seem perfect, including Alan King's (he plays Rabbi Lembeck as a gregarious sport with a heart of gold), Judith Malina's (her all-out comic hysteria—big emotions stream indecorously out of her—falls away to reveal her heartbreak when she tells Herman she wants a grandchild "to name for the murdered Jews"), and those of Rita Karin and Phil Leeds and Mazursky himself in smaller roles. Silver and Huston are American, Olin is Swedish, and Stein is Polish, but in this movie they seem effortlessly bound, as if they'd lived together for years in these period settings (which were meticulously designed by Pato Guzman and warmly photographed by Fred Murphy, who also shot *The Dead*). Mazursky's an astonishing filmmaker. What he's always been able to do for hip American subcultures (in movies like *Bob and Carol and Ted and Alice*, *Blume in Love*, *Next Stop, Greenwich Village* and *Down and Out in Beverly Hills*) he's learned to do for immigrant subcultures, too. Up to now, my favorite of his movies was *Moscow on the Hudson*, in which he captured the bittersweet flavor of Russian émigrés searching for community in Manhattan. *Enemies* extends his triumph in that earlier picture—it has an even richer texture.

Mazursky gives you a complete picture of what it meant to be a Jew in New York after the war; he uses the differences in the neighborhoods Herman hangs out in to delineate economic and social distinctions. Rabbi Lembeck's expansive apartment on Central Park West, in mid-renovation when we first see it, isn't in the same world as the flat Tamara shares with her uncle and aunt on the Lower East Side, where Herman has to peer past the Hebrew printing on the poster boards and through the close, intimate crowds to read the street numbers. Coney Island, where Herman lives with Yadwiga, is lower-middle-class, and though the neighborhood is largely Jewish, Yadwiga is accepted here. The Bronx, where Masha lives with her mother, is on a higher financial scale than Coney Island, but both these places have a Jewish–Europeaan flavor. There are scenes in beachfront cafeterias, where customers drink tea in glasses and choose between the cheesecake and the fruit compote; and in Catskills resorts, where the P.A. recruits players for afternoon canasta games, and women exchange opinions on which Hollywood leading men are Jewish.

Mazursky's so confidently immersed in this time and this place that he can use editing and soundtrack to make jokes. At the end of their first reunion, Tamara kisses Herman on the mouth and sends him home to have Sabbath with his Polish peasant; Mazursky cuts to blonde, blue-eyed Yadwiga, a veil over her head, solemnly reciting the blessing over the Friday-night candles. Herman hesitates in front of subway signs for Manhattan, Brooklyn and the Bronx, while we hear the Andrews Sisters singing "Joseph, Joseph, Make Your Mind Up." *Enemies* is a marvel—a study of transplanted intellectuals, skeptics who can't *not* believe in a God they feel has dealt them out some incomprehensible punishment. ("There is no God," Herman yells at Yadwiga, "and if there were, I would defy him." A couple of scenes later, he reads aloud to her from the Torah—but he won't go to synagogue with her on the high holidays, refusing to mingle with assimilated Jews who only pray once a year.) These are people whose years of deprivation have left them ferociously hungry for life. And Mazursky's group portrait is a banquet for movie lovers.

January 1990

GLORIOUS COMPROMISE

• • •

In the counterculture classics of the late sixties and early seventies, like *The Graduate*, *Easy Rider*, and *Five Easy Pieces*, compromise was a dirty word, associated with the middle-class standards you were supposed to be getting away from. Compromise meant getting into plastics, joining the straight world, being a concert pianist—or even, for Jack Nicholson's Bobby Duprea, ordering what was on the menu of a hash joint when it wasn't what you felt like eating. Young audiences admired the heroes of these movies for resisting the pull of the bourgeois world; at the end of the picture, when it turned out that there was no escape from the moral and spiritual ugliness of that world (or of America, generally), the hero's recognition of his own defeat—Captain America's "We blew it" before his highway death in *Easy Rider*, Benjamin Braddock's fallen face on that bus with Katharine Ross at the conclusion of *The Graduate*—was the Vietnam era's version of romanticism, just as surely as Bogart's joining the Resistance at the end of *Casablanca* had been for World War II audiences.

Those sixties movies sentimentalized defeat, and by the mid-seventies we'd all grown weary of the easy cynicism of American pictures especially, which assumed that the system was corrupt from the top down and no one was free of its taint. (Perhaps the last popular vestige of this way of thinking was *The China Syndrome*, which came out in 1979.) Still, there was something refreshing about the way they leveled with you, assuming you were canny enough not to buy the official line, assuming you lived in the real world and understood something about the way it worked.

In the eighties, that kind of honesty was rare in movies. And when it came, often it was in films where the ability to compromise could be as heroic as the inability to compromise used to be. Movies like Ron Shelton's raucous baseball comedy *Bull Durham* (like Shelton's script for *The Best of Times*, which Roger Spottiswoode directed) and Steve Kloves's sexy romantic drama *The Fabulous Baker Boys* (which ought to have been a *Casablanca* for the eighties) recognize that we live in a messy, complicated world where adults with brains and sensibility and experience learn to accept less than they dreamed of when they were younger—not in defeat, but in gratitude for what there is of beauty and grace in the life they've agreed to settle for.

The films covered in this section illustrate and offer different varieties of compromise. It's the strength of Gus Van Sant's *Drugstore Cowboy* that it refuses to supply a happy ending for its addict protagonist, played by Matt Dillon, the way *Clean and Sober* does; Dillon's Bob turns back to the straight world in the middle of the movie, but he never embraces it. (Admirable in many ways, chiefly in its acting, *Clean and Sober* gives off the clinical smell of therapeutic virtuousness; it might have been commissioned by a drug-awareness group.) Bruce Weber's one-of-a-kind documentary *Let's Get Lost*, which has indirect links to *Drugstore Cowboy*, focuses on the jazz trumpeter Chet Baker in his final months, when a lifetime of drug abuse has all but wrecked his singing voice, ravaged his face, and worn down most of the people who ever loved him. Weber's portrait of Baker is loving and searing, revering and exposing him by turns; it tells us that we can never resolve our feelings about the people we love, whether intimately or from a worshipful distance. Nor are there absolutes in Robert Towne's *Personal Best*, set among pentathletes working toward the benighted 1980 Olympics.

The heroine, Chris Cahill (Mariel Hemingway), comes of age when she forges an idiosyncratic standard out of what she's learned from the two athletes she's loved, a woman and a man (no absolutes here, either). In her coach's eyes, that's a stupid compromise—because it softens her competitive ruthlessness. But it allows her a personal triumph.

My Left Foot, written and directed by Jim Sheridan, and *Driving Miss Daisy*, Bruce Beresford's adaptation of the Alfred Uhry play, both released (like *Baker Boys* and *Drugstore Cowboy*) in the final months of the decade, feature characters dealing with severe handicaps—physical in the case of Daniel Day-Lewis's Christy Brown, moral (an inherited series of prejudices) in the case of Jessica Tandy's Daisy Worthan. These movies could be said to be about winning out over adversity, and I imagine it's that side of them that earned them popular and critical acclaim and various Academy Awards. I wouldn't argue with that assessment (and I'm grateful for their success), but I'd modify it: What makes them unusual and memorable (and, in the case of *My Left Foot*, truly great) is their acknowledgment of the depths of loneliness and despair in their protagonists' situations—Christy's cerebral palsy, Miss Daisy's obstinate aristocratic widowhood—and the limitations of these characters, who can grow but only so far.

Christy's relationship with his unyielding, undemonstrative father darkens his domestic life, and his sexual frustration brings out a bullying, masochistic side that is no less horrible for being poetic and pitiful. A friend told me that *Driving Miss Daisy* made him furious because at the end Daisy still clung to bad old habits; her treatment of the chauffeur, Hoke (Morgan Freeman), who'd become her closest companion, still tended toward the patronizing and the insensitive. That's what I *loved* about the movie: It doesn't pretend that human beings effect miraculous transformations (especially at Daisy's age). Daisy compromises her archaic standards; she doesn't throw them away—and the compromise is a kind of miracle in itself, a *realistic* miracle.

In an era when moviemakers are so often torn apart by two absolutes, Hollywood conservatism and political correctness, compromise can be a sweet surprise. The people who put together these movies didn't make *artistic* compromises: In fact, of the seven pictures highlighted here, six were the work of writer–directors who brought visions to the screen that were entirely their own.

The Unembarrassed Camera

• • •

Personal Best, a film about the coming-of-age of a rising pentathlete, Chris Cahill (Mariel Hemingway), is daringly unconventional, and yet the approach Robert Towne (who wrote, directed, and produced it) has taken to the material is so logical that when I'd left the theater I couldn't imagine any other way he could have achieved his results. Towne's dialogue captures the rhythm and mood of his characters perfectly. It's spare and precise, so naturalistic and so efficient that you don't notice at first how good it is. But it's written to be filled in with the athletes' main way of expressing themselves—through body language. What the characters say to each other is less revealing than what their legs and torsos and shoulders say; we're continually astonished at how eloquent their bodies are.

Moments before Tory Skinner (Patrice Donnelly), the older and more experienced Olympic candidate who befriends Chris at the Hayward Field tryouts in Eugene, Oregon, on the day Chris blows her chances for the 1976 Olympic team, actually makes a pass at her, the balance of tension and relaxation in their juxtaposed forms tells us a sexual relationship between these two young women is imminent. Tory is very perceptive about Chris. She knows the younger woman choked on the field, anticipating a tough time with a highly skilled rival; she knows Chris's father gets on her ass for not being an aggressive enough competitor. Tory's honesty disarms Chris, and then it makes her angry. Their lovemaking actually begins as competition—an arm-wrestling match that becomes very intense because there's so much going on, emotionally. We can read Chris's determination to show she's not a wimp, Tory's amazement at Chris's inner and outer strength and control, Tory's own competitive instincts, her understanding that they could be a match, and the sexual feelings she's beginning to have for Chris.

Towne and the actresses use the physical contact between the two women to convey all of these emotions. And, since part of an athlete's training is learning how to read other athletes' bodies, they're the best interpreters of each other's body language. We see by the way Tory lifts Terry Tingloff, her coach (Scott Glenn), up off the ground, playfully, after she does well at the field trials, that they're close, and we see Chris watching them wrestle together—a clue to us, and to her, that they used to be lovers. The way Chris and a male athlete at a party edge subtly toward each other infuriates Tory: They're flirting with each other. Later, the way Tingloff massages Chris's leg tells us he's attracted to her, and when Tory sees her leaning easily against him, she clearly reads the potential for a sexual relationship *there*. It turns out that Denny Stites (Kenny Moore), a former Olympic star Chris grows to love, has known about her relationship with Tory long before she's agreed to reveal it to him. "It wasn't a secret," he says—and we realize that *of course* other athletes would figure out who's sleeping with whom faster than anyone else could.

The physical details delineate the differences between the women. Donnelly's taut Indian face is in striking contrast to Hemingway's wider, freer one, and when they arm-wrestle we see two kinds of concentration. The closeness of the athletes is emphasized in the way they horse around together; these are people who express themselves more easily through their bodies than they do verbally. So Towne shows us a football game among the women (to the distinctly Southern California sound of the Doobie Brothers' "What a Fool Believes"), a trick that a big, bearded guy at a party does with his belly, the women lounging in a steam bath, perfectly comfortable with each other's nakedness. (The relationships he shows us among them—both those that exist during the course of the movie, and the ones he hints at that existed before the beginning of his story—are an extension of that intimacy and comfort.) Sometimes these physical details provide fresh, surprising comic moments. Towne trains the camera on the struggle of the two women to jog up a sand dune, and then he cuts to Tingloff, lying on top of the dune, relaxing in the sun with a cooler and a radio, silently commanding them to repeat the exercise. After the fierce strain of those legs in friction with the sand, Tingloff's position—his legs are bent and the arm that motions them to start over hangs loose—makes you laugh.

With almost no dialogue that you remember afterwards (because it refuses to call attention to itself), *Personal Best* says a lot more about athletes and sport than the endlessly chattering *Chariots of Fire. Chariots of Fire* pretended to be about something higher and deeper than merely winning (something I don't think I got—I came out of the movie with the idea that if you believe in God, you can be a great runner), which was presumably why the director, Hugh Hudson, didn't bother placing the camera where we could see who was ahead in the climactic race. *Personal Best* isn't a conventional sports movie, either; it's about the expenditure of physical and emotional energy, and about the search for a balance between friendship and the drive to win. And yet Towne, who thinks like a filmmaker, not a Sunday-school teacher, doesn't sacrifice the excitement of the greatly satisfying final race. In motion (and there are exquisite montages of hurdling and high-jumping and shot-putting that take you right back to Leni Riefenstahl's *Olympiad* and then build on it), the bodies are extraordinarily beautiful; Hemingway and Donnelly look so great when they run together that their physical relationship seems like the most natural thing in the world. The photographer, Michael Chapman, uses a pallette reminiscent of the painter David Hockney's—a sensuous array of pastels, in harmony with the SoCal soundtrack—and the clarity of the bodies against what is sometimes a hazy, dream-like background is overpowering, as in hyperrealist art.

All the physical connections in *Personal Best*, including the sexual ones, are gloriously free of self-consciousness; no one in the theater giggles when Chris and Tory lie in bed together (the way an entire audience did the night I saw *Making Love*, during that painful first kiss between Michael Ontkean and Harry Hamlin). Later, when we see Chris in bed with Denny, we can enjoy the sweetness and good humor of their intimacy in a way usually denied us in love scenes in the movies, because Towne doesn't try to use this encounter to score points for or against any of the characters. We're not meant to make a judgment about whether Chris "ought" to live with a man or a woman; that's not the point of her moving from Tory to Denny. It's just a step in her growing up.

The movie is framed by two sequences at the Hayward Field trials, one in 1976 (where Chris does badly) and one in 1980 (where she makes the Olympic team). In between, she becomes an adult. At the beginning, the major force in her life is her father, who bullies her and to whom she feels the need to apologize for her disappointing performance at Hayward Field; whining and weeping, she's a little girl, and he's tough on her. Once she starts to work out with the team (Tory persuades Tingloff to let her), Terry takes Chris's father's place. He's a strange sort of father figure, but he's tough on her, too (though his style is different), ragging on her for her lack of "killer instinct." We know she's still a child when Terry lets her run and she's so flustered that she trips, and then she's so embarrassed at tripping that she doesn't even realize how well she's done. (This is also a function of her modesty—one of the qualities we like best in her.) We know it when she doesn't get a masturbation joke another woman makes in the steam bath; when, ignoring the administrators' warnings, she stupidly eats fruit in Colombia, where the women are competing, and gets Montezuma's revenge; when she begs Tory to stay up with her that night and hold her, which results in Tory's exhaustion and poor performance on the field the next day. We know it when, after sustaining an injury at the high jump, she can't stop crying in the hospital—not out of pain, but because she's afraid Terry's angry at her.

Tory first steps into Chris's life when Chris is sick after the Eugene field trials and almost passes out. She plays mentor, adviser, older sister, even mother to Chris, and after they become lovers, she doesn't relinquish these other roles. That's the main problem between them; their break-up is inevitable, because Chris moves past her need for a maternal girl friend. More significantly, though, she moves past Terry Tingloff's competitive vision. Terry's a great coach, but he's often wrong—his saving grace is how often he's willing to admit it. (When Tory gives him hell for behaving badly toward Chris during workouts, treating her like a flunkey, he pulls back and gives her a chance to run. That's when he sees for the first time that Tory's right about Chris's abilities: "I misjudged it all," he confesses.) Yet Tingloff's still sure that the only way to win is to kill your competition; he's suspicious of Tory's motives when she counsels Chris in workouts, and he succeeds in poisoning their relationship when Chris is hurt in the high jump and he suggests that Tory is responsible.

It isn't until after Chris has struggled to recover from her injury, and begun to see Denny, that she really starts to mature. She learns from Denny, who's more bemused than dazzled at winning his gold medals, that athletics is about "whipping your own ass," not someone else's. Towne puts the phrase "personal best" in the mouths of the sportscasters in the final sequence, back at Hayward Field. It's the first time we've heard it, but it sounds like a summation of what we've discovered ourselves in the course of the movie. At the end, it's Chris who bucks Tory up, encourages her to race after an injury "because that's what you are," and proves Terry wrong by performing at her own personal best while making a place for her friendship with Tory.

Towne could have set the movie earlier in the seventies, but he elects to show these athletes training for the boycotted Moscow Olympics. Even before the sportscasters make it clear at the end that the athletes won't be going to Moscow (one says they're "all dressed up with no place to go"), every time we hear the slogan "Moscow in '80" we register that it isn't going to happen. This irony underscores the movie's point about "personal best" by finally removing any and all outside competition. That's not the reason these women train so hard; the lack of an Olympics doesn't undercut the value of what they've accomplished.

This is Towne's directorial debut, after nearly a decade of being Hollywood's premier screenwriter. (He's the author of *The Last Detail*, *Chinatown* and *Shampoo*.) The writing is as sharp as ever here, but all through *Personal Best* he wears a brand-new suit—and one that doesn't resemble at all what anybody else is wearing. After seeing the picture, I couldn't decide whether I was more impressed by the visual conception and working-out of the film or by the way he uses his cast. Mariel Hemingway and Scott Glenn are the only professional actors in the movie; Patrice Donnelly, Kenny Moore, Jodi Anderson (who plays the other major Olympic candidate, Pooch), and the others all are athletes who have never appeared in a movie before. Obviously Towne has to be credited with the absolutely consistent, naturalistic performances of the nonactors, but since Hemingway and Glenn also give unaffected, nonactorish performances, you can see he's done as much work toning down the pros as he has toning up the amateurs. It helps that he cast the roles of Chris and Tingloff brilliantly: Hemingway and Glenn are two of the most believable and unflamboyant featured players to surface in the late seventies and early eighties. No one in *Personal Best* has a false moment that I could spot, and Donnelly, like Hemingway and Glenn, is really superb. Deep-dyed authenticity is integral to what Towne wants to bring off here: Watching *Personal Best* is like being invited to observe the most private moments of a young woman's rite of passage—and then discovering that you don't have to feel embarrassed at being there. Towne may have invented a new kind of elation for an audience.

March 1982

Hail Compromise!

• • •

Ron Shelton is one of the few American screenwriters of recent years with a distinctive comic voice. He's both a realist and a cockeyed romantic—maybe the best combination for making comedies in the post–myth-deconstructing, post–renegade Hollywood of the eighties. His movies about Americans approaching middle age and learning how to get the best out of the compromises they've been forced to make in their lives (*The Best of Times*, which he wrote for Roger Spottiswoode, and *Bull Durham*, which he wrote and directed) are tremendously satisfying emotionally: They have a canny, worldly buzz, so their upbeat tone doesn't make you feel cheap or used. And their knowingness isn't smirking. Shelton's heroes embrace their lives with a whole heart.

In the wonderful 1985 comedy *The Best of Times*, Spottiswoode generously mutes his own finesse to underscore the whirling idiosyncrasies of Shelton's script. And it's quite a script. Shelton is in the Preston Sturges line—the picture is reminiscent of Sturges's knockabout, Rube Goldberg–contraption farces about small-town American life, *Hail the Conquering Hero* and *The Miracle of Morgan's Creek*, with their casts of eccentrics, their rapid-fire talk (like Sinclair Lewis, but with a dry spin on the lines), and their all-American obsessions. But it has a warm heart—a touch of Jonathan

Demme. Shelton's hero, Jack Dundee (Robin Williams), a banker in a gone-to-seed SoCal town, hatches a loony scheme to replay, close to twenty years later, the football game he lost for his high-school team when he fumbled a pass from his best friend, Reno Hightower (Kurt Russell), the star player (who now is an easygoing auto mechanic who paints copies of Van Gogh and Michelangelo on vans as a sideline). Shelton's focus is Jack's dream of returning to the past to do something right that he screwed up years ago. It's a movie for adults, because that's a dream only adults could understand; Jack's blasé, punked-out teenage daughter thinks he's crazy. (If the movie has failed to capture the audience it deserves on video, where good, badly promoted movies sometimes do, it's because Embassy packaged it to look like a farce for teens—the worst possible market for this particular film.)

Shelton uses the rematch as a metaphor for all the ways in which the characters put a new bloom on their lives: The town gets dressed up for the ceremonies and shows a new eagerness and sense of purpose, and Jack and Reno reexamine their marriages, which have grown worn, and find new romance in them (and a new commitment). The game works a kind of magic, all right, but it's magic we can all believe in: fresh perspective, an acceptance of who we are. Holding out a sweet balance of dreams and compromise as the hope of Americans sailing into middle age, *The Best of Times* is the best antidote for yuppie *angst* ("thirtysomething"'s specialty).

Bull Durham shares that theme and that vision. It's set in Durham, North Carolina, home of the minor-league baseball team, the Durham Bulls. (Bull Durham is a famous brand of chewing tobacco—an item as solidly and peculiarly American as baseball.) The Bulls' manager, Skip (Trey Wilson), has just acquired a new pitcher, Ebby Calvin LaLoosh (Tim Robbins), who has talent but no skill; his mighty, strong-arm pitches go wild half the time. Twelve-year veteran Crash Davis (Kevin Costner) is brought in, ostensibly as catcher but really to "mature" LaLoosh. Crash is close to beating the minor-league record for hits, but he doesn't publicize it; he's never gotten over his disappointment at not making the majors—"the show," as the players call it, speaking the phrase with a mixture of envy, awe, deprecating humor, and griping disdain. (Crash was picked up by a major-league team once, but he lasted only twenty-one days.)

The other character who takes a hand at seasoning LaLoosh is Annie Savoy (Susan Sarandon), the movie's on-again, off-again voice-over narrator. Annie tells us she worships at "the Church of Baseball" (she's rejected all the other religions she's tried) because she finds it guilt-free and never boring—just like sex, which she also loves. These two preoccupations overlap: Every year Annie adopts a player she thinks is promising, takes a close interest in his game, sleeps with him, and remains faithful to him for the season. (It's her own slightly skewed form of serial monogamy.) This season, Annie feels forced to choose between Ebby and Crash. When Crash, obviously interested in her but insulted by the competition, withdraws, she takes up with LaLoosh. She gives him the nickname "Nuke" and gets to work refining his lovemaking—which, as the Bulls' steadiest groupie, Millie (Jenny Robertson, in a funny, clear-eyed performance), observes, is as wild as his pitching.

Nuke LaLoosh, whose gifts outweigh his intelligence by about twenty to one, is a wonderful comic creation, and Tim Robbins is splendid in the role. He's a little like Michael Keaton without nerves. Nuke ambles through life drunk on his own sexual and athletic energies, his own supercharged young maleness. And he gets hilariously confused whenever someone challenges him—when Crash outtalks him or makes him look bad (every time Nuke ignores one of Crash's signals, Crash trips him up by informing the player at bat what Nuke's planning to send across home plate), or when Annie frustrates his expectations by tying him up in bed and then reading Walt Whitman aloud to him all night. Robbins can do great things with his eyes (like peeling them so they look like marbles), and he's physically equipped for comedy right down to the rolls of baby fat under his cheekbones. When Nuke concentrates, he pulls a long face and all that flesh stretches out like plasticene to give him a double chin, so he looks like an irate rooster.

But the movie isn't about LaLoosh; uproarious as he is, his role is to be the catalyst for the relationship between Crash and Annie. World-weary but vital, in love with the game but exhausted by the dead-end gyrations his second-rate pro-ball career keeps twisting him into ("Fuck this fucking game" are his first words about baseball, and that's about as charitable as he gets on the subject), Crash is a grizzled life force. He's kept himself alive by developing a highly idiosyncratic approach to ball: He plays it for his own amusement

and for the enjoyment of his teammates. (There's a wonderful moment when he hits a homer and, running the bases, dances sideways
for the benefit of the other guys on the team, throwing his hands
up to his face in an expression of mock amazement at his own prow-
ess. Their response is equally deadpan: They do a dugout version of
a stadium wave.) Instructing Nuke on pitching tactics, he explains
that strike-outs are fascist and ground balls are democratic. Later,
as the kid begins to shape up and acquire a following, Crash teaches
him a list of clichés for quick access during interviews. When Annie,
ticked off because he won't fight for her, asks him what he believes
in, he retorts with a series of abstractions that's as sexy and romantic
as it is funny. And that's the point at which Annie, like the audience, falls in love with him.

Kevin Costner had a standout freshness in Lawrence Kasdan's
stone-dead western *Silverado*, but he gave thin, lame performances
in *No Way Out* and *The Untouchables*—so the work he does in *Bull
Durham* comes as a lovely surprise. His voice has a craggy-smooth
underlayer that gives off heat when he speaks, and his pace is
slightly slower than you expect and fuzzy around the edges, as if he
were a little high. He hits a weird note that's somewhere between
laid-back and revved-up; the wilder his scenes get, the more fun it
is to watch the relaxed part of Crash lock in with the part of him
that likes to bounce off walls. (The best example is a yelling match
with an umpire—probably his most sheerly pleasurable scene.) This
is a star turn, and more than that, it's the kind of turn an actor
usually pulls off only after he's been a star for ten years or so. It's
like a veteran performance from Paul Newman.

Annie is as distinctive a personality as Crash, and—thanks to
Shelton's dialogue—she's as snappy and inventive a talker as he is.
(In this movie, an offbeat articulateness is evidence of strength of
character, as witty talk always is in the romantic comedies of the
thirties Shelton is spinning off from. Nuke talks too dumb to be the
central character.) Annie's conversation is a high-voltage mix of
Zen, baseball jargon, pop psychology, quantum physics, and innu-
endo. That's how she advises Nuke on his pitching, and that's how
she tutors both men in her own approach to the world. Annie bears
a family resemblance to Darla, the hooker–therapist in *The Best of
Times* (played by Margaret Whitton), but Shelton's developed her
more, made her upfront seductiveness and kooky warmth the center

of the picture. I've loved watching Susan Sarandon for years—those huge doe eyes, ringing changes like a slot machine, are enough reason to see her in even a crummy picture like *Tempest*—but this is the role she's been waiting for; it gives her a shape to pour her zingy, playful comic talents into. (Before it, the closest she came to finding a part to bring her out was as the journalist who turns detective in *Compromising Positions*.)

What gets these two interested in each other is sex; each can tell at a glance the other is terrific at it. But it takes the movie a long, long time to get them in bed together, because on the way they discover they have potential for a deeper bond, and at first that terrifies Crash. My favorite scene is the one in which Annie marches into Crash's apartment after Nuke has stopped sleeping with her, to demand an explanation. (The Bulls are on a losing streak, and Nuke, on Crash's advice, has decided to redirect his sexual energy into his game.) To her own surprise—and breaking her own rules—she ends up propositioning Crash, who responds with a triple-take stutter and tries to throw her out. (No doubt he's as amazed as she is; it's hard to believe this man has ever turned down an offer from a woman as beautiful and sexy as Annie.) She challenges him, accusing him of being scared of her, and his reply— "Maybe I am, but I still think you should leave"—catches her off guard. (This is Costner's best line reading in the whole film.) What he's scared of is emotional, not sexual, and on one level the picture is about how he conquers that fear and comes back to her—how they both learn to know themselves well enough to accept that they're not going to find other partners they like half as well. For Crash, that also means accepting his life in minor-league baseball, away from "the show."

In the last twenty minutes of the movie Shelton slows the motor down, and on a purely visceral level it's a disappointment: You want more of the fun you've had for the first hour and a half, and Crash's return to Annie seems so inevitable that you're not sure why Shelton lavishes so much screen time on it. Then you realize how much it takes for him—and her—to bring themselves to a full stop and allow that coming together. The movie's earned the right to a long, slow dance at the end.

August 1988

Chet's Blues

• • •

Chet Baker's trumpet playing has a languid mournfulness that stops somehow short of being precious, and when he sings—with the amazing, offhand purity of his early recordings (in the fifties) or the wrecked blurriness of his middle age—you can't work out how he sustained the mood of romantic masochism with so little apparent effort. (His life ended abruptly in 1988 at age fifty-eight, when he allegedly fell from an Amsterdam hotel window.) This is music to wallow in, like the great jags of Billie Holiday, whose exquisite cornet voice was scraped down, like Baker's, to a shockingly effective wavering husk by years of heroin abuse. Baker holds onto his sadness with cockeyed pride; he presents it as self-definition. He's the most appealing kind of narcissist—the gifted-artist kind, the hurting-bad-boy kind. And in the fifties, when he was devastatingly handsome, driving fast cars, experimenting with dope, and posing for record covers with a variety of gorgeous women, hipsters and alienated teens adopted him just as they did James Dean (whom he resembled somewhat).

In the documentary *Let's Get Lost*, the photographer-turned-filmmaker Bruce Weber explores the appeal of that narcissism—for both the women in Baker's life and his male admirers, like the wonderfully articulate screenwriter Lawrence Trimble (who places Baker in his cultural context), the photographer William Claxton (who "discovered" him as a camera subject), and Weber himself. The movie is much more than a portrait of Baker; it's also an essay on the erotics of jazz—a dimension glaringly absent from the two big-deal jazz bios of recent years, *Round Midnight* and *Bird*—and a study in the nature of obsession. And that's something Bruce Weber, who shot the controversial Calvin Klein "obsession" ads, surely understands.

Many people found the unabashed homoerotic content of those ads distasteful, and in the first, puritanical media sweep of the AIDS crisis they vanished from the pages of national magazines. But Weber likes to push and probe and get underneath the things that magnetize us, as DePalma does (though he's not playful like DePalma); he works off his *own* obsessions. In his first film, *Broken Noses*, he used his ostensible subject, the training of young boxers, to investigate how machismo starts and how it operates, and he refused to shy away from the spectacle of boys posing bare-chested in shorts or jabbing at punching bags, their movements echoed by silhouettes as meticulously crafted—and as self-conscious—as turn-of-the-century photographic prints. I liked *Broken Noses*, which featured father-and-son encounters (some real, some surrogate) that gave off startling reverberations, but it's in *Let's Get Lost* that Weber shows he's a genuine director.

In a series of jaunts along the highways and beaches and through the clubs of southern California, he surrounds the fifty-seven-year-old Baker with mirror images—the musician Chris Isaak and Andy Minsker, the star of *Broken Noses*, both of whom look strikingly like Baker in his early twenties, when he played with Charlie Parker and Stan Getz and Gerry Mulligan and then became an idol in his own right. (Weber and his cinematographer, Jeff Preiss, ingeniously lend these scenes a style reminiscent of the French New Wave directors, who were the first to transfer the irony and romanticism of fifties jazz and poetry to the screen. The whole film is in shimmering black and white.) This doubling, as well as the juxtaposition of photos and rare footage of the sleek young Chet with the craggy Chet of 1987, and the way Weber shoots Baker's look-alike son Paul (who has a glint of wildness in his eyes), both focuses the issue of narcissism and sets up the theme of this jazz hero's awful physical degeneration. Weber's turning-back-the-hands-of-time approach achieves at least one Proustian moment: as a recent Baker performance of "Just Friends" segues without warning into a much older recording, footage of Cannes in 1987 (where Chet entertains festival crowds with an impromptu rendition of "Almost Blue") slips magically into the Cannes of the fifties and early sixties—where Belmondo and Moreau, Bardot and Signoret are caught in the careless spotlight of their celebrated youth.

Let's Get Lost is shaped so we grow more distant from Baker—with his soft western lisp, his beguiling cool, and his impeccable raconteur's timing—as we hear the testimony of some of his past and present dependents. His sometime girl friend Diane Vavra calls him a con man and a Jekyll-and-Hyde; the singer Ruth Young, whom he lived with while he was still officially married to his third wife, Carol, says he's a liar who slowly drained her of her money; Carol talks about the time their son Dean was run down by a drunk driver and Baker, alerted on a European tour, never even bothered to phone. In a stunning moment his mother, Vera, admits to Weber that he disappointed her, and pauses before absorbing this disturbing truth once again into her near-perfect composure. The man who emerges from these reports is certainly a shambles as a human being. And when we see a clip of him playing at the 1956 San Remo Jazz Festival, his small, hard eyes deflecting the camera's gaze, it's not hard to believe all the things these women say he's capable of.

But, except for Vera, they aren't exactly paragons themselves. Diane, who has a wasted, aging-hippie look, seems as crazily hooked on Baker as he is on junk; you can't believe she'd keep coming back for more punishment after some of the stories she tells, yet there she is at his side at Cannes. Ruth is abrasive, vindictive, and self-aggrandizing (and she wears killer earrings). Carol, who hung onto the role of the abandoned but still-faithful wife for close to twenty years, grins like a conspiratorial schoolgirl as her daughter Missy recounts a creepy story about getting revenge on Ruth (when Missy was fourteen) by stealing all her jewelry and hocking it for ninety bucks.

Weber's interview with the Baker family at their Oklahoma house is one of the movie's most haunting sequences. Carol, Vera, and Carol's three kids sit silently, listening to Baker's "Blame It on My Youth"—the ironic anthem of a man who's made a life out of getting blissfully lost and skipping out on responsibilities. The camera pans slowly from face to face, fixing each family member in our heads the way Sidney Lumet does at the end of *Long Day's Journey into Night*. Then, asked if they want to say a few words to their dad, Chet's children can't think of anything except "Stop screwing around" and "Don't be a stranger" and "We could use some financial assistance." And then they disappear into the night.

A friend who saw the movie with me said Weber does such a good job of dismantling Baker that there's finally nothing to like about him but his music. I think, though, that he makes a fair bid for our sympathy in the last few minutes. Weber (off camera, as always) tells Chet how painful it's been to watch him whacked on heroin (you think he's going to nod off every time he has to speak)

and Baker replies that, at fifty-seven, he couldn't possibly have
made it through the shooting any other way. The pathos of this
scene may come less from Baker's suffering than from something
much broader: a recognition of the tragic way we all waste time
and time wastes us all. *Let's Get Lost* is about the choices we make
in our youth, and about losing control of our lives as we get older,
and it's not judgmental—it views Baker and those who tell tales on
him with the same sadness. And, yes, it participates in the Chet
Baker myth it undertakes to examine: It plays both sides of the
fence, just as Baker does when he recites the Eddie de Lange lyrics
of "Deep in a Dream" for the camera, flavoring the smoky reverie
with a trace of self-mockery. Weber's a canny romanticist and one
hell of a filmmaker. What rescues Chet Baker in this movie, finally,
is the magnificence of Weber's obsession with him.

June 1989

Riffing on the Downbeat

• • •

The astonishingly lyrical and quick-witted *Drugstore Cowboy*,
which Gus Van Sant co-wrote (with Daniel Yost, out of a novel
by James Fogle) and directed, is set in Portland, Oregon, in 1971,
and every movie it reminded me of comes from the sixties and early
seventies—*Bonnie and Clyde*, Godard's *Band of Outsiders*, *Mean
Streets*, *M*A*S*H*, and the long-forgotten Ivan Passer film *Born to
Win*. In *Born to Win*, George Segal played the first legitimate
junkie hipster in the movies, a man who had to shoot up because
being straight was too boring, and in *Drugstore Cowboy* Bob (Matt
Dillon), chief of a quartet of low-grade desperadoes who rob drug-
stores, and filch pills and Dilaudid from hospitals, explains that

staying high releases the pressures of the everyday—like tying your shoes. Bob and his band—his wife, Dianne (Kelly Lynch), soft-spoken, rabbity Rick (James Le Gros), and his novice girl friend, Nadine (Heather Graham)—are rebels against respectability. They're not much different from thousands of enclaves of young people of the same era, who sat around getting stoned and laughing at antidope ads on TV—the lame propaganda of the straight world—except that they use pharmaceuticals instead of grass and hallucinogens, and that's *all* they do. Scoring and staying ripped form the wobbly arc of their lives.

Van Sant, whose style is rambunctious and playfully experi-mental and rag-taggle–poetic, keeps up with them by creating a leapfrogging rhythm out of odd, slanted angles and quick cuts, and a skewed vision of the world out of his unpredictable, often magical focus on unexpected objects (or ordinary objects seen in extraordi-nary ways). When Bob boils water for tea in a little tin pot in his room, Van Sant's camera practically dives into the bubbles (like Go-dard zeroing in on the cup of coffee in *Two or Three Things I Know About Her*); when Bob switches on a light, Van Sant gets in close enough so we can read the wattage on the bulb. And there are free-form sequences where the implements of Bob's lifestyle (capsules, spoons, matches), as well as tiny trees—and at one point a blue gun—float by like the uprooted bits of Dorothy's farm during the cyclone in *The Wizard of Oz*. They're the disconnected shreds of Bob's consciousness; Van Sant allows us to see the world as he fig-ures a junkie must see it.

A painter with a film degree from the Rhode Island School of Design, Van Sant has a gift for this kind of lopsided allusiveness and home-grown collage surrealism. He also has a gift for conveying outsiders' perspectives. His previous movie, *Mala Noche*, based on a short story by Walt Curtis, was shot (also in Portland) in black and white and sixteen millimeter, and though it has a perfectly lin-ear narrative, everything in it seems to be communicated indirectly, by feeling. The hero, Walt (played by the wonderfully expressive Oregon actor Tim Streeter), is a young man, working in a conve-nience store, who falls in love with a Mexican teenager, Johnny (Doug Cooeyote), an illegal alien, and subjects himself to a pro-tracted—and futile—series of games and humiliations to earn his affection. In place of his love object, who first refuses his advances and then disappears, Walt sleeps with Johnny's friend, Pepper (Ray Monge), who later gets shot by cops during a drug deal. The movie is about the follies of passion; plaintive and deeply impassioned itself, it takes the point of view that these can't be explained and don't need to be defended. Walt allows himself to be left on the outside of Johnny's and Pepper's camaraderie—to be the gringo on whom they can take out their frustrations with white society. He's smart enough to know that when Pepper has sex with him, his aggressiveness is meant to victimize Walt, and he's sane enough to resent it; but he's also strung out on his own homosexual romanticism, and he keeps exposing himself. When he wrestles with Pepper and gets on top of him, Streeter's Walt looks ravaged, melted down by his desire for the boy, and there's desperation behind the good-buddy grin he flashes at Johnny on the street when he invites him to come by the store for a visit. Lacerated Walt is the most nakedly emotional gay character in a movie since the runaway Lilica in *Pixote*, and *Mala Noche*, with its manic–depressive tone and its mysterious ashcan lyricism (Pepper's shooting is like a classic *film noir* scene that's been split apart—it's shot like a pointillist photograph), seems to ride on his brain waves.

Working on a budget of $7 million in *Drugstore Cowboy*—many times what it cost him to bring in *Mala Noche* (which was his second independent feature)—Van Sant manages to sacrifice remarkably little of the looseness, the adventurousness, the improvisatory feel of the earlier picture; he still has a knack for taking us into corners we've never come across before. And his actors seem to trust him completely, as Tim Streeter must have in *Mala Noche*. Matt Dillon gives his best performance to date as Bob, whose peculiar gift as a put-on artist is that, on some level, he's always telling the truth—he's straight and bent at the same time. (He and Dianne unsettle Nadine with a rap about the superstitions that govern their lives, several of which they claim she's stepped right into. It's hilarious—a blitzed Nichols and May routine—but when the motel Bob's gang is holed up in turns out to be housing a cops' convention, Bob blames the hex he says Nadine's inadvertently put on them, and he's dead serious.) Dillon's grown smarter and surer and a lot more skillful as an actor, but I think it's his on-camera instinct, the quality that made him a star when he was a teenager, that makes him the perfect actor for Van Sant; I doubt the director could have connected with a more technical actor in quite this way, or gotten him to skate on his mood shifts as Dillon does here. This is Altman-caliber acting, where the performer manages to pick up the *feeling* of a film—which is semisubmerged in the script (terrific as it is) but evident in the camera movement, the photography (by Robert Yeoman), and the editing (Curtiss Clayton)—the way a vocalist can catch on to the subtleties of a jazz combo.

Tall, aristocratic Kelly Lynch, who was a sour, leggy blank in *Cocktail* and *Roadhouse*, riffs superbly with Dillon, especially in a wonderful seriocomic gag where she tries to get him into bed but he's more turned on by scoring more dope. Lynch's Dianne has a tough, swinging presence, but she's lost underneath it. When Bob, fed up with the turn his luck has taken, decides to enroll in a methadone program, she feels betrayed: How can he consider such an alternative when he knows she can't? Lynch has worked out her performance fully in physical terms—when she leaves him for the last time, the way she bops down the corridor of his apartment building, slightly disconnected from her surroundings, is touching, pathetic.

Bob isn't always likable: When Nadine O.D.'s on Dilaudid, his response is callous and self-absorbed. And one of his pranks almost gets a cop killed. Van Sant isn't interested in dividing up his characters so we'll know which ones we're supposed to like; the officer on Bob's case, Gentry (James Remar), is capable of both brutality (provoked by the injury to his partner, he beats Bob up) and generosity (when Bob resurfaces in Portland, in the methadone program, Gentry warns him that he might be in danger). What Van Sant looks for in his characters are surprises, the unanticipated twists that people are always capable of—the ones that throw us and then lead us to uncover unsuspected areas of those we thought we knew: Bob's capacity for lonely contemplation, Dianne's blurry vulnerability, Nadine's bravado, Rick's tenderness.

The entire cast is excellent: Le Gros and Graham, James Remar (cast against type), Grace Zabriskie as Bob's mother, Max Perlich as a druggy teen named David—a Michael J. Pollard type who's a lot creepier than he seems at first; and William S. Burroughs, with his weird, distended drawl and his hawk face, in an uncategorizable cameo as a junkie priest. Burroughs isn't really an actor, but he has a mesmerizing presence, and he stirs our associations with him as the literary junkie gospel—you can't help wondering if he wrote his own lines.

The soul of the movie is in the interaction of the younger actors, though. Bob and his "crew" are a stoned parody of the perfect TV-style American family. Bob is the harassed breadwinner who has to take all the risks on himself, give orders, get everybody cracking when they'd rather sit around and enjoy their high. (He even yells, "Honey, I'm home!" when he walks in the front door after barely escaping being caught on the prowl for drugs in a hospital ward.) Dianne, the scolding wife, complains about Bob's behavior ("Do you have to fix in the car? Why can't you wait till we get home, like everybody else?—as if every family in America did drugs together on Saturday night) and about his neglecting her ("You never fuck me and I always have to drive"). They treat Rick and Nadine like their teenage children, commiserating when they're alone about how difficult it is to relate to these "TV babies," and Nadine rebels against their authority by shooting up more than she can handle. In one of the first young-rebel movies to come out of Hollywood, *Rebel Without a Cause*, the characters played by James Dean, Natalie Wood and Sal Mineo formed a kind of mock family, too, out of a longing for the kind of loving family each had been denied. Here the family setup is a good black joke—even a sick joke, when you add David, who is *Drugstore Cowboy*'s version of the neighborhood kid who's always hanging around (like Eddie Haskell). The irony is that David sells crystal meth, and, tired of being treated like a little boy, he responds with a surprise rebellion, too. (Bob turns out to be right: There *is* something scary about these "TV babies.")

Van Sant mixes his tones with a painter's confidence, setting up the big transition, two-thirds of the way through, from anarchic comedy (in the *Bonnie and Clyde*-ish robbery scenes and the scenes involving the gang relaxing) to bluesy low gear (once Bob makes up his mind—with no feeling of triumph or joy, or even simple satisfaction—to give up dope). At this point, half an hour from the end, the movie slows down and the style becomes more gritty and naturalistic. When we see Bob learning how to operate a drill or in a drug therapy session, watching the minutes tick by, the tea bag soaking in the hot water, the butts accumulating in the ashtray, while the music gets jazzy and balladeering, we get a taste of how different it feels for him to be straight.

The scene that prepares us for where the movie's going is Bob and Dianne's visit to his mother, a diminutive, apple-cheeked woman in a bouffant and high heels, who, screaming that Bob's a dope fiend and Dianne's a nymphomaniac, refuses to open the door until she's hidden her valuables. It's a wild sketch with a core of melancholy that kicks in a moment or two before Van Sant passes on to something else—and in that moment you get a glimpse of what's underneath the movie's wayward knockabout humor. In a way the end of this scene, seeping into our consciousness, is like the opening shot of the Mexican kids traveling in boxcars in *Mala Noche*: Van Sant never returns to it, but its mood haunts the film. Alienation's a great deal funnier in *Drugstore Cowboy* than it is in *Mala Noche*, but both movies come from the same impulse: to find a style appropriate to characterizing the lifestyles of people who are closed out—or close *themselves* out—from the mainstream. The downshift in *Drugstore Cowboy* is Van Sant's way of keeping faith with that impulse.

November 1989

Slumming on the Road to Romance
• • •

The Fabulous Baker Boys are a brother act, duo pianists, who've played low-rent, ersatz-glamor dives in the Seattle area for fifteen years—places like the Starfire Lounge, where it's best to count what's in the pay envelope. (They're paid by a sleaze who reminds them they're not playing for "the niggers down on State Street.") Frank (Beau Bridges), who's forty-four, gets a little extra for managing the act, which job he's well equipped for: Married, responsible, and square, he isn't eaten up alive by having either to make nice to the people who hire them, or to sport a Hawaiian shirt for a gig. He even gets into the hushed, Las Vegas-y patter. Jack (Jeff Bridges) doesn't; he can barely get it up to appear on stage every night. He's been collaborating with his brother, as amateur and professional, for thirty-one of his thirty-eight years, and he's as fed up with Frank's meticulousness and anxiety and big-brother advice as he is with some of the wretched songs they have to play ("Feelings" is, Frank feels, an indispensable part of their repertoire). Jack copes by retreating—by staying detached, ironic, sealed off. But when he listens to the glittering arpeggios a wizardly young pianist gets off in his favorite after-hours jazz bar, he grows sick with envy and self-disgust, because he knows that's the kind of music he wanted to play before he got trapped in the lounge circuit.

The Fabulous Baker Boys, written and directed by Steve Kloves, is about what happens to the brothers' relationship when, because they've started to lose jobs to snazzier acts, Frank decides to hire a singer. Susie Diamond (Michelle Pfeiffer) is a tough cookie—she's been biding her time working for an escort agency—with a cannily concealed underlayer of childlike dreaminess, and when she sings, the combination heats up an audience. With her streaky blonde bangs and funky jewelry and red beret, Pfeiffer suggests the little-girl sensuality of a Rickie Lee Jones, and her tense, emotive singing style is midway between Greenwich Village, circa 1955, and Starfire Lounge. She's not a great singer, but she has a throaty, soulful contralto and she wears a lyric tight to her skin, like a zipped-up sleeping bag. The moment she starts to sing, every man in the club (and the moviehouse audience) gets woozy and longs to fall into bed with her. She's a hotel-lounge wet dream.

Not surprisingly, Susie views Frank with a certain incredulous amusement—she calls him "Egghead" and can't help spiking him sometimes, which his brother must have stopped doing years ago, when he lost the energy for it—and she's temperamentally drawn to hip, laconic Jack. When Frank's son has a bicycle accident on New Year's Eve and Frank is called home, the parental influence is removed, and Jack and Susie, inevitably, become lovers. (Frank, who's seen his kid brother float through a series of one-night stands for years, has warned Jack to keep his hands off Susie. He's worried that Jack's inability to behave like a responsible adult will damage his professional relationship with her.) The love affair brings all of the semiburied tensions between the brothers to the surface.

The setup may be a cliché, but the movie isn't. Kloves is a romantic with an edge of self-consciousness, and that's where his three superb actors take up residence. The movie isn't smug or sneering, but it's aware of its romantic-comedy conventions (Kloves is very playful about them in the anticipation scene that follows Frank's New Year's Eve departure) and also its infatuation with blue moods, wee-hours wakefulness, which Kloves is extraordinarily good at evoking and which his cinematographer, Michael Ballhaus, graces with a grungy lyricism. Kloves has drawn Jack Baker out of that awareness. The way Jeff Bridges's Jack holds himself in check, refusing any kind of commitment, is actually an emotional indulgence: He gets to nurse his own loneliness, and though it makes him angry and restless (you can see that in one beautifully acted scene where he goes to pick up his dog at a pound), he's at home with it.

Kloves isn't an iconoclast, exactly, but he knows how to push the inside of the conventions he's working with so that they reveal something genuine—and surprising. When Jack and Susie make love, they're on the stage of a deserted hotel ballroom; he unzips the top of her gown and, nuzzling her back, begins to play it gently, like an instrument. You can feel a thrill running through the audience; it's the kind of bliss a couple as incredibly sexy as Michelle Pfeiffer and Jeff Bridges can bring you to, the kind that makes you giggle at yourself a little. What you may not look for is the wit and sharpness of the morning-after scene: Susie, waking up and seeing Jack pulling on his trousers across the room, sensing his accustomed distance from a woman he's found in his bed, quips, "Look, I didn't expect you to go out and buy me a corsage this morning. . . . Your high-school ring is safe." Kloves (with the brilliant collaboration of his two actors) does wonders with the disenchantment in this scene.

Kloves is also phenomenal at conveying fraternal tension, competitiveness, the difference between the kind of sparring that's sanctioned between brothers and the deep, bitter, O'Neillian kind of anger that such sparring can mask. When the Baker boys finally have it out, their rage triggered by a Mickey Mouse charity benefit Frank's landed them, where Jack brawls with the M.C., they hurl awful accusations at each other, and we know that, on both sides, truth is being spoken. Jack tells Frank he's lost any dignity he ever had, Frank calls Jack self-indulgent and self-deceiving, and we can hear three decades of resentment in their squabbling. When the fight turns physical, Jack, getting the upper hand, bends over his brother (who's sprawled on the pavement) and twists his finger. Kloves isn't afraid to make Jack mean enough to go for what, in professional terms, is his brother's jugular, any more than he's afraid to show Frank spraying his bald spot with black paint before the brothers go on stage. (The finger-twisting is a remarkable, multileveled bit: You can also read it as Jack's cruel disparagement of Frank's talent, and an expression of self-loathing—Jack's talent is in his fingers, and this is what he's allowed himself to believe the Baker Boys act has done to it.)

Jeff and Beau Bridges must have been waiting most of their lives for a chance at a scene like this one—especially Beau, whose career didn't go where it should have after his charming, youthful performances in *Gaily, Gaily* and *The Landlord*. Neither of the brothers has ever been better. They've internalized their characters so completely that when you see the way Jack listens to Susie talking about the guys her escort service hooked her up with—how he shows us the soft stirrings of the emotions just under the surface of his languor and sexual assurance—or the way Frank's permanently quizzical eyebrows rise when he sees the silent connection between Jack and Susie, you understand exactly how each of these men functions.

Michelle Pfeiffer has an appealing collection of numbers: some are great old show standards (Rodgers and Hart's "Ten Cents a Dance" and "My Funny Valentine," "Makin' Whoopee," "More Than You Know"), some are middle-of-the-road but very amiable ("The Look of Love," "Can't Take My Eyes Off of You"), some are pure schlock ("Feelings," of course), but Susie makes them *all* sound good. *The Fabulous Baker Boys* could do with a better instrumental score than the one Dave Grusin's provided, though; it starts off with brio, but by the last half hour it's disintegrated into drippy sludge. And Kloves has included an obligatory scene in which Jack takes out his anger at his own inability to forge a relationship with Susie on Nina (Ellie Raab), the kid upstairs, and then has to run up onto the roof and make it up to her. Until then, the scenes between Nina and Jack—Nina hangs out in his apartment whenever her mother brings home one of her boy friends—are pleasantly casual; Kloves is content to show us Jack's impulse for a more permanent connection with another human being without underlining it.

Kloves is an impressive young talent (this is his first movie); he knows how to direct his actors to strike the perfect balance between glamor and grit, he can write dialogue that's both ticklish and stinging, he has fine timing, and he's remarkable at ambiance. And his movie really keys into something, I think. It plays on the conventions of old-style Hollywood romantic melodrama, which had exotic settings, a poetic–fatalist hero who disguised his broken heart with cynicism, a beautiful heroine, and a bittersweet ending. Some of these are reversed, others modified—but you never doubt that Jack and Susie, whose styles (his is hip and laconic, hers is low-key and double-take) are magnificently suited to each other, are half in love with these romantic clichés, even while they're sneering at them. The ironic tension between the conventions and the realism that undercuts them, moving to an even more ironic embracing of them in the second half, suggests what the movie is about: finding some genuine meaning in the clichés, approaching them fresh and using them to resurrect your life (which is very different from just recalling them and relying on them, the way a movie like *Field of Dreams* does).

Baker Boys, like *The Best of Times* and *Bull Durham*, presents compromise as life-affirming *if* it's approached with real emotional commitment. Susie doesn't become a big star at the end of the picture, and Jack never will, either, but they can get to do the things they love, and they can get to share their lives with each other if they're smart enough, careful enough, passionate enough. *The Fabulous Baker Boys* rescues the idea of romance. When the picture's over, you want to go straight home and listen to every Sinatra record you've got.

November 1989

Actor/Director

• • •

Jim Sheridan came to movies from years in the Irish theater, and his first film, *My Left Foot*—which he also scripted, with fellow playwright Shane Connaughton—has a fully formed sensibility that isn't like anyone else's. Based on the autobiography by Christy Brown, a working-class Dubliner born with cerebral palsy who became a writer and an artist, *My Left Foot* belongs to the same genre as *The Miracle Worker* and *The Wild Child* and *The Elephant Man*: movies about the victory of intelligence that's been incarcerated by physical or environmental forces. But its temperament and tone (it's a fierce-souled, coruscating tragicomedy) belong to another world entirely; they're more easily traceable to the legacy of Irish playwrights like Sean O'Casey and John Millington Synge. *My Left Foot* is a debut the way Olivier's *Henry V* was. We don't have to wait around for Sheridan to develop.

The day Christy is born, his father Paddy (the late Ray Mc-Anally, in a superb sendoff performance) goes to his local pub for a jar. When an acquaintance jeers at him for fathering a cripple, Paddy charges him, head first, like a bull and knocks him on his ass. It's a rough neighborhood and a tough time to grow up: the Depression and the Second World War. At one point Paddy loses his job for slamming his boss on the head, and the family has to start going to bed after supper to conserve coal. Christy, who's played first by the marvelous child actor Hugh O'Conor and then by Daniel Day-Lewis, inherits not only his father's thick skin (he plays street hockey with his brothers and their friends, employing his head, Paddy-style, as a battering ram and biting the legs of his adversaries), but also his mother's perceptiveness, and a ferocious independence that's their shared inheritance. The fact of that independence in a body incapable of propelling itself except by crawling, with only one working limb—Christy's left foot—is a stinging irony that Christy, with much torment, turns into a triumph of spirit and creativity. But Sheridan and Connaughton, whose work is bracingly free of sentimentality, aren't reticent about dealing honestly with Christy's most painful side: his sexual longing and the black rage that results from it.

It's Mrs. Brown (the intuitive, understated actress Brenda Fricker) who first catches on to the idea that Christy, assumed from birth to be retarded, has a driving intelligence. Using his left foot as a hand, he scrawls on a chalkboard the answer to an equation that's eluded his siblings, and he writes his first word—"Mother," of course—in the same manner. These scenes have an almost unbearable emotional suspense. As Christy grows older, he learns how to speak, though he can't enunciate his consonants, and when he's nineteen Mrs. Brown, who's secretly been squirreling money away for a wheelchair, brings home Dr. Eileen Cole (Fiona Shaw), whose specialty is developing linguistic skills in the physically handicapped. She becomes his mentor—by slow steps, because he has to acknowledge his dependency before he can progress past it. She encourages his painting, and even gets him an exhibition. But he's fallen in love with her (the filmmakers are careful to include childhood scenes that locate Christy's sexual stirrings and the agony they cause him), and when, the night of his opening, she tells him at a restaurant celebration that she's engaged to the gallery owner (Adrian Dunbar), he erupts. As the camera rocks back and forth, picking up the turmoil in the air, Christy gets extravagantly drunk, summons all his withering wit to mock them both (articulating ferociously—his way of spitting in Eileen's face), smashes dishes, and resists every effort to wheel him out of the room.

This relentless, horrifying scene resembles something out of Strindberg; it matches the displays of churned-up emotion in *Last Tango in Paris* or *Shoot the Moon*. Daniel Day-Lewis's physical and vocal transformation in this role is Olivier-like (the way he animates the pocket between his lower lip and his chin, which is a crucial speech passage for Christy; the flourishes of ironic romanticism he manages to orchestrate with his left foot), but it's the interplay of wit and passion in his performance that really gives the lie to the thinking that Dustin Hoffman's studious mimicry in *Rain Man* was great acting. Day-Lewis invests Christy's feistiness with a sly jokesterism. It's that Beckettian kind of mischievous humor—he's ribbing the universe, fully knowing who's going to get the last laugh. He also defines, not just Christy's struggles and his feelings, but his *style*. Exasperated at one point in his work with Eileen, he holes up in his room with the copy of *Hamlet* she's given him to read. She finds him buried under a blanket with the book in front of him; coaxed, he thrusts out his foot and drags the book into his improvised tent. First he's telling her he's nothing but a lump; then he's saying, "Yeah, but lumps can surprise you sometimes."

Daniel Day-Lewis's performance is sheer genius; he's the best young actor in movies today. In a scene where Paddy, hearing that his unmarried daughter is pregnant, initiates a dreadful domestic argument, Christy emits a frightening howl. It's as if, with enormously evolved sensitivities trapped in a three-fourths-dead frame, he'd become a magnet for all the ugliest energies in the house—an emblem of them. This moment prepares us, as much as anything can, for the restaurant scene, where Christy in effect does the same thing, only now he's personalized those energies, and now he has the skills for sharpening them into weapons and aiming them with precision.

Sheridan and Connaughton's screenplay is vivid and crisp, and the dialogue is often so beautifully wrought that phrases ring in your ears months after you've heard them. When Eileen asks Christy for his response to Hamlet, he characterizes him succinctly: "Cripple. Can't act." She points out that he does act in the end, and Christy answers, "Too late." Mrs. Brown is Christy's prime motivator—when he feels defeated she goes full tilt at him, refusing to let him wallow—but she grows fearful when Eileen helps him improve his speech and she starts to hear something new: "Too much hope in it," she tells Paddy.

The acting is impeccable: If this picture and *The Dead*, which also draws on the resources of the Irish theater, are an indication of the quality of acting over there, then the Dublin season must be dazzling. And it must be Jim Sheridan's theatrical background that gives him his unconventional visual sense—he thinks like a filmmaker, all right, but sometimes the imagery is pointed, punched, so it resonates the way a great stage image might. I loved a scene where Mrs. Brown takes Christy into a church, amid rows of smoking candles, and a Halloween outing that begins with a shot of a puppet on a bonfire, like a flaming crown, recalls the celebrated Halloween sequence in *Meet Me in St. Louis*. But no one besides Sheridan could have come up with the moment when the family returns home to find Paddy collapsed on the floor from a heart attack, and Christy crawls next to him, this man whose pride and obstinacy he inherited, for whom the communication of feelings had to be couched in a sort of rugged code—and nuzzles his mouth to his father's ear.

December 1989

Duet

• • •

Jessica Tandy has a proud, tough-bird humor in the role of Daisy Werthan, the aging southern–Jewish widow of *Driving Miss Daisy*, Bruce Beresford's movie of the Pulitzer Prize–winning Alfred Uhry play, which covers a period of two and a half decades (from 1948). Miss Daisy leads a solitary life in her Atlanta house; her only steady companion is the laconic, no-nonsense cook, Idella (Esther Rolle), and her significant routines aren't daily, they're weekly— mah jongg nights and Saturday mornings at the temple, where she meets with other elderly ladies in her set. But when she demolishes her automobile and her son Boolie (Dan Aykroyd) insists on hiring her a black chauffeur, she stubbornly opposes him. Morgan Freeman, gray-haired, bespectacled, and armed with a gentle, respectful persistence—a resilient charm just as obstinate as Miss Daisy's irritated detachment—plays the chauffeur, Hoke Colburn. *Driving Miss Daisy* is about how Hoke and Miss Daisy become the most intimate of friends without ever violating the division between their social roles. It's a flirtation, a dance, and the footwork by these two magnificent actors is delicate and dazzling. You can't imagine better performers in these parts.

Miss Daisy denies she's prejudiced, but she can't get used to the idea of a black man hanging around her house; she keeps expecting

him to expose himself as lazy or greedy or dishonest. (She's so used
to Idella that she's probably stopped seeing her as a black woman—
and Idella, as ironic and self-possessed as her employer, has earned
the privilege of telling her off on occasion.) But though the story
does have its messagey, earnest-liberal side, Uhry (who served as his
own adapter) is too smart to score points against Miss Daisy: The
movie isn't primarily concerned with the racial education of a white
southerner. (It's not about beaten-down minorities against the
world, either, thank heaven.) Uhry makes it clear that Miss Daisy's
reluctance to accept Hoke as part of her household has more to do
with her terror of admitting that she's losing her self-reliance. Hoke
finally breaks Miss Daisy down by shadowing her in the car when
she sets out to walk to market. Embarrassed, aware that her neighbors are watching, she has no choice but to concede. That car crawling behind Miss Daisy, who hates to be referred to as wealthy but
keeps a queenly distance from the rest of the world, is a sweet visual
joke—a cartoon.

Uhry and Beresford are very canny; they avoid all the traps of
this kind of material. Hoke drives Miss Daisy to the cemetery so she
can visit her husband's grave, and she asks him to locate a relative's
headstone in the next row. That's when she learns that he can't read.
But she used to teach school, so she goes ahead and gives him a
lesson. Think of all the maudlin, awful ways of doing this scene—
but Tandy and the filmmakers circumvent the sentimentality by
having Miss Daisy respond with a schoolmistressy sternness, an *intolerance* for Hoke's embarrassment. And when, later in the film
(and eight years on in their relationship), Hoke drives her to Mobile
for her brother's ninetieth birthday party, and her distress over a
missed turn and the lateness of the hour makes her unreasonable
about letting him stop to relieve himself by the side of the road, the
scene isn't treated as a lecture on race relations—even when Hoke
explains to her that he couldn't use the whites-only washrooms at
the gas stations they passed. You get the point, but the filmmakers
serve it to us indirectly, through a dramatically more interesting
observation: Miss Daisy's so self-absorbed and unconscious that she's
been treating Hoke as a child who has to ask for permission to pee.
(There's an extraordinary shot of Tandy's Miss Daisy alone in the
car, scared, that tells you the real issue here has nothing to do with
race.) Uhry slips up only once, in an encounter with a pair of red-

neck cops. But Beresford tamps it down: He and the photographer, Peter James, give the scene a spare, Edward Hopper visual tension that draws you away from the temporary melodrama in the writing.

I never thought I'd have a kind word for Beresford, but the movie is wonderfully directed. In the past he's shown an understanding of how to work with actors (*Crimes of the Heart*), but none of how camera and editing can collaborate with them; here, you can't separate out the visual rhythms from the exquisite performance rhythm Freeman and Tandy have going. (Mark Warner edited.) Beresford knows he's working with two of the best actors in the country, and it brings something poetic out in him. One example is the scene where, after Idella's death, Hoke and Miss Daisy pay her tribute by serving up her fried chicken recipe and then eating it—she in the dining room, he in the kitchen.

The two performances are a miraculous combination of grace notes and the kind of seamless acting that makes you forget to watch for technique. Freeman gives Hoke, in his bow tie and suspenders and moustache, a gentlemanly elegance: Hoke doesn't bow and scrape to Miss Daisy—his deference is tinged lightly with amusement, and it doesn't emasculate him or threaten his self-esteem. Tandy made her first New York stage appearance in 1930 and her first movie in 1932, but I can't imagine she's ever been better, even as Blanche DuBois on Broadway. Only an actress with superb theatrical training could make Miss Daisy's loveliest speech—about the first time she ever tasted salt water—sing the way Tandy does. But this is one of those performances (like Edith Evans's in *The Whisperers* or Peggy Ashcroft's in *A Passage to India*) where you feel that a lifetime of experience has become bound up with a lifetime of acting. When Miss Daisy, retired for decades, wakes up one morning and becomes confused about where she put her schoolbooks, Tandy's acting tells you something about old age that no one has ever expressed before. At least not quite in this way.

On stage, *Driving Miss Daisy* came across as thin, insubstantial. You could tell Uhry was trying not to be obvious and manipulative, but there was so little going on that his restraint seemed a negative virtue. Plays that aren't all they're cracked up to be tend to get exposed cruelly on screen, but the "opening up" of *Driving Miss Daisy* has the surprising effect of grounding it, and, with the characters fleshed out by Tandy and Freeman, the lines suddenly have the unstressed compactness of dialogue written directly—and skillfully—for the movies. Maybe Uhry should have been a screenwriter all along.

There are a couple of additions—nice, small roles for Esther Rolle and Patti LuPone (as Boolie's wife, assimilated Florine, whose idea of heaven, Miss Daisy says, is socializing with Episcopalians). And Dan Aykroyd, beautifully cast, is a revelation as Boolie Werthan. Boolie's inherited his mother's sense of irony, but he has admirable reserves of patience: Years of dealing with two women who tend to dig in until they get their own way have made him philosophical. Aykroyd plays this man as if he'd been doing straight drama all his professional life; he even *ages* in character.

When Boolie is cited Atlanta's Businessman of the Year, and acknowledges how proud his father and grandfather would have been, you don't have to be told what kind of legacy a Jewish merchant has in a southern Protestant society. *Driving Miss Daisy* is a modest, satisfying comedy about different ways of living with dignity; the characters in it—Miss Daisy, Hoke, Boolie, even Idella—learn to respect each other's. The best compliment you can pay the filmmakers is to say that they give their performers the same kind of room to express themselves that the characters afford each other.

December 1989

THE EMPEROR'S NEW CLOTHES

• • •

If you respond full-heartedly to a movie like *Shoot the Moon* or *Pennies from Heaven* or *Casualties of War*, if you feel that a director like Jonathan Demme or Fred Schepisi engages all your circuits, then you can't help being baffled, over and over again, not only by the products that Hollywood coos over, but by the readiness with which the country accepts them as the best the industry has to offer. This disjunction between what is truly great and what Hollywood likes to think of as great (and consequently Oscar-great) wasn't original with the eighties, of course. But it's appalling to look back at *The Great Ziegfeld* and *The Life of Emile Zola*, *Mrs. Miniver* and *Going My Way*, *Ben-Hur* and *West Side Story*, and realize that the esteem with which they were held in their day derived from all the same fake criteria Hollywood is still applying: size, budget, "importance" of subject matter, earnestness, prestige (i.e., expensiveness) of source material.

It seems amazing that a culture can pass through *M*A*S*H*

207

and the *Godfather* movies and *Cabaret, Sounder, Deliverance,* and *One Flew Over the Cuckoo's Nest*—popular, Oscared (or Oscar-nominated) movies that were also terrific—and end up back where it started, jumping up and down over *Ordinary People, Chariots of Fire, Gandhi, The Color Purple, Broadcast News, Rain Man, Crimes and Misdemeanors,* or the two representative "big" movies I've focused on in this section, *Amadeus* and *Out of Africa.* What these films offer is a kind of respectability—the façade of engagement with significant issues and the veneer of that favorite old Hollywood phrase, "production values."

"Production values" means you can *see* the money the studio lavished on the project. It *doesn't* necessarily mean that it was well spent, or that it was used to buy the best craftsmanship available—though that's always the implication. Have you ever noticed that the Academy Award for Best Editing almost unfailingly goes, not to the year's most exciting picture, but to the longest, dullest epic? That's an example of what Hollywood means by "production values." You feel older at the end of one of these movies—not exhilarated and smarter, the way you do after *The Godfather, Part II* or *Nashville.* Just older. Audiences may believe the promoters' delusion that they've gotten their money's worth because they've put in so much time or watched so much money paraded in front of them (the same way they do when they pay upwards of a hundred bucks for a pair of seats to *Les Misérables*), but there's nothing up there worth looking at. The Emperor isn't wearing any clothes.

The Consequences of Inflation

• • •

After seeing Peter Shaffer's *Amadeus* twice on stage (once on Broadway and once in San Francisco), and sitting dutifully through all two hours and forty minutes of the film version, directed by Miloš Forman and with a revised screenplay by Shaffer himself, I confess I still don't see in it what the New York critics and so many theatergoers apparently have—though perhaps I understand what lends this heavy, stuffed-shirt play its appeal. Shaffer has a knack for hatching dramatic ideas that *sound* fascinating until you examine them carefully, and he's the shrewdest of used-car salesmen when it comes to second-guessing his audience.

In the 1973 *Equus*, Shaffer streamlined drama for liberal intellectuals that responded superficially but precisely to then-current psychological fads. Writing a play about a boy with a stereotypical strict-religious upbringing who commits an atrocity out of an inability to reconcile sexuality and religion, Shaffer gave his emotionally lacerated victim/hero an analyst who's experiencing *his own* sexual frustrations. A humanitarian, Dr. Dysart fears that by "curing" the boy he will be taking away his passion and consigning him to the mediocre, emotionally dead world in which Dysart himself is a permanent resident. This Laingian shell-game of an argument begged the central sociological question of the play—how should society deal with a boy who has done something horrible (he blinded several horses) but who clearly deserves our sympathy for the agony he is in?—as well as the central humanistic question—what can the psychiatrist do to alleviate the boy's suffering?—by shifting the focus to the (considerably less interesting) analyst. Logically, it's nonsense to insist that we use the doctor's jaded, embittered vision of the life of the psychically well adapted as a normative point of view, but Shaffer carried it off dramatically, relying on liberal audiences to accept his evasions as profundities—just as they'd accepted, in other eras, the pseudo-probing of such plays as *The Children's Hour* and *The Crucible* and *Inherit the Wind*.

In *Amadeus* the shell game has become more complicated as

209

well as bewigged and petticoated, since it takes place (mostly) in the court of Emperor Joseph II of Austria during the 1780s and early 1790s, when Antonio Salieri was official court composer and Wolfgang Amadeus Mozart a brilliant young upstart threatening Salieri's superior position. This time the issue is the form of genius, and Shaffer begins with what seems to be a revisionist view of musical history's most redoubtable one. Mozart's gifts are couched in a grotesque form—a facetious, arrogant, scatological twit (played in the film by Tom Hulce) who paws his bosomy bride-to-be Constanze (Elizabeth Berridge) under a sweet table in a palace reception room while his music is being performed for the pleasure of the Emperor (Jeffrey Jones) in an adjacent salon.

The paradox is that such a revolting spoiled brat could produce such magnificent music, or as Salieri (F. Murray Abraham), who is watching this display of juvenile lust unseen by the participants, expresses it, that God should choose "an obscene child to be his instrument." Shaffer has rigged it so that Salieri alone, the favorite of the Emperor and therefore of the cowardly, blank-minded, shoe-licking Viennese aristocracy, has the vision to comprehend the revolutionary complexity of Mozart's music and thus (and this is Shaffer's prize irony) to acknowledge—and rage privately about—his own pitiful inadequacy. Salieri interprets this solitary curse as God's blight on him and declares war on God, with Mozart as the battleground. He sees to it that Mozart can't get ahead in the Austrian court, and that Mozart and Constanze (now married) and their child remain on the verge of starvation even as Mozart continues to create one glory after another—*The Abduction from the Seraglio, The Marriage of Figaro, Don Giovanni, The Magic Flute*—glories that only he, Salieri, can appreciate.

But this kind of cynical approach to an established view of greatness, which would have been swallowed whole by audiences in the late Vietnam years, is démodé for the eighties, and Shaffer knows it. So he pulls back from Salieri's venomous perceptions halfway through the drama and shows us what Salieri himself can't see: that Mozart is no silly, dimpled weakling, no foul-mouthed jerk, but a man of *passion*. Passion is Shaffer's "Open sesame!" once again; as in *Equus*, it throws everything fashionably out of kilter. Mozart writes such inspired music not just because he is prodigiously equipped to, but also because his soul, unlike Salieri's shriveled one, bulges with the life force, and that is why obscenities pour unseasonably from his mouth. For wouldn't you expect impropriety from a man who, his pores ever open in his all-embracing tour of life, laughs too heartily and drinks too deep and makes love with too much gusto? Shaffer supplies supposedly ironclad proof of Mozart's moral superiority over the spiritually constipated Salieri (who stuffs himself on pastries alone): The *people* adore Mozart's music. The Emperor's servants applaud his court performances, and the fun-loving crowds devour *The Magic Flute* at the Theatre auf der Wieden, where the impressario Schikaneder (Simon Callow) plays the first Papageno.

Never mind the extreme implausibility of Salieri's being the only educated man in Vienna in the late eighteenth century to appreciate Mozart, and never mind the contradiction inherent in Shaffer's dramatic construction: that Mozart is too intricate for Salieri's colleagues to understand, and yet the untutored audiences at Schikaneder's theater (if indeed such audiences would ever have found their way to the opera in this period or any other) intuit the composer's greatness instantly. Never mind that the movie begins with the tempting proposition that the only man in Vienna smart enough to see the visionary genius in Mozart is in the greatest danger from it (and therefore must plot to suffocate it), and ends by throwing that idea out for the more democratic (and highly debatable) one that true genius belongs to the people, and they will always recognize it. Shaffer can have it both ways because he puts his audience in a plum position, congratulating us continually on our hindsight. When the court censor, Count Orsini-Rosenberg (Charles Kay), urging Mozart to abandon *The Marriage of Figaro*, asks him why he wastes his spirit on such rubbish, we can snicker because *we* know what the "rubbish" will end up sounding like.

It must have been the combination of deep-seeming popular ideas and all the period pomp that drew Miloš Forman to this project, as well as such assorted luminaries as choreographer Twyla Tharp and the world-renowned Czech set designer Josef Svoboda. Forman has made his reputation on "important" properties. First there was Ken Kesey's *One Flew Over the Cuckoo's Nest*, which he turned into a terrific popular entertainment; then *Hair*, which became a provocative, powerful, but unlikable (and financially unsuccessful) movie musical, and finally the E. L. Doctorow novel

Ragtime, which he wrecked—but in such a broad, respectable manner that it won him praise anyway. Because I don't care about the
play *Amadeus* and I did care about Doctorow's book, I could watch
Forman's movie version without the anger I felt during *Ragtime*.
But it's such a *heavy* movie—long and boring, and cluttered (as
Ragtime was) with overdressed extras who evidently have no idea
of what they're supposed to be playing. If Forman has a bone in his
body that isn't weighed down by his eastern-European sensibility
(he's a Czech émigré), he hasn't revealed it in any of his movies; the
"jokes" in *Amadeus* (like the way Salieri's father meets his end in
the flashback montage) hit the floor like ten-ton weights, and then
Forman clears space for them as if by staring at them we'd find
them funnier. The only humorous moment that really comes off is
the one most dependent on exaggeration: When Constanze's over-
bearing mother (Barbara Bryne, playing essentially the same role as
she does in *The Bostonians*) screeches at Mozart for failing to provide properly for her daughter, he looks at her monstrously over-
worked mouth and fierce eyes and his imagination starts to con-
struct the most horrific of all mothers-in-law, the Queen of the
Night in *The Magic Flute*.

Many reviewers have praised Forman for reproducing so much
of Mozart's music in this picture, but we don't get to enjoy it, because there are so many distractions—like the bad dubbing (why
didn't Forman just shoot real singers in the opera scenes?), and a
very odd, disjunctive conceit by which the libretti always begin in
German or Italian and then switch into English. Besides, since the
entire movie is framed by his recounting the story of his rivalry with
Mozart at a distance of several decades, to a shocked priest in a
hospital ward, that unbearable Salieri is always around to tell us
how marvelous the music is, as if we couldn't decide that for ourselves.

In the hospital scenes, poor F. Murray Abraham has to wear
one of those overaccomplished make-up masks (designed by Paul
LeBlanc) that seem to become characters in themselves and efface
the flesh-and-blood actors behind them—like the one Dustin Hoffman suffered in for *Little Big Man*. Forman probably means something by all those close-ups of Abraham's wizened old "face," with
its detailed ugliness, while he's describing the beauty of Mozart's
music, just as he insists on showing us a ward full of stage-set luna-

tics (not once but repeatedly), and the blood all over Salieri's face when he hemorrhages, and the most unsavory details of Mozart's burial. (It reminded me of historical films set in the Middle Ages where directors show they've done their homework by training the camera on the excrement in the courtyard.) If Forman were really interested in authenticity, anyway, he'd have had someone show Tom Hulce how to conduct, and he'd have cast someone else as Constanze—someone who didn't have Elizabeth Berridge's contemporary New York looks.

Both F. Murray Abraham and Tom Hulce have their moments, but as Shaffer has built the play neither role can work straight through. Since the script begins by embracing Salieri and his view of Mozart and ends by discarding it, Abraham is at an advantage in the first half of the movie, when we find Mozart intolerable, and at a disadvantage in the second half, when Mozart's humanity emerges and Salieri's disappears. I saw Ian McKellen and then John Wood, both fine actors, struggle with the role of Salieri and fail to find a path through it; Abraham is less mannered than either of them, but the movie eats him up in the final analysis. As Mozart, Tom Hulce, whose casting you might think utterly bizarre based on his previous screen appearances (like the innocent undergraduate in *Animal House*), gives a bad, flamboyant, and anachronistic performance for most of the movie's length—though he gets to wear Paul LeBlanc's best proto-punk wig, a white powder puff dusted with orange, when he conducts one of his operas. But surprisingly, in his feverish deathbed scenes, he shows some skill.

Every now and then, Forman and Shaffer do something genuinely clever (a sequence in which Mozart transforms Salieri's dull welcome march in his honor into a splendid trifle by improvising a variation on it) or genuinely affecting (Salieri transcribes the dying Mozart's final opus by dictation). But not often. Shaffer endows Mozart's father with so much power over him that, after the old man's death, Salieri can throw the young composer into a state of nervous collapse (and physical disrepair) by arriving at his door in a carnival costume Mozart père once wore and demanding a mass for the dead. In the play, this semimystical, semi-Freudian mumbo-jumbo was rather bewildering; in the movie, which Shaffer has padded out with a real on-screen version of Leopold Mozart (played by Roy Dotrice), you can't take it seriously for a moment. Leopold's

initial appearance in a black cape, his arms outstretched like a vampire bat's wings, is meant to be ominous (though Forman botches
the moment), but as soon as he settles into the role of the visiting
in-law, forever nagging his son and berating his daughter-in-law for
her poor housekeeping, he becomes so insignificant that Mozart's
resurrection of him, as the Commendatore in *Don Giovanni*, seems
a joke the filmmakers neglected to punch properly. And if Mozart
is supposed to be such a life-lover, couldn't Shaffer and Forman
have depicted his marriage to Constanze as the nurturing force they
want us to believe it was, rather than as a series of inane dirty jokes
and banal domestic scuffles? It's not enough to star Wolfgang Amadeus Mozart in your movie and fill the soundtrack with his music;
you have to be worthy of him, too. In *Amadeus*, Peter Shaffer and
Miloš Forman have inflated *themselves* with Mozart's greatness.

October 1984

Precursors

• • •

Out of Africa is a puzzle. This two-and-a-half-hour chronicle of
the years Karen Blixen, who later became the writer Isak
Dinesen, spent running a coffee farm in Kenya (1914 to 1931) has
all the elements of spectacle: an African setting; safaris; World War
I; and a passionate romance between a tough, independent Danish
woman who threw her dissolute husband out some time after he
gave her syphilis, and a stout-hearted English big-game hunter who
lives off the sale of ivory. But the filmmakers, screenwriter Kurt
Luedtke and director Sydney Pollack (who also collaborated on *Absence of Malice*), seem to have something else in mind. Despite
David Watkin's superb photography, the scenes that you might ex-

pect to have an "epic" feeling, like Karen's trek through the countryside to bring supplies to her husband's regiment or the Armistice parade, are competent but obligatory.

Did they want to celebrate the courage of this woman, who grows from a petulant, spoiled heiress—she marries Count Bror Blixen-Finecke because her real lover, his brother, has deserted her, and she needs the security of marriage to feel she isn't a failure—into a figure of Hemingwayesque proportions, running the farm singlehandedly and eventually gaining the hard-won admiration of the male-dominated British ruling class in East Africa? (There are deep connections between Hemingway and Isak Dinesen: Her memoir, *Out of Africa*, one of the four sources for Luedtke's script, has a Hemingway-like leanness and reserve, and Bror Blixen furnished Hemingway with the model for the safari hunter in his story "The Short Happy Life of Francis Macomber.") If that was their aim, then the filmmakers and Meryl Streep, who plays Karen, haven't cracked her shell.

Karen's Edwardian clothes are the best Streep has ever worn on screen, and her early scenes with Klaus Maria Brandauer as Bror have an unaccustomed snap. By letting her play off a character with unusual caches of warmth and wit (especially for a self-centered profligate who in another movie would certainly be a thoroughgoing villain), Brandauer brings out more interesting colors in her than she usually shows, and she drops that great-lady pose for a while. (She's better cast here than in *Silkwood* or *Plenty*, too.) She's very convincing as the willful countess, and she's refreshingly funny in Karen's first encounters with the Kikuyu, the native Kenyans— a European émigré trying to assume a position of control over these Africans, who are far more comfortable in this setting than she can ever be, and getting twisted in the inevitable breakdowns in communication and cross-cultural confusions.

But the more adept Karen gets at managing this life (and the less we see of Brandauer), the more Streep retreats behind her Danish accent. Yes, yes, it's an impeccable accent, an amazing accent; Streep shows us what I don't think even Olivier ever did in one of his foreign incarnations—that nonnative speakers blur the contours of their English sentences in moments of anxiety. It's the blurriness at Karen's *core* that I'm objecting to: In the second hour (or perhaps even earlier), Streep starts becoming increasingly more distant and unfathomable. When Karen learns she has syphilis, and much later when she receives sad news that supposedly affects her even more, the actress refuses to give us any indication of what this woman might be thinking. Pauline Kael once wrote of Marlon Brando (in *Last Tango in Paris*), "He's an actor: When he shows you something, he lets you know what it means." With Meryl Streep, you're never sure. Just before Karen leaves Africa and her bankrupt farm behind, the men who were shocked by her forthrightness when she first arrived (and even suspected her of German sympathies when the war broke out, though Luedtke's script merely hints at this) invite her into their club for a drink, breaking with male tradition. She toasts them, downs the drink in a single gulp, and marches out again. There's no suggestion of what this "honor" means to Karen— whether she's touched by it or disdains the men for waiting until the day of her departure to finally welcome her. And so the scene serves no purpose, except perhaps as an echo of an earlier one, in which she walked into this private club by mistake and was summarily *thrown* out.

It may be that a script with Karen Blixen at the center of it just won't yield the emotional force needed to drive a movie, especially one of this size. (What audiences are responding to is more likely the familiar Hollywood-epic elements—the big money, the picturesqueness, the potential for high drama and romance in the story—rather than the movie itself.) Her book *Out of Africa* is written in a beautifully fluid style, but it's somewhat cold and certainly elusive: She never mentions Bror, and her references to Denys Finch Hatton never identify him as her lover (though it's easy to read between the lines; her obituary for him is the most emotionally accessible passage in the book).

In any case, as the film is constructed it's difficult to know what Pollack and Luedtke latched onto when they read *Out of Africa* and Judith Thurman's acclaimed biography of Isak Dinesen— in other words, why they wanted to make this movie. They don't banalize the dramatic elements of Karen's Africa years, like the syphilis and the financial collapse of the farm; this isn't soap opera, and it isn't *Cross Creek*, either. But the issues tied up with the farm (like Karen's attempts to doctor the natives and set up a school for their children) and the whole business of the clash between her indomitable spirit and the conservative, misogynistic British establishment are relegated to pockets of the movie, as if *they* didn't much interest the filmmakers, either.

Nor is *Out of Africa* about the birth of a writer, even though the famous opening phrase of Dinesen's memoir, "I had a farm in Africa, at the foot of the Ngong Hills," is repeated several times in a voice-over spoken by an aging Karen. (Predictably, the voice Meryl Streep adopts for Karen's old age—craggy but not cracked, still elegantly bred but stripped down from the inside—is a prodigious piece of craftsmanship.) Dinesen didn't become a writer until after she had left Kenya; her first collection, *Seven Gothic Tales*, was published in 1934, and *Out of Africa* came out three years later. And so the only allusion to her eventual vocation in this picture, aside from the framing device of having her recall her life in Africa as she sits hunched over her writing desk, is her fondness for spinning stories, a talent that delights her frequent guests, Denys Finch Hatton (Robert Redford) and his best friend, Berkeley Cole (Michael Kitchen). (Finch Hatton is not yet her lover at this point.)

The tale that Karen entertains these receptive visitors with after dinner one evening sounds a lot like Thomas Burke's "The Chink and the Child," the source of D. W. Griffith's *Broken Blossoms*, and Streep tells it well—but we hear only the beginning. Then Pollack fades her voice out and focuses on the rapt expression on Redford's face as he listens. (Pollack used this technique once before, in *The Way We Were*, when Redford, as a college writer, responded to his own story being read aloud in class. In both cases you get the feeling that the director is using it as an escape hatch— that he's afraid, perhaps with some justification, that the story wouldn't be sufficient to hold *us*.) It's Finch Hatton who urges Karen to start writing her stories down, and when she does, after his death, we can guess that she's fulfilling an unspoken promise to him, or reaping the fruits of his inspiration, or perhaps keeping their romance alive by doing his bidding. But the movie never tells us which.

The relationship between Karen and Denys takes up the greater part of the film's second half, but if it's passion the filmmakers were interested in, they certainly picked the wrong actors. In the hands of emotionally recessive Streep and granite-faced Redford, this romance is a bad joke; as far as we can see, they never connect. Who *could* connect with Robert Redford, anyway? He hasn't given a performance since *The Way We Were*. Sydney Pollack, who's worked with him half a dozen times, has a blind spot where Redford is concerned: In an interview in *The New York Times Magazine* he's quoted as arguing, "Let's say you have a guy who's a loner—he's terrifically intelligent, he has a sense of humor but he also has a dark side. Women find him very, very attractive but he wants more out of life. Well, if you cast Bob Redford, you don't have to write as hard." Actually, I'd say Redford is one actor who needs all the help he can get from a writer. And, as it happens, Kurt Luedtke has written harder for this role than for Karen: Redford has all the best lines that don't belong to Klaus Maria Brandauer. (Luedtke must understand these men better than he understands Karen Blixen, which isn't very surprising.) But Redford doesn't give much in his tête-à-têtes with Streep, and the scenes in which he *does* act—like the one in which he visits the dying Cole—are so terrible that you end up feeling that, like Clint Eastwood, he's better off not even trying. Of course, he's also better off in some other movie. What's he doing playing a man named Denys Finch Hatton, anyway? He doesn't even use an English accent. (Apparently he rehearsed one, but Pollack got him to drop it during the filming—reasoning, I suppose, that it would sound pathetic next to Streep's brilliantly accomplished Danish one.)

A movie is in trouble when so much of it depends on the emotional interaction between two actors as ill-matched (and ill-suited for displays of emotion) as Streep and Redford. This one is stolen with no apparent effort by Brandauer and Kitchen. These actors burn down into their roles; their scenes let off a human steam. When Brandauer passes out of the film, it shifts into low gear; when Redford bows out, we don't experience any grief because he barely seemed to inhabit the screen in the first place.

I'm reluctant to suggest that what might have drawn the filmmakers to *Out of Africa* was the juxtaposition of a protofeminist and a great spirit who teaches her to respect the identity of a country and culture she is alien to—the politically correct elements of the material. (The *Stanford Daily* critic Steve Warrick observed that Redford's mission in eighties movies seems to be to play the soul of continents—North America in *The Natural*, Africa in *Out of Africa*.) That particular subtext, of course, is the most uncomfortable part of the film, as well as the silliest, because Finch Hatton was a great white hunter, not a mystery-man naturalist; and Karen Blixen, though no doubt a benevolent mistress to her Kikuyu servants, inevitably brought a master-race condescension to her new colonial home that never entirely left her. (You can hear it in her prose; it's the legacy of her background and of the period in which she ran that coffee farm.) Besides, Finch Hatton and Berkeley Cole, too, were first drawn to Karen's supper table and hearth because she represented the trappings of white European civilization, the bone china and the fine cuisine, that they had left behind them in England: Dinesen makes a point of telling us that the two men kept her wine cellar well stocked.

This movie suggests that Finch Hatton thought little of Karen's old-world objects; that he taught her to lose her attachment to them just as he taught her, with conveniently avant-garde sagacity, to work toward self-actualization and to value her personhood just as he valued his. Granted that we can't help filtering history through our own contemporary perceptions, but this mid-1980s view of Dinesen and Finch Hatton doesn't enrich them as personalities—it reduces them to precursors.

January 1986

ART-HOUSE VISIONS

• • •

Sometime in the late eighties, the Harvard Square movie theater in Cambridge—which had gone from a popular second-run cinema in the sixties and seventies, housing occasional first runs of foreign and independent pictures (Claude Jutra's *My Uncle Antoine* played there in 1973), to a first-run art house—began to add big commercial releases to what had previously been a fairly classy roster. Those of us who wrote about movies in Boston balked at the crassness of Loews's salesmanship strategies, but the fact is the management was responding to a dramatic change in the college audience that had occurred sometime in the late seventies and become shockingly clear in the eighties. You couldn't rely on even Harvard audiences to support movies like *Wish You Were Here* and *Withnail and I* (both of which did in fact play at the Harvard Square, to small crowds); to bring in business, you had to screen the same damn movies any suburban shopping mall was offering.

When the counterculture disappeared, so did the student audience that longed to see offbeat and foreign films. Most of my students have to be coaxed toward *anything* with subtitles; they approach it dutifully, as if given a difficult reading assignment. An adventurous young audience these days is one that goes out for the latest Jim Jarmusch. Not that *Stranger Than Paradise* or *Down by Law* is any worse than some of the shallowly hip movies of the Vietnam era; hell, they're *both* preferable to *El Topo*. But Jarmusch fans don't tend to supplement his pictures with, say, *The Unbearable Lightness of Being* or *Enemies, A Love Story*, or *The Dead*. They're more likely to line up for *Rain Man*, the epitome of conventional, sentimental Hollywood filmmaking.

You know the art house is dead when the movie that more discriminating filmgoers—the ones who'd rather slash their wrists than have to endure *Terminator 2*—want to talk about at a dinner party is the latest from France. The imports from Europe are even more dispiriting than domestic pictures these days (unless they hail from England, where filmmaking came suddenly and unexpectedly to life in the mid-eighties and is still holding on). And the French ones are the worst, unless they have Louis Malle's name on them, or occasionally Andre Téchiné's or (less and less frequently) Bertrand Blier's. The French, at least from the looks of what makes it to these shores, divide their energies between cutesy comedies about Gallic family life—most of which, like *Three Men and a Cradle*, end up as Hollywood remakes—and witheringly dull period pieces, usually derived from Marcel Pagnol stories and/or featuring Gérard Depardieu.

Certainly there are worthy Pagnols in the history of French film (*Harvest, Marius, The Baker's Wife*), but *Jean de Florette* isn't among them. Bearing the seal of the French Academy under Pagnol's name in the credits like an imprimatur, this static, simpleminded pastoral melodrama gives you nothing to look at, nothing to think about. Depardieu, idiotically cast as a saintly hunchback, plants lettuce and raises rabbits, cheerfully unaware that among his neighbors is a pair of villains (Yves Montand and Daniel Auteuil) who are plotting against him. It's hard to get up much sympathy for a character who can't figure out what the slowest child in the theater would grasp the moment these two show up in their black hats, throwing poisonous looks in his direction. (Depardieu's character is so dense that, when the friend who accompanied me saw him gamboling among his rabbits, he quipped, "This movie is like *Of Mice and Men* from Lennie's point of view.")

Depardieu was a staggering presence in such French films of the seventies as Blier's *Going Places* and *Get Out Your Handkerchiefs*, and even in supporting roles like the one he played for Claude Sautet in *Vincent, François, Paul and the Others*; and in Marco Ferreri's *The Last Woman* he gave one of the greatest performances ever recorded by a camera. In the eighties, however, he became an emblem of what had gone wrong with art-house filmmaking. Suffocating his gifts in period costumes and roles he had no business playing (he welcomed in the nineties by taking on Cyrano de Bergerac, a part he's as utterly unsuited for as Brando would have been at his age), he was no longer an original in the line of great French virile unclassifiables like Michel Simon and Jean Gabin. He'd turned into a fake, getting by on his famous energy and robustness and sliding noisily over the surface of the characters he was supposed to be getting under the skin of. His movies have become increasingly stodgy and tiresome: When I saw *Jean de Florette* I stopped complaining about *The Return of Martin Guerre*, and *Cyrano de Bergerac* made me almost wistful for *Jean de Florette*.

The eighties were dotted with quirky movies by directors with atypical, skewed visions—movies that by rights should have been art-house favorites, though few of them were. I've selected some for this section that stayed with me, because they were such unexpected takes on familiar genres (the gangster movie *The Long Good Friday*, the musical *True Stories*), or because they experimented in memorable ways with mixed styles or tones (*Hour of the Star, The Funeral, Mélo*), or because they weren't like anything else I'd ever seen (*The Eyes, the Mouth, Alice, Superstar: The Karen Carpenter Story*). The Scottish director Bill Forsyth, who came to prominence in the early eighties with his entrancing comedy *Local Hero*, doesn't make movies like anyone else does; that's why a failure like the 1987 *Housekeeping* haunts you in a way that more successful films don't. Between these two pictures he made the bittersweet, quickly departed *Comfort and Joy*. Only 1989's *Breaking In*, his most overtly commercial effort, made little impression. It was the only one he didn't write himself (John Sayles did), and the farther Forsyth gets from material shaped by his own peculiar sensibilities, the less chance he has to roam freely through it. *Housekeeping* originated in a novel by Marilynne Robinson (which is what's wrong with it), but at least Forsyth did the adaptation himself.

When PBS telecast the Dennis Potter–Jon Amiel *Singing Detective* in 1988, it became clear that if the art house has relocated anywhere, it's probably television. Who ever would have thought it? I don't think it's too much to say that no one attempted anything in movies during the decade as daring or as ambitious as *The Singing Detective*, though two of the films Potter had a hand in (*Pennies from Heaven* and *Dreamchild*) were quite amazing. And audiences responded to it: It acquired a cult following, the way the great first season of "Wiseguy" did; viewers prescient enough to videotape these episodes needed to draw up waiting lists to accommodate everyone who wanted to see them. (The Brattle Theatre, Cambridge's superb revival house, screened the entire *Singing Detective* on two occasions after the local PBS channel had run it.) I include a review of it here because I think that, even more than the theatrical films in this section, it represents the kind of art-house viewing many of us dream about.

The Godfather as a Comedy of Menace

• • •

John Mackenzie, the director of *The Long Good Friday*, has a quiet style that seems offhand at first; then the small, jagged bits of Barrie Keeffe's script slide swiftly into place, and you realize how carefully the film has been crafted. *The Long Good Friday* is a modest picture, but it's consistently intelligent, and it holds a few surprises. Harold Shand (Bob Hoskins) has thrust himself up from his slum roots to captain the biggest gangster-run network in London. He's eliminated or cowed all his rivals, has politicians and policemen in his pocket, and is about to clinch the most ambitious deal of his career: a translatlantic corporation that will ally him with the American Mafia. The film begins with the arrival of the American connection, Charlie (Eddie Constantine), and his lawyer Tony (Stephen Davies), and charts the descent of one of the most powerful men in England as Shand's associates are killed off and his property destroyed by an unknown enemy. It's *The Godfather* in reverse.

It takes a while to get used to Bob Hoskins's aggressive approach to acting, and to see that he's not simply trying to make a virtue out of gruffness, but rather is stylizing the gangster-movie clichés that Keeffe's built the character of Harold Shand on. Shand's ghetto background sticks out: He eats at the finest restaurants (he seems to own most of them) and lives in a penthouse, but he doesn't seem comfortable in the high life. The filmmakers even include a sequence that's a variation on an archetypal encounter from 1930s movies like *Dead End* and *Angels with Dirty Faces*, in which Harold returns to the slums in search of information and admires the ingenuity of hard-boiled twelve-year-olds who charge him protection money for parking his fancy car on the street. His girl friend, Victoria, began a few rungs farther up the social ladder, and she's subtler, more patient, and—unexpectedly—a lot smarter. She also seems to be genuinely in love with him. (As Victoria, Helen Mirren looks smashing in her Julie Christie hairstyle, and gives a solid performance.)

225

Mackenzie and Keeffe have found new approaches to an old genre. *The Long Good Friday* may not be novel in presenting a vision of big business as gangsterism, or in showing the modern expansion of the underworld into the international scene (*The Godfather, Part II* did all that)—but no one has ever dealt with these issues *comically* before. The filmmakers get early laughs out of Shand's initial blustery dominance of the London scene, and as his power begins to slip away from him, and his bulldog belligerence is inadequate to cope with the enormity of the crisis, Shand becomes steadily funnier. So does the movie. The thin ice of diplomacy cracks in the final clash between Shand and his intended partners: The Englishman and the Americans tell each other what they've really been thinking all along. Charlie and Tony call England a banana republic, and Shand responds with an attack on sloppy, big-talking Yankees. It may be the most hilarious face-off in the history of gangster movies. (It highlights the movie's one casting flaw, however. Mackenzie must have wanted Eddie Constantine for the associations that European audiences might have with him—he played Peter Cheyney's detective hero Lemmy Caution in a series of French thrillers beginning in 1953 and reprised the role in Godard's *Alphaville*—but, despite his hefty presence and that great granite face, he isn't enough of an actor to carry off what he's given to do.)

The joke about Harold's classlessness is that the movie has him stand in for British stick-to-it-ive-ness—he's a sort of hoodlum Winston Churchill. And then he loses the war. The film's most unusual twist turns out to be a political one: The *real* threat in this story is the IRA. They terrify even the cops and the city councilors: "Those boyos don't know the rules," Parky, Shand's top contact on the force, tells Harold. (Dave King is terrific in this role.) The England of *The Long Good Friday*, Harold Shand's England, is falling apart despite every effort of tough-sounding jingoists to hold it together. In the end, all of Shand's guns and paid flunkies are as useless as the slogans and nostalgia in John Osborne's *The Entertainer*, a portrait of Britain in an earlier epoch; the decay continues. As cruel as a Harold Pinter "comedy of menace" and considerably more fun, *The Long Good Friday* provides an insider's view of a country on the wane.

May 1982

Goodbye to Cruelty

• • •

In his youth, the amazing Italian director Marco Bellocchio was a satirist. His first film, *Fists in the Pocket*, made while he was still in his twenties, featured the *bourgeoisie* as a race of lustful, murderous monsters. The appalling family he depicted bore resemblance to characters in Cocteau and Buñuel, but perhaps they were too outrageous to appeal to even an art-house audience: When the most pernicious of them, the incestuous Alessandro (Lou Castel), began to kill off the others, a viewer could begin to see the validity in this Swiftian solution to the problem of the middle class. In *The Eyes, the Mouth*, Bellocchio no longer sees his characters as monsters, but rather as life-embracers, their peculiarities and madnesses signposts on the road to survival.

That road literally leads away from the grave. The movie begins with the gathering of three generations of a family after one of the sons, Pippo, has committed suicide. His mother (Emmanuèle Riva) has been told his death was an accident, and her brother (Michel Piccoli) and her two surviving sons (Lou Castel and Antonio Piovanelli)—one a bachelor, the other a widower with three children of his own—plan to keep her from discovering the truth. To that end, they urge Pippo's fiancée Vanda (Angela Molina), who's carrying his child, to appear at both the memorial service and the funeral breakfast, and to behave in a "normal" fashion throughout. But she's distraught and uncontrollable—even when her greedy, socially ambitious father coaxes her to calm down, convinced that with a little effort she can redeem her losses and gain access to Pippo's wealthy family through the unwed Giovanni (Castel). Vanda and Giovanni do in fact become lovers, but their relationship is far from the crass business transaction her father's schemes point to; the romance has the beauty of a found connection between two fiercely eccentric individuals.

The title refers to a prank Giovanni and Pippo enjoyed playing as teenagers to entertain the neighborhood girls. They used to dive into the water, shutting themselves off and flirting with death

("We'd close our eyes, our mouths"); now, Giovanni realizes, "That's no way to impress a girl." *The Eyes, the Mouth* (which Bellochio co-wrote with Vincenzo Cerami) is about how you keep yourself from plunging so deep into despair that you can't come up again—how you keep breathing. According to Giovanni, the promise of a home and family represented for unhappy Pippo the end of all his suffering. However (though we don't know exactly what precipitated his suicide), presumably at some point Pippo no longer had faith in the possibility of *that* solution. Giovanni grew up close to his brother, and identifies with him strongly enough to fantasize lying in his coffin, to make love to his girl, and even—in the movie's most extraordinary scene—to masquerade as his ghost and visit their grieving mother. In the world of the film, this identification is seen as a positive step: Giovanni, an actor by profession, "doubles" for Pippo in an effort to bring the carelessly abandoned threads of Pippo's life to some sort of completion, and in doing so to affirm his own survival.

For Bellocchio it doesn't matter how neurotic you are (*everyone* in the movie is, to a greater or lesser degree—with the possible exception of the Michel Piccoli character), as long as your neuroticism allows you a means of reaching for dry land, of keeping your eyes and mouth open. Vanda—played by the magnificent Angela Molina as a young Anna Magnani might have played her—hurls herself from room to room, screams and struggles with her father, refuses to abide by the rules of social convention. And her total immersion in love, over and over again, continues to bring her heartbreak. But she can tell Giovanni "I won't kill myself," and mean it; crazily overcommitted to life, she's actually out of danger.

For Giovanni, survival is all tied up with acting. He was a sixties renegade who became a movie star for a brief period because his fugitive looks and uncompromising attitude spoke articulately to an audience of his peers. "They needed an angry, antisocial type," he tells Vanda after she's seen him act for the first time—in *Fists in the Pocket*, showing at a local repertory theater. (Bellocchio's use of his own debut film may be the most overt, and the most suggestive, example of self-reflexive moviemaking since Erich von Stroheim and Gloria Swanson, in *Sunset Boulevard*, watched a scene from a film he'd directed her in two decades earlier.) "But I haven't changed," Giovanni continues. "I'm dated. Your generation doesn't know I exist." With his unfashionable long hair, Lou Castel (who gives a superb performance) looks like a young rebel who never grew out of that phase. His refusal to play dead for hack directors—his insistence on retaining his integrity as an actor—has cost him dearly, and even his uncle is weary of his obstinately unseemly "clownish" behavior: "Enough of fists in the pocket," he castigates him. We understand, however, that Giovanni's apologia for his wrecked career ("Even in the tackiest, the dumbest films I always tried to convey something—a detail, a joke—so I wouldn't be canceled out, so I would exist") is the cry of the creative artist in the wilderness (that is, in the industry), the cry of a young Marlon Brando. And not only is it Giovanni's means of staying alive, but it also allows him to reach out to others. While his uptight, celibate brother frets about his children, Giovanni plays wild, preposterous games with them, swinging them through the halls of the mourning household on rugs; he's not afraid to act the fool in order to enchant them. (Or to strip, in the fireplace of Vanda's apartment, and crawl along the floor.) His actor's freedom and inventiveness culminate in his greatest role—as his brother's ghost, bringing solace to his damaged, anxious mother. Vanda calls the scene from *Fists in the Pocket* in which the protagonist pushes his mother into a ravine "too cruel." Giovanni's final performance in *The Eyes, the Mouth* turns cruelty to pity.

February 1985

American Tales

• • •

David Byrne's voice is light and airless; it seems to be floating, yet there's no lift in it. And he tells offhand jokes with so little inflection that you always catch them on the rebound. When he sings in *Stop Making Sense* he's a star; when he speaks in *True Stories*, which he co-wrote (with Beth Henley and Stephen Tobolowsky) and scored and directed, he's—deliberately—less than a presence. We hear his dry, detached voice-over as he shows us slides of Texas's history and prehistory (they include a shot of Raquel Welch in *One Million B.C.* and other small amusements); then he appears in front of the screen, steps through it, and assumes the role of our tour guide through mythical Virgil, Texas, where the citizens are celebrating the state's 150th anniversary with a "celebration of specialness." Garbed in a variety of archetypal Texan costumes that look as flamboyant on his slender, geometric frame as the "big suit" he wore for the "Swamp" number in *Stop Making Sense*, he glides down the highway in a grape-colored Chrysler, introducing us to the inhabitants of Virgil—all-American straight arrows with (it turns out) eccentric curls at the edges.

Byrne's wry, paper-thin line readings and the smalltime blackout-sketch style of the first few segments (involving the workers at Virgil's center, the Varicorp computer factory) couldn't sustain a movie by themselves, especially since the dialogue really isn't as witty as it could be. So if that was all there were to *True Stories*, the film would be nothing but a doodle pumped up to two hours. The immensity and purity of the film's visual conception, which Byrne worked out with his gifted photographer, Ed Lachman, supply a context for watching these people. The reviewers who've objected to Byrne's attitude toward Virgil and its citizens as condescending and disdainful can't have been paying attention to the breathtaking landscapes—the skies, at various times during the picture, seem to have been painted by Wyeth (monolithic blue), Maxfield Parrish (mauve, with white–orange clouds), and Van Gogh (a cloud like a comet spun across a morning azure)—or to the muted, shivering ambers and crimsons of traffic lights and neon in the nighttime streets of Byrne's invented city. And they can't have been watching the tiny, incidental moments between the sketches and the musical numbers. A man stands on a stage that's being erected for the variety show at the climax of the celebration (it looks like a 3-D platform supported, impossibly, by scaffolding) and sings opera *a cappella*. Another, glimpsed through the window of a skyscraper, executes a slippery, jagged little dance that could be a tribute to Vernel Bagneris's mournful ballet in *Pennies from Heaven*.

The sketches themselves are of variable quality. The best ones involve John Goodman as Louis Fyne ("The Dancing Bear"), a burly fellow with a hyperbolic fashion sense and a self-presentational style who goes to humorous lengths in his search for a wife; Jo Harvey Allen, as The Lying Woman, whose whoppers, delivered with sober confidence, become more elaborate and more audacious as the movie goes on; and Alix Elias (she was the cheerful, itinerant truckers' prostitute in Jonathan Demme's *Citizens Band*) as The Cute Woman, whose pink-and-blue print dress matches the cushions on her davenport, and who reminds Louis, her face delicately strained with worry, that "there can't be enough sweetness in the world."

Swoosie Kurtz plays The Laziest Woman in the World, who lives in bed, switching the channels on her TV and glancing at magazines on an automatic page turner while a feeding machine proffers one spoonful of dessert at a time. The joke is that her thirties-style satin bedclothes are always fresh, and she's always impeccably, glamorously dressed. But it's a very little joke, and, despite Kurtz's expansive charm, this is one running gag that must have looked better on paper. If you've seen Kurtz's inspired performance as Bananas O'Shaughnessy in the New York revival of *The House of Blue Leaves*, you feel a little cheated when you see how Byrne uses her in this movie. Still, she has one moment that makes you grin: When she catches Louis on television, urging interested young ladies to call 844-WIFE, she presses a button and her upper bed lifts toward the set as if she were on a magic carpet. (She *really* sits up and takes notice.)

Matthew Posey makes a promising appearance as a computer executive, but his two brief scenes are even more drastically underwritten than the rest of the film. The monologist Spalding Gray has the worst sequence: As a Varicorp chief, he delivers a business lecture at the dinner table, illustrating his points with canapés and vegetables. Part of the problem here is Gray himself, whose style—ironic intensity—is so much more patented than everyone else's that he comes across like a plastic flower in this garden of living curiosities.

True Stories is a new kind of musical, or more accurately a contemporary variation on the musical revues produced in New York in the twenties and thirties. The most famous ones were sleek, art-deco urban entertainments with self-contained numbers and often parodic, occasionally satirical, skits interspersed among them. Byrne employs a similar structure, but the urban settings (like the shopping mall—a sequence filmed in Dallas's North Park Center—and the rock and salsa clubs) are mixed in with rural elements (fields, highways, country roads) to produce a contemporary down-home esthetic. And the numbers are genuine originals: videos conceived in cinematic terms. There are eight of them, and except for a political–evangelical song called "Puzzling Evidence" (performed by John Ingle), which is as inconclusive as its title indicates, they're so delightful that you find yourself revving up from the moment the music starts. (The nonvocal music, stretching between numbers, manages to be both eerie and quaint.)

"Dream Operator" is the theme song for the wildest fashion show ever put on film (most of the clothes are organic—they have plants and grass sprouting all over them); Annie McEnroe plays the moderator, a fastidiously coiffed and outfitted suburban woman who gets carried away by the beat. Pops Staples, in a wonderful cameo as a benevolent witch doctor The Dancing Bear consults for assistance with his love troubles, leads the "Papa Legba" number, which includes a nifty, inventive segment spotlighting shadow puppets. Talking Heads lend their voices as well as their instruments to these musical interludes, and they star in one, "Love for Sale" (a comment on Louis's quest for a mate), where they get dipped in chocolate and wrapped in gold foil.

Both the first number, "Wild, Wild Life," and Louis Fyne's performance at the variety show, "People Like Us," near the end, are like smaller-scale chunks of Robert Altman's comic folk epic, *Nashville*. In "Wild, Wild Life," Virgil's best take the microphone at a nightclub, one at a time, to lip-sync the words to the Heads song; the overall effect is a four-minute musical embodiment of one of *Nashville's* themes—that the boundaries between stardom and anonymity are more easily crossed than we might guess. "People Like Us," with its strenuously apolitical–populist lyric, is close kin to Keith Carradine's "It Don't Worry Me," which Barbara Harris performs in the last minutes of *Nashville*. The similarities with the earlier picture (including Byrne's way of turning up the same characters over and over again, in different settings and different combinations) are obviously no accident, especially in a movie in which Altman's frequent associate Allan Nicholls (who was in the rock trio in *Nashville*) served as executive in charge of production; and there's a note of thanks to Joan Tewkesbury, *Nashville's* screenwriter, in the end credits.

But when you start thinking about Altman's idiosyncratic vision of America, now more than a decade old, you recognize the limits of David Byrne's. Byrne's style is to shy away from emotional commitment, and it's partly his playful irony that gives *True Stories* its distinct flavor—but it prevents the movie from taking hold of you completely. It's a charming musical comedy, and Byrne and Ed Lachman achieve something extraordinary in the quiet, open-air images. When he tells you at the end that it's only by first noticing all the details of a new place, and then forgetting them completely, that you can see it as it really is, you've been shown enough evidence to realize that he knows what he's talking about, and that his perspective is fresh and welcome (God knows) in American movies. But if he's going to be a first-rank filmmaker, he'll have to relinquish some of the detachment that's so precious to him.

November 1986

Removing the Obstacles Between Audience and Character

• • •

The Brazilian moviemaker Suzana Amaral has released dozens of short films and documentaries, but *Hour of the Star* is her first feature, and it's a small miracle. Based on a novel by Claire Lispector, the movie is about the emotional awakening of Macabéa (Marcelia Cartaxo), a nineteen-year-old country orphan who comes to São Paulo and finds work as a typist, lodgings in a tiny, squalid room that she shares with three other young women, and, everywhere she looks, mysteries she can't seem to penetrate. Macabéa doesn't have anything going for her. Her face is homely—puffy and flat at the same time, as though someone had started out with Isabelle Huppert's or that of one of the baby-doll heroines in French films of the thirties and then drained the transformative sensual glow out of it. She's slobby and slow: Only her boss's pitying good nature keeps her from losing the sub–minimum-wage office job she pecks away at dully and deliberately. Apologetic and obedient, she stumbles through the world, comprehending almost nothing she sees or hears; sheltered, unschooled, and accustomed to poverty, she possesses so little basic information that it's startling.

There are few enough movies about the unexceptional struggles of ordinary folk, and they're almost always inadequate or, more likely, wrong-headed. American directors tend to either condescend to these characters or ennoble them (the classic example, John Ford's *The Grapes of Wrath*, does both), and when European filmmakers make an attempt, the result is usually something earnest and plodding, like *A Special Day*. The rare ones we remember are filtered through a highly original sensibility (the Taviani brothers' movies) or informed by a shocking vision of the world (Buñuel's *Los Olvidados*) or illuminated by a beauty of craft so all-encompassing that it disappears—paradoxically—inside the movie (Renoir's *A Day in the Country* or the masterpieces of De Sica). So far, Amaral's craft is still fairly elementary. You can see her setting up the plot, leading us too schematically to Macabéa's discovery of her own needs and desires, and when she moves away from Macabéa's point of view near the end of the picture, the shift is clumsy and jarring. But she does something more important that justifies the comparison to De Sica or Renoir: *Hour of the Star* has the emotional clarity of great art. Somehow Amaral and her leading actress, Marcelia Cartaxo, manage to remove all the usual obstacles between the audience and the character, so that we have direct access to Macabéa's feelings. And every action she takes, every object she picks up, becomes suffused with those feelings.

Macabéa's emergence from her rural Catholic sleep (which is depicted here as a kind of sensory deprivation) is gradual and full of painful shocks. After overhearing one of her employers saying she's a hag, she stares in the dirt-streaked office mirror and then in the tiny, dark looking glass in her room, touching her face tentatively to see whether the remark can be true. She dresses under the covers, as the aunt who brought her up taught her to do, until her roommates balk at her modesty. The thought of sex doesn't seem to enter her head until a fellow worker, Gloria (Tamara Taxman), who's pregnant by her married boy friend, begins to question her about her sexual experience, and counsel her on ways to build up her body to attract men. Then, as if a wall had been torn down, Macabéa starts to notice men in the street, in restaurants, in the subway. Out by herself on a Sunday, she flirts like a high-school girl with strangers whose interest in her is purely her own imagination; sandwiched between the armpits of two strangers in short-sleeved shirts on the train, she experiences their masculine odor as something inexpressibly heady and potent that she's never encountered before. That night she masturbates in bed, pulling her bedclothes up to her chest after her orgasm in a touching, maidenly way and making the sign of the cross.

There's an amazing scene in which Macabéa, having followed Gloria's example by taking a private holiday from work, celebrates her freedom by dancing in her slip to the "Blue Danube Waltz" played on her little transistor radio (a gift from one of her roommates) with a sheet wrapped around her shoulders like a cape. Then she stops before the mirror and holds the sheet to her head like a wedding veil. *Hour of the Star* is about the birth of romantic desire in a woman for whom romance is beyond the borders of possibility.

When she does meet a man who looks twice at her, he's moody and small-minded and ungenerous. Olimpico (José Dumont), who's a steel worker, acts aghast at Macabéa's dearth of knowledge, but in truth he knows almost as little as she does: When she asks him questions, he just covers up his ignorance with disparaging, repressed responses like "That's for faggots" and "Girls who ask such things end up in whorehouses." Because of the way Amaral and Cartaxo work, Olimpico's treatment of Macabéa, who isn't sophisticated enough to protect herself against his insults, both infuriates us (we're indignant for Macabéa, whose sensitivities haven't evolved as far as indignation) and wounds us (because we can feel what she feels).

Macabéa's questions originate in the bits of information she's picked up on "Time Radio," which she listens to religiously, recording them on a pad so she can bring them up at lulls in the conversation with Olimpico (which is almost *all* lulls). It's as if she'd discovered the empty places in her heart and her head at the same time; she moves through the world now with purpose, trying to cram it into the gaps inside her. And when this unhappy little man, whose way of dealing with his own bewilderment at the world is to close himself off from it, drops her unceremoniously (he tells her he's found a girl, as if she'd never counted as one), she munches aspirins, trying to cure her headache and her heartache together.

You don't want to make too big a fuss over a movie as small and unassuming as this one. The friend I saw it with identified Amaral's problem as a sensibility that's far in advance of her technique. But somehow I wasn't bothered by her inadequacies; I kept thinking of all the superlative technicians (like Amaral's classmate at N.Y.U., Jim Jarmusch) who haven't come up with anything worth making movies about, and all the pictures I've sat through, week after week, that couldn't provide a single moment of honest emotion. At its best, *Hour of the Star* is so pure that it pops open, in a series of epiphanies: Macabéa standing with a flower in her hand, her head tipped to one side, her eyes dreamy and half-closed, transfixed by a bridal dress on a shop-window mannequin; Macabéa weeping silently as a tenor sings "Una furtiva lacrima" on the radio; Macabéa so distraught by the loss of her beau that she stuffs food into her mouth until she's sick, her face frozen in a humiliated smile as she watches Gloria make immediate sexual contact with a stranger across the table. By the end, when the film switches from pathos to tragicomedy, from naturalism to magic realism, Amaral's technical limitations seem to be beside the point—the movie has blossomed past them.

April 1987

Decorum
• • •

A friend whose mother died a few years ago has an anecdote about a neighbor who came to pay her respects after the funeral: Pumping the arm of one of the mourners, the neighbor blurted out "Sorry about that!" The point of the story is that the visitor's blunder provided a burst of comic relief—and also (though I'm not sure my friend saw it this way) that on such a solemn occasion, a ritual that ill fits the messy emotions associated with death, people can always be counted on to behave inappropriately.

That's the theme of *The Funeral*, the Juzo Itami comedy—his first picture—that's found distribution here thanks to the success of his second, *Tampopo*. For the first two-thirds the movie is like a Kaufman and Hart farce done in Robert Altman free-style, with Buñuel touches. A man (Koen Okumura) dies of a heart attack in the countryside outside Tokyo. His widow (Kin Sugai) decrees that the funeral should be held there, so it's up to her daughter and son-in-law (Nobuko Miyamoto and Tsutomu Yamazaki, the ramen queen and king of *Tampopo*), who own the country house, to supervise the event. We see the family viewing the body for the first time, dealing with the undertaker (an obsequious fellow in shades and a beret, probably meant to suggest a movie director, played by Neko-hachi Edoya), ordering food for the wake, handling hysterical guests, guests drunk on sake, guests who make scenes or overstay their welcome. There's even a moment that parallels my friend's tale: An aging man, a croquet buddy of the deceased, who bows to the family on his way out of the wake and assures them, "It really was a great tragedy," as though he were complimenting a meal.

The hosts of the funeral, Wabisuke and Chizuko, are actors— as are Itami, a film performer for twenty-five years, and Miyamoto, his real-life wife. (Itami got the idea for the picture when Miyamoto's father died and Itami found himself in Wabisuke's position.) When the news arrives of the old man's demise, they're filming a commercial in which Chizuko plays a geisha serving Wabisuke sake, while half a dozen Japanese men in suits and ties watch them on a monitor and laugh in amusement at the quaint, antiquated scene. Chizuko is still in costume when she receives the phone call; then we see her spin out of her kimono, with the help of a dresser, and reappear in slacks, smoking a cigarette. Itami wants us to see that the rituals surrounding the funeral belong to an earlier, more formalized time, and that for contemporary Japanese to put them on requires performance skills, skills that are particularly hard to summon up when you find yourself with an unexpected case of stage fright. (Though Wabisuke acts professionally, he gets so nervous in anticipation of the speech he's supposed to make after the cremation that his leg can't stop shaking.)

Itami gets a lot of comic mileage out of his idea of a funeral as a type of performance. There's a hilarious scene in which Chizuko and Wabisuke study a video called *The ABC's of Funerals* to learn how to comport themselves the next day, and another in which the psychiatrist next door (Masahiko Tsugawa), who called the ambulance on the night of his neighbor's attack, comes by with his wife (Michiyo Yokoyama) to exchange sober, well-worn banalities about his dilemma over which hospital to call. And Wabisuke's friend Aoki (Takashi Tsumura) roams around during the funeral preparations, capturing everything in a home movie. When we see the final product, we notice that everyone's smiling through it—we might be watching a birthday party or a summer-camp romp played back on eight millimeter. What makes it affecting is the combination of the silence and the feeling of people caught between their natural impulses and their straining to rise to an official occasion.

The film is overlong, and some of the sequences misfire due to clumsy staging or bad timing. (An interlude between Wabisuke and his flighty mistress, played by Haruna Takase, seems interminable.) As *Tampopo* shows, Itami isn't a farceur as much as a parodist, and in *The Funeral* he hasn't yet tapped the cuckoo extravagance that makes the later film such a deluxe treat; he keeps getting tripped up by his lack of invention. (Three sequences shot from the point of view of the corpse are at least one too many.) In the last third, however, the farce turns melancholy, as the members of the family begin to liberate their feelings of loss. This is Ozu territory, and Itami brings in Ozu's favorite actor, Chishu Ryu, to play the priest—the movie's representative of the Japanese traditions Ozu always examined in his pictures. It's an ambitious direction for Itami to take, and it doesn't quite seem to work until, perhaps ten minutes from the end, the widow, replacing her son-in-law, makes an extemporaneous speech in tribute to her husband at the crema- tion luncheon. (Kin Sugai is terrific in this scene.) What we respond to here may be as much Itami's intention as his achievement, but the poignancy of the characters' managing to break through the boundaries of the funeral—or to use them to find a passage into their own emotions—is what you take away from the movie.

November 1987

Mood Piece

• • •

Marilynne Robinson's 1981 novel *Housekeeping* is a very odd coming-of-age story. The first-person narrator, Ruthie, remembers her childhood in Fingerbone, a small town in Washington State: her last glimpses of her mother (her father had left long ago), who deposited her and her younger sister Lucille with their grandmother and then committed suicide; the seven years before the grandmother's death; the few months when two old maiden great-aunts moved into the house, fretting themselves nearly into apoplexy over their charges. These early episodes have a musty, Edwardian quality—they're reminiscent of the domestic growing-up tales you may have dug out of the library as a child, like *Five Little Peppers and How They Grew* or *Mrs. Wiggs of the Cabbage Patch*— but they're pleasantly rendered in Robinson's cozy, seamless prose. You don't know what the author is up to until the two spinsters are replaced by the girls' aunt, Sylvie Fisher, an indigent who agrees to settle down in Fingerbone for a while and take care of the kids.

Sylvie is an unsettling presence in the house; her adolescent charges are charmed and fascinated by her eccentricities, but her previous lifestyle and her habit of wandering out at unusual hours exacerbate their fears of being abandoned once more. Eventually she serves as a catalyst for their emerging personalities: Lucille, more conventional and yielding to social pressure, becomes embarrassed by Sylvie, rebels against her want of authority, and finally adopts another guardian, while Ruthie, who has never craved company outside the family (she's awkward and shy with other teenagers), grows more and more like Sylvie. It's really Ruthie's story, the story of a girl who discovers what she is (Sylvie) and what she's not (Lucille). The problem is that Sylvie isn't as appealing to us as she is to Ruthie (and, obviously, to Robinson). Unruffled, slightly addled, with a faraway gaze, she's more of an absence than a presence, yet there she is at the center of Robinson's novel, and the revelation that Ruthie is her kindred spirit doubles the vacuum. At this point, the dippy domestic feminism that's been the book's most irritating characteristic moves aside to make room for a crack-brained vagrant romanticism that *really* tries a reader's patience. And the prose spreads like honey to fill in the cracks: "Anyone that leans to look into a pool is the woman in the pool, anyone who looks into our eyes is the image in our eyes, and these things are true without argument, and so our thoughts reflect what passes before them." What, no "dear reader"? You feel the need to wash the stickiness off your hands when you finish reading.

I've dwelled so long on the book because I think it's central to an understanding of what's wrong with writer–director Bill Forsyth's movie version. It's a beautiful film, probably the best anyone could have made of a novel that's conceptually so dreadful. Ruthie's voice-over narration basically comes from the book, but Forsyth has drained the preciousness out of the writing, as well as sharpened the focus and buried the cockeyed feminism. But he can't get rid of the idea of dreamy Sylvie as a free spirit; or repopulate the thinned-out landscape of the story (since that's the point: It's Ruthie's sufficiency unto herself, and Lucille's need for others, that break them apart—and Robinson strands us, along with Ruthie and Sylvie, in that house). You may wonder what drew the wry, dry-eyed Scot Forsyth to this material in the first place. Very early in the picture, though, you're grateful that if someone *had* to bring the novel to the screen, it turned out to be a filmmaker of his remarkable, off-center gifts for getting tones and moods no one else can come close to.

In the opening scenes Helen (Margot Pindivic), the girls' mother, holds her arms akimbo and smiles mysteriously, as if hinting that she's holding onto a wonderful secret. When she drives her car into the lake, Forsyth keeps his camera at a distance, giving the scene a serene, sealed quality, like a Vermeer. Working in America for the first time (and shooting in breathtaking Nelson, British Columbia, where *Roxanne* was also filmed), he's been fitted with a new cinematographer, Michael Coulter, and a new composer, Michael Gibbs—but the movie is such an assured, subtly crafted mood piece that it's hard to believe they all just became collaborators. There's a marvelously understated sequence at the funeral reception where the grandmother's elderly friends and relatives attempt to entertain the silent orphans, whose eyes hover uncertainly on the outskirts of a situation they can't comprehend. And the early scenes with Sylvie (Christine Lahti), in which the girls, panicked at every step she takes toward the door, try to latch onto her distant, informal style, have a displaced, delayed humor. (You always laugh a moment too late.) When the spring floods come to Fingerbone, the girls tiptoe downstairs one morning to find Sylvie wading through the ankle-deep water, undisturbed, waving cheerily at them and tossing her cold coffee remains into the pond at her feet as if it had always been there; a rat floats by on a log. It's a little like the "Pool of Tears" chapter in *Alice in Wonderland*, with the hysteria of the swimming creatures flattened out of it.

Forsyth's eye for casting is as acute as ever. With scarcely a line to say, Georgie Collins, as the grandmother, conveys both the aristocratic reserve that has kept her daughters at a remove from her and the chasm of grief underneath it. Anne Pitoniak and Barbara Reese, as the worry-wart aunts, talk in fragments and finish each other's thoughts, like an old folks' vaudeville team. And the girls are perfect. Leah Perry, who plays Lucille as a child, has a porcelain-doll face with a purse-clasp mouth and a nose that seems to have been stuck on by accident; she grows into Andrea Burchill, whose face, with its traces of teenage hauteur, is almost glamorous around the obstacle of that upturned nose, and whose clear, expressive eyes always show an edge of anxiety. (It's matched by the edge of disapproval in her voice when she begins to feel cornered by Sylvie's presence.) As Ruthie, Tonya Tanner has a more reflective, cautious face; her teen counterpart, Sara Walker, is tall and gawky, with long stick arms and stick legs, and the more conscious she grows of their length, the more she draws attention to them by grasping her elbows or bending at the neck like a broken swan and staring at the ground. Yet she has a tomboy delicacy. In one scene, she polkas merrily and un-self-consciously with Sylvie while Lucille stares out the window. (Forsyth, typically, doesn't stress it, but this is an emblematic moment, delineating the approaching separation between the girls.) Later, running away from a group of schoolmates who make her uncomfortable, Walker's Ruthie pads through the street without making a sound.

The girls give terrific performances—especially Walker, who has the greater range of emotions to convey. Christine Lahti doesn't, but it isn't her fault, or Forsyth's; it's Marilynne Robinson's. Who could play this drably flighty character and make you care what happens to her? Lahti is a fine actress who has created luminous characters in *The Executioner's Song, Swing Shift,* and even the desperately mediocre *Just Between Friends*; I assume Forsyth cast her because he hoped she'd vivify Sylvie and provide a force at the center of the movie. But though Lahti is warm and empathic, and her line readings are fresh, full of sprung rhythms, she doesn't work on the role—*it* works on *her,* fuzzing up those wonderful sharp lines in her personality and making her seem a little mushy-headed.

Forsyth is so amazing at charting the tiny but significant shifts in the girls' attitudes, and the expanding gap between their temperaments, that you keep hoping the movie will turn into *The Member of the Wedding.* It can't, though, because where Carson McCullers's heroine, Frankie Addams, was the portrait of a poet as a young woman, *Housekeeping* is the portait of a young hobo, and—good as Sara Walker is—Ruthie inevitably becomes less compelling as she starts turning into Sylvie.

The picture is tenderly observed, though, and it has scenes of unstressed splendor—like one where the girls, playing hooky from school, trek through the forest, smoking branches and singing "Oh, My Papa"; and Ruthie's first view of the woodlands on the other side of the lake, its frosted greens as exotic as a sudden glimpse of another planet. The best scenes, like these, are drenched in melancholy, much as Forsyth's *Comfort and Joy* was—though the two movies aren't comparable in any other way. In both cases, though you can see what the *intended* source of the sorrow is (Bill Paterson's destroyed love affair in *Comfort and Joy,* the mother's suicide in *Housekeeping*), you sense it comes from something much deeper and more concealed.

In the most memorable scene, Sylvie and Ruthie row out over the lake, under the train bridge, in the darkness, and Sylvie hoists herself up so the light of the passing train flickers across her face. Standing on the bow, with the mist bubbling up around her and beads of light shimmering on the surface of the water, she looks (for the first time) as if she were tuned into a magic wavelength that's denied the rest of us. Then she lies back, her arms outstretched, and she and Ruthie sing "Good Night, Irene." This is a scene that leaves you feeling inexpressibly sad. It's also an example of how a great filmmaker can bring so much of himself to a project that he can make something out of nothing.

December 1987

Film and Theatre

• • •

A lain Resnais' *Mélo* (from "mélodrame") is at least the fourth screen treatment of a 1920s boulevard play by Henri Bernstein about a young woman who is driven to self-destruction when she has to choose between her devotion to the man she's married to and her passion for his best friend. (The most famous version, *Dreaming Lips*, was directed by Paul Czinner in 1937 and starred his wife, the German actress Elisabeth Bergner.) No one writes dramas in this style any more, but at one time they were fantastically popular; the twentieth-century equivalent of the well-made plays Scribe and Sardou wrote in the early 1800s, at their best they were marvels of dramatic construction and had a heartbreaking chic delicacy that passed for depth. (They were also very influential: Noël Coward's *Private Lives* and Jean Cocteau's *Les Parents Terribles* both are variations on boulevard melodramas.)

Resnais's decision to return to perhaps the best-known example and remake it more than half a century after playwrights stopped working in this genre suggests either perverseness or a genuine wish to explore the potential in this form for illuminating certain themes. Actually, I think it's both. Resnais is the snow king of filmmakers: An astonishingly graceful technician with a highly developed appreciation for décor but without a sensuous bone in his body, he uses his skills as distancing devices, freezing out the audience, forcing us to respond to his movies esthetically rather than emotionally. But he's up to something in *Mélo*, which is an oddly compelling picture—a museum piece that freely admits that's what it is and then sets out to find its own peculiar resonance; a stage play that proclaims itself a stage play yet insists it can be a movie, too.

Mélo begins in a charmingly antiquated manner. In an old-fashioned theater, a pair of feminine hands flips through a playbill containing the names and faces of the actors, then Resnais focuses on the folds of the thick crimson curtain, which dissolve into the first act. The three central characters—Pierre Belcroix (Pierre Arditi), his wife Romaine (Sabine Azéma), and their dinner guest, Marcel Blanc (André Dussollier)—are seated on a terrace; behind them is a garden, framed by a quaintly arched tree, with a gate and the rear of another house beyond, set against an unnaturally blue nighttime sky, a perfectly round moon, a few decorative stars. It's a stage set, magically idyllic. And in the long first section of the film (roughly one-third), Resnais never exceeds the parameters defined by the proscenium arch; we don't shift perspectives or wander into the kitchen with Romaine when she disposes of the dinner dishes. This is no third-row-center view of the action, however: Restricted by the shape of the stage, Resnais' camera can nonetheless roam through it, exploring its depth in a way that a spectator in the audience wouldn't be able to.

At one point Marcel, who is a famous violinist, tells his friends the story of a woman he loved who betrayed him by flirting openly with a stranger in a concert hall while Marcel bowed helplessly on the stage. Resnais zeroes in on Dussollier's face and holds him in close-up for the entire monologue, which must take a full five minutes, and the effect is startling: We feel the way we do in the theater when the precision of a fine performance draws us in (Dussollier's reading of the speech is remarkable), but here it's the camera, and not just our fascination with the actor, that determines our focus on him.

Resnais is certainly not the first director to bring a movie audience inside a stage play; that was Olivier's famous trick in his *Henry V*, which began as a Globe Theatre performance and transformed itself when the young warrior king sailed for France. And with much less formality that's what the most memorable filmed plays have always accomplished: *Les Parents Terribles, Long Day's Journey into Night, The Member of the Wedding, A Streetcar Named*

Desire, Street Scene, the 1931 version of *The Front Page,* and especially John Frankenheimer's movie of *The Iceman Cometh,* which
never strayed from the back room of Harry Hope's saloon. But Resnais makes you conscious of stage space in a way none of these other
pictures did except *Henry V,* and he *keeps* you conscious of it.

In every new setting (the first act is followed by a series of
much shorter scenes) he plays variations on the same stage/screen
paradox. In a restaurant we see only the three protagonists directly;
everyone else—patrons dancing or drinking, waiters carrying flaming shish kebabs through the aisles—is reflected in a set of mirrors
behind Marcel and Romaine (who have begun their affair) and
drunken Pierre. In Marcel's apartment, when Romaine, distraught
because Marcel's about to go on tour without her, hurls herself on
the rug, everything in the frame—Azéma's lithe flapper's body twisted as eloquently as a ballerina's, the carefully arranged lighting,
the Mondrian-like stained-glass windows behind Dussollier—draws
attention to the theatricality of the scene. (A few minutes later, Resnais quotes *Private Lives:* The lovers sit on the couch, their legs
criss-crossing in the famous scissored position assumed by Noël
Coward and Gertrude Lawrence in the second-act photographs of
the play.)

In a Resnais movie, I usually feel there's nothing to do but admire the decors (Jacques Saulnier was the art director for *Mélo*) and
the costumes (these are by Catherine Leterrier) and the gorgeous
fluidity of the camera (Charlie Van Damme and Gilbert Duhalde
photographed). And there's no denying that in *Mélo* Resnais has
found a context for accentuating all the visual frissons he wants to
concentrate on anyway. In this case, though, he has a point. Romaine's attempt to conform to two sets of respectable conventions—
to be a devoted wife, at Pierre's beck and call when he grows ill,
and to be a devoted mistress, waiting in the wings for Marcel to
return from his concert tours—tears her apart. She drowns herself
in the Seine, and Resnais, for the first and only time, breaks the
boundaries of the stage frame to lead us, along with Romaine, to
the river. In the final scene (three years after her death), Pierre,
about to leave Paris, drops by Marcel's apartment to say goodbye
and ask him if he and Romaine were lovers. (Only in a play of this
type can the cuckolded husband get away with being so stupid for
so long.) Looking around Marcel's apartment, Pierre disdainfully

declares his taste "chic," and the phrase echoes back through the movie; we see the limitations of art—Marcel's, Bernstein's, Resnais's—to express the passion bubbling underneath.

Does Resnais's experiment work? Formally, yes; emotionally, no—except, briefly, during Dussollier's first-act monologue. Sabine Azéma, in the crucial role, doesn't bring it the neurotic passion and the quicksilver shifts of mood it cries out for; you spend the whole performance recasting Romaine in your head. (I came up with three actresses I would love to have seen attempt it: Margaret Sullavan in the thirties, Anna Karina in the sixties, and Blythe Danner in the seventies.) But it's clear that Resnais wants the crisp, highly polished quality of Azéma's acting—that he doesn't want a transcendent actress. Only Resnais, a master of technique and restraint and nothing else, would select a play and a method of shooting it that prove drama and film can't ever get beyond technique and restraint; his conclusions are Q.E.D.

"The cinema calms the spectator, the theater excites him," André Bazin wrote in "Theater and Cinema." Olivier, Cocteau, Frankenheimer, and the other men who directed the most spellbinding stage-to-screen adaptations, used their cameras to *invade* the space behind the proscenium arch, not to *preserve* it, and shattered the calm of the cinema with the excitement of great theater. (Unlike Resnais, of course, they were working from magnificent texts.) Using *his* camera to barricade the borders of the stage, Resnais ends up becalming the play and putting us at an even greater remove than we would be in any theater.

March 1988

Children's Gothic

• • •

There's a musty obsessiveness about Jan Svankmajer's *Alice*, a free-form adaptation of Lewis Carroll's *Alice in Wonderland*. The Czech animator Svankmajer, whose style is a cut-and-paste collage that uses dolls, puppets, found objects and live actors, is a hero of the Quay brothers (one of their short subjects is dedicated to him), but he doesn't reside in the shadowy, Kafkaesque world of their *Street of Crocodiles*; he's creepy in a different—homier—way. Alice is a restless, pouty child who finds it intolerable to be cooped up in her room with only a book and a cup of cold tea for company. (We assume she's been consigned there as a punishment.) She props up a doll with the book in her lap—making it a double for her sister, whom we saw reading to her by the river bank in the opening moments of the film—and tosses pebbles into the tea; the splash they make is the languid sound of childish boredom. Alice drifts into a fantasy that has a nagging, self-abusive quality; it's the kind of story a shut-in child might concoct as a form of rebellion against the surroundings that have begun to eat away at her.

This *Alice* gets going, as Carroll's does, with the appearance of the White Rabbit. In Svankmajer's film, he's a stuffed animal in a glass cage who comes to life, dons a pair of gloves and a dress suit, and smashes his way out of his cell with a pair of scissors, nicking himself in the process. He bleeds sawdust; the watch he pulls out is coated with it. But, pragmatic creature that he is, he pins the hole closed and replenishes his dwindling supply of sawdust by eating a bowlful with a spoon. The field he gambols across, with Alice in close pursuit, is all hard earth and rocks; this is not the rich green terrain of an idyllic childhood. And instead of vanishing down a rabbit hole, he dives into an open drawer in an ancient wooden desk—the kind you associate with Victorian schoolrooms. When Alice gives chase she pricks her finger on a compass and finds, to her dismay, that the desk is littered with discarded geometry instruments and notebooks. Svankmajer's film is full of the debris of childhood: not only desks (which pop up everywhere) and classroom chairs, but also household implements, which clutter the White Rabbit's house, and unidentified cans and jars stacked up on high closet shelves and on the tiers that line the insides of dumbwaiters. There they are, in confused and fascinating abundance, the playthings of kids who spend their idle hours alone, investigating the mysteries of the indoors instead of seeking the company of other children in the sunshine.

Svankmajer's film owes as much to Mary Norton's *Borrowers* books (where diminutive creatures take up residence in the undisturbed corners of houses and build their lives around the bits and pieces they've lifted from the owners) as it does to Lewis Carroll. It has a recluse's resourcefulness and tendency toward inwardness. When Alice peeks through the locked door at the garden she longs to enter, what we see is a tacky, watercolor wing-and-drop stage set of the sea. Floating on the pool of her own tears, she encounters a sailor mouse with a trunk tied to its tail who lands on her head, hammers a handful of sticks into her skull, and cooks a can of soup over a fire started with a few dry locks of her hair. The bottle she drains in order to grow smaller is full of ink, and the jars she opens in the kitchen closet contain unpleasant but oddly compelling surprises—rusty tacks, oily keys, meat that walks away on its own.

This movie is considerably more violent and painful than other film versions of the *Alice* books (though the Muppets in the fantasy sequences of *Dreamchild* are fairly horrifying), but in its nerd's nightmare way it's quite faithful to Carroll's version, which has its own relentlessness and nastiness. And Svankmajer's persistently whining heroine isn't far away from Carroll's, with her litany of "Please, sirs" and her mannerly insolence. (One way of reading the books is to see the impossible creatures Alice meets up with as skewed reflections of her own wilfulness and doggedness: bad-mood Alices.)

Svankmajer has dramatized two early, borderline-masochistic chapters of *Alice in Wonderland* that most filmmakers ignore ("The Pool of Tears" and "The Rabbit Sends in a Little Bill") and given less emphasis to the second half; he's eliminated the Duchess, and the Queen of Hearts appears only once. It can't be said that he's not working off the text, even though, watching *Alice*, you know you don't want to send children to see what he's come up with. (That's especially true of his setting of "The Rabbit Sends in a Little Bill," which offers a crew of skeletal creatures and a climax in which Alice tumbles into a barrel of milk and emerges looking like a bloated, sickly porcelain doll.)

Alice is more intellectually absorbing than it is pleasurable to watch, and it has its share of unexplainable annoyances, such as the inserted close-ups of Alice's mouth whenever she adds a phrase like "said the White Rabbit" to the dialogue. (At times you can see her saliva and the stains on her teeth. And you can't be sure it's the same actress who plays Alice in the rest of the film; the figure in the close-ups seems redder and poutier, though it's not clear why Svankmajer would want to use a second child.)

An hour and a half may be half an hour too long for what Svankmajer is trying to accomplish; the movie begins to wear down around the Mad Tea Party (the dreariest sequence). And there's an unmistakable dullness at the center of the film. But *Alice* is *about* dullness, the dullness children are likely to find in themselves after long hours of solitude; it's about an irritated child's visions of home, school, and play. When Alice shrinks she turns into an expressionless poppet, with wide black eyes and synthetic hair; this might be the fate she's afraid she deserves, or even the way she sees herself when she feels at the end of her rope. And after the extended flamingo-croquet game, when the White Rabbit rushes around with his scissors, beheading cards at the Queen of Hearts's bidding, the movie builds to a moment of triumphant chaos. Svankmajer makes the Queen's court a parody of a classroom, where Alice is required to read her confession out of an exercise book. But she rebels: She shoves all the tarts in her mouth, scandalizing the jury, and stands up to her tormentors and dismisses them. Then she filches the White Rabbit's scissors and cuts off *his* head—to pay him back for leading her into a world where the creatures are just as infuriating as any adult.

December 1988

Barbie and Kens

• • •

Karen Carpenter died in 1983, at the age of thirty-two, from an overdose of ipecac, one of the two substances she took at various times in her life (the other was Ex-Lax) as a way of keeping her weight down. It was a grotesque death—but then, there'd *always* been something grotesque about Karen Carpenter. Her voice had a peculiarly toneless smoothness and sweetness; you got the feeling someone had surgically removed all traces of emotion and sexuality from it like tumors. And you'd think Americans would have had to perform the same kind of surgery on their brains to look around at this country in the seventies, peer through the Vietnam carnage *and* the White House carnage, and hear the music of Richard and Karen Carpenter, like some Pied Piper's, luring them away from it all. (The duo reached their greatest popularity in 1973–74.) The Carpenters remain an unsettling emblem of the move from the hippie culture to the culture of narcissism, where the focus of individual Americans turned sharply (and, so far, irrevocably) inward. It's creepily apt that Karen Carpenter died of a disease—anorexia nervosa—that's defined by its skewed perception of outward appearances. It's the physical manifestation of a distortion by a mind that can't look outside itself for confirmation.

In the short film *Superstar: The Karen Carpenter Story*, Todd Haynes uses Barbie and Ken dolls to dramatize the horrifying tale of Karen's demise. Haynes's point is obvious: The prepackaged wholesomeness of The Carpenters was basically an invention of consumer experts who anticipated that Americans would be looking for an alternative to hard rock, with its allusions to drugs, Vietnam, and the assassinations. And from the movie's feminist perspective, the rigorous demands of the pop culture Karen was enslaved to (as well as the misplaced attentions of an overprotective mother, a kind of Harriet Nelson or Margaret Anderson monster) forced her to flush out her own identity—i.e, her own body—and conform to a model of bland Barbie-doll perfection.

What's surprising about *Superstar* is how effective Haynes's technique turns out to be. The washed-out photography and the messed-up, decaying sets are like a nightmare miniature of southern California. And the off-screen voices matched to unmoving mouths and the clunky-gliding movement of the dolls underscores the way the culture manipulates everyone—even the people who manipulate Karen's life, like her mother (who won't let her move away from home) or her producers. Haynes has come up with a theatrical device for getting at Carpenter's story that resonates on more than one level. When you hear Herb Alpert, the president of A & M Records, lecturing Karen and Richard on the new appeal of "young and fresh" media figures, his demonic tones flash back to the dummy that takes over Michael Redgrave's personality in *Dead of Night*; when the Karen doll suddenly starts coughing during the "Close to You" recording session and then swears in exasperation, the moment is Brechtian.

The pop-cultural material in the film generally works better than the feminist text, which is rather heavy-handed, but Haynes, a confident ironist, scores points on both fronts. He juxtaposes "Rainy Days and Mondays" with the moment when, just before a concert, Richard has to rouse Karen from a lethargy brought on by too many laxatives. And there's a chillingly funny bit where, following an explanation by a female voice-over narrator of how anorexia restores young women to a prepubescent state, and abstaining from food produces a state of natural intoxication, we hear Karen singing, in that airbrushed voice, that she's on top of the world. At times during the film you can't imagine a better metaphor for southern California during the Me Decade than Ken and Barbie dolls: When Karen sees her husband-to-be for the first time across a restaurant, she mistakes him for her brother. All Kens look the same.

February 1989

Brecht and Freud

• • •

There are songs to sing. There are feelings to feel. There are
thoughts to think. That makes three things. And you can't do
three things at the same time. The singing is easy. Syrup in
my mouth. The thinking comes with the tune—so that leaves
only the feelings. Am I right? Or am I right? I can sing the
singing. I can think the thinking. But you're not going to
catch me feeling the feeling. No, sir.
—Philip Marlow in *The Singing Detective*

Film and television are so easily the province of naturalists that
screenwriters and directors whose response to the world is
framed in nonrealistic modes always seem a bit weird to us; we tend
to squint, puzzle, scrunch up our faces, and wonder if we're missing
something. So anyone who works against the realistic grain has to
be especially courageous, because he or she is bound to be misunder-
stood. For some artists, however, there seems never to have been a
choice. Martin Scorsese is a born expressionist, and so is the Spanish
writer–director Pedro Almodóvar; David Lynch is as instinctual a
surrealist as Luis Buñuel was. And the English writer Dennis Potter
is, of all things, a natural Brechtian.

Clearly this claim needs some explanation. Since Brechtian, or
"epic," theater is by its nature highly self-conscious (as *evolved* as
art can possibly be), the phrase "natural Brechtian" is something of
a paradox. Moreover, we tend to associate Brecht solely with agit-
prop drama, which Potter has no interest in. Brecht's famous (and
famously mistranslated) "alienation effect," a technique that piles
on songs, music-hall patter, narration, direct address to the audience, and strips of expressionistic drama, collage-style, aims to keep

an audience on its guard, on the prickly edge of surrender to the narcotizing lull of fiction, continually aware of the tricks and mechanisms of theater. He wants to dazzle us with the sunlight of constant (political) revelation, and for that he needs us to be fully conscious all the time.

But Potter, author of the musical *Pennies from Heaven* (first a 1979 BBC serial starring Bob Hoskins; two years later an M-G-M movie with Steve Martin in the lead), the 1985 fantasy *Dreamchild*, and the six-part series *The Singing Detective* (produced on BBC in 1986 but not telecast on PBS until two years later), *lives* on that edge between realism and antirealism, theatrical illusion and blatant theatricality. Brecht is wary of emotion, concerned that an audience overpowered by empathy won't have any energy left for political action, and so the alienation devices are meant to serve as dividers, sealing us off from the feelings we might have expended on his victims of poverty and capitalism. For Potter, stylization—whether in the form of the Depression-era production numbers of *Pennies from Heaven*, or the fantastical encounters in *Dreamchild* between the octogenarian Alice Hargreaves (Coral Browne) and the creatures Lewis Carroll created out of love for her when she was a child, or the mix of *film noir* and forties pop in *The Singing Detective*—is an *expression* of emotion, as well as a comment on its place in the characters' lives.

Rather than operating as a distancing device, stylization for Potter charts the distance that *already* exists between his characters (Arthur, the pathetic song plugger of *Pennies*; Mrs. Hargreaves, who has worn her Victorian corset straight into the twentieth century; disease-wracked Philip Marlow in *The Singing Detective*) and their feelings, which are too excruciating to be borne, while providing a bizarre outlet for those feelings. The self-conscious art in Potter's work is a form of psychological displacement; in his hands, Brecht turns Freudian. And *The Singing Detective*, his masterpiece, is actually *about* the Freudian process. So, in it, form and content are indistinguishable from each other.

The Singing Detective might best be described as a Freudian musical murder mystery with strong autobigraphical overtones, made up of four interwoven sections. In the frame story Marlow, the hero (Michael Gambon, in a brilliant performance) suffers—like Potter himself and like John Updike (who wrote eloquently

about his tribulations in a *New Yorker* piece a couple of years ago)—
from psoriatric arthritis, a horrendous skin disease that is both dis-
figuring and agonizingly painful. When we meet Marlow, he is undergoing an attack so extreme (every inch of his skin burns with it)
that it causes him to be hospitalized for several months. During that
time, plagued with fever and memories and a sense of professional
impotence, he begins to reconstruct in his head a novel called *The
Singing Detective* that he published some years earlier. (As he tells
one of the doctors, being named Philip Marlow—though, significantly, without the final "e"—has fitted him for nothing *but* writing
detective fiction.) Once his estranged wife, Nicola (Janet Suzman,
with her cool, taunting line readings and her razor eyes), begins to
visit him, the plot of his mental wanderings alters.

Overlaid on the second story, the "singing detective" story—
where Marlow himself doubles as a gumshoe who moonlights as a
big-band vocalist, and a slippery character named Mark Binney
(the gifted Patrick Malahide) is the client/victim/villain—is a variation, in which Binney becomes Finney, Nicola's lover, who con-
spires with her to steal a screenplay from Marlow and sell it to a
studio under his own name. The fourth and most compelling plot
is the Freudian mystery that eventually explains the obsessions that
define the other three. While he's undergoing medical treatment
in the ward, Marlow simultaneously (and over his own strenuous
objections) sees the hospital psychiatrist, Dr. Gibbon (Bill Paterson,
of *Comfort and Joy*), ostensibly to help him deal with the psychological implications of his disease but really, it turns out, in order
to discover its cause. In the course of these sessions, Marlow relives
his grim childhood in the north of England—D. H. Lawrence territory, the setting of *Sons and Lovers*—where his father (Jim Carter)
labors in the coal mines and his London-born mother (Alison Steadman), out of place among her husband's family, grows more perilously restless every day.

Potter and the director, Jon Amiel (who also collaborated with
him on the BBC *Pennies from Heaven*), effect the transitions between sections by keeping us, almost all the time, in Marlow's head,
wandering among the four worlds of his consciousness. (The only
time we leave Marlow's point of view is in perhaps half a dozen
scenes between two of his neighbors in the hospital ward—crotch-
ety, fastidious Mr. Hall, played by David Ryall, and a semiarticu-

late young man named Reginald, played by Gerald Horan. These are the least satisfying scenes in the series, though you can understand why Potter couldn't resist throwing them in: The murder mystery that Reginald is constantly absorbed in, to the everlasting irritation of Mr. Hall, is *The Singing Detective*.) The chief concern of the drama is certainly the unraveling of Marlow's psyche, through a series of clues that we, like Marlow, learn to read as we journey through the maze with him—details of the detective story that are actually dissociated remnants from his childhood, fictive corpses that change face every time he visualizes them, characters (like Binney/Finney) who turn out to have their roots in his past.

Potter includes brief *hommages* to two cinematic sources, *Citizen Kane* and *Blow-Up*, both of which center on the quest to solve the unsolvable. Marlow complains at one point that most novels are "all solutions, and no clues," whereas his detective stories capture "the way things are. Plenty of clues. No solutions." However, Potter, unlike Welles and Antonioni, concludes that by this kind of probing you *can* eventually get to the bottom of the mystery.

He treats other themes, too. Physical illness is seen as a metaphor for trauma: Marlow's disease, which makes him literally untouchable (even his own tears scald him), is a symbol for the agony he feels when Gibbon tries to reach an even more tender part of him. There's the great Dickensian theme, the tyranny the adult world exerts over children, which is glimpsed through Marlow's past and paralleled in his present by the enslavement he feels, in the hospital, to the tyranny of physical impotence. And peripherally (and less successfully), Potter examines and parodies how fiction is created: The "script" story includes a couple of mysterious thugs who suggest a mixture of the ambiguous assassins in Pinter's *The Basement* and the unfinished characters milling about in Gilbert Sorrentino's comic novel about writing, *Mulligan Stew*.

The idea of skin—Marlow's protective armor, which rebels against him—is everywhere in *The Singing Detective*. In the opening detective-story sequence, for example, a vocalist at a club called Skinscape's croons Cole Porter's "I've Got You Under My Skin." (On the first page of Potter's 1986 novel *Ticket to Ride*—which, incidentally, carries an epigraph from D. H. Lawrence—we read the following sentence: "The windows . . . have a double skin, and are shaped like a screen. They are separating you from the land and the air. They cannot be opened." *Ticket to Ride* is a murder mystery about the fragmenting of a personality.) In the hospital, Marlow's psychological skin is being stripped away while his actual epidermal layer is flaking, turning painfully into ash as the fever in his blood burns its way out of his body. Horrifying as it is, that's the healing process.

But he's stripped down in another—negative—way, too: The humiliation he and his fellow patients undergo as a result of their physical incapacities strips them of their dignity, and they find themselves (like the inmates of *One Flew Over the Cuckoo's Nest*) forced to either submit to the sternly maternal ministrations of the no-nonsense head nurse (Imelda Staunton) or rebel in tiny ways that are humilating in themselves—sulking, or refusing to speak, or tainting with an edge of sarcasm the replies they're trained to give. This system turns the patients into quivering cowards: When the man next to Marlow dies of a heart attack, the nurses make up the bed as if it had never had an occupant, and Marlow, terrified, goes along with the ruse. It also turns them into miniature tyrants: Marlow's sadistic ranting prods another of his neighbors, a sputtering old man named Adams (Charles Simon), into a heart attack of his own. And Potter and Amiel show us, in schoolroom scenes as ghastly as anything devised by Dickens or Charlotte Brontë, how this power-by-humiliation strategy is instilled in Marlow as a child (beautifully underplayed by Lyndon Davies). We see him terrorized by a teacher (the frighteningly effective Janet Henfrey) whose threats of corporal punishment are less disturbing than the evangelical fervor—the threats of *divine* reprisal—that informs her officially sanctioned ravings.

Helpless even to reach for a cigarette, treated like a naughty child, swaddled around the waist like an infant (or a Christ figure), lying on display for a team of doctors to scrutinize, Marlow feels desperately trapped in his own flesh. His peculiar form of rebellion consists of mockery, fueled by a John Osborne–like facility with invective, and a relentless sour-spiritedness. It's a credit to Potter's fair-mindedness, and to the complexity of Michael Gambon's acting, that even though we're positioned to see the hospital staff through Marlow's inflamed skin, we can still appreciate how difficult he is to deal with. There's a remarkable scene in which the hospital registrar (Thomas Wheatley), trying to convince Marlow to agree to visit Gibbon, mentions he'd like to read one of Marlow's books. His remark obviously arises more out of politeness than genuine interest, and because of his natural power (as a healthy hospital administrator, over this ailing patient) there's an inevitable strain of condescension in his request. But when Marlow snaps back that all his books are out of print, the way he shuts the registrar down is unsettling. We may admire his integrity in refusing to go soft in the ward (resisting tranquilizers, for instance), and certainly we can see where his crotchetiness comes from, but the registrar is so transparently well-intentioned, and so demolished by Marlow's superior wit, that we can't help wanting to shake Marlow—especially since we sense that therapy may be his only chance. And so it is. Gibbon's wry humor is a match for Marlow's raging wit, and his tone of unsurprised, unsentimental sympathy leads Marlow gently into lowering his guard: Marlow's past begins to leak through into his sessions with Gibbon and, more and more, into the feverous fiction he constructs and reconstructs in his head. Amiel and Potter's technique for building the story of Philip's childhood, which contains all the answers to the mystery of his character, is a combination of jigsaw puzzle (as in *Citizen Kane*), gradually enlarged focus (as in *Blow-Up*), and a dream-like substitution of images (displacement, as in *Dreamchild*). Philip's past is recreated by bits and pieces: his sweet, melancholy, cuckolded dad, wasted in the mines and finally cut out of his life entirely when his mother takes Philip to live with her parents in London; his embattled relationship with his schoolmates when his cleverness earmarks him as superior to the life they've all been born to; the hellish classroom; the boy's dialect, scorned by his mother and sneered at by her relatives, the loss of which symbolizes his estrangement from his father. In one astonishing scene Marlow imagines himself, grown and garbed in his hospital pajamas, sitting in the pub where his father used to entertain his friends by lip-synching the words to popular songs. When Marlow's disease prevents him from applauding, another miner censures him for never having given his father any credit while he was alive. When Marlow, refusing to believe his father is dead, begins to shout at him, he reverts movingly to dialect: "Dad! Thee's know how much I'd care about tha—."

The central images for the unscrambling of Marlow's past are the forest near Philip's home, where he spies on a lovemaking cou-

ple, and where, high in a tree overlooking the woods, he has a private conference with God; the classroom and the spinster schoolteacher, whose face he sees later on a scarecrow he glimpses from a
train; the train itself, which carries him and his mother away from
his father; the tunnels of the London tube station, where he runs
away from her; and the woman's corpse dragged out of the Thames
in the "singing detective" story. The woods and the tunnels are traditional Freudian symbols. The tunnels are the tortured corridors
of Philip's mind, and all his grueling rites of passage occur in the
woods—where he sees his mother with her lover, where he hides
from his father after her death brings him back home, and where,
in his talk with God, he lays the ground for his later "detective
work" (both as a writer and as an analysand):

> Everything will be all right. When I grow up, *everything*—
> . . . Everything ool be *all right.* (Tiny, uncertain pause.) Won't
> it? Won't it, God? Hey? Thou's like me a bit—doosn't, God?
> Eh? (Longer pause.) When I—When I grow up, I be going to
> be—a *detective.* . . . I'll find out. I'll find out things! . . . I'll
> find out who did it!

The faces of the woman in the woods, and of the victim in the
detective plot, keep changing. At times they're Nicola, at other
times Philip's mother—who are to Marlow doubles of the same eternal female, like the women in his story, each of whom is a whore
and each of whom has her turn in the Thames. Marlow the adult
fiction writer has to keep executing her for the heinous crime he's
never forgiven his mother for—sex. It isn't until Gibbon challenges
him to a breathtaking word-association game, towards the end, that
Marlow is at last able to recognize the connection. (Bill Paterson
gives an impeccable performance as the psychiatrist.) And, as we
learn, he's suppressed even more, too: the nature of his private act
of revenge against his mother's lover. The treetop sequences are
drawn by a compass that describes a greater and greater arc; each
time Amiel's camera returns to that tree, we learn a little more
about what took Philip there in the first place.

There's a Joycean thrill in watching *The Singing Detective,* not
only because Potter's method is a Brechtian kind of stream-of-consciousness, but also because what seems at first like an arbitrary

collage—with intricate references discharged so rapidly we feel they're whipping by us, like faces glimpsed from a merry-go-round, impossible to get a reading on—comes into clearer and clearer focus as the episodes collect. And the dramatic power accumulates as Marlow's story yields more and more layers of meaning. The individual sections of the teleplay are masterfully rendered; the range of the dialogue alone is amazing (angry-young-man expressions of rebellion and despair for the hospital scenes; mock–Raymond Chandler prose for the detective scenes, which are also peppered with musical jargon and allusions to pop tunes; self-reflexive humor for the "script" story). As in Joyce, there are both emotional revelations (which we experience along with Marlow) and intellectual ones (which we come upon by ourselves)—like the way he employs *film noir* and musical comedy, two essential film genres of the forties, the era of Philip's childhood, to expose the psychological underpinnings of his central character.

Noir, with its atmosphere of psychic doom and its obsession with the sordid, is exactly the right kind of thriller for Marlow, whose own mystery hovers like the smoke in crowded Skinscape's. And musical comedy, with its manufactured optimism and its aura of romance, is *noir*'s perfect opposite. For Potter, popular music is inescapably haunting; its very cut-rate quality seems to imbue it with melancholy (perhaps by emphasizing the fleeting nature of things). Potter and Amiel have chosen an affectingly lagging arrangement of "Peg o' My Heart" for the theme song, by Max Harris and His Novelty Trio, and it's an inspired selection: The beat hobbles, anticipating its end from the first chorus, and a harmonica hangs in the air (much like Bobby Bruce's violin in the rendition of "Pennies from Heaven" you hear in the movie).

The Singing Detective contains a great deal of music, and at least a dozen production numbers, in which (as in *Pennies*) the characters lip-sync the lyrics while period recordings spin on the soundtrack, and upon several of which Amiel superimposes a medley of images, segueing from the hospital to Philip's childhood or the club haunts of the singing detective. Two of them, built around Fred Waring's "Dry Bones" and the Harold Arlen–Johnny Mercer "Accent-tchu-ate the Positive" (Amiel and Potter use the the original version, by Bing Crosby and the Andrews Sisters), are really wild, and flamboyantly sardonic. "Dry Bones"—which has stylistic links to the Walt Disney *Silly Symphonies* of the early thirties and also suggests a dryer, more modest variation on the heart-attack number in Bob Fosse's *All That Jazz*—is Marlow's vision of the hospital. The doctors, dressed in white tuxes and black ties, mouth the words while the nurses play lab skeletons like percussion instruments and the skeletons bob their heads on their rib cages as if possessed. "Accent-tchu-ate the Positive" is the song Marlow puts in the mouths of a hospital evangelist groupcalled The Awakeners, foisted on unsuspecting patients with no choice but to listen; its relentless upbeatness devastatingly undercut, this number is a black-comic parallel to the soppy wartime tune, "It's a Lovely Day Tomorrow," drummed into Philip's head by his schoolteacher. You can see why Marlow's singing detective refuses to smile while he performs with the band, and why he distances himself by only mouthing the words—he knows (i.e., *Marlow* knows) how potent even kitsch can be.

That's quite a different tactic from the way Potter uses music in *Pennies from Heaven*, where the characters sing when they're so welled up with emotion but so poor of expression that they need to shape their feelings in the words and voices of others. Marlow has seen his father do just that (during the pub amateur nights that are his only creative outlet), his sad, saucer eyes registering the romanticized pain of "It Might as Well Be Spring" and "Do I Worry?" and the Mills Brothers' "Paper Doll" and "You Always Hurt the One You Love"—while we, along with the remembering Marlow, register the ironies of the lyrics about unrequited love and betrayal that escape Philip's dad, who is sharing the stage with his wife and her lover, his best friend. (With almost no dialogue the outsize, lumbering actor Jim Carter gives a remarkably emotional performance as Mr. Marlow.) No wonder the detective, whose big-band appearances stand in for Marlow's father's hometown gigs, tells us he'll sing the singing but he won't feel the feeling: Feelings are much too painful, and they only give you away, make it easier for other people to wound you.

It's that pain and risk that Marlow has to learn to embrace, with Gibbon's help. His breakthrough comes when he's able to tell young, pretty Nurse Mills (Joanne Whalley), who has been kind to him despite his ill temper, "You are the girl in all those songs. Dee dum. . . . The songs you hear coming up the stair. . . . When

you're a child. When you are supposed to be asleep. Those songs."
In the final number, "The Teddy Bears' Picnic," we hear Marlow's
own voice for the first time—a crucial moment in a Dennis Potter
musical, where it represents, for good or bad, the merging of previously separate realities. (At the end of *Pennies from Heaven*, Steve
Martin sings the reprise of the title song himself, on the scaffold.)
That's when we know Marlow is ready to move past the singing
detective—to feel the feeling at last.

May 1988

ENTERTAINMENTS

• • •

As Pauline Kael pointed out in her famous essay "Trash, Art, and the Movies," few of us start going to the movies because we're looking for great art, and God knows few of us *keep* going to them for that reason. Slogging through crap most of the time, we're more than happy to settle for a good time. Of course there's a difference between art and entertainment, but it's overrated—not just because the best art is almost always entertaining (like the Taviani brothers' *Night of the Shooting Stars*, the finest movie I saw in the eighties), not just because great entertainment can come so close to art (like *E.T.* and *Batman, Dressed to Kill* and *The Stepfather, Local Hero* and *Women on the Verge of a Nervous Breakdown*), but because the discrepancy between them has caused more trouble than it's worth.

Most people assume that art is something they're supposed to appreciate (which generally means something that makes them feel straitjacketed while they watch) and entertainment is something they don't need to think about. I felt chained to my seat during *Jean de Florette*, but I don't think it's art (well—maybe calendar art); *Casualties of War*, which gripped me at every moment, certainly is. And isn't engagement of the mind as well as the senses one of the pleasures of great entertainment? If you didn't bother trying to follow the plot in *The 39 Steps* or *Charade*, you'd probably find these light-fingered, suspenseful thrillers dull—as audiences (and many critics) found Fred Schepisi's 1990 *The Russia House*, where the plotting of the Tom Stoppard script (out of John le Carré) is a marvel. You could decide it's too much trouble to scan the overlapping dialogue in *His Girl Friday* or *M*A*S*H*, or that theatrical satires like *Singin' in the Rain* and *The Band Wagon* can only be appreciated by those who have some background in the theater, or you could be put off by the shift of styles and tones in *The Manchurian Candidate*—and that would kill those movies for you, too. It's a popular misconception that entertainment is supposed to be mindless, as the high-tech Schwarzeneggers are. Generally I go as crazy with boredom at those as I did at *Jean de Florette*.

I had a terrific time at a wide variety of movies during the eighties—at, for instance, *Tootsie, Roxanne*, and *All of Me*; *Divine Madness* and *Hairspray*; *So Fine, A Private Function*, and *The Man with Two Brains*; *Splash* and *Big*; *Home Movies, My Favorite Year* and *Weeds*; *Barbarosa, The Year of Living Dangerously*, and *Never Say Never Again*; *Fast Times at Ridgemont High* and *Say Anything*; *Star Trek II: The Wrath of Khan* and *The Adventures of Buckaroo Banzai*; *Dreamscape* and *True Believer*; *Near Dark, The 4th Man* and *The Stepfather*; *Songwriter* and *Vampire's Kiss*; *A Room with a View* and *Tequila Sunrise*; *Bizet's Carmen* and *Nutcracker*; the first half of *The Fly*, the first forty-five minutes of *Empire of the Sun*, and the George Miller and Joe Dante episodes of *The Twilight Zone: The Movie*.

Most of these pictures weren't hits; it's become increasingly rare for even a first-rate entertainment, a movie you anticipate giving pleasure to millions of people, to last more than a couple of weeks in the suburbs. That's why the success of Norman Jewison's *Moonstruck*, which came out at the end of 1987, was so cheering. So I've included *Moonstruck* here, along with four more of the best entertainments I found during the decade: the Jonathan Demme–Talking Heads collaboration, *Stop Making Sense*, Woody Allen's

The Purple Rose of Cairo, Albert Brooks's *Lost in America*, and *High Season*, a lovely farce, though virtually unknown, by the English moviemaker Clare Peploe.

Rockin' Out

• • •

Rock concert films and documentaries containing concert footage ("rockumentaries"), even when they lack a controlling vision or aren't very well shot or edited, can be more compelling and more entertaining than more intelligent and craftsmanlike movies. Preserving an active, vibrant moment, they offer us the opportunity to see, at close range, performers we may have missed our chance to see live. *Woodstock* and *Ladies and Gentlemen, The Rolling Stones* and the posthumous collage *Janis* give us exciting, if secondhand, experiences; we still have immediate access to the performers, years after the (often hastily assembled) film has become historical documentation. But when sophisticated musicians plan a series of concerts in terms of the movie they intend to release afterwards, and a first-rate director takes charge of the filming, the results can be thrilling—maybe even more thrilling than landing tickets to see the band live. Martin Scorsese's *The Last Waltz*, which was lovingly shot by perhaps the most prestigious collection of cameramen ever gathered together on a single project, provided a more enviable vantage point for The Band's farewell concert than the luckiest patron at Winterland could have had. And Jonathan Demme has turned Talking Heads' appearance at the Pantages Theatre in Hollywood in December of 1983 into an ecstatic film, *Stop Making Sense*.

Talking Heads's enthusiastic following among intellectual rock aficionados can be explained by David Byrne's dry, sneaky word-game lyrics and the unusual rhythms, which mostly derive (on the later records) from African music. While the strands of harmony and counterpoint multiply—especially on an album like *Remain in Light* or *Speaking in Tongues*—the lyrics, beginning as tight kernels, carefully pared-down portions of banal phrases evoking a range of contemporary obsessions (sex, urban living, the Bomb), bounce off each other like billiard balls and veer away in unanticipated directions. The lyrics have a toying, exploratory quality, the music often is startlingly beautiful, and the relationship between the two elements shifts constantly. Watching the Heads in *Stop*

267

Making Sense, you become conscious of a second kind of tension. The musicians are impeccably polished, and Byrne—who wrote most of the tunes, sings lead vocal on all but one, and even designed the stage lighting (with Beverly Emmons)—has clearly exercised complete authority over the show. Yet the band's joy in playing both music and games goes hand-in-hand with improvisation and spontaneity. The result is generous restraint, controlled frenzy, red-hot cool.

The band can maintain this weird balance in part because each of the members demonstrates such a distinctive personality on stage. Jerry Harrison, who plays guitar and keyboards, has dark, curly hair and a reticent half-smile. He seems always slightly agog, while Chris Frantz, the drummer, sits back confidently on his stool, leaping into the air on a particularly lively chorus and waving his sticks like a military bandman gone mad. Chris's wife, Tina Weymouth, the bassist, has lacquered blond hair and perfect little china-doll features; she's a mischievous sphinx, smiling in secret delight and never letting on what amuses her and keeps her eyes so unnaturally wide. (Her mute-musician mystique continues for almost the entire film: She doesn't sing a note until, perhaps twenty minutes from the end, she and Frantz lead a version of "Genius of Love," from an album on which they perform as The Tom-Tom Club.)

The rest of the band, except for Byrne, is black—two women and three men, all recent additions to the Heads contingent. Bernie Worrell, the keyboardist, is the most enigmatic of the men; he has cat's eyes and a cat's tautness, and he doesn't convey pleasure (until the very end); he just increases his intensity when things heat up. Alex Weir, who plays guitar, has a measured warmth and crinkles up his face when he gets excited, but Steve Scales (the percussionist) really busts loose—marching back and forth, exhorting the audience, grinning puckishly. (He's the world's tallest elf.) The two backup vocalists, Edna Holt and Lynn Mabry, are also livewires. During "Slippery People" they face Byrne and, lifting their feet with exaggerated care, they mimic his motions (including his broad, slap-happy guitar style) like gifted children playing mirror games.

But David Byrne is the star of Talking Heads, and of *Stop Making Sense*, and he gives a brilliant virtuoso performance. I'm not sure that any rock performer since the young Mick Jagger can have demonstrated such an overwhelming combination of precisely directed energy, razor wit, and versatility. With his mongoose neck and scarecrow body, his hair slicked back except for a furtive patch that explodes over one eye, he looks like a demented Walker Evans figure, or like the "Psycho Killer" he sings about in his opening number—except that everything he does is funny. You hardly expect that gawky frame to be lithe, but he does amazing tricks with it: throws it back into a surprised arc, as if he'd been pummeled by a volley of beebees; or executes a series of absolutely symmetrical bowlegged moves; or, in a single step, transforms a pigeon-toed lunatic into The Hunchback of Notre Dame. He imports props (a floor lamp with a flexible stand becomes an object of wonder), or uses his microphone and mike stand as substitutes—or his costumes (glasses; a red baseball cap; a jacket worn open and sagging like an exhausted scientist's lab coat; an outsize suit with squared-off shoulders)—or else he appropriates a slice of the air and mimes what he can't produce. Like Jagger and Bette Midler, he never stops mocking himself; if he did, his fierce physical commitment to every number would be frightening—he *would* be the "Psycho Killer." As it is, he can be science–fiction hero and villain, mutant, devil and evangelist, nerd and obsessive, and yet remain the crown prince of nonsense, a New Wave Edward Lear.

You can't tell where Byrne's authority left off in this film and Jonathan Demme's began: Demme seems to have devised the movie from inside Byrne's head. His photographer, Jordan Cronenweth (who shot *Blade Runner*), adapting what was evidently an intricate stage-lighting plot, has done a beautiful job: The autumn-bonfire reds and Halloween shadows of the "Swamp" and "What a Day That Was" numbers, the neon whites and smoky blues of "Take Me to the River," are among the most exquisitely lit "theatrical" interiors a moviehouse has ever seen. Demme's direction isn't just a matter of taste and tact; he constructs the movie the way Byrne constructed the concert. It starts simply and elegantly, one man alone on a bare stage with a guitar and a boom box (providing the full requisite background for "Psycho Killer") and erupts when all nine musicians are finally in attendance (on "Burning Down the House," a conflagration of a song). And it keeps erupting, until, on "Girlfriend Is Better," the theatrical/cinematic metaphor begun with the illusion of a band on stage turns gleefully on the audience.

Byrne, who's already thrust his mike in front of a techie creep-

ing around on stage with a lighting instrument, eliciting a sung response, now points the mike at the camera—at *us*. This song, which
proclaims that it's always showtime, is the movie's theme. Byrne
sings that when we get older we stop making sense, and as he dances
around in the "big suit" that Gail Blacker designed from him, we
understand that by "stop making sense" he and Demme mean to
start making theater. The two numbers that follow, "Take Me to
the River" (by Al Green) and "Crosseyed and Painless," have a relaxed feel; the lights go up, Byrne slips out of his Goliath-shouldered
jacket, and even Bernie Worrell breaks into a grin. Byrne and
Demme think of everything: They even work up a curtain call set
to music.

November 1984

A New Sensibility

• • •

The Big Chill was a cautionary (and hypocritical) fable about
the evils of yuppiedom and the need to preserve the ideals of the
sixties. Both *The Sure Thing* and *Desperately Seeking Susan* contain
yuppie characters in important supporting roles, but they function
in the place of their stuffed-shirt predecessors in screwball comedies—to provide a contrast with the hero, so the heroine, realizing
what a mistake she's made by allowing herself to be straitjacketed
in a dead relationship, can move herself (and the plot) forward. But
Lost in America is the first real comedy *about* yuppies, and it has
an entirely new kind of energy, because the director–star, Albert
Brooks (who also coauthored the script, with Marcia Johnson),
doesn't make movies like anyone else in the world.

Brooks's previous picture, *Modern Romance*, which he also

starred in, was a weirdly muted examination of the end of an affair, and for the first half—before the main character's obsessiveness about the woman who's left him began to wear down our patience—it was hilarious, though in ways difficult to explain. The humor didn't punch in, it wasn't cumulative, and, though it clearly derived from the eccentricities of the protagonist's style, there were many glitches in his behavior not attributable to any reasonable motive. And perhaps *that*, as much as any other element in the movie, was the source of the laughter. (I noticed in *Lost in America*, too, that not everyone in the theater was laughing at the same lines, but everyone was laughing at *something*.) The paradox at the heart of Brooks's style as a comedian *and* as a filmmaker, his affectless intensity, turns out to be the perfect instrument for getting on screen (and sending up) a new wrinkle on the American sociocultural canvas.

In *Lost in America*, Brooks plays David Howard, who banks on capping eight years at a big-time advertising agency in Los Angeles (the last two spent in the capacity of "creative director") with a promotion his boss has *practically* promised him. David and his wife, Linda (Julie Hagerty), a personnel manager, have bought a new house in anticipation of their ascent to this new social and economic plateau, even though both are experiencing severe anxiety, too: They feel tied to the future they've worked toward—robbed of their freedom to control the course of the rest of their lives. Then David is handed a transfer instead of a promotion, and he's so furious at his treatment that he explodes in his employer's office, and ends up fired. (This scene recalls Gene Hackman's rebellion against his boss in *All Night Long*, another comic original, but the two movies couldn't be farther apart in tone or style.) Responding manically to this turn of events, David decides that fate has freed him and Linda up to drop out of society (like the heroes of his favorite movie, *Easy Rider*). So he persuades her to quit *her* job. They then liquidate all their assets, buy a motor home, and drive off to look for America and themselves.

Brooks and Johnson aren't writing off the top of their heads; they have literary and cinematic models, and that explains why *Lost in America* has such a classical feeling to it—despite its weird, dissociated approach to comedy. (It also explains to some extent why it's a much more satisfying movie than *Modern Romance*.) The

Howards are sensitive enough to experience the moral and esthetic dislocation in the pattern of their domestic lives, and complex enough to struggle with it, but out on the road in quest of their destiny they can't help thinking like yuppies; they're Reagan-era Babbitts. The first shots of Brooks (whom we've already heard on the phone with his Mercedes dealer) behind the wheel of his spanking new Winnebago, with the Steppenwolf recording "Born to Be Wild" pounding on the soundtrack, are priceless: A biker pulls up beside him at an intersection, and, feeling an immediate camaraderie with this fellow free spirit, David flashes him a "thumbs up" sign from his elevated seat. He's so wrapped up in his fantasy of the open road that he doesn't realize how completely his cottage-sized vehicle, with its built-in microwave oven, makes him look like a slumming monarch. (The biker answers by flipping him off.)

If one source of *Lost in America* is Sinclair Lewis, the other is Preston Sturges. The Howards are like the filmmaker Joel McCrea played in Sturges's *Sullivan's Travels* who gave up making trivial comedies and walked off in search of the agonized, trod-upon little man he wanted to build his next picture around. But McCrea's character took no real risks: A studio van followed him at a discreet distance to see that he didn't get into any real *trouble*. In *Lost in America*, David and Linda intend to spend the first night of their new existence camping out under the stars, and then signal their regenerated commitment to each other by walking through a second wedding ceremony. But the town they pick for this symbolic act is Las Vegas, where blue neon bells adorn the façade of the church they plan to wed in, and they wind up sleeping in the kitschy "junior bridal suite" of an expensive hotel.

The next phase of the movie follows the *Sullivan's Travels* model, too. Sullivan gets more than he bargained for when a bum knocks him out, steals his wallet, and leaves him at the scene of a crime. Arrested, unable to prove his identity, he lands on a chain gang and discovers the down side of life with a vengeance. Then the Howards tumble into their own nightmare perversion of a wish come true when Linda gambles away all their money and they have to settle down wherever they stop for the night—Safford, Arizona, as it happens—and look for any kind of work they can get.

The opening shot of *Lost in America* (which was photographed by Eric Saarinen) looks like a straight version of Magritte's "The

Empire of Lights," and there's something Magrittish about this whole movie. Brooks puts together scene after scene that reproduces the veneer of reality but is preposterous underneath—*cinéma vérité* gone haywire. Because Brooks's performing and directorial style (austere flakiness) is so completely his own and so thoroughly worked out, and because he's terrific at getting deadpan performances out of the other actors in the cast, some of these scenes are truly prodigious—especially the confrontation with his boss (Michael Greene, with Tom Tarpey as the ad man who wants to employ David in New York), the scene in which he tries to talk the casino manager (Garry Marshall) into giving him back the money Linda has lost at roulette, and the dialogue between David and the employment agent (Art Frankel) he visits in Safford. The most amazing scene in the 1978 drama *Straight Time* situated Dustin Hoffman in an employment agency, desperate for a job but forced to confess to the agent that the gaps on his record were due to the spaces of his life spent in prison. In *Lost in America*, a man whose last job netted him an average of a hundred thousand a year is offered a job as a crossing guard.

Other moments don't pan out: An encounter with highway cop (Charles Boswell) shifts comic gears in the middle without the needed transition, and our glimpse of David as a crossing guard doesn't live up to its build-up. And then the whole movie takes a sudden plunge to its ending, before we've had a chance to get used to the Howards' newly enforced lifestyle; it feels as though someone pulled out the plug. But overall it's a delightful movie, anyway. Albert Brooks and Julie Hagerty are terrific together; they give first-rate comic performances that are in perfect rhythmic opposition to each other. He maintains a bizarre balance between executive cool and hyperkinetic enthusiasm. When David attempts to sell the casino manager on the proposition that if he returns their money, he'll receive a million dollars' worth of free publicity, he slides into an ad man's pitch line ("I have chills") with all the taut, poker-faced underplaying of his profession. But Brooks plants this ploy right in the middle of one of David's worst attacks of nervous energy, so we can hear the frantic tension in his voice at the same time as we hear him playing it cool.

Julie Hagerty approaches her role differently. She plays only one emotional state at a time, but it consumes her completely, and it's always seated smack in the center of her eyes. The wide-eyed comic innocence of *Airplane!* and *A Midsummer Night's Sex Comedy* has become wide-eyed intensity in *Lost in America*, and sometimes it makes her look really crazed—especially in the casino, where she does probably the funniest impression of a compulsive gambler ever put into a movie. The bonus in her performance is that walking out on her job wipes the Mary Hartman *angst* off her face. She doesn't smile until then, and when she finally does, her radiance makes *us* grin; we feel that throwing all that money down the drain actually liberates her. Reluctant at first to trust David's impulses, she turns out to be the true convert to his dropout philosophy, while he proceeds to fall apart under the pressure of losing his money. But there's a real connection between Brooks and Hagerty on the screen. Somehow they make these two specimens of corporate burnout, each caught in a different psychic loop, a perfect match.

March 1985

Coming Up Roses

• • •

Woody Allen's *The Purple Rose of Cairo* is a slender film, like his perfect minicomedy *Zelig* was, also running under ninety minutes and restricted to a single comic conceit. But I think it's a marvel—ineffably sweet, imaginative, and suffused with feeling. Allen himself doesn't appear; he performs the ultimate act of submersion into the material by turning it over to Mia Farrow. She plays Cecilia, a poor working-girl in the New Jersey of the Depression, married to an insensitive lug (Danny Aiello) who squanders her wages—eked out at a hash joint where she and her sister (played

by Stephanie Farrow, Mia's true-life sibling) are employed as wait-
resses—on craps and liquor, and then brutalizes her. Returning
night after night to the local moviehouse, the Jewel, where she
knows the manager (Irving Metzman, an asset to *any* comedy) and
his staff by name, and they greet her like a member of the family,
she loses herself in whatever she sees up on the screen—and then
carries it with her through the next day, so that she resides in a
permanent daydream and functions at only a semiconscious level in
the restaurant.

When Cecilia's distractedness loses her the job, and she inadvertently catches Monk (her husband) with another woman, her
only recourse is to run back to the Jewel and retreat into the feature.
It's a programmer called *The Purple Rose of Cairo*, and as she
watches it over and over, savoring the scene in which the juvenile,
explorer Tom Baxter (Jeff Daniels), is taken out on the town by his
New York socialite friends, we see this scene again and again, too.
We become so familiar with every gesture, and the timing of every
phrase, that we gasp when, suddenly, Tom pauses for a moment
and looks directly at Cecilia. (It's an amazing moment: When
Woody Allen's technique is in perfect sync with his ingenuity, he's
untouchable.) Then Tom Baxter steps down off the screen and confronts her.

From that point on the movie operates on several narrative
(and comic) levels at once. Tom wants to be "free to make my own
choices," and he begs Cecilia, whom he's fallen in love with, to
show him *her* world. These scenes parody movie conventions, as
Tom learns to his dismay that his play money won't buy him dinner
in a real restaurant, and to his bemused delight that when he kisses
a real woman there isn't an automatic fade-out. Meanwhile, the
characters he's abandoned up on the screen can't play out the rest
of the story, so they panic and argue, and then they begin to insult
individual members of the audience, who have grown restless and
started to complain out loud. This section of the film (the most inventive), which is peerlessly acted by Edward Herrmann, Zoe Caldwell, John Wood, Deborah Rush, Van Johnson, Milo O'Shea, and
Karen Akers, parodies both the conventions of fiction and the concerns of contemporary criticism in a way that suggests parts of Gilbert Sorrentino's marvelous runaway novel, *Mulligan Stew*.

Tom's unheard-of behavior alarms both the studio executives, who see lawsuits in their future, and Gil Shepherd, the actor who played Tom in the film and who is terrified that his character run amuck will endanger his own burgeoning career. (He's hoping to play Charles Lindbergh next time out.) So he shows up in New Jersey, too, to try persuading Tom to rejoin the other characters on the screen. Meeting this movie idol in person is the most exciting thing that's ever happened to Cecilia (even more exciting than meeting his fictional character), and Gil is first flattered by her wide-eyed response to him, and then so touched that *he* falls in love with her, too.

The Purple Rose of Cairo is a full-length variation on one of Allen's best stories, "The Kugelmass Episode," in which a middle-aged Jewish man, unhappy with his life and bored with his marriage, is transported into nineteenth-century rural France to have an affair with the woman of his dreams, Emma Bovary. (*Broadway Danny Rose* also spun off from one of Allen's stories, "The Shallowest Man." Both can be found in the third Allen anthology, *Side Effects*, published in 1980.) But the movie is very different in tone. Although Cecilia, the movie characters, and even the members of the audience at the Jewel respond to the preposterousness of their new circumstances with typical Woody Allen casualness (after being courted by Tom, helping him to hide out, and struggling to keep her activities secret from her jealous husband, Cecilia confesses, "It's been a strange day"), the film is at heart a romantic fantasy. The scenes between Cecilia and Tom harken back to the tender looniness of Fellini's *The White Sheik*, and those between Cecilia and Gil are reminiscent of *It Happened One Night*—especially the one in which he croons "Alabamy Bound" and "I Love My Baby, My Baby Loves Me" while she accompanies him on the banjo. (The makers of *The Sure Thing*, who tried so hard to make a contemporary version of *It Happened One Night*, would probably cut off their right arms for the unstrained ambiance that Allen brings to this interlude.) I've never seen a Woody Allen movie that was gracefully charming in quite this way. It's the kind of movie you can't make, I imagine, until you have spent nearly two decades directing and have had to sweat to find a style to frame exactly what you wanted to say.

Jeff Daniels brings a fresh boyishness to Gil Shepherd—he's an ingratiating narcissist, an ego with a heart—and he looks smashingly in period in his casually elegant wardrobe of pastel sports jackets and argyle sweaters. He's not quite as fine as Tom; he lacks the aged-in-Hollywood crispness of the other actors in the film-within-the-film (particularly Edward Herrmann, who really has never been better, Zoe Caldwell and John Wood), just missing the very lightly parodic veneer (although his make-up is very funny). I don't know how one goes about playing a fictional character set loose in the real world, but I bet Steve Martin would have some idea. The problem is that if you cast someone as dynamic as Martin in the part, the romance would lose its balance, because Cecilia isn't written as a force to be reckoned with—and that's just what you would need opposite Steve Martin. Daniels is much closer to what the movie needs.

The scenes between Cecilia and Monk tend to repeat themselves (we hear essentially the same argument three times), and this part of the plot has narrative glitches. Cecilia never tells Monk she's lost her job, though he depends on it for his income, and when he finds her with Tom in a church (trying to explain religion to him), he's furious at her apparent relationship with this stranger. But he doesn't register that she ought to be at work. The odd scene fizzles—brief glimpses of the moaning studio executives, and one sequence in which a friendly prostitute (wonderful Dianne Wiest) leads Tom to a brothel, where she and her colleagues try to explain the difference between sex and true love. (This scene must have looked great on paper.)

Finally, however, these shortcomings don't dampen the film at all, not only because Allen's invention soars through so much of it, but also because it has a soul: Mia Farrow. Allen knew just what he was doing when he entrusted the bulk of the acting in *The Purple Rose* to her: Though she's given lovely performances before this, no previous director has seen in her what Allen clearly sees (and he's right). At first, listening to her brightly colored, run-off-at-the-mouth line readings—sometimes she sounds like a female Woody Allen here—and watching how her face lights up the moment she enters the Jewel, and how she can't wipe off her foolish grin or keep her hands still when she meets her movie star, I thought she was giving the most purely charming comic performance that any actress has since Shelley Duvall in *Popeye*. That's only half of it, though. Cecilia wears all her emotions right out on her face: Gazing up at the screen, she's an enraptured waif, and when someone breaks her heart, her face blurs, as if tears could erase it. She changes expressions so dramatically and yet so naturally that the long close-ups she takes, especially in the last scene, seem like magical transformations. The delicate intensity of her acting recalls Lillian Gish's—and, really, I can think of no higher compliment.

It's possible to see this movie as condescending, the way Frank Capra's comedies often were and the conclusion of Preston Sturges's *Sullivan's Travels* was, with the ambitious director realizing that the greatest mission on earth was to make the mass audience bury its sorrows in laughter. After all, the film-within-the-film is (intentionally) fairly terrible, and yet Cecilia responds to it with every fiber of her being, just as she responds later to something that really *is* great: Astaire and Rogers dancing to "Cheek to Cheek" in *Top Hat*. But *The Purple Rose of Cairo* has a bittersweet underlayer; the relationship between Cecilia and the movies she fills her head with isn't far from the relationship between the characters in *Pennies from Heaven* and the songs they sing to give shape to their blocked-up emotions. (The sensuousness of the thirties reconstructions in parts of this picture connect it to *Pennies from Heaven*, too—and to Robert Altman's *Thieves Like Us*.) Besides, the "magical glow" that Gil ascribes to her transforms even the clichés of a third-rate screen romance; it's her glow that brings Tom down off the screen. That's the meaning of the fairy tale. (It transforms Gil, too, and makes him fall in love with her.) I don't know whether Woody Allen could have found another actress to bring this off. Mia Farrow does; she is sublime.

April 1985

Clair de Lune

• • •

The Italian New Yorkers in *Moonstruck*—which was written by an Irishman (John Patrick Shanley) and directed by a Canadian WASP (Norman Jewison)—are half-mad, benighted lovers. They're comic-opera Italians, like the family in *Prizzi's Honor*, and they have the same fanciful, *buffa* accents. (The actress and acting teacher Julie Bovasso coached both casts.) The resemblance ends there. *Moonstruck* is a comic love story, so the characters' flair for melodrama, their penchant for turning the slightest irregularity into a domestic crisis, their air of deadpan exhaustion, their colorful non sequiturs and folk-fable superstitiousness and hilariously over-stated fatalism are at the service of a lopsided romanticism. They can see just enough out of their starry eyes to know they're behaving like fools.

Rose Castorini (Olympia Dukakis), who knows her husband, Cosmo (Vincent Gardenia), is seeing another woman (Anita Gillette), warns her daughter, Loretta (Cher), not to marry a man she loves: "When you love 'em they drive you crazy 'cause they know they can." When Loretta falls hopelessly in love with Ronny Cammareri (Nicolas Cage), the estranged younger brother of her fiance, Johnny (Danny Aiello), Ronny tells her, "Love ruins everything. It ruins your life. It makes things a mess. We are here to ruin ourselves and break our hearts." The enchanting *Moonstruck* is a celebration of that messiness.

I've tried to read Shanley's plays (*Danny and the Deep Blue Sea* is the best known), but I never get farther than the first act: His miserable, low-life, dead-ended men and women are like the bums in *Barfly* taken straight, and the shaggy confrontational–masochistic tone is a pain. But the doom that beckons the characters in *Moonstruck* is the wages of love, and they aren't dragged down into it—they fly up to it. When Ronny carries Loretta to bed she throws back her head, embracing her fate, and cries "I don't care, I don't care!" And when she confesses to her mother that she loves him "somethin' awful," she has a crinkled, slightly embarrassed smile on her face.

It's a very funny script, but I can't imagine what it would have been like in the hands of another director. Norman Jewison's superb craftsmanship, and his warmth and love of idiosyncrasy, give the movie shape and emotional texture. He's at the top of his form; he orchestrates scenes like a master. When Johnny proposes to Loretta in the neighborhood *trattoria*, the entire staff gets into the act, and when she insists he drop to his knees and do it right, Jewison cuts deftly to a customer (John Mahoney) who asks one of the waiters, in discreetly hushed tones, "Is that man praying?" And there's a wonderful sequence in which Loretta, obeying Johnny's request, visits Ronny at the bakery he runs (in order to invite him to the wedding), and Ronny, wielding a bread knife, launches into a semicoherent diatribe about the "bad blood" between himself and his brother. Nicolas Cage, acting with flamboyant confidence and without self-consciousness, is like a nasal, low-rent Pagliacci here. While he philosophizes, a young woman who works in the bakery (Nada Despotovich) gazes adoringly at him and confides to her friend, "This is the most tormented man I ever met. I love this man, but he doesn't know." (The scene is like something out of Ettore Scola's lovely *Pizza Triangle* played at a faster speed.)

Moonstruck has as distinctive a comic vision as a screwball comedy from the thirties or a Sturges picture from the forties. Like them, it thrives on curve-ball lines that ring in your head afterwards ("My scalp don't get enough blood sometimes," Johnny complains, scratching his head nervously as he delays proposing to Loretta, and Cosmo says his daughter, a widow, is bad luck: "Your mother and I were married for fifty-two years and no one died. You're married two years and somebody dies"). But it also thrives on a large cast of eccentrics, and the whole cast is perfect. Olympia Dukakis plays Rose as world-weary but still passionate, and Vincent Gardenia mugs endearingly: his frown is so oddly fastidious it's as though he'd turned his mouth down, fold by fold. Danny Aiello follows up his surprise turn as the hash-joint Romeo in *The Pickup Artist* with an even better performance here as the grown-up baby-boy Johnny.

Loretta's extended family includes a magnificent-looking grandpapa (Feodor Chaliapin, the son of the celebrated Russian opera star), who feeds his five dogs from his own plate and takes them out to bay at the full moon, as well as Rose's brother, Raymond (Louis Guss), and his wife, Rita (Julie Bovasso), who run an Italian epicurean shop. Under the moon, Raymond grows nostalgic and amorous—and Rita, giggly as a ticklish child, shies away from him in bed, her face lit up with pleasure. (Guss and Bovasso are so good you want to whistle and stamp your feet every time they show up.)

The head waiter at the restaurant is as solicitous as an uncle and has a discreet concern for the family issues of his customers. Dinner scenes in this setting are always punctuated by the quarrels of a middle-aged NYU communications prof (the talented Mahoney) and his much younger girl friends. And remember the woman (Helen Hanft) in the audience in *The Purple Rose of Cairo* who claimed her husband was a student of human nature? She has a cameo as a liquor store owner who tells her husband, "I see a wolf in every man I ever met, and I see a wolf in you!"

Cher is sensationally funny and charming as Loretta—it's a bona fide star-comedienne performance, as glamorous and stylish and sustained as Claudette Colbert's in *It Happened One Night* or *Midnight* or *The Palm Beach Story*, or Carole Lombard's in *Twentieth Century* or *My Man Godfrey*. There's a moment when Loretta decides to trade in her silver-tinted raven curls for an ultra-ultra 'do with the gray dyed out and her hair ribboned high on her head, and you worry that the movie has made the conventional mistake of ironing out the kinks in the heroine's appearance. But her new look gives Cher's Loretta a lilt she hasn't had before; she practically dances down the city streets. After a few scenes you realize how Loretta's newfound glamor, with its fifties-Hollywood excessiveness, matches up with the use of Dean Martin's "That's Amore!" on the soundtrack at the beginning, and the gloriously overemotional Renata Tebaldi recording of *La Bohème* (which is dubbed in during the Met performance Ronny takes Loretta to, in the movie's climactic sequence)—and that impossibly gorgeous full moon, which shines on a Manhattan as stylized as the Italians who inhabit it. Jewison and the photographer, David Watkin, create a New York so magical it *deserves* that moon.

March 1988

Summer Vacation

• • •

High Season, set on the island of Rhodes, is about culture and heritage and how these things can't help being tainted by the clumsy thumbprint of progress—both in the world outside and in our own complicated lives. But the movie, which was directed by Clare Peploe, isn't cynical, or even serious; it's a lustrous, effervescent comedy in which most of the characters are cheerful fakes. The movie takes place amid the first tourist boom after an airport has been built on Rhodes. Katherine (Jacqueline Bisset) is an English photographer who lives on the island with her 13-year-old daughter, Chloe (Ruby Baker); she's separated from her husband, Patrick (James Fox), a sculptor who resides nearby. They're fond of each other but can't help scrapping, partly because he's a compulsive philanderer and partly—mostly—because they don't have much respect for each other's work.

And they're *both* right. Patrick accuses Katherine of artistic dishonesty, because her latest coffee-table compilation, presumptuously titled *The Light of Greece*, contains nothing that's been built in the last two thousand years. She complains that his art is vulgar, and she's incensed that he's agreed to supply a sculpture called *The Unknown Tourist* for the dedication of a local boutique, which has been refurbished by its ambitious young owner, Yanni (Paris Tselios), to take advantage of the British tourist trade. Yanni now calls his shop (which formerly bore his dead father's name) "Lord Byron," trading on the centuries-old English romanticism about Greece. Katherine's photographs buy into that same romanticism—though her love of preservation doesn't prevent her from rejoicing when she's finally able to install a modern toilet in her cottage.

In fact, Katherine's book hasn't been doing well, and so, to stave off the necessity of giving up her house, she gains permission from her most devoted friend, Basil Sharp (Sebastian Shaw), an aging art historian, to sell to a Greco–English tycoon, Konstantinis (Robert Stephens), a vase Basil gave her years ago. The tycoon, wary of being obstructed by the Greek government when he tries to carry off this precious sample of the national heritage, asks Sharp to sign an affadavit declaring that the vase is only a copy. This scheme is overheard by Carol (Lesley Manville), a not-overbright tourist who's staying next door with her husband, Rick (Kenneth Branagh). Restless, and under the spell of the island, Carol's fallen for Yanni (*and* for all his "Isles of Greece" nonsense). She's here under false pretenses but doesn't realize it: This vacation is a cover for Rick's official business in Rhodes. (We don't learn what that business is until late in the picture.) Meanwhile, Rick's become hopelessly enamored of Katherine.

Watching over all these Feydeauesque developments with a mixture of amusement and disdain is Yanni's mother, Penelope (Irene Papas), who's furious at her son for soiling his father's name by selling bikinis and tennis rackets in his shop. She persists in wearing black and proclaiming her husband died in the fight for Greek independence, though in fact his death was far more ignominious (and far funnier). Penelope's no fool, however: While she fuels his myth and takes her stand against the barbarism of the invading tourists, she hoards American make-up and stashes it in a bureau under the altar she's erected to her beloved husband's memory.

Carol isn't alone in falling under the spell of Rhodes: The way that Peploe and the photographer, Chris Menges, have shot it—in luminous, sun-drenched panoramas—you do, too. There's a peculiarly pastel quality to the light in the daytime exteriors in this movie, and at night the island's even dreamier in misty blue, and the ocean is speckled with starlight. I'm not sure I've ever seen a farce that looked as breathtaking as *High Season*. Peploe uses the splendor of the setting, and the magnificent spectacle of the actors against it, as choreographic elements—the sinuous way that Bisset walks up a mountain path, her frizzy hair trailing down her back and her handbag swinging from her shoulder; the visual harmony struck by the landscape and Sebastian Shaw's sad, pellucid eyes; and the line of Lesley Manville's leg as, lying on her bed, she prods the chandelier with her toe, all are as much a part of the movement of the film as the couplings and uncouplings (and not-quite couplings), the high-spirited shadow play of façades, that make up the plot.

This sensuous romp, orchestrated with amazing precision, is Peploe's first feature, but she's married to Bernardo Bertolucci and has worked on his pictures and also on Antonioni's. And her brother, Mark Peploe, who coauthored the script, has screenwriting credits on *The Passenger* and *The Last Emperor*. Perhaps Rhodes took the crick out of his writing: The dialogue in *High Season* has a graceful fluidity that's nowhere in evidence in his previous work, and the ironies aren't the mechanical, abstracted ones he's normally so fond of—they're breathing human ironies. He and his sister have written a genuine high comedy.

The script demands a high level of ensemble acting, and indeed the whole cast is wonderful. Jacqueline Bisset has always been a feast for the camera, but the sour stiffness of her acting has generally gotten in the way. Not here, though; she's as free-spirited as she is loose-limbed. And in a couple of back-to-back scenes—drunk and making love to Rick in the moonlit ocean, she mistakes her eager suitor for Patrick, retreats when she realizes her error, and marches off to wake her husband (who is in bed next to another woman)—she shows some of the sexy, blurred-edge comic finesse of Julie Christie in her early, love-child days. As her daughter, Ruby Baker has a pert, natural wit (and a naturally free physicality: Chloe is certainly her mother's daughter). Of the young women in the cast, Lesley Manville carries off the trickiest scenes; Carol has an innocent sexual adventurousness, a schoolgirl eroticism, under her spoiled-English-tourist petulance. We root for her adulterous fling with Yanni, just as we root for Rick to get it off with his dream lover, Katherine: These *amours*—silly and inconsequential—seem as much the natural effect of the island's magic as the cavortings of the bewitched humans are an outgrowth of the woodland sorcery in *A Midsummer Night's Dream*.

James Fox (a trim, glowing forty-eight when he made this movie) and Kenneth Branagh give finely tuned comic performances at opposite ends of the comic spectrum: Fox is merrily understated as the confident sexual athlete, and Branagh, as the mooning dupe whose face shows the strain of his aching erection, sputters hilariously. Robert Stephens does one of those distinctly English chameleon turns as Konstantinis; he's practically unrecognizable. But good as all these actors are, and good as Paris Tselios is in the role of the aggressive entrepreneur, Yanni, the movie's sweet, motley soul resides in the performances of Sebastian Shaw and Irene Papas. Shaw (who is in his eighties) is like a great Noël Coward actor in late bloom: His voice quavers, his brittleness is affecting, but through the bemused, expansive wisdom the years have lent him you can still discern a bee-stung wit, a madcap panache. His portrayal of "Sharpie" Sharp is full of serene surprises that go off like tiny firecrackers as the character reveals more and more of himself.

Papas, one of the world's supreme tragediennes, gives a full-scale comic performance here (as she did in the 1984 *Erendira*), and it's masterfully controlled. In her biggest scene she hoists her husband's rifle, slings a bandolero across her chest, and rides her donkey into the village square to do battle against the forces of commercialism she believes are wrecking her island home. This is a fabulous lunatic image: Papas's Penelope, knowing how ridiculous a display she's putting on, glories in it. You have to be as canny as Papas, the great Antigone and Electra and Helen of Troy of the screen, to carry off a parody of Greek heroism like this one. It clinches Peploe's theme, and it caps the luxuriant pleasures of *High Season*.

June 1988

DIRECTORS

• • •

In the sixties, film students discovered the *auteur* theory, which made a big fuss over directors who left the imprints of their style on every picture they turned out. Mostly a glorification of mediocre talents without the range or inventiveness to stretch beyond mere repetition, it was a silly vision of the way movies get made (it ignored all the constraints of the studio system and dismissed the fact that movies are a collaborative art form). But at least, for maybe the first time, directors' names meant something to the audience. For a brief period, film lovers rushed to see the latest by Truffaut or Altman or Bergman: Even if it wasn't any good you had to be able to argue about it, because everyone else was going to see it, too. You recognized the voices of these filmmakers; you felt they were part of an international treasure. People still feel that way about authors, still snap up the most recent García Márquez or Pynchon novel, but especially young moviegoers aren't conscious of a controlling presence behind the camera. The audience that recognizes the director's name in the credits is shrinking every year, except in the case of a handful of superstars the media make a lot of noise about (Francis Ford Coppola, of course, and now Kevin Costner, who most moviegoers probably believe directed *Robin Hood, Prince of Thieves* in addition to *Dances with Wolves*).

During the eighties, directors with an unusual sensibility and a taste for offbeat projects really had to scramble, because their movies didn't make money and studios stopped wanting to back them. That's what happened to Carroll Ballard, who made maybe the greatest children's picture of all time, *The Black Stallion*, at the very end of the seventies. That film *did* make money (kids adored it, and parents loved taking them to see it), but *Never Cry Wolf*, released in 1983, bombed. (It was an unsatisfying, unshaped movie, but it had exquisite passages.) Ballard was a slow, painstaking, expensive director on both these movies, and even though he proved he could work fast and cheap when he shot *Nutcracker* in 1986, he'd acquired a reputation for being unbankable (as much because of the nature of his movies as because of their expense). *Nutcracker*, designed by Maurice Sendak and danced by Seattle's Pacific Northwest Ballet, was lovely, but it was treated shamefully by its distributors (in Boston, where I live, you could see it only at suburban moviehouses, and only during the afternoons), and the press, misunderstanding that it was more than just a filmed stage production, dismissed it with the kind of condescension it still saves for small, unprotected movies. (You'd never catch that supercilious tone in reviews of *Ghost* or *Terminator 2*.) Ballard couldn't land another job for the remainder of the decade.

There aren't many great directors left, anywhere in the world, who can afford to continue to work the way they'd like to; their idiosyncratic approach—the thing that makes them great—has become a more serious liability than ever. Akira Kurosawa, the unrelenting ironist, the brutal humanist, the master of spectacle, still makes movies his own way: *Ran* is an example of the kind of experience a towering, unflinching artist can give us when there are no obstacles in his path. But lately a number of the leaders of the world filmmaking community have had to *unite* to finance his ventures—and, given the current atmosphere, I don't see how the projects could come about otherwise. There *are* other world-class directors who somehow follow their own paths, like Satyajit Ray, Kon Ichikawa (though he churns out a lot of potboilers, too), the Taviani Brothers, Jacques Rivette. But often you can't see their movies here, except at festivals or in brief runs in one or two or three cities. When Ray, the embodiment of the spirit of Renoir and De Sica, died in 1992, he hadn't had a movie distributed in the United States since *The Home and the World* (in 1985), and I discovered when I set out to write an article on him at the end of the decade that the companies that handled his older films had allowed the contracts to lapse—so even a retrospective would have been nearly impossible.

The current art-house idea of an *auteur* director is Woody Allen or Jim Jarmusch. But Jarmusch's movies (like *Mystery Train*, included in this section) are minuscule achievements; he's the cinematic equivalent of Spalding Gray, who can't be bothered to put on either a character or a costume when he shows up on stage. (These men are like the self-satisfied guests who sit smiling patronizingly at dinner parties while their wives or girl friends implore them to tell some treasured anecdote. They give in at last, but they never let you forget they're doing you a big favor.) And except for *Zelig* and the charming, plaintive *Purple Rose of Cairo*, and two-thirds of his throwaway short, *Oedipus Wrecks* (one of the three segments in 1989's *New York Stories*), Allen's output in the eighties, prolific as it was, was a bust.

A whole generation of moviegoers—the *Annie Hall* generation, alienated by the mostly imbecilic teen cycle of the mid-eighties—breathed a sigh of relief when *Hannah and Her Sisters* came out in 1986, and embraced it as the first comedy for adults in many moons. But *Hannah* was no *Annie Hall*. Sure, it had all the Allen trademarks—the tasteful, self-assured style, the focus on comic self-doubt, the banter of the New York *cognoscenti*, the cast of sensitive, intelligent neurotics—but there was something brand-new in it, too: His usual downbeat open-endedness had given way to a happy resolution. The philandering lawyer (Michael Caine) returned to the comforts of home; the alcoholic (Barbara Hershey) left her lover for a more accommodating (and attractive) man; the coke freak (Dianne Wiest) found a successful career as a writer and married the hypochondriacal producer (Allen himself, of course), bearing him the child he'd been told he could never have. As Hannah (Mia Farrow) and her extended family sat down to Thanksgiving dinner, the sound you heard, for the first time on the soundtrack of a

Woody Allen film, was the buzz of contentment. Sadly, even
Woody Allen, who'd helped define the zeitgeist in the seventies, had
buckled under to it in the eighties. He followed *Hannah* with the
poky *Radio Days*, with its preposterously glazed view of the past (it
was tailor-made to be double-billed with Barry Levinson's *Avalon*),
and ended the decade with the preachy, complacent *Crimes and
Misdemeanors*.

Several American directors distinguished themselves in the
eighties, and I try to pay tribute to some of them here. John Huston
in *The Dead* (his glorious final movie, released posthumously) and
Philip Kaufman in *The Unbearable Lightness of Being*, a triumphant
adaptation of the Milan Kundera novel, behaved like artists—embracing
projects that didn't stand a chance of ringing in at
the box office, rising to stylistic challenges that must have looked
impossible. The irrepressible Robert Altman, who spent the first
half of the decade discovering theater and looking for ways to transfer
it to the movies (most excitingly in *Come Back to the 5 & Dime,
Jimmy Dean, Jimmy Dean*), returned to his roots in TV for the
HBO miniseries *Tanner '88*, bringing to the small screen the sophistication
and complexity and passion for experimentation he'd explored
on the large one. David Lynch and Jonathan Demme came
into their own as moviemakers in the eighties; the release of Lynch's
Blue Velvet and Demme's *Something Wild*, complementary films
in many ways, within a month and a half of each other in the autumn
of 1986 was a sharp reminder that the problem with movies
wasn't a lack of talent out there. A few talented American women
appeared behind the camera during the decade as well (especially
Barbra Streisand), though the most extraordinary woman director
of the eighties was an Australian, Gillian Armstrong. Her finest picture,
High Tide, barely surfaced here; for all but a handful of American
cities, it was a straight-to-video release.

Something Wild failed to attract the audience it deserved (until
they discovered it on video), and Demme managed to make terrific
pictures all through the eighties without once scoring a hit—even
with the Talking Heads rockumentary *Stop Making Sense* or the
daffy, sweetly insubstantial comedy *Married to the Mob*. (He remained
hitless until 1991, when he dressed up a creaky Thomas
Harris Gothic, *The Silence of the Lambs*, that he was eminently
wrong for but that critics and audiences were dying to see.) The last

entry in this section chronicles Demme's biggest heartbreak, *Swing Shift*. To the double challenge of his first big-budgeted, big-studio experience (following *Melvin and Howard*, which many critics loved but audiences didn't go to) and his first period piece, he responded by making his best movie—a great movie, I think. But it was subtle, idiosyncratic. Warner Brothers and the star, Goldie Hawn, didn't understand it, so they took it away from Demme and released it in a radically reworked (and horrendous) version—to date, the only *Swing Shift* that audiences have ever seen.

Lear Without Tears

• • •

The thesis of *Ran*, Akira Kurosawa's gloss on *King Lear*, is explicated at the end of the picture, after almost all the bloodshed has taken place and the handful of survivors is stumbling toward peace. Kyoami (Peter), the Fool, weeping over the death of his master, Hidetora (Tatsuya Nakadai), says that the gods are cruel and rejoice to see men cry. But Tango (Masayuki Yui), the loyal lord in disguise who represents Shakespeare's Kent, argues that men create their own disasters; it's the gods who cry. By having the most dependable character on screen refute Gloucester's famous line, "As flies to wanton boys are we to th' gods; / They kill us for their sport," Kurosawa takes *Lear* out of the nihilistic world many critics and directors have placed it in—especially in our time, when the most celebrated critical reading of the play (Jan Kott's, in his essay "*King Lear*, or Endgame") and the most famous stage interpretation (Peter Brook's) have linked it to existentialism and the Theater of the Absurd. Kurosawa's resetting of the play is profoundly humanistic, though his tone is deeply pessimistic.

Kurosawa and his collaborators on the screenplay (Hideo Oguni and Masato Ide) have worked it out ingeniously. Hidetora is a war lord who owes his kingdom to his own bloody conquests of neighboring lands; two of his three sons are married to women who were themselves the spoils of war, and whose families he annihilated in order to annex their castles. When he dreams up the crackpot idea of dividing his land among his sons but retaining both the title of ruler over all of it, and the banner that symbolizes his imperial power, his youngest, Saburo (Daisuke Ryu), balks at his father's lack of understanding and foresight. He calls the old man a senile fool to expect that he and his brothers, sons of the cruel age that Hidetora himself has spawned, could share his land and live in peace. (In other words, *this* Cordelia's exile is brought about for speaking to Lear's face the line Shakespeare has Regan confide in private to Goneril: "'Tis the infirmity of his age; yet he hath ever but slenderly known himself.")

293

And indeed, in Kurosawa's conception the destruction of Hidetora's kingdom is a direct response to the old chieftain's brutality and mercilessness: Lady Kaede (Mieko Harada), the proud, arrogant wife of his son Taro (Akira Terao), engineers it in revenge against the killer of her father and brothers. First she demands that Taro reclaim Hidetora's banner and force him to sign a document that places him entirely at her disposal. Then, when Taro is murdered in battle by his brother Jiro (Jinpachi Nezu), Kaede seduces Jiro and asks him for the death of his passive wife (Yoshiko Miyazaki) as a prize—so she can once more enjoy an empress's power. When at last the kingdom is torn apart by civil war, Kaede is at the helm of the destruction. (Her death, at the hands of Jiro's chief minister, one of the few morally untainted characters in the film, does her full justice.) *Ran*, which means "chaos" in Japanese, could be Kurosawa's answer to the question that lies at the heart of *King Lear*'s mystery: "Is there any cause in nature that makes these hard hearts?" In this film the atrocities that the characters commit are evidence of perpetuation rather than invention.

Like Kurosawa's 1957 *Throne of Blood* (a samurai *Macbeth* starring Toshiro Mifune), *Ran* can better be appreciated as a variant on Shakespeare than as a production of one of his plays. The doubling subplot with Gloucester and his son has been eliminated, though bits and pieces of it find their way into other characters: Lady Kaede is a cross between Edmund and Cornwall (and a direct descendant of the Lady Macbeth whom Isuzu Yamada played in *Throne of Blood*), and Tsurumaru (Takeshi Normura), who's related by marriage to Jiro and has lived a reclusive life in a hovel since Hidetora had him blinded, is both Gloucester and Edgar as Poor Tom. Still, *Ran* is a much closer parallel to *Lear* than *Throne of Blood* is to *Macbeth*. And that turns out to be a liability, because the prose approximations by the screenwriters and the translators leave you hungry for Shakespeare's verse—especially in the reunion scene, where Hidetora speaks, like Lear, of being taken out of his grave, and of his willingness to drink poison. In *Shakespearean Tragedy*, A. C. Bradley writes of passages that make one worship Shakespeare, and for most people I know the reunion scene in *Lear* is one of them; it's a scene that can make you weep even in a poor production. As Hidetora, Tatsuya Nakadai (who played the dual roles at the heart of Kurosawa's last film, *Kagemusha*) does his finest work in this sequence, but the discrepancy between his words and Shakespeare's rankles the viewer who knows the original.

Sticking so close to its source, *Ran* encounters another problem. *Lear* is the most emotionally overpowering of Shakespeare's plays, and watching this film, we anticipate emotional clinches that Kurosawa denies us. Part of the difficulty may lie in the peculiar fairy-tale construction of the play itself. The opening scene presents two arbitrary acts—Lear's division of his kingdom, and his insistence on a love contest between his daughters to win the shares he's already chosen for each one—that continue to bewilder you even after many readings. Actors and directors justifiably view this scene as the great obstacle of the play, and it's true that a staging that can (or a performer who can) make sense of it without alienating the audience from Lear is likely to triumph. (In reading the play you can more easily place this scene in context and leap past it, but on stage the obstacle is much greater. That may be partly why it's become commonplace to refer to *Lear* as a great tragedy that never works in performance, though I don't think that's true.) I've only seen that kind of triumph achieved once: When Olivier played Lear on television as a truly "foolish, fond old man" who initiates the competition out of a childish desire to hear his daughters tell him how much they love him.

In *Ran* this scene (which of course has a very different texture because of the substitution of warrior sons for daughters) is played, as it often is, as ritual. It's an obstinate piece of filmmaking: Kurosawa keeps his camera at a distance, preventing us from identifying with anyone on screen. (Shakespeare uses his own form of closeup: He lets Cordelia speak in asides.) Kurosawa seems determined that if we're going to like the characters—*any* of them—it will be because we accept them on their own rough terms, not because the direction has made it easy for us. The consequence of that choice is that we remain uninvolved for a long time.

Furthermore, when Lear is recast as a merciless, bloodthirsty chieftain, we have less reason than ever to care about what happens to him. And in any case, when fate binds Hidetora to his wheel of fire, he doesn't learn how to love, the way Lear does. He sees his soldiers dying around him under Taro and Jiro's siege, he meets up with the young man whose blindness he commanded, and he learns to feel *guilty*, which isn't the same thing. Kurosawa even omits the moment when Lear shows pity for his Fool, who is shivering on the heath. In *Ran* there's ample evidence that the Fool cares for his master—in one beautiful sequence Kyoami, desperately afraid in the midst of the battle, tries to abandon Hidetora and finds he can't—but Hidetora doesn't reciprocate. Our closest sympathetic link to this man is that the "positive" characters—Kyoami, Tango, Saburo—do care about his welfare, and fight to keep him safe.

There's a terrible purity about the conception of this movie, a tough, unyielding humanism that you have to wrestle with (and that is light years away from the humanism in Kurosawa's *Red Beard* or *Dodes-ka'den* or *Dersu Uzala*). Kurosawa, seventy-five when he made this film, seems to be saying that if we're going to feel compassion for Hidetora, it will have to be because he's old and weak and mad and helpless, not because he's earned it from us. And we can infer a different but parallel message about *Ran* itself: We're going to have to respond to the film because it's brilliant, not because it's likable. This time out, Kurosawa doesn't give us the sweeping, exciting battles he's famous for; the panoramas aren't magnificent, as they were in *Kagemusha*; he doesn't edit for comic irony or surprise. (A reference to the famous opening of *Yojimbo*—in the aftermath of the siege, a soldier holds his own severed arm—might be intended as a reminder of how drastically he's changed his tone and his style.) The first hour is so measured that he hardly seems to be editing at all, and the battle sequence that climaxes it (the siege on the castle where Hidetora is holed up) begins as a long series of tableaux, like the hands-off battle in Peter Weir's *Gallipoli*. Set to peculiar music by Toru Takemitsu, a sort of mock-romantic theme jarringly unlike the rest of his score, this sequence contributes, like the emphasis on long and middle shots, to the steady distancing of the audience.

Then, mysteriously, something extraordinary begins to happen. Soldiers on horseback start to move around the castle, setting it ablaze with hundreds of flaming arrows, and the movie slowly mobilizes into more activity than Kurosawa has allowed thus far. He cuts to the interior, where Hidetora sits amid the fire and smoke and corpses, the bones of his face bulging through his skin, his cheeks swollen, his blood-cracked eyes the color of jaundice. Kurosawa follows this great image with an even greater one: The defeated ruler, drifting out of the room as if hypnotized, appears at the top of the outside steps, and Kurosawa's camera takes in the burning castle, the smoke billowing out from under the roof, and at the bottom of the screen the victorious soldiers waving yellow and red banners. Two medieval traditions merge in a single shot. This is a samurai representation of the Hell Mouth of the old morality plays.

From this point on, *Ran* is a far livelier picture. Kurosawa brings his camera closer to the action, quickens the pace, and offers richer visual contrasts in the landscapes. Mieko Harada moves into the foreground as Lady Kaede, and her bracingly witty performance energizes every scene she's in. Her seduction of Jiro is a bravura piece of acting, audacious and wildly funny. Offering him her dead husband's helmet, she leaps on top of him and, drawing a knife, nips his neck; then she rushes to the edge of the room, draws the screens, rends her own gown, and slithers across the floor toward the disarmed warrior, throwing away her weapon at the last moment before kissing him full on the mouth and applying her tongue to his wound.

We recognize Kaede as belonging to Kurosawa's world; she evokes not only Isuzu Yamada in *Throne of Blood* but also Machiko Kyo as the wife in *Rashomon*. And a scene between her and Kurogane (Hisashi Ikawa), Jiro's minister—a comic variation on the interaction between the wicked queen and the kindly huntsman in *Snow White*—also returns us to this director's distinctive sense of humor. But even in its second and third hour *Ran* is an oddball movie that resists easy categorization, just as it resists emotional involvement. I walked out thinking it was impossibly stiff-necked and chilly and unrelenting; I longed for the splendor of the battles in *Kagemusha*, and wondered if *King Lear* wasn't simply the wrong tragedy for Kurosawa's temperament. But even if that *was* the case, still I had to confess (finally) that on his own terms he's conquered this great, paralyzingly difficult play.

It's surely no accident that the mood and look of the film change after the first hour. Kurosawa didn't just wake up. He signaled the turning point in both the narrative and Hidetora's journey toward self-discovery: The old man suddenly stops behaving in the regal, frozen style of the tyrant ruler he has been for most of his life. He's so overwhelmed by the horror he's caught in that he neglects to do what is expected of him—that is, commit *seppuku* (ritual suicide). (In Kurosawa's terms, that means he's gone mad, just as confronting the horror turns Lear's brain.) *Ran* may give Shakespeare scholars headaches for years to come; its strategy appears to be based as much on frustrating our expectations as on anything else. But I think they'll have to contend with it, because it *does* address *King Lear*. And, likable or not, it's a brilliant movie.

January 1986

Mini-Jokes

• • •

The problem with Jim Jarmusch's movies isn't that he's not funny or clever; it's that his jokes are so tiny, and his imaginative grasp so reduced, that you can almost feel the film shrinking while you watch. I understand that the minimalism is itself a joke, a hip sliver of postmodernism that's also a parody of the postmodern impulse. But knowing how to read Jarmusch doesn't help much when you're stuck in the middle of *Mystery Train*, certain that you could take your brain for a walk for twenty minutes at a time and not miss anything important.

Jarmusch's first picture, the 1984 *Stranger Than Paradise*, was like a cartoon illustrating the old Carl Sandburg poem "The Sins of Kalamazoo," where the citizens of that town, constrained by their own lack of vision, look over the world and "come back saying it is all like Kalamazoo." The protagonists of *Stranger Than Paradise* start off in New York City, travel to Cleveland, and end up in Florida, but all three places look pretty much the same to them. To us, too—because Jarmusch shoots each of them as an underlife blur: crummy motels, freeway signs, grimy skies. His second film, *Down by Law* (1986), operated on the Penelope principle, continuously unraveling its own story. The heroes (again there are three) are thrown in jail, they escape; one gets lost on the way, they rescue him; the boat they take to scramble through the Bayou swamps develops a leak, so they end up back on dry land; they fight and split up, but they wander back to the same site and take up with each other again. *Mystery Train* adopts yet another kind of parallelism: It consists of three tales, all set in Memphis on the same night, all ending up in the same fleabag hotel. (The clerk is the black singer Screamin' Jay Hawkins, whose wild-man number, "I Put a Spell on You," was the theme for *Stranger Than Paradise*.) Jarmusch sure loves to work in threes.

The first episode, "Far from Yokohama," is a typical Jarmusch mixed-culture gag. Teenage Japanese lovers (Masatoshi Nagase and Youki Kudoh), touring America's rock 'n' roll landmarks by train, stop in Memphis to visit Graceland and Sun Studios. The joke is that these empty-headed kids from Yokohama are walking American pop dolls, and the laughs derive from the contrast between her spacey enthusiasm and his deadpan cool; their dialogue is like a stoned tennis match with a huge pause every time someone drops the ball. There's a lot more chatter in the second segment, "A Ghost Story," in which a young Italian woman, Luisa (Nicoletta Braschi, who appeared in the last half hour of *Down by Law*), escorting her husband's coffin back to Rome, gets delayed in Memphis overnight. First she's accosted by a scammer who tells her a weird story about seeing Elvis Presley's ghost—but then, sharing a hotel room with a down-and-out stranger named DeeDee (Elizabeth Bracco) who's leaving her boy friend, Luisa sees the ghost herself. In the third part, "Lost in Space," we meet the boy friend (Joe Strummer, late of The Clash), a drunken, unemployed transplanted Brit who gets himself and two pals, including DeeDee's brother (Steve Buscemi), in trouble by shooting a liquor-store clerk. This section, with its grubby trio (Rick Aviles plays the third and liveliest), is the most Jarmusch-like. Stuck in one enclosed space after another—a barroom, the liquor store, a car, the hotel room where they hole up overnight—and growing increasingly drunker, the men start bouncing off the walls, and off each other. Their lethargic scrambling suggests what the Three Stooges might be like on valium.

The triple rhyming pattern in *Mystery Train* is both graceful and dryly self-conscious: Every time Jarmusch repeats a snatch of a radio DJ's spiel (the voice belongs to singer–songwriter Tom Waits, who played an out-of-work DJ in *Down by Law*), to signal us that the three stories are being played out simultaneously, the audience I saw the movie with laughed at the blank, throwaway manner affected by the narrative. After a while, though, the laughter started to sound desperate—Jarmusch doesn't give you much, in any department. He's working in color this time, with the superb photographer Robby Müller, who brings his trademark underlit warmth to this meager party. But even *that's* used sparely: Almost everything is in shades of red and black. That's one of several visual borrowings from *Diva* (most of them are in "Far from Yokohama"), but they're more like parings from some small corner of Jean-Jacques Beineix's glittering pop junkyard.

Jarmusch is the damnedest director. You can identify the themes in *Mystery Train*—stasis versus forward movement, the inevitability of enclosure, how American pop culture has become a dead-end joke and how non-Americans relate to it—but you know none of them is really the point. Nor is the flaky triumph of his characters, who (as in his other two pictures) survive everything. The point is the form. *Mystery Train* is an intricate jack-in-the-box with three compartments and—you discover over and over again— no pop-up surprise. The audience laughs at the joke that their expectations have been frustrated. It's not much of a joke—and that's supposed to be funny, too.

January 1990

Serving the Text

• • •

John Huston began his career as a film director in 1941 with the taut, feisty, definitively masculine proto-*film noir*, *The Maltese Falcon*, and ended it with a breathtakingly graceful and muted adaptation of "The Dead." The movement from the flamboyant, line-drawn, misanthropic mannerism of Dashiell Hammett to the broad weave of James Joyce's story, in which the commonality of human experience glows through the idiosyncrasies of individual characters, is the logical journey of a young man into old age (though, ironically, Joyce himself was only twenty-five when he wrote "The Dead," in 1907—ten years younger than Huston was when he made *The Maltese Falcon*). What the two movies share—along with Huston's versions of Stephen Crane's *The Red Badge of Courage* (1951), Carson McCullers's *Reflections in a Golden Eye* (1967), and Kipling's "The Man Who Would Be King" (1976), and the best parts of *Moby Dick* (1956) and *Wise Blood* (1979)—is Huston's uncanny gift for employing the deftness and flexibility of his craftsmanship to capture on screen the sensibilities of writers he loved.

Of all American filmmakers, Huston was truly the greatest reader; the "literary" part of his career in Hollywood, which grew proportionately larger through the years, is a single, beautiful act of sympathetic extension. (When he failed, as he did with the 1985 *Under the Volcano*, at least he failed big.) For thirty years he wanted to bring Joyce to the screen, and though others have made attempts, it's easy to pass over the Joseph Strick versions—his briefly controversial *Ulysses*, with its intelligent staged readings (with living illustrations) of the famous passages, and his puny, academic *Portrait of the Artist*—and say that Huston was the first director to do so. That "The Dead," a story that is an affirmation of life through an acceptance of its transience, was the project to which Huston devoted the final months of his life, is poetically appropriate; that, wracked with emphysema, he managed to direct it from a wheelchair between inhalations of oxygen, is miraculous. Anjelica Huston, who plays Gretta Conroy in the film, said (in the Decem-

ber 1987 issue of *Interview*): "I watched my father at the end of his
life; physically his possibilities became narrower and narrower. As
they grew narrower, his mind expanded and he became more
gentle, more loving, more giving, more vulnerable, more creative.
. . ." No one who sees *The Dead* can doubt this.

In Joyce's story, which is placed at the end of his collection
Dubliners, nothing happens—and everything happens. (Its closest
dramatic equivalent would be Chekhov's *Uncle Vanya* or *The
Cherry Orchard*, in both of which the action can be paraphrased
in a couple of sentences, but the characters are profoundly and irrevocably changed by the final curtain.) The subject of "The Dead"
is the importance of community. The protagonist, Gabriel Conroy,
is withdrawn and self-absorbed; he lives in his head (and so do we,
for most of the story). The darling of his two maiden aunts, who
brought him up, he feels himself the centerpiece of their annual
New Year's dinner party. He accepts their attentions—their expressed reliance on him to protect the delicate flow of the evening
(to escort the inveterate tippler, Freddy Malins, through the room
without causing a major upset, for example), to carve the goose, to
give the post-dinner speech—as a traditional burden, and he dis-
charges it with a combination of self-conscious graciousness and
nervous irritation.

Gabriel is appalling, though not in any way we can't understand. What's horrifying to a reader of the story is that, as Mary
McCarthy wrote of the everyday crimes of Ibsen's characters,
"These are the things one knows oneself to be capable of." Gabriel
is a husband and a father, yet he's absented himself from life as
surely as the melancholics and misanthropes of Shakespeare's comedies who refuse to take part in the final rejoicing, and though we
may want to throttle him, we can't help seeing parts of ourselves in
him. There are other stories that force us to identify with characters
we want to reject; Tolstoy's "The Death of Ivan Ilyich" and James's
"The Beast in the Jungle" come immediately to mind. There's a
difference, though, and it makes *all* the difference: By the time Ivan
Ilyich and James's John Marcher learn what fools they've been, it's
too late (Ivan is dying, Marcher is at the grave of the woman who
might have changed his life), but Gabriel experiences his revelation
while it can still do him some good.

There probably isn't a piece of fiction that inspires the kind of loyalty "The Dead" does; it's the favorite story of almost every reader I know. For a long time—until the final few moments— screenwriter Tony Huston's adaptation stays out of Gabriel's head, and there are Joyce enthusiasts who will complain that the movie denies us the pleasures of the story's double consciousness: In Joyce, we see the Morkans' party filtered through Gabriel's limited vision while at the same time our perspective allows us to judge Gabriel with an objectivity he obviously lacks. (This is most clear in the comic section involving his altercation with his fellow professor, Molly Ivors.) One Joyce aficionado I know says the movie has no point of view; what he means, of course, is that it doesn't have the *story's* point of view. Yet it seems to me that to throw away Huston's *The Dead* on the grounds that we don't experience it in exactly the same way as we do the story would call into question the possibility of *ever* doing justice to a literary work on screen, in which case we'd have to forget our pleasures—however diluted—at the movie versions of *Lolita, The Scarlet Letter, Outcast of the Islands, Great Expectations, The Turn of the Screw.*

More importantly, it would be to lose sight of Huston's achievement. I don't think any moviemaker has ever come this close to reproducing the *emotional* experience of a work of fiction. During the years in which Huston waited to film Joyce, his favorite writer, he seems to have mysteriously gotten inside the man's head. When you see the Morkans' house, lamp-lit from the street, with the figures of the guests dancing in silhouette behind the drawn curtains, and then from the inside, where Aunt Kate (Helena Carroll) and Aunt Julia (Cathleen Delany) wait anxiously at the top of the stairs for Gabriel (Donal McCann) to arrive, while Lily (Rachael Dowling), the maid, rushes about in a state of perpetual consternation, the images so approximate the shared picture of the setting we have from reading and rereading the story that what we experience is a kind of déjà vu.

Huston's strategy for getting Joyce's story on screen is, appropriately, Chekhovian. The interaction of the hostesses and the guests at the party is orchestrated magnificently; everything is conveyed in telling, understated details, like Gabriel's distractedness during the performance portion of the evening (when different principals offer their amateur talents for singing, playing piano, recitations as part of the entertainment), or his inattention to Lily's embarrassment when he presses a coin into her hand. Donal McCann is a marvelous actor; he shows us the fine distinctions among Gabriel's emotions by the degree of warmth in his face, and he has a fish-eye distance from the others—a slightly affected hauteur that can pass for world-weariness or elegant reserve among people who are inclined to give Gabriel the benefit of the doubt. Similarly, his care with old Mrs. Malins (Marie Kean), who wants to chat with him about the vacations she takes with her daughter and son-in-law, or with Freddy (Donal Donnelly) when he turns up sloshed, is as remote and professional as an orderly's.

It's no mean trick for a performer to let us see Gabriel's snobbish cool without losing our interest in him long before his "generous tears" redeem him. And it's even more difficult for a director to allow us just enough sympathy with Gabriel's feeling of displacement among the other guests to understand him (even if we think he's behaving badly) when he removes himself emotionally from the party. McCann and Huston accomplish both of these during the "amateur night" section of the film. When Mary Jane (Ingrid Craigie), the music teacher, plays piano, her angular form bends stiffly over the instrument, and her nervous concentration creates a breathless tension that her listeners can sense. She's awkwardly earnest, and although her show-off musical technique is all training, the ferocity of her attempt to please her audience touches us. But not Gabriel—and that's where we part company with him.

Huston's all-seeing generosity, on the other hand, lets us take note of Mary Jane's faults and then pass over them. Something similar happens when Mr. Grace (Sean McClory) recites, with a practiced melodramatic intensity, an ominous Irish lyric that no one in his audience quite comprehends but everyone projects his or her own feelings onto. (This is a charming scene.) And when Aunt Julia is persuaded to sing, her thin, faded voice is an emblem, for everyone who hears her, of the lifetime that has preceded this moment—and Huston, picking up on their associations and her own, pans through the house, showing us mementos of her past.

In terms of dramatic structure, *The Dead* can be seen as a four-act play, with these pre-dinner theatricals highlighting Act One, the feast constituting Act Two, the post-dinner preparations for leaving the Morkans' taking up all of Act Three, and Act Four depicting Gretta's story about Michael Furey (her dead suitor) and Gabriel's transformation in the hotel room. The key moments in Acts Two and Three develop Joyce's idea about the value of popular art and how Gabriel's inability to appreciate it cuts him off from the companionship of his fellow man. I mean "popular art" in its most literal definition: art (even if it lacks artistry) that makes a direct connection with its audience, requiring no niceties of education to provide access to it. Gabriel's speech at the conclusion of the banquet is all artistry with no content and no sincerity—empty form. And yet, as Huston's camera travels slowly away from Gabriel, down the table to the three women to whom it's addressed (his aunts and Mary Jane), we see how their warm response takes it away from him and transforms it into something heartfelt and meaningful. Later (in Act Three), Gabriel sees Gretta (Anjelica Huston) on the stairway, transfixed by the rendition of the ballad "The Lass of Aughrim" by the tenor, Bartell D'Arcy (Frank Patterson), in the parlor above. Gabriel stands apart from her, feeling excluded, jealous, unable to extend himself to an understanding of (or even a respect for) the depth of her emotions. This extraordinary moment marks Huston's most complete identification with Joyce—it's the point at which story and film merge. The image of Anjelica Huston, silhouetted by the stained glass on the landing behind her, her figure casting a shadow on the peeling wallpaper, a white scarf thrown loosely over her hair, her eyes glistening, tipping her head ever so slightly as she burrows into her past, may be as great as any movies can offer us.

Of the cast, only Anjelica Huston and Dan O'Herlihy (as Mr. Brown), he with a gorgeous white mane and that unforgettably rich baritone, are recognizable to American audiences. Most of the others are Dublin stage actors, and their unfamiliarity works in the movie's favor. The uncanny casting is in fact further proof that Huston achieved some mysterious communion with the story. The acting could almost be called a collection of epiphanies: Helena Carroll's hearty, spirited Aunt Kate, reminiscing in her crackling voice about the tenor she adored in her youth; the moment when Marie Kean's Mrs. Malins declares, her face pinched and her eyebrows raised superciliously, that she doesn't attend Verdi's operas because of the composer's "dubious" morals; Dan O'Herlihy's drunk scene, when his hair becomes comically disheveled and his eyes tragically blurry and old. And the moment when Maria McDermottroe (as

Molly Ivors), departing before dinner has begun, declares with a delicious taste of scandal that she's off to a union meeting, and when Katherine O'Toole (as Miss Furlong) pulls herself up to her full height at the table and pronounces judgment on the "vulgarity" of the production she saw a few nights earlier, munching determinedly on a lettuce stalk to punctuate her point. As Freddy Malins, drowning in spirits, Donal Donnelly executes a brilliantly sustained farce turn that's also suffused with feeling; when he downs a whiskey for courage and slides across the room to face the merciless eyes of his mother (whom he's disappointed by breaking the abstentioner's pledge he swore four days earlier), Donnelly makes you feel the reluctance of a little boy who knows he's about to get his wrist slapped—and Kean's Mrs. Malins is just the matriarch to do the slapping.

If you saw Anjelica Huston's sly performance as the conniving Maerose in *Prizzi's Honor*, her father's next-to-last movie, you may gasp at how different she is here. As Maerose she used her unusual height comically; in one scene, clad in black, she put on pale make-up and turned herself into a Modigliani figure to gain sympathy for her revenge plot against a faithless lover (Jack Nicholson). As Gretta she has a dainty, flirtatious elegance; she treads as lightly as a ballerina, and her entrance from the cold night, arms pressed to her sides, hands drawn together as if in prayer, posed on point as she stamps her feet to warm herself up, is so delicate you could swear she'd dropped six inches. This is the kind of physical transformation, effected entirely through acting and with no effort you can catch, that you associate with only a handful of actresses—Gish, Hepburn, Redgrave, Maggie Smith, Blythe Danner. In the climactic scene where Gretta pours forth her sad tale of Michael Furey (the youth she loved, now long dead, who used to sing "The Lass of Aughrim"), Huston, her hair flowing down her back, twists her body, heaving with sobs, away from Donal McCann; her right shoulder carries the burden of her sorrow for the camera and becomes the focus of the shot. It's as if a Degas had come to life.

As Joyce tells the last part of the story, Gretta's confession awakens a rapid series of emotions in Gabriel. His longing to make love to her in the hotel room mixes with "a dull anger," so his first verbal responses are careless and insensitive. He pities himself for not being as important to her as Michael Furey. He feels "a vague terror" when he begins to realize the intensity of Furey's young passion for Gretta. He's touched by her grief and "shy of intruding" on it. And when she's cried herself to sleep, "a strange friendly pity for her entered his soul"—and then the "generous tears." Huston keeps Donal McCann in sight through Anjelica Huston's full-hearted reading of Gretta's memory speech, and this astonishingly subtle actor lets us see each of Gabriel's shifts; he scans the emotional spectrum. But Huston knows there's no way to film Joyce's final paragraph, Gabriel's epiphany—possibly the most sublime ending given any story—without taking us right inside Gabriel's head. So for the first time he goes to a voice-over, while the cinematographer, Fred Murphy (who has done superb work straight through the picture), travels through the January night, tracking the snow that is "general all over Ireland." It's the only choice Huston could have made—at least the only one that makes sense: Having evoked the story so grandly from the opening glimpses of the Morkans' house, he concludes by maintaining an almost perfect alignment with Joyce. It's Huston's way of saying "You can't improve on this; listen to how beautiful it is." He's like a stage director who knows it's pointless to even try to recreate a storm on stage in the heath scene of *King Lear* because Shakespeare's language is all you need.

When the aunts' party is over, there's a very moving exterior shot of the house: The yellow lamplight seems old, and suddenly we are conscious of the passing of time in a way that Joyce couldn't have intended, because for us, for the world we live in, the Dublin of 1904 is long dead. And of course we're aware of fleeting time on another level, too, when we see John Huston's name on the film. It's impossible not to view *The Dead* as Huston's eulogy for himself—one of the most splendid an artist of this century has made. For nearly fifty years critics and other filmmakers have pointed to *The Maltese Falcon* as a model of how to get the spirit of the hard-boiled detective fiction of the twenties and thirties onto the screen. Now they will point to *The Dead* as a paragon of literary adaptation—proof that a man of talent, adapting the work of a man of genius, can create something unforgettable.

February 1988

The Epic Impulse

• • •

Philip Kaufman, who made *The Unbearable Lightness of Being*, is one of the few gifted American directors who persisted, in the face of the videoization of Hollywood and the imaginative melt-down of the mass audience in the Reagan era, in taking on daring, ambitious projects without assured box-office prospects. Kaufman, who made student films in the sixties and released his first commercial feature, *The Great Northfield, Minnesota Raid*, in 1972, still thinks like a moviemaker of that expansive, experimental era; he brings to a project a combination of instinct, craftsmanship, and an adventurous intellectual's vision of movies as an ideal medium for stretching outward to embrace a world of possibilities. He still treats his audience as intelligent, reflective individuals with the education and quickness of wit to process a wide range of allusions and weigh their implications, and to follow lightning shifts in tone or style.

You feel all your circuits are being kept busy at a Kaufman movie. In his deliriously enjoyable 1978 remake of *Invasion of the Body Snatchers*, Kaufman and the screenwriter W. D. Richter turned the familiar tale of the alien pods that plant a colony in California, first forging themselves into identical copies of the human inhabitants and then replacing them while they sleep, into a crafty, hilarious satire of late-seventies American lifestyles. With its therapist villain and retro-sixties rebel heroes, the movie was roughly the cinematic equivalent of Tom Wolfe's essay "The Me Decade and the Third Great Awakening" or (without its doom-and-gloom self-seriousness) Christopher Lasch's sociological treatise on the seventies, *The Culture of Narcissism*. It was also an ironic new twist on an old genre—maybe not quite the equal of the rerouted genre pictures Arthur Penn, Peckinpah, Altman, and Coppola produced in the years when Kaufman was starting out, but a stream-lined, wittily layered horror comedy. Working with the photographer Michael Chapman (*Taxi Driver*), Kaufman found spooky visual emblems for a world gone mysteriously haywire. The four heroes cast weird, de Chirico–like shadows as they ran through the

San Francisco streets; distorted or opaque reflections were everywhere you looked. The growing pods resembled monster fetuses and
made horrendous snorting and groaning sounds as they assumed the
features of their victims; when Brooke Adams was "snatched," the
life was sucked out of her body like air out of a punctured tire,
and then her double sprang out of the bushes, nude, like a pop-up
Botticelli Venus.

With a crooked finger in each of several film genres—the western (*The Great Northfield, Minnesota Raid*), the explorer adventure (his affecting, wonderfully muted *The White Dawn*), the teenage rite-of-passage picture (*The Wanderers*), and science fiction/
horror (*Body Snatchers*)—Kaufman might have continued to make
smart, hip entertainments. Instead, he took a quantum leap in 1983
with his three-and-a-quarter-hour, $27 million adaptation of Tom
Wolfe's comic chronicle of the NASA program, *The Right Stuff*.
And the result was a smart, hip entertainment on an epic scale—a
madcap epic. Kaufman hadn't been dwarfed or co-opted by the size
of the project; you could feel his finely tuned mind behind every
frame. There were sequences where the mesh of styles and the casual flip-flop of tones proved too jarring (like the John Glenn flight,
with its heavenly choirs and half-dozen Aboriginals executing a ritual dance), and others where the deliberately divided heart of Kaufman's conception—he wanted to both parody and celebrate the astronauts—created insurmountable problems (the barbecue party at
the Houston Astrodome, which had Sally Rand fan-dancing under
cathedral lighting). But you could always see the outlines of his
ideas. And the best-achieved scenes were extraordinary: the mock-
mythic meeting of Chuck Yeager (Sam Shepard) and the great
rocket plane, the X-1, which breathed fire like a fairy-tale dragon;
the medical testing of the astronauts, who treated the procedure as
if it were a championship athletic match, psyching each other out
and working up strategies; the domestic scenes, in which the astronauts and their displaced wives coped with their yearning for community.

Though Wolfe's book is unified by his distinctive tone of ur-
bane astonishment, it's really not a novel at all. It's a series of essays
on a single broad topic or, if you will, a single, outwardly spiraling
digression on everything having to do with the space program. So
Kaufman's decision to bounce from one style to another in the

movie made perfect sense; it was the response of a first-rate filmmaker who's also a first-rate reader.

On the other hand, *The Unbearable Lightness of Being* certainly *is* a novel, and a wonderful one. But it's tough to categorize
(except under a catch-all phrase like "postmodern" or "novel of
ideas")—and, I would have said, impossible to film.

There is a strong narrative, set just before, during, and just
after the Prague Spring of 1968. It's constructed around the relationships of a Czech doctor named Tomas with two women: Tereza,
a photographer whom he meets at a hotel where she's waitressing
and who eventually becomes his wife, and Sabina, an artist who
continues to be his mistress even after he marries. But it's presented
in a nonlinear fashion, with flashbacks and flash-forwards embed-
ded in an allusive, anecdotal style, and each time Kundera moves
on to another section (there are seven) the dominant point of view
changes. Moreover, much of the book takes the form of a discourse
on the relative values of "lightness" and "heaviness," ascribing these
qualities to a variety of abstractions: sex and love, freedom and
commitment, art and kitsch, life and death. Life, says Kundera, is
unbearably light: Since we live only once, and are thus prevented
from making experimental life decisions and then reversing them,
"The sketch that is our life is a sketch for nothing, an outline with
no picture."

What keeps the novel from bogging down in these philosophical explorations is a combination of the brief chapters (thin, flavor-
ful slices of text), the airy, spun-dry diction, the companionable,
coffeehouse feeling of the nonnarrative passages (they're like late-
afternoon conversations you remember having in grad school), and
the fact that, in his unsentimental way, Kundera manages to lay
open some substantial emotional issues. But how do you translate
this wry little novel to the screen, when the very elements that make
it such an unlikely subject for filming—the smoke rings of philosophy and the crisply rendered comedy of fatalism—are the same
things that keep it swimming around in your head? The best you
might hope for is a beautifully shaped film of the *story*, removed
from its philosophical context—something like the Visconti version
of Camus's *The Stranger*.

Incredible as it may sound, however, *The Unbearable Lightness of Being* is *both* an authentic version of Kundera's book *and* an

authentic movie. (It's a *big* movie, too, like *The Right Stuff*; it weighs in at two hours and forty-five minutes—road-show length.) Kaufman and his co-screenwriter, Jean-Claude Carrière, have trimmed the narrative and rearranged it into a linear framework; they've turned Tomas from an oversexed early-middle-aged physician with one discarded marriage into a seductive young surgeon, played by that witty chameleon Daniel Day-Lewis in a sleek, mock–Don Juan style. Here Day-Lewis is garbed in a black turtleneck with dark pants and corduroy jacket that accentuate his olive skin. (He was pale, almost sickly-looking, in *My Beautiful Laundrette* and *A Room with a View*.) With a sly smile, amused little rat's eyes peering out from behind shades that slide down his nose (as if he were disrobing), an upswept coiffe, and aggressive, bushy eyebrows, he looks predatorily sexy, wolfish. In a parody of caddishness, when he lunges for a woman he desires, he leans over sideways in her direction, one hand on his hip, and he gives his lines (many of which come straight out of Kundera) a prickly ironic edge.

For the first half hour or so, while Tomas darts around Prague and the provinces, officiating at operations and pursuing *amours*, and Janáček's *Fairy Tale* plays ferociously on the soundtrack, the movie is a peerless farce. His fellow doctors watch from a darkened operating chamber while he goes to work on a nurse in the next room; even the patient sits up to peek at his celebrated technique. Driving merrily to one hospital, Tomas passes a troupe of women in nightdresses performing calisthenics on the lawn; Altman-style, the camera swoops past this nutty image, allowing us just enough time to take it in. Inside, as if infected by the general mood of joyous insanity, everyone participating in the operation picks up the rhythm of the march being played out on the lawn. Tomas hums as he saws away at his patient's skull, a nurse whistles along, and the oxygen bag inflates and deflates to the beat. Hilariously carefree, Day-Lewis's Tomas is the personification of "lightness."

Kaufman's movie is a series of dramatic variations on Kundera's light/heavy theme. Tomas and Sabina (Lena Olin) share a perfect light-handed relationship; their lovemaking, blissfully free of emotional ties, has a playful, let's-try-it-on quality. When Olin (she was the young actress with designs on Erland Josephson in Bergman's *After the Rehearsal*) stands before her mirror in her lacy black underwear, a black bowler hat tilted over one eye, she evokes insouciant movie heroines of the past (Dietrich in her androgynous Sternberg roles, Liza Minnelli in *Cabaret*), and she gives a remarkable, quicksilver performance. Her supremely confident, cosmopolitan sexiness suggests what the Soviets wanted to suppress in Czechoslovakia—she's a walking example of what it means to be truly free. Sabina, as protective of her liberty as Tomas is, gives him the ultimate compliment: "You are the complete opposite of kitsch."

For Sabina, romantic commitment is something sticky and clinging, like the thick bad taste she believes is turning the world ugly; she recoils from it just as she recoils from the Soviets when the Russian tanks roll into Prague. Setting herself up in a studio in Geneva, she begins a new phase in her work—sculpted mirror pieces—and takes a married lover, Franz (Derek de Lint), who follows her around like a puppy dog. One day he walks out on his marriage and arrives on Sabina's doorstep with his bags and a vow of commitment to their relationship; he tells her he wants to live in a glass house, with no secrets from the world. But Sabina, who deals in art that entices the world but hides its own core—both seducing and frustrating intruders—and for whom lovemaking is another form of art, doesn't want Franz's see-through sex. When he returns, she's run away, leaving him only a few shards of mirror in an empty studio.

Tomas courts Tereza (Juliette Binoche) in the same free-wheeling gamesman's spirit in which he initiates all his other affairs—but it's not in her nature to settle for romantic games. Responding joyously to his advances, she skips along the street as if she were in a three-legged race; it's easy to see why he's so enchanted with this ingenuous gamine with astonishingly clear, brown doe's eyes. What he doesn't see at first—but *we* do—is the nakedly needy expression in those eyes. Binoche (who played the Juliet figure in André Téchiné's *Rendez-vous*) wears her hair in tiny prickles along the top of her brow; she looks like Isabella Rossellini from some angles, and in close-up she recalls some of the French movie actresses of the thirties, with their skewed, unarranged, somehow semiformed beauty—women like Orane Demazis and Sylvia Bataille. Of the three central characters in *The Unbearable Lightness*, Tereza gets to illustrate the greatest emotional range, and Binoche's performance is a tour de force.

Along with Tomas, we first see Tereza when she dives heedlessly into the pool on the grounds of the provincial hospital he's visiting and disturbs a floating chess game. Tereza's an innocently disruptive force, and Tomas is attracted to her immediately. He has to walk through steamy corridors to track her down—like a fairy-tale prince in search of an incognito princess—at the hotel bar, where she's a waitress. On the basis of a few moments' acquaintance with him (they don't even make it to bed), Tereza packs up and moves to Prague, where one day he finds her at his door—as Sabina will later find Franz—with bag and baggage. When he starts to make love to her, she sneezes (she caught a cold on the train); when she has her orgasm, she screams; when morning comes, he discovers his hand tightly clasped in hers, and an unfamiliar weight on his life.

Tereza's faithful eagerness has a hold on Tomas; he chafes against it yet grows attached to it. And suddenly he finds himself avoiding some of his mistresses and keeping an eye on the clock when he makes love to Sabina. And, watching Binoche's Tereza, we can understand why. She has a playful, giggly side: When she catches him showing his discomfort at her dancing with another man, she waltzes around the room, crying in delight, "He's jealous! He's jealous!"—and she's as voluptuously schoolgirlish as Amy Irving in *Yentl*. But she's passionate, too. She clings to him. And though he keeps pulling in the other direction (he won't give up *all* his mistresses), her conviction is something he's never experienced before, and despite himself he falls in love with her. Unlike Sabina, he becomes a traitor to his own "light" nature.

Anxious to do justice to Kundera, Kaufman and Carrière transform some of the philosophical passages in the text into dialogue (mostly for Tomas). This takes a little getting accustomed to, but it's used sparingly, and somehow you accept it as part of the coffee-and-wine atmosphere of the first section. In these scenes Kaufman, production designer Pierre Guffroy, costumer Ann Roth, and photographer Sven Nykvist (doing his most imaginative work in years) achieve an emotional fullness in the period recreations of Alexander Dubček's "enlightened" Prague that's almost miraculous. The filmmakers realize that in order to transpose Kundera's world to the screen, they need to do more than reproduce his eastern-European dryness and irony: They have to supply their own vision of what the Czech humanism of the sixties meant. Then, brilliantly, they

decimate it in the Soviet invasion sequence, where Tereza, fed up
with Tomas's infidelities, storms into the night and is nearly run
over by Russian tanks plowing through the narrow streets like ghost
silhouettes with an advance guard of searchlights.

The invasion scenes are the most accomplished moviemaking
Kaufman's ever done; they have such a convincing documentary
feel that you're startled to see Tomas among the protesters pounding
away at the sides of a tank, and Tereza in the midst of the violence,
snapping photographs of the invaders. (Perhaps Binoche's best acting is in the economical way she shows us Tereza's politicization
during the Prague Spring: This national crisis, which comes at a
time of personal crisis for her, matures her—it brings out her courage while it turns her into a political artist.) This sequence is tense
and chilling in the way that *Z* or *State of Siege* or *Under Fire* is.
While Nykvist alternately bleeds the color out of the compositions
and insinuates it back in, we experience the events with some of the
shock and dislocation of the Czechs themselves. And we can see
Tomas and Tereza's story turning into history.

The Unbearable Lightness is in four parts that function like
symphonic movements. The picture moves from Prague to Geneva
(where Tomas and Tereza, temporarily abandoning their homeland, relocate and meet up with Sabina once again), then back to
Prague (to which Tomas follows Tereza, who feels useless in Swit-
zerland), and finally into the countryside (where Tomas and Tereza
take up a new phase of their lives, on a farm). The Prague and
Geneva sections are the most immediately impressive. There's an
amazing sequence at Sabina's Geneva studio, where Tereza, advised
by Swiss editors to give up on candid news shots and try art photography, insists on shooting Sabina in the nude. This scene is like an
emotional Dance of the Seven Veils performed as a pas de deux.
Tomas is neither present nor alluded to, but he's the tacit subject of
every move the women make, the invisible third person in the room.
They play-act their respective relationships to him and to each other
concerning him. When Sabina repairs behind a curtain to undress,
Tereza follows her, catching her before she's ready, as if she were
catching her in bed with Tomas; she sees her as she imagines Tomas
sees her, and approaches her tenderly, as she feels Tomas would.
(It's the first time we've seen Sabina nude, so we too are seeing
something exposed that we haven't seen before.) Tereza wants erotic

photos depicting a woman looking up at a lover. And Sabina looks at Tereza with the understanding that Tereza knows she's watching her husband's lover; you see fear, shame, defiance, amusement alternately in her eyes. Then the tables turn: Sabina insists that Tereza strip ("Take off your clothes," she says—Tomas's seduction line) and that they switch roles. For a while the tone turns schoolgirlish, while they play hide-and-seek with the camera. Then Sabina mounts Tereza and with both fierceness and tenderness removes her panties. She's trying to see what Tomas sees in Tereza. And when she pins back Tereza's arm and demands, "Look at me, Tereza," it's a challenge: she's asking her friend to see her as Tomas's lover. Little is spoken during this scene, but the exchange is like a thrillingly revealing tête-à-tête that makes two friends almost frighteningly intimate. You keep wondering (as you might have in the love scenes in Robert Towne's *Personal Best*) how any man could have dared to film such a complexly sensuous encounter between two women.

At the end of the second section Tomas, feeling the tug of his love for Tereza when she returns to Prague, pursues her there. At that point Lena Olin leaves the picture (to reappear only once, briefly), Tomas learns the oppression of living under the shadow of the Soviets, and the movie—inevitably—becomes "heavier." But Kaufman knows precisely what he's doing: He wants us to feel the weight of Tomas's new life, both in Prague and (when he and Tereza decide they can't stand the city any longer) on the farm. But the third section—which is about Tomas champing at the bit, trying to rebel against the new bondage of the Russians and to adapt himself to marriage—has defects in rhythm, and an entire subplot (involving Tereza and a man she sleeps with, in a futile effort to mimic Tomas's "lightness" about sex) that just doesn't work. (This episode is a holdover from the novel, where Kundera provides a fuller thematic context.) However, it also has a terrific one-scene performance by the Czech actor Daniel Olbrychski, as a shrewd government manipulator who tries to trap Tomas into signing a disclaimer on an article he wrote during the Dubček days, when liberals were exercising what they believed was their right to freedom of the press.

Kaufman consciously turns the movie into a more conventional epic as the potential for frivolity slips quietly out of Tomas's life. But he's one of the few American directors left who still *understands* how to make an epic, and there are scenes in the last section, in the countryside, that might have been directed by Renoir. One, in which the dog Tomas bought Tereza on their wedding day has to be put to sleep, is a test case for directorial sensibility. Grounding the scene carefully in both the thematic issues of the film (Tereza argues that her love for the dog is unburdened by the jealousy that taints her love for Tomas—that it's "light") and in the bond between Tomas and Tereza, Kaufman transcends sentimentality.

By the third hour Kaufman's craftsmanship and Binoche's and Day-Lewis's acting have raised the stake we have in the characters' fates to an extraordinarily high level. Kaufman really cashes in on our identification with Tomas and Tereza in the last few minutes of the film, when he's able to bring off an astonishingly difficult final contrast between "light" and "heavy" by showing us how Tomas comes to accept and feel happy for the commitment he's made to Tereza—and then the exquisite brevity of that happiness. And Sabina, who's now in California, living the life of a hippie artist—she's literally gone to the end of America to find her freedom—returns to the movie to acknowledge, finally, her own "heaviness": her love for Tereza and Tomas.

"Einmal ist keinmal," Tomas believes at the beginning of Kundera's novel, underscoring the futility of a life that can't be tried out, experimented on, and then replayed if things don't work out. "What happens but once . . . might as well not have happened at all." (It's his justification for the unfettered lifestyle he chooses for himself.) In Kaufman's film, these lines become first ironic, then ineffably moving, as we come to realize, along with Tomas and Sabina, that once can be everything.

February 1988

For Reel

• • •

At first glance the Robert Altman–Garry Trudeau HBO series, *Tanner '88*, seems no more than an elegant curio—a hip, clever, deftly assembled and beautifully acted satirical comedy about the selling of a presidential candidate that, combining Altman's off-hand eavesdropping style with Trudeau's distanced canniness, comes across like a collage put together by experts. The experts have distinctive voices and personalities: *Tanner '88* is a weird meeting of *auteurs* in which each maintains his autonomy. You can spot Trudeau's hand not only in the deep-inside political humor—which springs cooled-out barbs in the direction of almost every Democratic hopeful since the race began, as well as sending up the primary process itself—but also in the structure of scenes, which are like thematic clusters of small comic ideas that tend to culminate, like Trudeau's *Doonesbury* strips, in final-frame throwaway punch lines. And you can see Altman's right at home in the world of politics and the media. Watching his free-floating camera making passes at the images on TV monitors, or searching for clues to the characters' motives among the casual detritus in hotel rooms turned overnight into campaign headquarters and demographics testing centers, you recognize the director of *Secret Honor*, that semiabsurdist mock-confessional about Richard Nixon. And with Michael Murphy cast as Congressman Jack Tanner, the eleventh-hour Democratic candidate who emerges after Joe Biden's withdrawal, you make the connections to *Nashville* (in which Murphy played the politico who handles the Hal Phillip Walker campaign).

In the one-hour pilot, called "The Dark Horse," Tanner's crew, headed by T. J. Cavanaugh (Pamela Reed), camps out in New Hampshire, trying to shape an image that will help him pull ahead after a poor showing in Iowa. A New York would-be documentary filmmaker named Deke (Matt Malloy) has produced a bio videotape to introduce Tanner to the voters that mixes goofy pseudo-vérité glimpses of the candidate shoveling snow at his home in East Lansing, Michigan, and accepting a telephone invitation to join the race with stock footage meant to link him to JFK, Martin Luther King, and the other liberal touchstones of his generation. The control group polled by the demographers fails to respond to the tape, resisting the sentimental pull of the down-home segments involving Tanner's devotion to his daughter, Alex (Cynthia Nixon), during a childhood illness, and complaining that Tanner's platform is cribbed and fuzzy. Yet something about him, perhaps the combination of his sincerity and his professorial articulateness (he holds a Ph.D. and teaches at Michigan State), appeals to the New Hampshire voters: He comes in fourth, and (in Part 1, "For Real," and Part 2, "The Night of the Twinkies") moves up to third on "Super Tuesday" and rallies in Nashville, where the tag-along press joins the Tanner entourage.

It's amazing to see a TV program that conveys the sensibilities of both Trudeau and Altman—especially Altman, whose small-screen Pinter adaptations (*The Basement* and *The Room*) couldn't break out of the pinched confines of the forced-elliptical dialogue. (For the first half of *The Room*, I thought Altman and Linda Hunt had managed to create one truly memorable character, a woman who exposes a fresh fear every time she moves or speaks, but in the second half Hunt's shifting pools of emotional response solidified into a series of bizarre theatrical affectations.) But it's tough to find the center of "The Dark Horse," and at times you wonder if—except for Pamela Reed's fabulous performance and two or three moments that catch Tanner and his team off guard, depressed, and exhausted—the show is going to amount to more than just a lot of Altman frissons (like the farmer's wife, played by Pat Falkenhain, who collects photos of Democratic candidates), or Trudeau frissons (like the absurdities of the bio film), or bits that overlap the concerns of both (the running gag about how ordinary human activity—snow plows or pizza deliveries or quilting bees—keeps upstaging the serious speechifying).

The seductive ambiguity is clearly deliberate. Altman and Trudeau's theme is the way T. J. and her team turn everything Tanner says and does into a Tanner promo; every time he bursts into a tirade, Deke's camera is on hand to shoot it. And since you can't tell how conscious Tanner is of the way his words are being used to advertise him, you don't know how large a role he's playing in the creation of his own image. That's a great subject for political satire, and *Tanner '88* is enjoyable and intriguing from the first shots. But the tantalizing elusiveness of Altman's approach can be frustrating: At the end of "The Dark Horse," you're still not sure what you've got hold of. It's not until "For Real" that the conception begins to pay off—and it keeps paying off into "The Night of the Twinkies," which focuses on the slapdash, improvisational intrusiveness of the press.

The title "For Real" is a pun Altman suggests at the beginning of the episode, when, in a TV ad for Tanner, the phrase "for reel" appears on the screen and metamorphoses into "for real." (It's not clear whether that's a subliminal slip on Deke's part or a touch of expressionism on Altman's.) And as Tanner finds selected sections of his FBI file reproduced in his brochures and "real folks" performers like Waylon Jennings being hit up to perform at his rallies, the idea of T. J.'s manufacturing a media "reality" out of Tanner's real life becomes richer and funnier.

"For Real" plays like a series of comic riffs on the moment in Pirandello's *Six Characters in Search of an Author* when the Father, seeing that his story has caught the imagination of the actors he's asked to dramatize it, observes with horror that he can already hear an undefinable falseness transforming his words. Stringer Kincaid (Daniel Jenkins), the most gung-ho member of the Tanner team, instructs the candidate on which gestures he should get rid of because they "spell" other, jinxed politicians like Jimmy Carter; Jennings's choice of song for the occasion, "If Old Hank Could Only See Us Now," is about the commercialization of the "real" Nashville; a knife-wielding drunk, acting naturally (in pursuit of his wife's lover, not Tanner), accidentally makes Tanner a media celebrity. (The national press, like Opal in *Nashville*, misses the big event. Their bus has broken down a hundred miles from the city, and they're using their TV monitor as a poker table when the news report comes on.)

Tanner has a first-rate cast. Michael Murphy, who can make his face appear comfortably open and furtively anxious at the same time, is the perfect actor to play Jack Tanner; Altman makes the most of his hushed earnestness, his soft-slippered perfect enunciation, and his endearing shagginess. (Murphy may be the most underrated member of the Altman repertory company; each time I see *Nashville* or *McCabe and Mrs. Miller*, where he plays the company man who tries to buy out Warren Beatty, I'm struck by how many good moments he has that I'd never noticed before.) As chain-smoking T. J., Pamela Reed speaks her lines from somewhere deep in her tarry throat. The velvet hominess of T. J.'s exec style is purest eighties; she's like a tranquilized version of another initialed heroine, J. C. Wyatt (Diane Keaton), in *Baby Boom*. If we're never sure of the level of Tanner's self-consciousness, we can be certain of T. J.'s: She's *always* aware of the impression she's making. (That's why she's a pro.) She's not a fake, though, any more than J. C. is— and, in some funny way, the genuineness of these women redeems the superficiality of their demeanor, perhaps by showing us how feverishly dependent they are on their work to constantly reenergize them. There's so much going on in Reed's eyes that she often seems to be in two places at once, the present and the anticipated future, and in her best moment—a gaffe on the phone to Joe Kennedy in which she refers to him as "Bobby" (inevitably recalling Barbara Baxley's obsessesion with the Kennedys in *Nashville*)—the past comes crashing through, too. Reed does the finest sustained acting in *Tanner*, but there are a number of other performers who do themselves proud: Veronica Cartwright, Kevin J. O'Connor, and Richard Cox as reporters, Daniel Jenkins and Cynthia Nixon, Cleavon Little as Reverend Billy Crier, a wary Southern Baptist minister (an old pal of Tanner's from his Civil Rights days), Ilana Levine as a spacey, desperately well-meaning campaign worker who wears T. J. down.

Robert Altman has always been fascinated by behavioral details no one else notices and that can reveal whole new facets of personality (or deeper, unsounded mysteries). In *Nashville* he demonstrated that people expose even more of themselves when they perform for an audience or a camera and *think* they're in control of what they're putting out. His peculiar brand of naturalism, which depends as much on nuance as Chekhov's and as much on multiple perspectives as Virginia Woolf's, is brilliantly on display in *Tanner '88*, which is on one level a reverse take on the *Nashville* theme (here revealing moments are built into hype) and on another level fresh evidence that human interaction is full of surprises (Stringer Kincaid gets far from the effect he looked for when he leads the press to Tanner's private reunion with Rev. Crier). *Tanner '88* is small-scale, but the probing intricacy of Altman's work finds resonances

in Garry Trudeau's script that Trudeau himself might not have realized were there.

April 1988

How the Other Half Lives

• • •

Susan Seidelman's *Desperately Seeking Susan* and Martin Scorsese's *After Hours* were fake representations of emotional and sexual unrest among the baby boomers that ended up sublimating the
private perils they hinted at by either giving them a fairy-tale finale
or turning them into gags. However, in their trivial, exasperating
way, these pictures did draw attention to the disjunction between
the image we've accepted of ourselves as rooted, self-satisfied,
worldly in a material sense—down-home suburbanites—and the
renegade part of ourselves that recoils from the glaze of the happy
ending. David Lynch's *Blue Velvet* and Jonathan Demme's *Something Wild* concern themselves with the precarious balance of comfort and danger in the twilight of the Reagan era; and we might
call them, borrowing Martin Esslin's phrase for Pinter's plays,
"comedies of menace."

Watching David Lynch's *Blue Velvet* is like being under hyp-
nosis for two hours: When you emerge you feel logy and hung-over,
still drenched with the images, and the world outside the theater
suddenly seems eerily unfamiliar. The movie is set in a small North
Carolina town, but Frederick Elmes's lush cinematography has the
mysterious clarity of dreams, and the innocence of Lynch's Ameri-
cana is pitched right on the edge of a precipice with the hounds of
nightmare baying below. It's as if Norman Rockwell had peered

into a mirror and found the faces of Edward Hopper and Max Ernst staring back at him.

The movie begins with a springtime idyll. Lumberton is a lace-work of tree-lined streets with gracious, expansive houses and towering rose gardens. The sky is a passive blue. The local fire truck appears, a smiling man perched on its running board waving benignly at us as he floats past the camera. These images are startlingly sharp and close, but emotionally they have a far-away, half-submerged quality, like something stirred out of childhood memories. The mood suddenly shifts as a heavy-set man (Jack Harvey) watering his lawn grimaces, clutched by a stroke, and tumbles over; he falls onto the hose, which is caught stiffly at his crotch, obscenely spraying water that his yapping pet dog, excited and confused, laps up. The camera rushes past him, deep into the grass, where the magnified rustling of unseen creatures drowns out the hissing of the garden hose. (Lynch works once again with the sound editor Alan Splet, who's something of a genius.)

This must be the strangest perversion of suburban serenity since Tuesday Weld played the psychotic majorette residing on FreshAir Lane in the 1968 *Pretty Poison*, but Lynch's tone isn't mocking or satirical—it's seductive. He keeps drawing us through the innocence down the side of that cliff, but he never abandons the idyll; he keeps both in sharp focus, insisting with the passion of a native surrealist that they can coexist, just as the manglings of London's industrial hell and the gentle, cultivated grace of the damaged protagonist coexisted in his film of *The Elephant Man*. The incongruity of juxtaposing the sunny small-town world with its dark underbelly is often funny in *Blue Velvet*. What may seem to be a conflict of tones or an intrusion of warring styles is in fact implied in Lynch's vision.

Superficially, the story's a murder mystery without a corpse. Jeffrey (Kyle MacLachlan), the late-teen son of the stricken man in the opening sequence, is on his way to the hospital to visit his recuperating father when he finds a human ear in a field. He brings it to the police station, where he knows one of the detectives (George Dickerson) from the neighborhood. Later, Jeffrey calls on him at home, to ask about the progress of the case. The cop refuses to give Jeffrey any information, but his daughter, Sandy (Laura Dern), takes Jeffrey aside and tells him she overheard her father talking about a singer named Dorothy Vallens (Isabella Rossellini), who might be involved. His curiosity aroused, Jeffrey persuades Sandy to help him gain access to Dorothy's apartment; while he's there, posing as an exterminator, he pockets Dorothy's key so he can steal back inside that night before she's returned home from the club where she performs. She arrives before he can find any evidence, however, and he has to hide in her living-room closet. From that vantage point he sees her undress, and overhears a frightened, ominous phone conversation with a man who appears to have abducted her husband and her little boy. Later he watches, frozen, while the caller, a psychopath named Frank (Dennis Hopper), invades Dorothy's apartment and performs a bizarre, abusive sexual fantasy upon her.

As Lynch films the two women in this movie, their beauty is iconic. We first glimpse Laura Dern when she steps out of the darkness to speak to Jeffrey outside her parents' house: Tall, blossoming, with lustrous hair like the gold in Renaissance paintings, she's an unbelievably rich teen dream. Dern's mixture of natural modesty and breathless sexual eagerness, which was the best reason to see *Smooth Talk*, is really explored in *Blue Velvet*. She plays the nice girl in the picture, but she isn't benign—her sweetness is heady, overpoweringly intense. The information she passes on to Jeffrey is a guileless seduction, and when he involves her in the adventure that follows, she falls in love with him; she equates Jeffrey with the mystery, and they *are* part of the same thing: romantic adventure. But she isn't prepared for the scary implications of that mystery, and she's shocked and upset by what she learns. Lynch and Laura Dern accomplish here what *Smooth Talk* wanted to: You really understand the potency of romantic ardor. We see Dern as the purest expression of Lynch's suburban dream. There's an astonishing moment when the camera pans across a mirror in Sandy's room which reflects rose-covered wallpaper, a pink-and-white pillow, and Sandy herself in a matching print dress weeping to Jeffrey on the phone: It's a breathtaking soft-erotic image.

When Sandy begins to comprehend the danger Jeffrey is getting caught up in, she feels guilty; "I got you into this," she insists. And she's right. *Blue Velvet* is about a young man's sexual awakening—Jeffrey's tender stirrings for this chaste golden girl transport him into a darker response to Dorothy Vallens. Using the most expressionistic pallette for an apartment setting since the dying-sunset colors Bertolucci came up with for *Last Tango in Paris*, Lynch and Elmes and the production designer, Patricia Norris, saturate Dorothy's flat in crimson and grape and the crushed pale blue of her emblematic velvet robe. When we first see Isabella Rossellini she's wearing a tight, Depression-style purple dress and a thick smear of red lipstick; at the Slow Club, where she's billed as "The Blue Lady" and sings the title song in a smoky blue spotlight, she's clad in a backless black gown, cut low between her breasts, and she wears blue mascara. In the privacy of her apartment, unaware that Jeffrey is peeping at her, she walks around in a black bra and panties and scarlet shoes. If Sandy's his teenage fantasy, wrapped in roses, then Dorothy, with her exotic, menacing sexual vibrancy, is the woman he desires with the unbridled part of himself that disturbs and frightens him. And it's she who makes love to him—ferreting him out of his closet hiding place, commanding him to strip, pointing a knife at his crotch while she kisses his genitals. Their first session in bed collapses when she urges him to hurt her and he refuses; when he returns the next day, he's more susceptible to her demands, slapping her across the face in the excitement of sexual heat. "You have my disease in you now," she whispers to him.

Shattered, neurotic Dorothy (Rossellini is superb—in some scenes she gives the character the terrifying fragility of a sorrowing princess) initiates Jeffrey into the world represented by that ear; following her lead, he travels down its dark, enigmatic canals. Dennis Hopper, in a surprisingly powerful performance, plays the destructive crazy who turns up at the end of every one. Snorting an unidentified drug through an oxygen mask, he dry-humps Dorothy, taunting her with his control over her child by calling her "Mummy" as he approaches orgasm. The next time he drops by he takes her and Jeffrey, whom he discovers in her apartment, on a nightmarish joy ride with his gang of creeps (including Brad Dourif, who has long, stringy, sociopathic hair; a drugged-out Dean Stockwell in an amazing, flamboyant cameo; and Jack Nance from Lynch's *Eraserhead*).

Frank is the origin of Dorothy's "disease"; he's a walking perversion. He finds more expressive ways to use the monosyllable "fuck" than anyone else since Richard Pryor. It's the moniker he uses for everyone, he swears he'll "fuck anything that moves," and when they take to the road, he tells his pals and his captives that they're going "out to fuck the country." In Frank's mouth, this synonym for copulation reverts to its most brutal, assaultive connotation; when he says he's going to "fuck," he means he's going to destroy something. When he touches Dorothy, Jeffrey, immobile up to this point, smashes him in the jaw. It's his second act of violence in the movie, and it's psychologically related to his first, against Dorothy. Frank hauls him out of the car and kisses him on the mouth, so that the lipstick one of his henchmen has decorated Frank's face with, in a fantastic pop-erotic ritual that focuses on the recitation of the lyrics to Roy Orbison's song "In Dreams," spills onto Jeffrey's face. "If I send you a love letter," he warns the boy, "you're fucked forever"—leaving no doubt about what sort of "love letter" he has in mind.

Lynch gets extraordinary performances out of the four leading actors, including Kyle MacLachlan, who has been so absorbed into the scheme of the movie that he's almost a *tabula rasa* for Lynch's imagination: We get so close to Jeffrey that we experience the movie through his skin. MacLachlan was pretty much a hole in the screen in *Dune*, his last picture with Lynch, but Lynch wasn't in control there—the movie was so crammed with characters and plot twists that even his phenomenal visual sense was upstaged. Lynch, who doesn't structure and organize while he works, was the last director *Dune* needed, probably, though he ended up providing its only memorable moments (the most abstract ones). Lynch isn't a storyteller. *Blue Velvet*, with its semicoherent murder-mystery plot and its throwaway scenes between Jeffrey and the police detective, proves that in *The Elephant Man*, where he was in the service of an extremely well-crafted script, his heart was really in the uncategorizable surrealistic sequences. They weren't like anything done in any other commercial movie (the closest equivalent, perhaps—in terms of sheer audacity—was the boat ride in Charles Laughton's *The Night of the Hunter*), and that didn't surprise you if you'd seen his cult film, the outrageous comic horror fantasy *Eraserhead*, another movie about erotic awakening, though completely different in tone and visual style. The real surprise in *The Elephant Man* was that he was able to find the particular kind of discipline called for by the narrative, with its overtones of Dickens and Mary Shelley. (That's where the script helped.) All of *Blue Velvet* has the same incredible daring as the individual touches in *The Elephant Man*: It's a full-length experimental movie that somehow made it through the deadening conformity of the studio system and got released. (I never thought I'd say this, but God bless Dino De Laurentiis, who initiated the project and released the results.)

David Lynch may be the first visionary American director who appears to work completely nonintellectually; if you wanted to be glib about *Blue Velvet*, you might call it the greatest simple-minded film ever made in this country. But that description, of course, wouldn't begin to explain how overpoweringly effective a scene arrived at by intuition can be. It wouldn't suggest the profound emotional connections Lynch makes imagistically in this picture: The eerie close-up of the severed ear links up with Dorothy's profession, the flashing light on a police car echoes both the blues we associate with Dorothy and the flame from the candle Frank lights on her mantle, which envelops the screen during her lovemaking with Jeffrey. It wouldn't suggest the altogether extraordinary ways in which he employs the title song (heard first in the classic Bobby Vinton rendition and then in a delicate, impassioned version by Rossellini at the club), Roy Orbison's "In Dreams," and a tune he and composer Angelo Badalamenti wrote for the film, "Mysteries of Love." And it wouldn't suggest the weird, skewed humor of the domestic scenes between Jeffrey and his mother (Priscilla Pointer) and his chatty, old-fashioned aunt (Frances Bay), or what you feel when you see Jeffrey watering the lawn in a pair of sunglasses after he's been beaten up by Frank, or when his two lives finally collide in what must be the funniest and most reckless emotional apocalypse in any contemporary American movie.

Intriguingly, the director whose work Lynch suggests at points in *Blue Velvet* is Orson Welles, who arrived at *his* results much more through intellection than intuition. There's a motel room scene here that recalls Janet Leigh's ordeal in *Touch of Evil*, and one sequence—sitting in Jeffrey's car in front of the stained-glass windows of a church, Sandy relates a benevolent dream about a thousand robins—reminded me of a scene in *The Magnificent Ambersons*, where Anne Baxter tells Joseph Cotten a symbolic fable. On paper I'm sure the speech is trite, but so was Anne Baxter's; as Lynch directs it, and as Laura Dern reads the lines, the cliché is so intensified that it becomes joyful, and the emotional color almost blinding. As a friend of mine expressed it, *Blue Velvet* makes you feel you've never seen a movie before.

There definitely are elements in *Something Wild* you've seen before in other movies, but because the director, Jonathan Demme, brings a lopsided, flyaway quality to them, nothing feels familiar. The traveling shot across the East River into New York City that opens the film has what you might call a fluid bounce. Demme and his superb cinematographer, Tak Fujimoto, manage to capture some of the intimacy and spontaneity, as well as the catch-as-catch-can excitement and the accompanying evanescence, that you can usually get only with a hand-held camera. And the David Byrne–Celia Cruz salsa duet on the soundtrack, "Loco de Amor (Crazy for Love)," helps provide a kinetic lyricism that bounds into the first scene, which is set in a down-home hash joint. Charles Driggs (Jeff Daniels), a tax consultant in the first flush of a vice-presidency, sits hunched over his pocket calculator; when the waitress (the Jamaican toast singer Sister Carol) presents him with his check, he casts an eye around quickly to see if anyone's watching and then slips it surreptitiously into his coat pocket. He makes it to the sidewalk before a young woman (Melanie Griffith) with Louise Brooks bangs and layers of metal and macramé jewelry accosts him and points out that he ran off without paying for his meal. Embarrassed, he tries to settle his bill then and there. But it turns out that she doesn't work in the restaurant; she's been following his movements from across the room and has identified him as a "closet rebel." Pretending to offer him a lift to his office, she decides to dig that rebel out: She tosses his calculator out the window, passes him a pint of scotch, and heads for New Jersey, where she pilfers some spending money from a liquor store cash register and then seduces Charlie in a motel room, literally jumping on top of him and ripping his shirt off. When she reaches inside her see-through, watermelon-print plastic purse, pulls out a pair of handcuffs, and dangles them over Charlie's head, he murmurs, "You're a funny girl."

Yes, this is the fable of the woman who's in touch with her instincts—and maybe a little crazy—bringing out the eccentric and releasing the emotional sublife in the stuffy businessman who has always lived entirely in his head. And it's so well known through decades of movies that these characters are practically archetypes.

We've seen them, or variations on them, in *Bringing Up Baby*, in *You Can't Take It with You* (where the heroine's family removes the starch from the collars of the hero's family), in *The Philadelphia Story* (where the roles are switched), in *One Touch of Venus* (where the aggressive female is literally a goddess come down to earth), and in dozens of other pictures; perhaps the last memorable time around was *The Owl and the Pussycat*, starring Barbra Streisand as a whore and George Segal as a bookstore clerk. But though this convention is the premise of E. Max Frye's script for *Something Wild*, he has something more daring in mind, and he's collaborating with Jonathan Demme, whose movies (like *Citizens Band*, *Melvin and Howard*, and the Talking Heads songfest *Stop Making Sense*) are anything but conventional.

Loosening Charlie up with sex and liquor, Lulu leads him into Pennsylvania, where Fujimoto's landscapes lose their urban grime and take on an immaculate silvery-blue mist that's almost otherworldly. She's seen the photo of a wife and two kids in Charlie's wallet, and after a series of escapades (she abandons her car, crashed drunkenly into a motel sign, buys another one off a used-car lot, treats Charlie to a spiffy blue suit that might be described as New Wave conservative) she removes her art-deco femme fatale wig to reveal her natural strawberry blonde hair, trades in her sexy black skirt for a rose-print dress, and tries on the role of the suburban bride who matches his corporate gleam. She tells him her real name—Audrey—and takes him home to meet her mother, a sweet, twinkly-eyed matron named Peaches (Dana Preu) whose life-style is like a living Norman Rockwell painting, complete with a terrier, a porch swing, and a spinet in the parlor. "See, Mama," she says, pointing proudly to the guy she claims to be wed to, "he's just the kind of man you always said I should marry"—and there's a whisper of melancholy in Melanie Griffith's voice as she speaks the line.

Demme is a marvel. His zany-lyrical approach to the screwball comedy that makes up the first half of *Something Wild* keeps it in constant motion, like an all-night party in a caravan. He's aided by the imaginative mixture of rock and salsa and reggae and rap on the soundtrack (the theme song is the old Troggs tune "Wild Thing," which Charlie and Audrey sing as they tool through Pennsylvania, and strains of which are picked up in both "Loco de

Amor" and the last number, performed by Sister Carol), as well as by the assortment of oddball characters he strews along the lovers' path. There's a liquor-store salesman with a Sherlock Holmes pipe (Tracey Walter), a motel philosopher (Jim Roche) who nurses Charlie's hangover and counsels him, "It's better to be a live dog than a dead lion"; a car salesman with a pencil-thin moustache (filmmaker/author John Waters, the prince of raunch), a restaurant proprietor (co-producer Kenneth Utt) with a hilarious, upbrushed fringe of hair across an otherwise bald head, and deep-ringed Mafioso eyes. John Sayles shows up, too, in a bit as a motorcycle cop, as does Demme regular Charles Napier, as a chef doubling as a bouncer. (When Audrey strands Charlie in Utt's restaurant without any money to pay the tab—she's testing him—it's Napier who emerges from the kitchen to troubleshoot when Utt indicates Charlie and mumbles in a broken-gravel bass, "Possible cash flow problem.")

Demme and Frye go much farther, though: They locate an emotional depth at the core of the screwball comedy. When Audrey, bereft of her Lulu get-up, sails out of her mom's house and into her tenth-year high-school reunion with this executive livewire on her arm, she's living out a cockeyed version of the small-town American dream that she really believes in. And she's pulled Charlie, whose life had become deadening before she disrupted it, right in with her. (She doesn't know yet that his wife walked out on him nine months ago, taking the kids.) The reunion scene completes the metamorphosis of Charles Driggs. He bumps into Larry (Jack Gilpin), an accountant from his office whose wife, Peggy (Su Tissue)—a diminutive woman with a pinched-in mandarin face mismatched to a pregnant belly—was in Audrey's graduating class. Charlie hems and haws, trying to come up with an excuse for being there, but Audrey, a gifted prevaricator, blows his cover by claiming him as the father of her unborn child. Unnerved by how close Audrey has brought him to the edge, Charlie considers retreating into his "boring, very safe life," but Audrey persuades him to live out the fantasy for the rest of the evening. It's an affecting moment, because you can hear the sadness, once again, in Melanie Griffith's plea, and you can see Jeff Daniels throwing off Charlie's last inhibition with schoolboy abandon and reentering the party with a newly confident—and romantic—swing. (The two actors are formidable.)

When they start to dance (to the Feelies' cover of David Bowie's "Fame"), it's Charlie who leads, inventing a sort of show-off marionette step that is disarmingly all his own. We can see that he's fallen for this woman, and that he's ready for anything—in Audrey's words, he's discovering how much he likes the way the other half lives (the other half of himself). However, that's precisely when Audrey's tight, sashaying, good-time-girl school pal Irene (Margaret Colin) glides up beside them with Audrey's ex-con husband Ray (Ray Liotta) in tow.

At this point Charlie's urban-escape dream begins to take on the color of a nightmare. But Demme doesn't change tempos, and in fact he keeps the movie poised on the edge of a tonal shift; it continues to be funny and romantic even when elements of violence and entrapment bleed into the picture. He can carry off this feat partly because of the depth his two leading actors provide, and partly because of Ray Liotta. Ray is a type, too—the psycho with the glittering blue eyes—but Liotta adds a few new wrinkles: When he flashes his goofy scarecrow grin he's very seductive, and his mockery of Charlie appears so open-faced and good-natured that he seems to be making jokes at his own expense. He's like a heavyweight who invites you laughingly to punch him in his hard belly and then knees you in the groin without diminishing one degree of his smile.

We know this creep is bad news from the way Peggy shrinks when he says hello to her at the reunion (she reverts instantly to her high-school role, the wimpy nice girl terrorized by a bully), but we don't know exactly when he's going to strike—and anyway, we can't help enjoying his company as much as Charlie does: He's the life of the party. When he sends Audrey and Irene to pick up a couple of six-packs and the two men are shooting the bull together in Ray's (probably stolen) car, Liotta's balance of danger and comrade-in-arms smoothness plays so deftly off Daniels's balance of surprised merriment and old-fashioned courtliness that Demme is able to make a transition work that must have seemed impossibly difficult on paper. Ray jokes his way into Charlie's confidence, then asks what Audrey is like in bed, taunting Charlie without losing his smile. "She looks like she could fuck you in half," he quips, falling over himself giggling, and Charlie replies, soberly and with dignity, "There's no call for that kind of talk." Then Ray mimics a gentlemanly apology so seamlessly you can't see the mockery in it at all, and Charlie's good humor returns immediately. It's a triple-shift moment.

This fake-casual insult, of course, is just a prelude to what Ray has in mind for Charlie after he's ditched Irene and taken him and Audrey for his own version of a joy ride. Frye has provided ingenious parallels here to the first half of the movie: Ray robs a liquor store, but he delivers both Charlie and the kid behind the counter a malicious beating in the process; he hauls Charlie and Audrey to a crummy motel, but this one has kids running loose outside around a flaming garbage can, and walls so thin he can kick a hole in one during a screaming fight with his next-door neighbor. There's even a replay of the scene in which Lulu–Audrey left Charlie to run out on his check, but the stakes are higher this time, and the game has darker repercussions. And meanwhile the movie continues to generate terrific new characters—a teenager at a motel gift shop (Kristin Olsen) who turns her dreamy eyes on Ray, a convenience-store salesman (Steve Scales, who played percussion for Talking Heads in *Stop Making Sense*) who keeps shifting his immense stature to stay at eye level with Charlie, trying to stay out of Ray's line of vision.

Jonathan Demme's movies are usually rich in character and incident, but they're not just eccentric human landscapes. They work because of an emotional commitment that isn't obvious as you scan the surface of them. He's the Renoir of screwball comedy. *Something Wild* deepens as it goes along; that's the crucial difference between it and comedies like *Desperately Seeking Susan* and *After Hours*. (Its closest equivalent is probably the sweet, muted 1981 comedy *All Night Long*, with Gene Hackman as a junior executive who becomes a clerk in a twenty-four-hour store after hurling his boss's chair out the window in a fit of justified anger.) And that deepening process supports the dark side of this picture, which is more disturbing than anything in *Citizens Band* or *Melvin and Howard*. The inevitable battle between the two men over Audrey is evidence of the movie's audacity and its integrity: Demme and Frye refuse to back off from, or soften, the implications of what they show us. And when the violence finally erupts, it doesn't look like the violence in anybody else's movies—it's shot close in, at angles that make it look like the characters are suspended in the air and have to grab hold of whatever they can to keep them from flying off into space. That's not a bad metaphor for violence. *Something Wild* begins as a wish-fulfillment fantasy, and the unbroken stream of music is Demme's way of signaling us that even when the movie crosses over into cruelty and violence, the party's still going on. But what happens to Charlie Driggs changes his life. Somehow Demme has found a way of keeping reality and fantasy in perpetual, complementary motion.

November 1986

Woman's Legacy
• • •

It's a fact of life in the movie world that even *talented* directors have to fight to make the films they care about, and then most of the time their best work drifts sadly in and out of moviehouses, almost unnoticed. And talented women filmmakers have the roughest time of it—especially, it seems, if their pictures convey a distinctly female sensibility. In the media, a particularly revealing and widespread perverseness seems to operate in connection with women's movies (though it's really just a more marked example of the perverse way in which *all* movies are handled). About once a year the media descend upon one new film by a woman director, invariably something truly awful like the pretentious, muddleheaded *Entre Nous* or the pop-shiny, empty-headed *Desperately Seeking Susan*, and declare it a breakthrough. Then an astonishingly large number of critics genuflect and write serious, reverent responses, as if Diane Kurys or Susan Seidelman were actually artists. (Can people still think that, even after *A Man in Love* and *Making Mr. Right*?) Meanwhile, the handful of movies that *gifted* women manage to get made that either express shades of feeling that men don't generally deal with, or depict male–female relationships, or parental feelings, or rites of passage, as men don't envision them, are either ignored or slammed with puzzling hostility by the mainstream press. I'm thinking of movies like Barbra Streisand's *Yentl*, or Amy Jones's *Love Letters*—which has some of the few sex sequences I've ever seen that are clearly shot from the woman's perspective.

Love Letters is an odd little melodrama—a romantic-triangle movie whose point of view is that of the adulteress. The unusual texture of the material (which Jones also scripted) draws a performance out of the star, Jamie Lee Curtis, that's emotionally denser and more ambiguous than anything else she's done on screen; there are gradations of anger and sexual jealousy here that aren't recognizable from any other picture I can think of. *Love Letters* is a small achievement, but a *real* one—yet it opened and closed in a week across the country; I found it by accident while looking for a video to rent that I hadn't seen. I wonder how many people will discover Gillian Armstrong's *High Tide* in the same way.

The Australian director Gillian Armstrong became a media darling in 1979 with her first film, *My Brilliant Career*—the only one of her four movies that didn't really come off. The better her pictures have become, the worse she's been treated. The coming-of-age story of a young woman in turn-of-the-century rural Australia, *My Brilliant Career* borrowed from a large variety of sources (notably *Little Women* and *The Sound of Music*), and the heroine, Sybylla, was baffling; her behavior amounted to a lot of protofeminist poses that weren't plausible in context. As a result, her independence came across as willful rather than liberated, the petty insurrections of a pouty princess. (When a perfectly decent landowner proposes marriage, she goes after him with a horsewhip; when tramps come to her door begging food, she suddenly acquires a set of political principles.) Still, Judy Davis, playing Sybylla, brought an entertaining spunkiness to the enterprise, and Armstrong edited the movie to Davis's rhythms. You could see these two women were in joyous sync.

Armstrong's second venture, the New Wave musical *Star Struck*, was endearing and had a spiky, dribbling style all its own. It was so spontaneous and unarranged-looking that you didn't realize at first that was part of the parody (of the Mickey Rooney–Judy Garland "Let's put on a show" movies of the thirties and forties).

Jo Kennedy plays a teenage singer whose cousin, a 14-year-old entrepreneur (Ross O'Donovan), gets her a spot on a local TV show.
Performing a tune called "Temper, Temper," Kennedy has some of
the charming marionette jerkiness of Cyndi Lauper, but the number's a genuine tour de force: Her face moves through cycles of emotional states, though they're somehow miniaturized, pixie-sized,
and she seems to be trying each one on like a new hair-do.

Amiable and fresh though it was, *Star Struck* didn't prepare us
for Armstrong's next movie, the 1984 *Mrs. Soffel*, a trenchant, poetic portrait of a woman, the wife of a prison warden in turn-of-
the-century Pittsburgh, who breaks out of her marriage. Diane Keaton (in a brilliant, uncompromising performance) plays Kate Soffel,
who falls in love with Ed Biddle (Mel Gibson), one of a pair of
brothers in jail for murder, and helps them to escape. Trapped in a
miserable marriage that literally makes her sick (she has bouts of an
unidentified fever), Kate responds to the romantic misery of this lost
man: When he tiptoes up to her bedroom and asks her to run away
with him and his brother Jack (Matthew Modine), she accedes,
flinging away the chance of ever returning to her home and three
children. Kate acts with a kind of daring that's both impulsive and
compulsive; behaving in a way she knows to be legally wrong, socially abhorrent, and contradictory to her religious convictions,
she's like a Dostoevski character whose heroism consists of a neurotic flinging-away of everything, a severing of all ties, in a single
motion. She isn't much like any other female protagonist in movies.
Her closest kin, perhaps, is Truffaut's Adèle H., who chases halfway
across the world after a man scandalously unworthy of her. Both
women surrender themselves to a romantic passion that represents
a release from the incarceration of respectability—and ultimately
defines them.

Mrs. Soffel has a fine script (by Ron Nyswaner, based on a true
story), and an ingenious, understated performance by Mel Gibson
(his best to date), but it's the collaboration between director and
actress that gives the film its special, agonized intensity. A male
viewer gets the sense he's never been permitted inside a woman's
psyche in quite this way before. There's a hard, glittering, Sylvia
Plath–like purity to this examination of Kate Soffel's personality
that's more than a little frightening. And that may explain the
strong negative response viewers often have to the movie—that, and

the film's refusal to judge Kate for acting with such utter abandon. Armstrong sees her as a tragic figure—not because she slips through the bars of her prison, but because she carries them with her, even on the road with the Biddles. (Armstrong's use of prison imagery throughout the movie makes Kate's entrapment clear, and so does the title, which conveys the opposite message from the title of *Hedda Gabler*: Hedda, unlike Kate, is never identified by her husband's name.) Yet this tragic figure is strangely triumphant—she brings her own liberation back with her when she returns to that prison, this time to live free in her own cell rather than chained to her husband. The movie's dark integrity *is* upsetting, mostly because you want to be able to like Kate Soffel more than Armstrong and Keaton will let you: They demand that you take her on her own unswerving, neurotic terms. Hardly anyone identified *Mrs. Soffel* as the feminist film it undoubtedly is. That would have required a kind of grudging respect, at the very least, from the politically correct.

High Tide is, in its way, equally uncompromising—but superficially, at least, it's more conventional. The photographer, Russell Boyd (Armstrong's collaborator since *Star Struck*), gives it a far gentler, airier look; *Mrs. Soffel*, which began with a flash of industrial fire against an inky sky, seemed to have been lit by lightning. And since *High Tide* is a movie that speaks to a wider audience, and is presented in the easily accessible form of a domestic melodrama, its failure to catch on is more bewildering than that of *Mrs. Soffel*. Laura Jones's screenplay is a variation on the oldest of soap-opera themes, the reunion of mother and child. Lilli (Judy Davis) belongs to a trio of female vocalists who travel through the small oceanside towns of Australia as backup to an Elvis imitator named Lester (Frankie J. Holden). It's a lousy, makeshift job, and Lilli doesn't manage well with authority figures like Lester feels he has to be, so she fights back by being insolent and half-disguising that as mischievous humor. One day, she alienates him enough that he gives her the sack. Her car's broken down, and she doesn't have the money to repair it, so she's stuck in the fishing town where she was let go, until she can earn enough cash (by performing as a stripper) to get back on the road.

For the time being, she puts up at a trailer camp, where she's befriended by a teenage girl, Ally (Claudia Karvan). It isn't until she catches sight of Ally's grandmother, Bet (Jan Adele), that she realizes the girl is her own daughter, whom she abandoned after her young husband died in a surfing accident when Ally was a baby. Bet, who works at a fish factory and also drives an ice-cream truck, has raised the child, telling her both her parents are dead. She's incensed when she sees Lilli hanging around Ally: She feels Lilli's reentry into the girl's life after all these years without contact is unmerited, and of course she feels her own position threatened. But, drawn as she is to her daughter, Lilli keeps her guard up by not telling Ally who she is. It isn't until a fisherman who's been taking Lilli out tells Ally the truth, and Ally runs to her for confirmation, that she's forced to confront her own penchant for running away. Having seen herself all these years as an adventurer, living the brave, independent existence of a woman eternally on the road, Lilli now admits to Bet to having been a coward. It's in the light of this new knowledge of herself that she has to choose whether or not to run one more time.

The story is as banal as a TV Movie of the Week, but there's tremendous potential power in banality—the power of the familiar—and Jones and Armstrong know how to draw it out. Richly and precisely detailed, and dense with the conflicting emotions of its three main female characters, *High Tide* is the most complex domestic drama anyone has made since the 1982 *Shoot the Moon*. In that movie, which was about the devastating effect that separation can have on the members of a family, the Marin County house that Diane Keaton and Albert Finney were raising their daughters in was a crucial element; here, Armstrong and Russell Boyd use the extraordinary setting of the shoreline town to explain the lives of the characters and underscore their dilemmas. The tacky oceanside fast-food stands, the trailer ("caravan," in local parlance) camps, the fifties feel of the bland, overdressed restaurants, the coffee shops with their graffiti-stained washrooms and video games crowded in too close to the dining area, the Saturday-night discos, the fish factory Bet works in, with its grimy plastic-curtain entranceway—all of these give the town a rambling, anonymous quality when we first see them, through Lilli's eyes. But, as Ally tells her, when you live in a caravan camp all caravans don't all look the same to you, and for Bet, who participates in amateur nights (performing "It Had to

Be You," she has a dully efficient contralto, a minor-league version of a "Your Hit Parade" vocal style), the local steak house has a fancy-treat aura. Not, however, for Ally, whom Bet and her boy friend, Col (played by John Clayton), drag there whenever Bet's set to sing. Ally begs to be allowed to accompany the kids she hangs out with, whose parents give them freer rein, to the disco.

High Tide isn't about the claustrophobic horror of small-town living, like Wish You Were Here; Armstrong focuses on the people for whom this place isn't generic or cut-rate, but home. And it doesn't take us long to see that Lilli's life, drifting around the country playing pseudo–rock 'n' roll in a mermaid prom gown and a blonde wig, is in no way more satisfying. The most vivid difference between these two movies' visions of life on the brink of the water is in the way they depict the ocean itself. In Wish You Were Here it's gray and misted over; its mournful beauty is a constant reminder of limits, mortality, the inevitability of despair. In High Tide, where its muted splendor carries us past the unconsidered visual ordinariness of the town, it's literally life-giving (everyone in town seems to live off the fishing industry) and inescapable. Lilli's husband died in the ocean, and she returns to it like a creature of the water (there's a lovely shot of her skipping stones over the morning waves); Ally, who carries her dad's surfboard around like a talisman, seeks her privacy lying on her back in a tide pool. You get the sense that the water has drawn these two together again, the way it will draw blood.

High Tide isn't horrifying like Shoot the Moon; it's not shaped as a tragedy. But Armstrong and Jones show the same knack for keeping us in close touch with all the main players in the central conflict, so we're sympathetic to each of them and at the same time painfully aware of the limitations to each of their points of view. Obviously you can't accomplish something like this without first-rate performers. Judy Davis is one of those actresses who appear to be half sorceress; her remarkable intelligence and the subtlety of her technique can't completely explain the delicate exactness with which she evokes moods or dramatizes mood shifts, or the way she uses what seem at first like distracted pauses to articulate previously unexpressed feelings. Lilli is Davis's most stunning creation—a woman who's lived the past decade and a half of her life in constant flight, but who's too smart and too sensitive to deny the primacy of the instincts that lead her back to the daughter she left behind. She can fight them, though, and *High Tide* is centrally the chart of her inward struggle. The way Davis and Armstrong capture, simultaneously, the unconscious parabola of Lilli's movement through her life, and her burgeoning comprehension of herself, poeticizes her; At times she's reminiscent of the woman in Joni Mitchell's autobiographical *Hejira* album, who's both a creature of the elements and a weary traveler, who wants to be all instinct but can't stop her habit of reflection. Davis has a magical moment at a motel room window with Mick, her fisherman beau (touchingly well played by Colin Friels, Davis's real-life husband), when she tells him about Ally, and explains that she ran away because her husband's death poisoned her—it made her hate her own life, and hate her baby. Mick, whose wife left him to raise one of their children alone, can't make sense of Lilli's choices. She berates him for living so unimaginatively, for taking the leavings and doing the best he can with them, but then he reminds her of the inadequacy of her own nomadic life. When she tells him, after a pause, that he's right about her—"That's what I am"—her haunted face at the window, framed by drenched red curls spun like webs around her head, has the distant, otherworldly aspect of a figure in a pre-Raphaelite painting.

Lilli doesn't ask for this reconciliation with Ally; it arrives of its own accord. But she can't prevent herself from skittering on the edges of the girl's life, trying to learn something about her while her own maternal feelings come in flashes she can't fathom and doesn't know what to do with. Happening upon Ally in the camp shower, she stops, smiling, to watch her using a razor on her legs, obviously for the first time. (This enchanting, revealing interlude is an example of what a gifted worman artist like Armstrong brings to movies; no male director would have thought to make a connection between mother and daughter in quite this way.) Later, Lilli stands outside Bet's caravan, spying on Ally. This is an archetypal estranged-mother-and-child scene. We saw it in *Kramer vs. Kramer*, where the male filmmakers made the mother creepy and menacing, and forty years earlier, in *Stella Dallas*, it rang the chimes of mother-sacrifice. In a gender variation it shows up in *Shoot the Moon*, where Keaton locks Finney out of the house, barring his access to his daughter—and, perhaps most famously, it appears in Saul Bellow's novel *Herzog*, where the hero, forbidden visitation rights, stands outside his wife's house and watches her lover bathe his children. In *High Tide*, Davis plays it with a mixture of curiosity and inchoate longing.

The talented Claudia Karvan plays Ally as a normal teenager with an abundant inner life she can't share with Bet or with her on-again, off-again caravan-camp pals. It's that private dimension—her quest for her parents in herself—that prompts the directness and insistence with which she pursues Lilli when she discovers their relationship. (It's interesting to think about what's in Mick's mind when he lets this information slip: how aware he is of what he's doing; how much he's motivated by the good intentions of a fellow parent and how much by his disappointment—because Lilli walked out on him in that motel room.)

Lilli appears at the moment when Ally is most in need of her as a self-defining element in her young life. When she asks Lilli outright if Mick spoke the truth, Lilli, frightened and not knowing what to do, at first says no. "Do you love me?" the girl wants to know, and Lilli shrugs. She tries to explain to Ally the debilitating emotional effect of her father's death. "Then you loved me before he died?" asks Ally, struggling to make sense of this—the kind of sense that will give her some hope that Lilli will love her again. But all Lilli can offer her is an apology. And, because she knows how feeble that is, she repeats it, hurling it furiously—"I said I'm sorry! Isn't that what you want?"—while Ally, her face averted, weeps silently. The scene is amazing: We understand the forces that propel both characters, and we see exactly why neither can win.

The movie's third major character, Bet, is given full human dimensions by Jan Adele. Big-boned Bet is tough, in the way you feel a woman raising a child on her own in rural Australia would have to be, and you don't doubt for a moment that Ally has always been able to find refuge in her warmth and her bulk and her strength. You can't blame Bet for her treatment of her daughter-in-law, even though it's unfair to hold Lilli responsible, as she does, for her son's death; to her mind, running out on Ally is evidence of the selfishness and irresponsibility she always perceived in Lilli. She can't help seeing Lilli's sudden interest in the girl as nothing but an impulse, potentially destructive to the bond she's formed with her granddaughter.

However, Bet is *not* especially sensitive to the needs of a lonely girl growing into womanhood; she's strict about the wrong things (like whether Ally ought to be allowed to party with her friends), and though you admire her brassy self-confidence about sex, and respect her for not allowing the fact of Ally to prevent her from having a life of her own, still the balance of time allotted for Bet's concerns, and time given over to Ally's in the caravan they share, seems disproportionate. When Lilli takes Ally out for a meal, a buddy embarrasses Ally by taunting her from the next table. "She's supposed to be my best friend," Ally explains, and Lilli says, "Oh— one of those 's'posed-to-be's."' Lilli, a loner, understands how inadequate friends can be. And though Ally loves Bet, that's what she's missing—an adult who can read her signals.

Just as *Mrs. Soffel* is framed by prison sequences, so *High Tide* is framed by rapid, almost abstract traveling shots of the highway taken from the point of view of a car whipping past. It's the road that deposits Lilli in this town and then removes her band, leaving her stranded. At the end, she asks Ally to come with her—and Ally says yes, insisting however that they first stop by the factory so she can say goodbye to Bet. The image of Bet peeking out through the strips of plastic at the factory entrance as Lilli drives Ally away (reversing the shot of Lilli standing outside Bet's caravan looking in at her daughter) segues into the racing white lines on the highway we saw at the opening. Lilli stops at a roadside restaurant for dinner, and, leaving Ally with the menu, she retreats to the car to contemplate what she's just got herself in for. We can see Ally sitting alone at the table as the camera pulls back, giving us the illusion that Lilli has run away again. But she hasn't: In a moment we see her stroll up behind her daughter and place her arms around the girl's shoulders. The temptation of the road, of escape, will always be there for Lilli; we don't know if she'll be able to alter this life and stay with Ally. For the moment, though, the road that first separated mother and daughter and then reunited them has moved on past them. This time the camera is measuring those white lines alone.

June 1988

Swing Shift: A Tale of Hollywood
• • •

There are plenty of tales of Hollywood injustices—of the good work of screenwriters destroyed by directors, of great scripts dumped at the whims of powerful stars, of movies nipped and carved by producers and studio heads after directors had given them their final shape. This particular story, sad and revealing, is about Jonathan Demme, Goldie Hawn, and *Swing Shift*.

Demme began shooting *Swing Shift* for Warner Brothers in the first half of 1983. *Citizens Band* (also known as *Handle with Care*) and *Melvin and Howard* had established his distinctly flaky, loose-limbed style, but this new project was the biggest of his young career. It starred one of Hollywood's most bankable performers, Goldie Hawn—who also takes a strong hand in the production of her own movies—and featured Kurt Russell and Ed Harris. A big-budget period piece, *Swing Shift* would begin the day before Pearl Harbor, end just after V-J Day, and focus on the introduction of a women's work force during the war; the action would take place in and around the MacBride airplane plant in Los Angeles. The large, promising cast Demme assembled included Christine Lahti, Fred Ward, Holly Hunter, Sudie Bond, Patty Maloney, Lisa Pelikan, and a few of his friends: Charles Napier (the bigamous trucker in *Citizens Band*), Susan Peretz (of *Melvin and Howard*), Stephen Tobolowsky (in two small roles), playwright Beth Henley (in a walk-on), and—as MacBride, who isn't glimpsed until late in the picture— Demme's mentor, Roger Corman. If you'd seen Demme's previous work, and you saw how graceful a touch he had with actors, the thought of what he could do with a sensational cast like this one was enough to make you salivate. And Warners, viewing the film as a prestige picture and a potential blockbuster, planned to put it out at Christmas. It finally opened in May, after a half-hearted, glossy publicity campaign that smacked of desperation. Demme renounced the movie, the press generally panned it, and audiences failed to come out for it. What was released as *Swing Shift* seemed to satisfy no one.

It takes a little digging to determine exactly how the *Swing Shift* that appeared in theaters in May 1984 (and can be widely seen, of course, on video) evolved. Demme, who in interviews at the time pronounced it the worst experience of his career, has long since stopped talking about it publicly. The film carries a screenwriting credit to one Rob Morton, who doesn't exist: At least four writers contributed at one time or another. Nancy Dowd came up with the original script, and since the story is so similar to *Coming Home*, which she also worked on, it's easy to make the assumption—as I did when I reviewed the movie for *Film Quarterly* in 1984—that she's mainly responsible for both. Kay Walsh (Goldie Hawn), the heroine of *Swing Shift*, is a housewife who grows out of her dependency on her husband, Jack (Ed Harris), after he goes off to war, and she gets a job in a factory and has an affair with her co-worker Lucky Lockhart (Kurt Russell). In *Coming Home*, Sally, played by Jane Fonda, acquires a new set of values—feminist and antiwar—when *her* husband goes off to Vietnam, and she signs up to do volunteer work in a vets' hospital and falls in love with one of the patients. However, Dowd's screenplay for *Swing Shift* was in fact heavily rewritten by Bo Goldman, and then Ron Nyswaner took over. The movie critic Michael Sragow reports that when he visited the set, researching an article on Demme for *American Film*, the shooting script bore Nyswaner's name, and Demme was using it exclusively. (Nyswaner, a gifted screenwriter, later furnished *Mrs. Soffel*.)

Goldie Hawn and her producing partner Anthea Sylbert, interviewed by Ben Brantley for a profile on Hawn in the September 1989 *Vanity Fair*, claim the problems began when Demme delivered his first cut to Warners and the executives didn't like it. Neither did Hawn, who says she felt that "the arc of [Kay's] character" wasn't clear, that "Jonathan's focus went off her at . . . very crucial moments. . . ." According to Sylbert, Demme's version made Hawn look like "this blonde extra who'd been overpaid"; Hollywood gossip had it that Hawn's real beef was that Christine Lahti, as Kay's best friend, Hazel, was stealing the picture. Jerry Bick was officially the film's producer, but Hawn had approval rights, and she insisted on reshoots, over Demme's objections. Scenes were rewritten (some by Robert Towne) and refilmed (it's not clear who stood behind the camera—only that Hawn was overall supervisor), and a new cut was prepared.

If you listen to Hawn and Sylbert's version of the story, the release print of *Swing Shift* was the best job well-meaning Hawn and her friends could cobble together under impossible circumstances. I've never met or spoken to Jonathan Demme, but anyone who's seen the pictures he's done since (*Stop Making Sense, Something Wild, Married to the Mob*) and the ones Hawn's been involved in (*Wildcats, Overboard, Bird on a Wire*) might be wary of trusting her point of view over his on artistic matters. As it happens, though, there's a smoking gun: a director's cut, dupes of which have been circulating for years. And the Demme version of *Swing Shift* is extraordinary—one of the best movies made by an American in the eighties. Taken together, the two cuts are the most powerful lesson I've ever had in how a first-rate director works. Moreover, they're an amazing document of Hollywood in the eighties—of art versus commerce, of course, like most Hollywood sagas, but more potently of how fear and insecurity and ego, in a system that breeds them, can override talent and intelligence and judgment.

The first thing you notice is the difference that Demme's impeccable film sense makes. Stiff and static, the studio cut of *Swing Shift* seems embalmed in the creamy, sunlit haze of Tak Fujimoto's cinematography; the movie dawdles, and the characters (especially Kay) have no apparent forward movement. Demme's cut is the same length but seems to move much faster: His editing gives it a flying density. You can spot the technical devices he relies on to achieve this effect (wipes in a montage showing the women getting accustomed to swing-shift life at the factory), and the way, in a workers' jamboree scene, he preserves the separate rhythm of each section, leading gracefully from Kay's reticence to join in the festivities to Hazel's reunion with her old boy friend, Biscuits (Fred Ward). (Hawn's editors intercut them.) The period markers Hawn took out—a speech by the factory's first war widow, Jeanie Sherman (Holly Hunter), commemorating the anniversary of her husband's death; the moment when the women listen, teary-eyed, to eulogies for FDR—place the individual scenes in a personal and historical context. What remains (like the announcement of the battle for Guadalcanal) isn't sufficient; it doesn't seem part of some overall pattern.

Worse, the commercial print feels anonymous, impersonal, with a slickness that reminds you of awful big-studio products of the forties, only without their gleaming conviction. The cheery Big Band-ish score by Patrick Williams beats on relentlessly, like thick icing slathered hopefully over the cracks in a poorly made cake. And when you see what's been left out—almost every trace of Demme's eccentrically democratic vision (that is, almost every sign of an artist's sensibility)—you can understand exactly why the picture feels the way it does. Demme's version is full of glimpses of women and men caught off guard at work and play: MacBride employees playing guitar and singing on their break; a gangly supervisor (Stephen Tobolowsky) pursuing broad-beamed Edith (Susan Peretz) at the jamboree; a female cabbie yawning as she picks up an early-morning fare. There's nothing emphatic about this stuff; it's all offhand. But it's precisely this casualness—like having the embarrassed young Marine who has to deliver the bad news to Jeanie and winds up with her, weeping, in his arms say his last line ("I've never done this before") off camera instead of on—that makes Demme's cut so un-slick, un-Hollywood-like, and authentic-feeling about the lives of these wartime workers.

The actresses who play Kay and Hazel's co-workers have wonderfully expressive faces and bodies, and Demme's cut gives us specific details about them at the beginning so we can keep track of them through the picture. Waiting on line to apply for jobs, the women strike up a conversation. Annie (Sudie Bond) mentions she's used to farm work, while the diminutive Laverne (Patty Maloney) says the best job she ever had was playing a Munchkin in *The Wizard of Oz*; later on we find out she came to MacBride from roller derby. None of this finds its way into the Warners version. And, since Demme *crafted* his, the omissions make for little peculiarities in rhythm and continuity. While the MacBride spokesman lectures the new workers, explaining that the jobs they've been given are ideally suited for them because "You women are used to repetitive tasks," Demme cuts to a close-up of Laverne looking back at him blankly—a shot that makes a point only if you know this woman's background, and how preposterous his statement must sound to her.

At first, you can't believe the people who put this cut together had any sort of constructive plan; they simply appear to have hacked away at Demme's. But most of the changes *are* deliberate—and, since Hawn supervised them, most of them concern Kay's character. The movie's title doesn't just identify the hours Kay and her friends work at MacBride (four to midnight). It also tells us what happens to her during the war: Her values shift, swinging her into a more profound (and more adult) understanding of the world. The Kay we meet in the opening scenes is sweet, but a little drippy—a well-brought-up Iowa WASP who offers hot milk or tea and sandwiches in a crisis. She's married to a guy who's even straighter than she is. Jack finds the clothes Hazel wears to the dance hall where she works (as a hostess and sometime singer) "cheap"; to him, she's a "tramp." But Kay's drawn to Hazel, who has a toughness, a gutsiness, that Kay envies—and turns out to have a capacity for. She's also drawn to Hazel's sexual forthrightness, which is a tacit encouragement to Kay to express her own sexual needs, during Jack's absence, with Lucky.

Kay's is a difficult role, but she's beautifully worked out in Demme's version. She sometimes behaves badly, she's inclined to revert to her old prissiness when she feels threatened, but she really does grow past Jack—past the point they're at as a couple when he leaves in 1941. The filmmakers show us everything that's inside Kay: how scared she is of going against the grain of old values the war and her new job are quickly rendering obsolete, how much it costs her every time she does, how much she gains by the risks she takes. Hawn says her character got lost in Demme's cut, but the truth is that all three of the other main characters in the movie are important mainly because of their relationships with *her*—because of the ways in which those relationships reflect the shifts in Kay. The main effect of the rewriting and restructuring of the picture is to blur what happens to her and make her benign, removing the ironic perspective through which we're meant to get her vision of the world—so it seems as if the movie *shared* that vision.

In Demme's cut, we see Kay's feelings for her husband most clearly the night before he leaves, when she touches his face tenderly as he sleeps. She dedicates herself to keeping Jack's presence alive by writing him, cherishing mementos of him, talking about him constantly—which, of course, is also her protection against the stirrings that Lucky arouses in her. He asks her out shortly after they've met, but she protests gently that she's married. The next time we see him approach her, she staves him off: "You've been asking me out every week for the last three months and I keep having to turn you down." At the jamboree, a stranger (Dick Miller) asks her to dance; when she automatically brings up the subject of Jack, he gets turned off and fades away. Lonely and blue, she listens to Lucky play trumpet on the bandstand and boldly approaches him on the pier afterwards, complimenting his performance. He drives her home on his motorcycle, takes her inside ("I think I just heard you ask me in," he says, picking up on what she's too scared to say), and what follows is as candid and deeply felt a love scene as you'll find in any movie of the decade. When he begins to make love to her, she cries, frightened of her confusion about what she feels and what she thinks is right. She wakes up in the middle of the night to find him lying nude beside her, his arm across her chest; automatically, she pulls the blanket across him, as if someone were peeking in. It's a delicately funny gesture. The next night, they go out to a restaurant, and when she spots a neighbor across the room she runs into the street. He follows her, but she begs him to leave her alone. "I'm married," she pleads. "Don't you understand? Don't you get it?"

Their relationship begins in earnest under the effect of exposed emotions after Jeanie's husband's funeral. Kay still has trouble reconciling her separate feelings for two men; she's worried that her fellow workers know about her and Lucky and think she's a tramp. But her self-sufficiency at the plant (she was promoted to "leadman" after saving another woman's life) and the easy carry-over of her work situation, with Lucky and Hazel, to the leisure time the three of them spend together, break down her resistance. Then one night in 1944, Jack shows up on leave. In the movie's best scene, they walk on the beach, and she hears in every word he says an attempt to affirm a state of mind she no longer feels part of. She chafes when he derides Hazel, when he says his wife shouldn't have to work, when he talks about his plans for their future; she keeps contradicting him. "Somebody's been putting funny ideas in your head," he tells her, bewildered. 'I can't even talk to you any more." And she replies, "Do you really think everything's going to be great? . . . You've been gone for three years." Finally she turns to him, her back to the tide, and confesses she's been seeing someone else.

Here's how the story's told in Hawn's version. We don't see Kay in bed with Jack, so her strong sexual need for him is not as firmly established. When Lucky approaches her at work, she says,

"You've been asking me out every week for the last *five* months" (you can actually see Hawn mouth "three" while her post-dubbed voice says "five")—presumably so we'll applaud her lengthier period of celibacy. Kay's freak-out at the restaurant occurs *before* she sleeps with Lucky, so it looks like an outburst of terrified chastity rather than postcoital terror. (It makes Kay look like a sexual hysteric.) In the new order of scenes, her approaching him on the pier appears more innocent; maybe she's trying to make up for her outburst outside the restaurant. When he drives her home, he *has* to come inside, because it's begun to rain and he's getting soaked. The scene that follows is a dopey retread from dozens of screwball comedies: His clothes drying, he putters around in one of her dressing gowns while he serves her one of his special omelettes. They end up in bed, but next morning they have a silly, unconvincing quarrel; she kicks him out; he comes back.

Hawn works like hell to reduce the relationship between Lucky and Kay to something superficial and farcical. We're supposed to think she's making a mistake, but it's all right, because she'll go back to Jack in the end. Hawn's version omits some of the footage of Kay and Lucky and Hazel together and, instead of the scene on the beach between Kay and Jack, includes an entirely new sequence, a confrontation that turns him into the victim of her carelessness. (Poor Ed Harris is strung up in this scene—he tries hard, but there's nothing he can do to make it work.) Somehow Jack intuits that Kay's been having an affair with Lucky (though this character isn't intuitive, and there isn't a hint of recognition in his face when he surprises the three of them dancing and swigging beer over at Hazel's), and Hawn makes a sad little face as she tells him, "I was wrong. I'm sorry." When he leaves early the next morning, we hear Kay's voice reading the note Jack's left her, full of clichés about how the war's taken its toll on both of them.

It's clear what Hawn's up to. She wants Kay to stay "nice," committed to the values Demme and his writers have her reject for a more complex, challenging way of interacting with the world. It's as if Hawn herself had never moved past the comfy, home-fires view Kay would have been seeing at the movies while her own life belied them. You can hear Hawn's attitude toward Kay in the song we hear Carly Simon perform over the beginning and end credits, "Someone Waits for You"—a reminder of what a soldier at war hopes for from his wife or sweetheart at home: a faithful heart. That's the ideal that Hawn wants Kay to embrace. I'm not trying to psychoanalyze Goldie Hawn; I have no idea how she really feels about fidelity and sexuality. But you have only to look at the movies she's appeared in since the mid-seventies (after *The Sugarland Express* and *Shampoo*—the only previous ones where she plays genuine, three-dimensional characters) to see how she wants her public to perceive her, and how frightened she is of veering from the huggable image she knows they adore. Demme asked her to play a woman who sleeps with two men and likes it, a woman who isn't always glamorous (certainly not in the scene outside the restaurant with Lucky, or the one where she cries when he touches her breast, or the one where she faces Jack and tells him she's been cheating on him) but is always real. And she did it. But then she got scared and threw the performance away, reverting to something she must have thought would keep her fans happy. In the attempt, Hawn managed to turn her character into nonsense: You keep wondering why the hell Kay can't seem to make up her mind about anything. The horrible irony is that Hawn didn't just slash Demme's canvases, but her own as well. Her performance in the *unreleased* version of *Swing Shift* is easily the finest work of her career.

Hawn has heartbreaking scenes in Demme's cut that remind you how gifted an actress she really is—especially the ones with Ed Harris during Jack's disastrous leave, where you see Kay's misery at having to make him so unhappy, and her sad understanding that she can't continue to lie to him. Even when the scenes Demme shot are lifted whole into the version Hawn approved, they don't mean the same thing; you lose the significance, the weight of some of her best moments. We all know that the director has a perspective the performer usually can't have, and that a good director can shape a piece of acting; that's why terrific actors are so often crucified by bad directors. But I've never seen so glaring an example of how the building of a character—that is, the overall editing of her scenes— can completely alter the way an actor comes across. When Kay protests to Lucky (outside the restaurant) that he has to stay away from her because she's married, you only grasp the complexity of the confusion Hawn is conveying if the scene comes *after* Kay's slept with him. Near the end, Lucky, hurt and angry at Jack's reappearance, has a one-night stand with Hazel. Kay finds out, and the two women make it up. But that night they go together to hear Lucky play at a local club, and Kay gets smashed and turns acerbic. The result is a screaming fight between the two women on the street, which ends with a drunken Kay, flat on the sidewalk, yelling after Hazel, "I was in love!"

A friend who watched the director's cut of *Swing Shift* with me marveled at the way Hawn played the fight scene, which had been so unmemorable in the release print; he could hardly believe me when I told him they were exactly the same. The difference is that, in Demme's cut, there's a moment in the previous scene where Lucky performs a second number—dedicated to "anyone who's ever been in love, ever been hurt by love, and is still trying to figure it out"—and Kay, looking over at Hazel, sees an intense longing in her eyes that seems to suggest more than a one-night stand. (She's misreading—understandably, in the circumstances.) Hawn's fantastic here; she looks dazzled by the pain of having lost, she thinks, her lover and her best friend at a single blow. *That's* what her reading of "I was in love!" plays off; it changes the whole meaning of that line.

The release print does minimize Hazel's influence on Kay. My guess, though, is that's less a case of jealousy over Christine Lahti's treatment than another indication of Hawn's insecurity over the way her fans might react to Kay. The Warners version contains cutie-pie, just-us-girls-together touches (like a shot of Kay and Hazel clowning in front of a mirror, cream on their faces), but no mention of the fact that Hazel coaxed Kay into buying a Victrola. After their fight, when Hazel, on her way home, pauses for a rueful moment in front of Kay's house, where music drifts from the parlor, we hear a ballad. But Demme's choice of tune was the Andrews Sisters' "Bei Mir Bist du Schön," the song Hazel was blasting from *her* record player in the opening scene, when Jack yelled at her to turn it down. The song is meant to remind us that Kay has changed irrevocably, largely through her friendship with Hazel, and to imply that the most important relationship in her life isn't the one she returns to at the end, with Jack (as Hawn and "Someone Waits for You" want us to believe), but the one with Hazel.

On the whole, Hawn's version of the movie doesn't wreck Lahti's performance; ironically, since we can't finally make much sense of Kay, it's Lahti's Hazel who moves into the vacuum Hawn's left

at the center of the picture. People who saw *Swing Shift* on its release tend to remember Lahti's terrific performance—and not much
else. But one of Hawn's changes *does* damage Lahti—from a mis-
guided effort to soften Lucky (Russell is Hawn's real-life live-in
companion). She omits a brief scene where Hazel, seeing Jack smoking on the porch of his apartment, and Kay moving around inside,
takes it for granted that their domestic situation is back to normal.
(She can't know what transpired on the beach.) Then, out of the
loneliness she's felt since she broke up with Biscuits, she decides to
accept Lucky's invitation to hear him play trumpet that night. They
wind up in bed together (Hawn cuts right to the morning after), as
they both knew they would. The way Demme and his writers have
it, it's really *Lucky* who's acting impulsively, out of anger: They're
careful not to include a scene where he considers *his* actions.

Kurt Russell actually suffers more than Lahti from the changes
Hawn supervised. His role is far better defined in Demme's version,
and he gets to play more low notes. That's especially true in his
farewell scene, where, having taken Kay home after her drunken
explosion at Hazel, he waits for her to wake up and then says he's
leaving. We know he's going to tour with a band; he's already told
her (in a scene left out of the Warners version) that she's the only
reason he's still working at MacBride's. (When she gives him a new
mouthpiece for his horn as a birthday remembrance, the gift means
more when we know what he's giving up to stay with her. Of
course, if Hawn doesn't want Kay's relationship with Lucky to have
as much weight as her marriage to Jack, she wouldn't want us to
see her offering in that light.)

The way *Demme* has it, Lucky sits miserably in the corner of
the room, drinking from a coffee cup with Jack's name on it (it's
unmistakable from this detail that he sees he can't compete with
Jack), and the camera pans slowly up Kay's legs—from Lucky's
point of view, so we can see Lucky's appreciation of what he's giving
up. (In Demme's version, sex has an emotional kick, the way it does
in life; he doesn't deny what it signifies to these characters, the way
Hawn's prudish version does.) Before he walks out, he takes a long
look at himself in her bedroom mirror, as if he were both remembering his role in this room—in her life—and understanding it in a way
he never has before. It's a bitter departure. We know—as Kay does,

reaching uselessly after him—that he's wrong about how little he's meant to her. But that's something he may never believe.

Russell is magnificent here: Much as I've loved watching him in *Used Cars*, *Silkwood*, and *Tequila Sunrise*, I've never seen him pull off anything as affecting as this scene. But you have to be prepared to watch a character you've been drawn to walk away harshly. Hawn evidently didn't want to. In the studio cut, the scene begins when Kay wakes up; you can hardly see the letters of Jack's name printed on the cup, and the look in the mirror is truncated. When Lucky tells Kay he's going away, he asks her to come with him—and she turns him down. A couple of minutes before the end of the picture, Hawn sticks in a brief sequence of Lucky riding through the countryside at night in a bus full of musicians, reading a letter from Kay (voice-over by Hawn) that—like the one we heard earlier, from Jack—is littered with optimistic clichés. "I'm hoping for the best," she writes about Jack's return from the war, and (by way of apology to Lucky) "Things got muddled in the end, but thanks." You'd swear at moments like this that Kay—the prim, smiley Kay who began the film, the Kay Goldie Hawn doesn't want us to think the character ever left behind—wrote the script.

On some level, Hawn seems to have understood *Swing Shift* as a protofeminist look at women on the work force in wartime. But feminism to her means *Private Benjamin*: women proving they can be as good as men, and twice as cute. (It doesn't mean, for example, sexual independence—that's too scary.) The studio cut omits the references to Laverne's show-business career and Annie's handling of farm machinery, but it makes a big deal about how working at the factory turns Kay into a stronger person because she makes a bigger salary than Jack and learns her way around equipment. One montage Warners added includes a shot of Hawn in her kitchen, fixing a coffee percolator; in another scene, a P.A. announcement advises the women to cut their hair or wear a hairnet (this is what they superimposed over Annie's farm-equipment line). Presumably that's so Kay's decision to cut her long blonde tresses—presented in Demme's cut as one more indication that she's trying on something new—will come across as determination to turn herself into the perfect little worker. (Since she has to wear a hairnet anyway, like all the other women, the change doesn't make sense.) In the same way, Hawn cuts the moment that explains why Kay misses the bus at the end of her first day's shift: Exhausted, unused to the hours and the exertion, she falls asleep at her station.

Of course, you don't buy this airbrushed portrait of Kay as a role model for women of the forties, which is presented in the most fatuous, sitcommy way, reducing Jack to a male chauvinist so the movie can score easy points against him. (Hawn's cut doesn't *like* Jack very much: He just fills a role—the someone who waits for Kay.) When Jack arrives on leave, he fails to understand the significance of her "leadman" shirt, and complains that the factory equipment she's brought home crowds his bedroom closet. Just what, exactly, is Kay doing with airplane parts in her closet? And we can't believe in Kay's growth when Hawn has sabotaged all the evidence of it in her relationship with her husband. The homecoming sequence in the studio print features an extra scene where Kay opens the door to their apartment with her own key, rather than letting Jack take the lead. But the second change is far more revealing: As soon as they get inside, Kay tells Jack she's planning a home-cooked dinner.

This unconvincing fake feminism substitutes for a genuine political subtext that's perhaps the most striking omission in the studio cut. Holly Hunter's Jeanie plays a far more important role in Demme's version. When her husband is killed, she becomes a convenient emblem for the war effort: Her "cute, tear-stained face" (as a MacBride executive puts it) makes the cover of *Life*, and a year later, dedicating a runway to her husband's memory, she gets to introduce a Marine who delivers a patriotic speech to the assembled workers (and whom she marries at the end of the picture). If it isn't clear enough how the filmmakers feel about this kind of sentimental patriotic manipulation, Demme makes it clearer by cutting away from the speech—to Kay and Lucky, who are using the cover of this special event to talk clandestinely in the storeroom. The Jeanie subplot works in tandem with the scene where the MacBride employees listen to the reports from Guadalcanal and then are coaxed to work harder for the boys at the front, as well as the key sequence where, as soon as the war is over, the women are laid off. With this subplot firmly in place, we can see that the movie is critical of the way the women were used and then discarded by the government and the factories. *Without* it, the layoff scenes don't have much resonance and the Guadalcanal scene reads as inspirational—exactly the *opposite* of what Demme intended.

Warners also cut a bit with Beth Henley as a Salvation Army lassie handing out Bibles to the departing soldiers (which implies a connection between the two "armies"—religion shoring up the war effort), and another where, outside the factory, Asian–Americans are carted off to internment camps while men on the street jeer "Japs, go home where you came from!" And what substitutes for these missing suggestions of the movie's political point of view? In a new scene between Kay and Jack on the morning after Pearl Harbor—replacing their scene in bed together—he explains solemnly to her why he has to go to war: "They started it. We gotta finish it."

I don't think it's fair to lay the political emasculation of *Swing Shift* entirely at Goldie Hawn's door, though. Hollywood has always been terrified of attacking sacred cows; you could hardly imagine Warners enthusing over Demme's take on World War II. But something that's lost its capacity to surprise you can still shock you, and that's the way I feel about what Warners did to Demme's movie. At the end of the studio's cut, Biscuits, reunited with Hazel, toasts each of the assembled couples and "No more war—one hell of a future." If there's any irony in this statement, I missed it. I missed the irony in the women's toast, too: "We showed 'em." Demme's version, which is understated and very moving, pays homage to the finale of William Wyler's celebrated 1946 movie, *The Best Years of Our Lives*. It picks up Wyler's tone of complex, tempered optimism in the vets' discussion of the new real estate on the market, the now ex–factory workers' philosophical attitude to the way their lives have turned around, and the fact that it's Jeanie, MacBride's cover-girl war widow, whose wedding they're attending. "We showed 'em" is echoed in the scene where Hazel and Kay reconcile: It means something different here—it's a measure of personal growth. And, instead of ending with a freeze frame of the two women hugging, Demme takes them down to the beach, and leaves them (in long shot) drinking beer and giggling and kicking up their heels. It's the final affirmation that Kay has moved a lot closer to Hazel's end of the spectrum than to Jack's. She still loves him, but if he wants the marriage to last, he's going to have to work to catch up to her.

The *Swing Shift* story is a Hollywood tragedy, like the hatchet job RKO did on Orson Welles's *The Magnificent Ambersons*.

Worse, because *Ambersons*, in release and on video, botched or not, is still a masterpiece. No viewing of the released *Swing Shift* will tell you what Demme and his writers were after—what, in fact, they achieved before their work was sabotaged by Hawn and the studio. Until some miracle occurs and Demme's cut is made available, *Swing Shift* remains a horrible mistake, a tribute to Hollywood mismanagement and paranoia.

June 1990

CONTRASTS

• • •

You can tell how smart *The Big Chill* thinks it is from the opening scene, where all the main characters—sixties folks now in their thirties—learn of the suicide of a college friend, while Marvin Gaye's "I Heard It Through the Grapevine" plays on the soundtrack and, intercut with their reactions, unidentified hands dress the corpse. The problem with this jazzy montage is that few of the shots tell us anything about these people or how they feel about the dead man, and the director, Lawrence Kasdan (who also co-wrote the script, with Barbara Benedek), includes so many close-ups of lips and legs and fingers that we might be watching a cosmetics commercial, while Carol Littleton's editing, which turns a corner on every beat, suggests a rock video. The combination of slickness and sexiness—the hands servicing the male corpse are unmistakably female—insulate the characters, and distances us from them, but it's disturbing in ways Kasdan couldn't have intended: Surely he doesn't want to sell suicide?

The Big Chill, which is about how these old friends confront their past and present lives on a weekend following the funeral, is propped up with a fantastic score (tunes by The Band, Aretha Franklin, Smokey Robinson, Percy Sledge, The Rolling Stones, and others). The musical selections not only determine the editing but also define the content of each scene, acting as a kind of cute dramatic shorthand. There's a lovemaking sequence scored to "A Natural Woman," and when Mary Kay Place, a corporation lawyer who's single but is desperate for a baby, talks on the phone to Kevin Kline and Glenn Close's little daughter, we hear "When a Man Loves a Woman" as Close looks meaningfully at Kline, whom—we quickly surmise—she intends to enlist as the father of Place's child. These scenes function like sound bytes. And so does the dialogue, a series of one-liners.

The music of the 1950s dominates the soundtrack of Barry Levinson's *Diner*: Chuck Berry, Bobby Vinton, Jerry Lee Lewis, Tommy Edwards, The Dell-Vikings. But in *this* movie it's not just a quick nostalgic fix, or a substitution for dramatic content. These characters care deeply about their music, and—like their feeling for sports, movies, and television—this passion is the key to everything that's wrong with their lives.

Set in Baltimore around Christmas of 1959, *Diner* is about a group of men in their early twenties who have gathered to celebrate the wedding of one of them, and to send off the decade that bore witness to their adolescence. (The title refers to their favorite neighborhood hangout, where several key scenes take place.) Eddie (Steve Guttenberg), the groom-to-be, has stipulated that he won't marry his fiancée, the unseen Elyse, unless she passes a football quiz he's prepared for her. Shrevie (Daniel Stern) quarrels with his wife, Beth (Ellen Barkin), because she refuses to treat his fastidiously catalogued record collection with reverence. Fenwick (Kevin Bacon) watches "G. E. College Bowl" and beats every contestant to the buzzer. Beth and Shrevie see the film *A Summer Place* with his friends, and afterwards, still lost in its romantic haze, she begs him to take her again; he suggests she go with Elyse. Each of these images resonates in an almost novelistic manner. We become conscious of other layers of meaning: that Eddie, still a virgin after five years of dating Elyse, is setting hurdles in the path of his wedding because he's terrified of marriage; that Shrevie's explosion is an expression of the gulf between him and Beth; that Fenwick, who's dropped out of college and hangs around unemployed, often drunk, is wasting a sharply honed intelligence; that Beth is starved for romance. And what binds these scenes together is a common theme—the investment these guys have made in their pop-cultural heritage.

When Shrevie (in what I think is the movie's best scene) yells at Beth because she doesn't know who Charlie Parker is, he's crying out against a denial of a part of himself; he feels that his marriage is threatening to submerge his identity. Music is the absolute against which the young men in *Diner* measure everything that transpires in their lives. Shrevie recalls which song was playing on the jukebox when he walked into the dance where he first met Beth, and Eddie leads an argument about who's the greatest singer of the era (Sinatra and Johnny Mathis are the prime contenders) that turns on their reminiscences of whose records they made out to in high school. (I've heard my brother's friends, also children of the fifties, hold almost the identical discussion.) When the guys sing along with their favorite rock 'n' roll tunes, they throw themselves into the choruses with a fierceness every one of us should recognize from our own experience projecting our most fervent emotions onto the music we listen to. After fighting with Beth, Shrevie drives alone through the streets of Baltimore, pouring his broken heart into the silly lyrics of the song he hears on the radio (Clarence "Frogman" Henry's irresistible "Ain't Got No Home," the quintessential silly song).

There isn't a cliché in all of *Diner*, as far as I can see. Not in the performances (the other major characters are played by Mickey Rourke and Timothy Daly), or the writing, or the direction. The movie approaches the young men's follies gently and comically— the improvised-seeming diner scenes are revue comedy sketches, extended triumphantly long past the point where you think any ensemble could sustain them. But it's not sentimental. *The Big Chill* is. Friendship wins out over the scariness of the world outside, and the women, who are all warm and maternal and a little dopey, band together to make the ultimate sacrifice to propagate the sixties spirit: Mother Close allows her hubby to sleep with her best friend so that she, too, can experience motherhood. In *Diner*, the men close ranks to try to protect themselves from the terrors of male-female relationships, but you can see what that does to Beth, who's closed out. (We never see Elyse's face; she represents the delayed end of Eddie's adolescence—"death," the guys' expression for any woman they admire. But Levinson is smart to include Beth among the major characters: He can't satirize the lifestyles of these men without admitting us to at least one woman's—one outsider's—point of view.) And you can see the bonding grow more desperate and more ineffectual.

The title *The Big Chill* refers to the cold world the characters never thought they'd have to face (and to their approaching middle age), but, except for a few minutes of William Hurt's performance, we never feel their terror, because Kasdan's quick-jolt method leaves no room for the kind of dramatic development that might connect us to the men and women on the screen. The *real* big chill is what we feel in the last scene of *Diner*, when we see the banner at the wedding that reads, "Eddie and Elyse: For the '60s and . . . forever," and we wonder if this marriage has a snowball's chance in hell of surviving—and we think ahead to what the sixties have in store for Eddie and his pals.

Robert Redford's *Ordinary People*, which won the first Academy Award of the eighties for Best Picture, defines its principal characters, the Jarretts, a family of Illinois WASPS, in its opening shots. We see carefully groomed trees in their autumnal splendor, a gazebo, a church, a school with the sounds of choir practice issuing forth from inside. The movie is about the agonies inadequately sheltered by this sturdy, classical Yankee style, suppressed by it until they have to explode, but the movie itself is so constricted and airless that it might have been *made by* the Jarrett family. Practically every shot has a point to make; watching the film is like sitting through a study session before a final exam.

The teenage protagonist, Conrad (Timothy Hutton), recently returned from a spell at a mental institution following a suicide attempt, comes down to breakfast after a mostly sleepless night. His mother, Beth (Mary Tyler Moore), serves him French toast—which he declines because, he says, he's not hungry, so she stuffs it down the disposal. Her gesture clearly tells us that (a) she's displeased, (b) she's putting a good face on her displeasure, and (c) she really wants Con to see through her pretense at nonchalance and feel guilty for making her get rid of the good food she prepared especially for him. Redford and the screenwriter, Alvin Sargent (adapting Judith Guest's popular novel), present this scene—indeed, *every* exchange between the characters—as flat slices of meaning, each one digestible in a single munch, with no crumbs left over to unsettle us. (And the revelations ring in regularly, like the "big" moments before commercial interruptions on TV dramas.) In a sense, once we receive and understand this moment of repressed misery between mother and son, we know everything we need to about both of them—especially Beth—and everything we're going to find out, short of narrative details. This tight, dehydrated, unadventurous movie seems to have been completely worked out before shooting even began: Good as the performers are (especially Hutton, and Donald Sutherland as his father, Calvin), they're not allowed the freedom to explore the corridors of their characters' psyches and discover anything the filmmakers haven't preset.

Shoot the Moon, written by Bo Goldman and directed by Alan Parker, is also about a family crisis: George and Faith Dunlap (Albert Finney and Diane Keaton) separate when she learns, some time after their marriage has begun to disintegrate, that he's seeing another woman. This movie deals with the process of estrangement between husband and wife, parents and children (the Dunlaps have four girls)—and with the interior conflict between love and resentment that separation causes to surface and that most people spend their lives trying to resolve. And, appropriately, *Shoot the Moon*— perhaps the greatest American film of the decade—resolves nothing. Goldman and Parker take us deeper and deeper into the characters (while Keaton's and Finney's performances expand), who constantly surprise us, the way the people we know in real life do. The final frame is a poetic resting-place that brings, in formal terms, a sense of closure. But their stories are far from over—we're not even sure of what will happen next.

The first moment on screen between Faith and George provides a fair sample of how the filmmakers work. Faith is dressing for a book-awards banquet that she's attending with George, one of the nominated authors. He's just finished a phone call to his girl friend, Sandy (Karen Allen); he's been crying, feeling torn between her and his family, not knowing how to handle the mess his life has become. He walks into the bedroom and, possibly as much out of guilt as good will, he compliments Faith's appearance. "You seem surprised," she snaps back. We can see from the expression on Diane

Keaton's face that Faith regrets the words as soon as they come out of her mouth, but she can't help herself. She tries to be nice and can't; she refers to the wine he spilled on her dress at last year's ceremony when another writer won instead of George. "You always remember the wrong things," he says.

In the breakfast-table scene in *Ordinary People*, the layering of emotion is as transparent as overlapping cellophane illustrations in an anatomy book: Beth feels one emotion (hurt), provoking one agenda (to make Con feel guilty), and she shields both with one kind of demeanor (cheerfulness). It's clever of Sargent to devise a single action (disposing of the French toast) that serves to illuminate all three—*merely* clever. His dramaturgy is too pat; it doesn't let the world in. It made me groan, like the moment in *Equus* where the disturbed boy, meeting his shrink for the first time, refuses to converse, singing jingles from commercials instead, and the shrink asks him casually which of his parents has forbidden him to watch TV. On the other hand, in the dialogue from *Shoot the Moon*, Faith's emotions are at war with each other; they coexist, in that messy, confusing way that real human feelings do. We can see all of them—Keaton's performance has the nonreductive clarity of great acting—but they don't fall neatly into line: She looks blurred and jagged at the same time (a brilliant strategy for expressing distress). And there's far too much stored up in Keaton's character for her to show us everything at once, the way Mary Tyler Moore does in *Ordinary People*. Faith is a gifted mother, balancing the four kids' needs and peculiarities in the air like balls she's juggling (George has to work much harder at being a parent, and so gets exhausted much more easily: After half an hour alone with the girls, he asks himself how the hell she does it.) But with George, she's all sharp angles: "I'd forgotten you stopped laughing," he says at one point. Keaton uses Faith's emotional equipment to vary her age, the way Katharine Hepburn does in *Long Day's Journey into Night*. It's a much younger Faith who flirts, half terrified, with Frank (Peter Weller), the workman who's contracted to build a tennis court in her backyard; a much older Faith who lies awkwardly to her dying father (George Murdock) about the state of her marriage.

Parker and Goldman's movie is elegantly worked out, but you don't think of that while you're watching it, because the feelings in it are so raw, and there's always so much going on that you don't have time to step back and see how they've put it all together—the way you do in *Ordinary People*, where the scheme calls attention to itself at every moment. You're too busy taking in the filmmakers' observations about how people who have separated move into a netherworld where no subject is safe, no words are trivial (Faith, stoned in the bathtub, repeating the lyrics of a Beatles love song and crying inconsolably); how a man can feel closer to his son-in-law (as Faith's father does) than he does to his own daughter; how many and complicated ways there are for children to react to the shaking-up of their lives. The younger girls exchange worried glances when Faith has trouble getting out of bed in the morning, and they check with each other about how they ought to respond to Sandy the first time they meet her—they want to please George, but they don't want to like her, because that would be disloyal to Faith.

Sherry (Dana Hill), the eldest daughter, takes over the role of head of the household, cooking breakfast and yelling at her sisters; she even uses George's favorite word, "goddamn," pronouncing it the way Albert Finney does. She's so much like her father that it makes perfect sense that she'd have the most difficulty adjusting to his departure. (She stops speaking to him.) Sherry's weird around Frank: She flirts with him, she's happy he likes her, she asks Faith if she can join them for dinner—but the sexual vibrations between Frank and Faith at the table turn her into a little tyrant, behaving like her mom's babysitter. The morning after he stays over for the first time, she roams through the living room, picks up his cigar butt, and mutters, "I hate Daddy." That makes perfect sense, too.

Parker and the photographer, Michael Seresin, animate the Victorian house where Faith remains with her daughters after she throws George out. It's not just a means of telegraphing the status of the characters and recycling a worn Hollywood irony (they may be rich, but oh, how they suffer), like the setting of *Ordinary People*. For George, the house—along with the tennis court, which was arranged for while he still lived with the family, but gets built in his absence—comes to represent everything he left behind when Faith called the marriage off and he went to live with Sandy. He comes by to bring Sherry her birthday present, but she's not home. Faith is outside with Frank, joking around, and it's obvious from their body language that they've become lovers. She basically ignores him, and his response is to make a derogatory comment about Frank's work on the court. That night, he comes back, but Sherry won't see him, and Faith locks him out. Enraged, he breaks in, puts

Faith outside, and goes after Sherry, cornering her in her bedroom and spanking her viciously. She pulls free and fends him off, weeping and stuttering, with a pair of scissors. George and Sherry reconcile on the night the tennis court is offically opened with a party, when she runs off and seeks him out at Sandy's. He drives her home and exchanges pleasantries with Faith and Frank. Faith suggests that the two couples have dinner sometime, behave like civilized human beings. George gets in his car, swerves around, and ploughs back and forth across the court until he's wrecked it completely.

The break-in scene is a nightmare that brings back all our worst memories of domestic quarrels we overheard or participated in as children; it resounds with all the ones we've had or witnessed as adults. And George's actions on the tennis court at the end of the movie remind us that the kinds of emotions a separation provokes and exposes don't resolve themselves neatly—may be, finally, unresolvable. The makers of *Ordinary People* provide a wise psychiatrist (Judd Hirsch)—a warm, open Jew—to release Con from his WASP straitjacket by helping him confront his anger and pain. Once he does, he's just fine—a little sad, but perfectly healthy. And, to clear the air of nasty emotions, they make Beth into the embodiment of everything that's wrong with the Jarrett family, and surgically remove her from the picture: She leaves Calvin, thereby allowing him and his son to reconstruct their relationship. Which movie is closer to the way human beings *really* behave? A married woman I knew at college was having an affair with one of her teachers. Her husband knew about it—he was seeing someone else, too—and one night the four of them got together for dinner, like civilized, modern people. After both their lovers went home, my friend's husband beat her up.

Audiences and the press, too, were much happier with the synthetic resolution of *Ordinary People* than with *Shoot the Moon*, which upset people—even made them furious. (A friend in another city told me that, at the end of the press screening he attended, one critic stormed out, slamming the door behind him.) *Shoot the Moon*—the title is a poetic metaphor for the death of romance, as well as an allusion to a move in a game of hearts whereby a player risks everything on a single play—is written in tears and blood, as O'Neill said *Long Day's Journey* was. It may be the most intense expression of domestic pain ever conceived for American movies— the cinematic equivalent of O'Neill's greatest drama.

A Selective Filmography

• • •

The following filmography is a selective list of movies, released between 1980 and 1989, that are discussed in this book. You won't find *Top Gun* or *Dead Poets Society* here: I've restricted the list to pictures I've spoken of favorably. Following the cast are, first, the studio that released the film (or, in the rare case of a television program, the network that broadcast it) and, second, the company that released the video. An asterisk indicates that, as of this writing, the movie had not been brought out in video.

*ALICE. Directed by Jan Svankmajer. First Run. 1987.

AU REVOIR LES ENFANTS. Written and directed by Louis Malle. With Gaspard Manesse, Raphaël Fejtö, Francine Racette, Philippe Morier-Genoud, François Négret, and François Berléand. Orion. Orion. 1988.

THE BEST OF TIMES. Directed by Roger Spottiswoode. Screenplay by Ron Shelton. With Robin Williams, Kurt Russell, Pamela Reed, Holly Palance, Donald Moffat, Margaret Whitton, M. Emmet Walsh, Donovan Scott, R. G. Armstrong, and Dub Taylor. Universal. Embassy. 1986.

BLOW OUT. Written and directed by Brian DePalma. With John Travolta, Nancy Allen, John Lithgow, Dennis Franz, John McMartin, and Deborah Everton. Filmways. Warner. 1981.

BLUE VELVET. Written and directed by David Lynch. With Kyle MacLachlan, Dennis Hopper, Isabella Rossellini, Laura Dern, Dean Stockwell, George Dickerson, Hope Lange, Jack Nance, Brad Dourif, Jack Harvey, Priscilla Pointer, and Frances Bay. DEG. Karl–Lorimar. 1986.

THE BORDER. Directed by Tony Richardson. Screenplay by Deric Washburn, Walon Green, and David Freeman. With Jack Nicholson, Elpidia Carrillo, Harvey Keitel, Valerie Perrine, Warren Oates, and Shannon Wilcox. Universal. MCA. 1982.

*BROKEN NOSES. Directed by Bruce Weber. With Andy Minsker. Zeitgeist. 1988.

BULL DURHAM. Written and directed by Ron Shelton. With Kevin Costner, Susan Sarandon, Tim Robbins, Trey Wilson, Robert Wuhl, William O'Leary, and David Neidorf. Orion. Orion. 1988.

CASUALTIES OF WAR. Directed by Brian DePalma. Screenplay by David Rabe, based on the article by Daniel Lang. With Michael J. Fox, Sean Penn, Thuy Tu Le, John C. Reilly, Don Harvey, Erik King, and John Leguizamo. Columbia. RCA/Columbia. 1989.

*THE CHANT OF JIMMIE BLACKSMITH. Written and directed by Fred Schepisi. Based on the novel by Thomas Keneally. With Tommy Lewis, Freddy Reynolds, Angela Punch, Steve Dodds, Jack Thompson, Elizabeth Alexander, Julie Dawson, Don Crosby, Ruth Cracknell, Ray Barrett, Brian Anderson, Peter Carroll, and Jack Charles. New Yorker. 1978; released in the United States in 1980.

A CRY IN THE DARK. Directed by Fred Schepisi. Screenplay by Robert Caswell and Schepisi, based on a book by John Bryson. With Meryl Streep, Sam Neill, Bruce Myles, and Neil Fitzpatrick. Warner Brothers. Warner. 1988.

DARK HABITS. Written and directed by Pedro Almodóvar. With Cristina Pascual, Julieta Serrano, Chus Lampreave, and Carmen Maura. Cinevista. Cinevista. 1983.

THE DEAD. Directed by John Huston. Screenplay by Tony Huston, based on the story by James Joyce. With Donal McCann, Anjelica Huston, Dan O'Herlihy, Helena Carroll, Cathleen Delany, Rachael Dowling, Ingrid Craigie, Donal Donnelly, Marie Kean, Sean McClory, and Frank Patterson. Vestron. Vestron. 1987.

DINER. Written and directed by Barry Levinson. With Steve Guttenberg, Mickey Rourke, Daniel Stern, Kevin Bacon, Timothy Daly, Ellen Barkin, Paul Reiser, Kathryn Dowling, Michael Tucker, Jessica James, and Tait Ruppert. MGM. MGM. 1982.

DREAMCHILD. Directed by Gavin Millar. Screenplay by Dennis Potter.

With Coral Browne, Ian Holm, Amelia Shankley, Peter Gallagher, Nicola Cowper, and Jane Asher. Universal. Thorn Emi/HBO. 1985.

DRESSED TO KILL. Written and directed by Brian DePalma. With Michael Caine, Nancy Allen, Angie Dickinson, Keith Gordon, and Dennis Franz. Filmways. Warner. 1980.

DRIVING MISS DAISY. Directed by Bruce Beresford. Screenplay by Alfred Uhry, based on his play. With Jessica Tandy, Morgan Freeman, Dan Aykroyd, Patti LuPone, and Esther Rolle. Warner Brothers. Warner. 1989.

DRUGSTORE COWBOY. Directed by Gus Van Sant. Screenplay by Van Sant and Daniel Yost, based on the novel by James Fogle. With Matt Dillon, Kelly Lynch, James Le Gros, Heather Graham, William S. Burroughs, James Remar, Max Perlich, Grace Zabriskie, and Beah Richards. Avenue. IVE. 1989.

ENEMIES, A LOVE STORY. Directed by Paul Mazursky. Screenplay by Roger L. Simon and Mazursky, based on the novel by Isaac Bashevis Singer. With Ron Silver, Anjelica Huston, Lena Olin, Margaret Sophie Stein, Alan King, Judith Malina, Rita Karin, Phil Leeds, and Paul Mazursky. 20th Century–Fox. Media. 1989.

THE EYES, THE MOUTH. Directed by Marco Bellocchio. Screenplay by Bellocchio and Vincenzo Cerami. With Lou Castel, Angela Molina, Emmanuèle Riva, Michel Piccoli, and Antonio Piovanelli. Triumph. RCA/Columbia. 1983.

THE FABULOUS BAKER BOYS. Written and directed by Steve Kloves. With Jeff Bridges, Beau Bridges, Michelle Pfeiffer, Jennifer Tilly, and Ellie Raab. 20th Century–Fox. IVE. 1989.

FORT APACHE, THE BRONX. Directed by Daniel Petrie. Screenplay by Heywood Gould, based on a book by Thomas Mulhearn and Pete Tessitore. With Paul Newman, Ken Wahl, Rachel Ticotin, Danny Aiello, Ed Asner, Pam Grier, Miguel Pinero, and Kathleen Beller. 20th Century–Fox. Vestron. 1981.

THE FUNERAL. Written and directed by Juzo Itami. With Tsutomu Yamazaki, Nobuko Miyamoto, Kin Sugai, Shuji Otaki, Takashi Tsumura, Haruna Takase, and Chishu Ryu. New Yorker. Republic. 1985.

GLORY. Directed by Edward Zwick. Screenplay by Kevin Jarre, based on books by Lincoln Kirstein, Peter Burchard, and Robert Gould Shaw. With Matthew Broderick, Denzel Washington, Morgan Freeman, André Braugher, Cary Elwes, Jimhi Kennedy, Jonathan Finn, Bob Gunton, Cliff DeYoung, Alan North, and Jane Alexander. Tri-Star. RCA/Columbia. 1989.

HAMBURGER HILL. Directed by John Irvin. Screenplay by Jim Carabatsos. With Dylan McDermott, Steven Weber, Courtney Vance, Anthony Barrile, Tim Quill, Michael Patrick Boatman, Don James, and Don Cheadle. Paramount. Vestron. 1987.

HIGH SEASON. Directed by Clare Peploe. Screenplay by Peploe and Mark Peploe. With Jacqueline Bisset, James Fox, Kenneth Branagh, Irene Papas, Sebastian Shaw, Lesley Manville, Paris Tselios, Robert Stephens, and Ruby Baker. Hemdale. Nelson. 1988.

HIGH TIDE. Directed by Gillian Armstrong. Screenplay by Laura Jones. With Judy Davis, Claudia Karvan, Jan Adele, Colin Friels, Frankie J. Holden, and John Clayton. Tri-Star. Nelson. 1987.

HOPE AND GLORY. Written and directed by John Boorman. With Sarah Miles, David Hayman, Ian Bannen, Sebastian Rice Edwards, Derrick O'-Connor, Sammi Davis, and Susan Wooldridge. Columbia. Nelson. 1987.

HOUR OF THE STAR. Directed by Suzana Amaral. Screenplay by Amaral and Alfredo Oroz, based on the novel by Clarice Lispector. With Marcelia Cartaxo, José Dumont, Tamara Taxman, Umberto Magnani, Fernanda Montenegro, Claudia Rezende, Lizete Negreiros, and Maria do Carmo Soares. Kino International. Kino. 1985.

HOUSEKEEPING. Written and directed by Bill Forsyth, based on the novel by Marilynne Robinson. With Christine Lahti, Sara Walker, Andrea Burchill, Margot Pindivic, Leah Penny, Tonya Tanner, Anne Pitoniak, Georgie Collins, and Barbara Reese. Columbia. RCA/Columbia. 1987.

LAW OF DESIRE. Written and directed by Pedro Almodóvar. With Eusebio Poncela, Carmen Maura, Antonio Banderas, Miguel Molina, Manuela Velasco, Bibi Andersen, Fernando Guillén, Nacho Martínez, Helga Line, and Rossy De Palma. Cinevista. Cinevista. 1987.

LET'S GET LOST. Directed by Bruce Weber. With Chet Baker, Diane Vavra, Ruth Young, Carol Baker, Vera Baker, Missy Baker, Lawrence Trimble, and William Claxton. Zeitgeist. BMG. 1989.

THE LONG GOOD FRIDAY. Directed by John Mackenzie. Screenplay by Barrie Keeffe. With Bob Hoskins, Helen Mirren, Eddie Constantine, Dave King, Bryan Marshall, and Geoge Coulouris. Handmade. Thorn Emi. 1981.

LOST IN AMERICA. Directed by Albert Brooks. Screenplay by Albert Brooks and Monica Johnson. With Albert Brooks, Julie Hagerty, Michael Greene, Tom Tarpey, Garry K. Marshall, Maggie Rosowell, Ernie Brown, Art Frankel, Joey Coleman, and Donald Gibb. Geffen. Warner. 1985.

LOVE LETTERS. Written and directed by Amy Jones. With Jamie Lee Curtis, James Keach, Amy Madigan, Bud Cort, Matt Clark, and Bonnie Bartlett. Vestron. Vestron. 1983.

*MALA NOCHE. Written and directed by Gus Van Sant, from a short story by Walt Curtis. With Tim Streeter, Ray Monge, and Doug Cooeyote. Frameline. 1988.

MATADOR. Directed by Pedro Almodóvar. Screenplay by Almodóvar and Jesús Ferrero. With Nacho Martínez, Antonio Banderas, Assumpta Serna, Eva Cobo, Julieta Serrano, Eusebio Poncela, and Carmen Maura. Cinevista/World Artists. Cinevista. 1986.

*MÉLO. Written and directed by Alain Resnais, based on the play by Henry Bernstein. With Sabine Azéma, Fanny Ardant, Pierre Arditi, André Dussollier, and Jacques Dacqmine. European Classics. 1988.

*MÉNAGE. Written and directed by Bertrand Blier. With Gérard Depardieu, Miou-Miou, Michel Blanc, and Bruno Crémer. Cinecom. 1986.

MONA LISA. Directed by Neil Jordan. Screenplay by David Leland and Jordan. With Bob Hoskins, Cathy Tyson, Michael Caine, Robbie Coltrane, Sammi Davis, Kate Hardie, Clarke Peters, Zoe Nathenson, and Pauline Melville. Island. HBO/Cannon. 1986.

MOONSTRUCK. Directed by Norman Jewison. Screenplay by John Patrick Shanley. With Cher, Nicolas Cage, Danny Aiello, Olympia Dukakis, Vincent Gardenia, Julie Bovasso, John Mahoney, Feodor Chaliapin, and Louis Guss. MGM. MGM/UA. 1988.

MOSCOW ON THE HUDSON. Directed by Paul Mazursky. Screenplay by Mazursky and Leon Capetanos. With Robin Williams, Maria Conchita Alonso, Cleavant Derricks, Alejandro Rey, Savely Kramarov, Elya Baskin, Oleg Rudnik, Alexander Beniaminov, and Tiger Haynes. Columbia. RCA/Columbia. 1984.

MRS. SOFFEL. Directed by Gilliam Armstrong. Screenplay by Ron Nyswaner. With Diane Keaton, Mel Gibson, Matthew Modine, Edward Herrmann, and Trini Alvarado. MGM. MGM/UA. 1984.

MUSIC BOX. Directed by Costa-Gavras. Screenplay by Joe Eszterhas. With Jessica Lange, Armin Mueller-Stahl, Frederic Forrest, Donald Moffat, Lukas Haas, Sol Frieder, Elzbieta Czyzewska, Magda Szekely Marburg, Michael Shillo, Michael Rooker, and J. S. Block. Tri-Star. Carolco. 1989.

MY BEAUTIFUL LAUNDRETTE. Directed by Stephen Frears. Screenplay by Hanif Kureishi. With Gordon Warnecke, Daniel Day-Lewis, Saeed Jaffrey, Roshan Seth, Shirley Anne Field, Rita Wolf, Derrick Branche, and Souad Faress. Orion. Karl–Lorimar. 1986.

MY LEFT FOOT. Directed by Jim Sheridan. Screenplay by Sheridan and Shane Connaughton, based on the book by Christy Brown. With Daniel Day-Lewis, Brenda Fricker, Ray McAnally, Fiona Shaw, Hugh O'Conor, and Ruth McCabe. Miramax. HBO. 1989.

THE NIGHT OF THE SHOOTING STARS. Directed by Paolo and Vittorio Taviani. Screenplay by the Tavianis, Giuliani G. DeNegri, and Tonino Guerra. With Omero Antonutti, Margarita Lozano, and Micol Guidelli. United Artists. MGM/UA. 1982.

NUTCRACKER, THE MOTION PICTURE. Directed by Carroll Ballard.

From a story by E. T. A. Hoffman. With the Pacific Northwest Ballet. Paramount. Atlantic. 1986.

PENNIES FROM HEAVEN. Directed by Herbert Ross. Screenplay by Dennis Potter, based on his BBC-TV miniseries. With Steve Martin, Bernadette Peters, Jessica Harper, Christopher Walken, Vernel Bagneris, John McMartin, Tommy Rall, Robert Fitch, Jay Garner, and Elizabeth Krupka. MGM. MGM/UA. 1981.

PERSONAL BEST. Written and directed by Robert Towne. With Mariel Hemingway, Patrice Donnelly, Scott Glenn, Kenny Moore, and Jodi Anderson. Geffen/Warner Brothers. Warner. 1982.

PERSONAL SERVICES. Directed by Terry Jones. Screenplay by David Leland. With Julie Walters, Shirley Stelfox, Danny Schiller, Alec McCowen, Victoria Hardcastle, Tim Woodward, Dave Atkins, and Leon Lissek. Vestron. Vestron. 1987.

PIXOTE. Directed by Hector Babenco. Screenplay by Babenco and Jorge Duran, based on a novel by José Louzeiro. With Marília Pera, Fernando Ramos da Silva, and Jorge Julião. Unifilm/Embrofilme. Columbia. 1981.

THE PURPLE ROSE OF CAIRO. Written and directed by Woody Allen. With Mia Farrow, Jeff Daniels, Danny Aiello, Irving Metzman, Stephanie Farrow, Ed Herrmann, John Wood, Deborah Rush, Van Johnson, Zoe Caldwell, Karen Akers, Eugene Anthony, Annie Joe Edwards, Milo O'Shea, Dianne Wiest, Alexander H. Cohen, and Michael Tucker. Orion. Vestron. 1985.

RAN. Directed by Akira Kurosawa. Screenplay by Kurosawa, Hideo Oguni, and Masato Ide. With Tasuya Nakadai, Mieko Harada, Akira Terao, Jinpachi Nezu, Daisuke Ryu, Yoshiko Miyazaki, Kazuo Kato, Peter, and Masayuki Yui. Orion. CBS/Fox. 1985.

THE RIGHT STUFF. Written and directed by Philip Kaufman, based on the book by Tom Wolfe. With Scott Glenn, Ed Harris, Dennis Quaid, Fred Ward, Veronica Cartwright, Mary Jo Deschanel, Pamela Reed, Sam Shepard, Barbara Hershey, Kim Stanley, Donald Moffat, Levon Helm, Scott Wilson, Scott Paulin, Charles Frank, Lance Henriksen, Harry

Shearer, Jeff Goldblum, and Royal Dano. Warner Brothers. Warner. 1983.

RITA, SUE AND BOB TOO. Directed by Alan Clarke. Screenplay by Andrea Dunbar. With Siobhan Finneran, Michelle Holmes, George Costigan, Lesley Sharp, Willie Ross, and Kulvinder Ghir. Orion. Orion. 1987.

*SEEING RED: STORIES OF AMERICAN COMMUNISTS. Directed by Julia Reichert and James Klein. Heartland. 1984.

SHOOT THE MOON. Directed by Alan Parker. Screenplay by Bo Goldman. With Diane Keaton, Albert Finney, Dana Hill, Peter Weller, Karen Allen, Viveka Davis, Tracey Gold, Tina Yothers, and George Murdock. MGM. MGM/UA. 1982.

*THE SINGING DETECTIVE. Directed by Jon Amiel. Teleplay by Dennis Potter. With Michael Gambon, Bill Paterson, Janet Suzman, Patrick Malahide, Jim Carter, Alison Steadman, Lyndon Davies, Joanne Whalley, Imelda Staunton, and Janet Henfrey. BBC. 1986.

SOMETHING WILD. Directed by Jonathan Demme. Screenplay by E. Max Frye. With Jeff Daniels, Melanie Griffith, Ray Liotta, Margaret Colin, Dana Preu, Jack Gilpin, Su Tissue, Tracey Walter, Jim Roche, John Waters, Kenneth Utt, John Sayles, Charles Napier, Steve Scales, Sister Carol East, and Kristin Olsen. Orion. HBO. 1986.

STAR STRUCK. Directed by Gillian Armstrong. Screenplay by Stephen Maclean. With Jo Kennedy, Ross O'Donovan, Margo Lee, Pat Evison, John O'May, Ned Lander, and The Swingers. Palm Beach. Embassy. 1982.

STOP MAKING SENSE. Directed by Jonathan Demme. With David Byrne, Jerry Harrison, Chris Frantz, Tina Weymouth, Steve Scales, Bernie Worrell, Alex Weir, Edna Holt, and Lynn Mabry. Island Alive. RCA/ Columbia. 1984.

*SUPERSTAR: THE KAREN CARPENTER STORY. Directed by Todd Haynes. 1988. This film was withdrawn from distribution at the insistence of Richard Carpenter, allegedly for copyright reasons.

SWEET DREAMS. Directed by Karel Reisz. Screenplay by Robert Getchell. With Jessica Lange, Ed Harris, Ann Wedgeworth, and David Clennon. Tri-Star. Thorn Emi/HBO. 1985.

*SWING SHIFT. Directed by Jonathan Demme. Screenplay by Ron Nyswaner, Bo Goldman, and Nancy Dowd. With Goldie Hawn, Kurt Russell, Christine Lahti, Ed Harris, Fred Ward, Holly Hunter, Sudie Bond, Patty Maloney, Lisa Pelikan, Susan Peretz, Stephen Tobolowsky, Roger Corman, Dick Miller, Charles Napier, and Beth Henley. Warner Brothers. 1983. The 1984 version available on video is not the one completed under Demme's control.

TANNER '88. Directed by Robert Altman. Teleplay by Garry Trudeau. With Michael Murphy, Pamela Reed, Cynthia Nixon, Veronica Cartwright, Daniel Jenkins, Kevin J. O'Connor, Richard Cox, Ilana Levine, and Cleavon Little. HBO. The first three episodes ("The Dark Horse," "For Real," and "The Night of the Twinkies") are available on HBO Video under the title *Tanner for President '88.* 1988.

*THY KINGDOM COME, THY WILL BE DONE. Directed by Antony Thomas. Roxy. 1987.

TRUE STORIES. Directed by David Byrne. Screenplay by Byrne, Beth Henley, and Stephen Tobolowsky. With Byrne, John Goodman, Swoosie Kurtz, Spalding Gray, Alix Elias, Annie McEnroe, Roebuck Staples, Jo Harvey Allen, Umberto Larriva, John Ingle, and Matthew Posey. Warner Brothers. Warner. 1986.

THE UNBEARABLE LIGHTNESS OF BEING. Directed by Philip Kaufman. Screenplay by Jean-Claude Carrière and Kaufman, from the novel by Milan Kundera. With Daniel Day-Lewis, Juliette Binoche, Lena Olin, Derek de Lint, Erland Josephson, Pavel Landovsky, Donald Moffat, Daniel Olbrychski, and Tomek Bork. Saul Zaentz. Orion. 1988.

WHAT HAVE I DONE TO DESERVE THIS! Written and directed by Pedro Almodóvar. With Carmen Maura, Luis Hostalot, Gonzalo Suarez, Ángel de Andres Lopez, Verónica Forqué, and Kiti Manver. Cinevista. Cinevista. 1984.

WISH YOU WERE HERE. Written and directed by David Leland. With

Emily Lloyd, Geoffrey Hutchings, Tom Bell, Pat Heywood, and Jesse Birdsall. Atlantic. Fries. 1987.

WITHNAIL AND I. Written and directed by Bruce Robinson. With Richard E. Grant, Paul McGann, Richard Griffiths, Ralph Brown, and Michael Elphick. Cineplex Odeon. Media/Cannon. 1987.

WOMEN ON THE VERGE OF A NERVOUS BREAKDOWN. Written and directed by Pedro Almodóvar. With Carmen Maura, Antonio Banderas, Julieta Serrano, María Barranco, Rossy De Palma, Kiti Manver, Guillermo Montesinos, Chus Lampreave, and Fernando Guillén. Orion. Orion. 1988.

A WORLD APART. Directed by Chris Menges. Screenplay by Shawn Slovo. With Barbara Hershey, Jodhi May, Linda Mvusi, Yvonne Bryceland, David Suchet, Albee Lesotho, Tim Roth, Jeroen Krabbe, Nadine Chalmers, Carolyn Clayton-Cragg, Merav Gruer, and Nadine Chalmers. Atlantic. Atlantic. 1988.

Index

• • •

376

377

383